The Turbo C Survival Guide

HARRISON
20 THORN ROAD
BRAMHALL
STOCKPORT
SK7 1HQ
061-439-7675

THE
TURBO C
SURVIVAL
GUIDE

Lawrence H. Miller
Alexander E. Quilici

WILEY

John Wiley & Sons
New York □ Chichester □ Brisbane □ Toronto □ Singapore

Another one for our families

Library of Congress Cataloging in Publication Data
Miller, Lawrence H.
  The Turbo C survival guide / Lawrence H. Miller.
Alexander E. Quilici.
    p.   cm. _
    Bibliography: p.
    Includes index.
    ISBN 0-471-61708-3 (pbk.)
    1. C (Computer program language) 2. Turbo C (Computer program)
I. Quilici, Alexander E. II. Title. III Series.
QA76.73.C15M552 1989
005.13'3_dc19   88-27608
                                                          CIP

PREFACE

C is a powerful programming language, one that is especially popular among professionals who program small personal computers. And Turbo C—with its sophisticat ed programming environment, its speedy compiler, and its special language features—makes programming in C a pleasure. But unfortunately C also has a reputation for being hard to learn and even harder to master. Its conciseness and complexity can overwhelm all but the most experienced programmer. *The Turbo C Survival Guide* will keep you from slowly sinking into a sea of confusion, and speed your journey from novice to expert C programmer. You'll find this book worthwhile if:

- *You've programmed in other high-level languages such as* BASIC, FORTRAN, *or* Pascal, *and now want to program in* Turbo C. We don't start from scratch and try to teach you how to program. Instead, we assume some prior programming experience and expend most of our effort describing how C differs from other high-level languages and investigating its unique and unfamiliar features.

- *You've programmed in C but you don't yet feel as though you've mastered it.* We cover the language completely, delving deeply into many issues that are often casually examined or completely avoided. You can't be a proficient C programmer without knowing how to put together large programs, how to produce portable and efficient code, or how to use pointers to effectively organize and access data—topics we emphasize rather than ignore.

- *You're familiar with C but not with Turbo C or* ANSI C. Turbo C implements the new ANSI C standard, along with some of its own additional features. We examine and exploit its ANSI C extensions such as function prototypes and implicit string concatenation. We explore the special Turbo C extensions, including its memory models, pointer modifiers, and graphics library. And we explain how to use the Turbo C programming environment, including the program builder and the debugger.

- *You're looking for examples of real-world C programs or are interested in obtaining a set of tools to improve your* DOS *environment.* We provide over 175 useful programs and functions, including a file display program, an indexed data base manager, a cross referencer, a function plotter, a file compression program, an octal dump program, a program to eliminate duplicate lines, various sorting and searching programs, and more. We also provide implementations of useful libraries, such as sets and queues, and utility functions to manage console input and output. All of these programs have been written, compiled, and executed using Turbo C version 2.0.

Special Features

This book has grown out of several years of teaching C courses to a wide range of students—from first year computer science majors to lifelong assembly language programmers, from casual computer users familiar only with BASIC to competent C hackers fine-tuning their skills. And we've concluded that there are several ways to ease the often difficult process of mastering a programming language, all of which we've incorporated here:

- *We provide complete, useful programs.* Our examples don't merely illustrate language features but illustrate them in a realistic way, as part of a useful function or program. And our examples are complete—we avoid potentially confusing program fragments and ensure that every function comes with a main program that shows how to call it and how to use its return value.

- *We provide sizeable programs.* Almost every chapter ends with a case study, a large, real-world application that cements the concepts covered in the chapter. We often construct these case studies from functions and programs written and explained earlier in the text, reinforcing our earlier examples and providing realistic examples of how bigger programs are built from smaller pieces.

- *We provide pictorial descriptions of data structures and algorithms.* Numerous illustrations help clarify complex concepts such as pointers, arrays, and dynamic allocation. These pictures simplify seemingly complicated data structures and algorithms, and ensure that our explanations are easy to follow.

- *We provide plenty of programming exercises.* We've included over 400 exercises spanning a wide range of difficulty. Some are simply modifications to our example programs that make them more efficient, more concise, more useable, or more user-friendly. Others range from small programs to sizeable programming projects, many of which are useful programs in their own right.

Organization

We divide the text into five parts. Part I is a tutorial introduction to Turbo C. Part II is detailed discussion of its basic data types (including pointers and arrays), operators, and statements. Part III covers constructing more complex programs, looking at functions, storage classes, and separate compilation. Part IV looks at data structures, from arrays of pointers to linked lists and trees. Finally, Part V covers special Turbo C features such as its graphics library and its memory models, studies real-world concerns such as portability, efficiency, and debugging.

Part I—A Tutorial Introduction to Turbo C • *Chapter 1* presents our first C program—one that computes the interest accumulating in a bank account—and uses it to introduce the basic C data types, operators, and statements, and to explain how to use the Turbo C development environment to compile and run programs. • *Chapter 2* provides three more example programs—an extension to the interest rate accumulator, a program to reverse its input, and an implementation of insertion sort—and uses them to introduce several additional control structures and operators, and the basics behind arrays and functions. This chapter also examines input/output (I/O) redirection and explains how it turns these programs into useful tools. Together, these two chapters provide an excellent feel for what programming in Turbo C is like.

Part II—Data Types, Operators, and Statements • *Chapter 3* describes data types, placing extra emphasis on how to manipulate characters, including discussions of character input and output and character testing. It concludes with our first case study, a program to display its standard input a page at a time. • *Chapter 4* addresses operators, paying special attention to the shorthand assignment and bitwise operators, and to automatic type conversion and casting. Its case study is a program to compress and uncompress files. • *Chapter 5* studies statements, showing the most appropriate uses for each, and concluding with a case study that dumps its input in octal. • *Chapter 6* presents pointers, arrays, and strings, emphasizing the relationships between them. It also introduces the standard string functions and uses them to write a useful tool to detect duplicate input lines.

Part III—Constructing Complex Programs • *Chapter 7* focuses on functions, exploring the details of how they can communicate with each other through parameter passing and return values. It also covers the closely related topics of pointers to functions, generic functions, and functions that can take variable numbers of arguments. Its case study is a recursive implementation of binary search. • *Chapter 8* studies storage classes and separate compilation, and discusses Turbo C's program builder. Its case study shows how to create abstract data types, illustrating them with a package that implements sets. • *Chapter 9* presents the preprocessor, describing how we can use it to make our programs easier to read and debug, as well as more efficient. The case study uses macros to create a simpler interface to functions with complicated arguments.

Part IV—Organizing and Accessing Data • *Chapter 10* discusses multidimensional arrays, showing how we can use pointers to access them efficiently. It dramatically illustrates their use in an implementation of the Game of Life. • *Chapter 11* presents arrays of pointers, showing how we can use dynamic allocation to initialize them, and how we can use them to access command-line arguments. Its case study is a string sorting program that takes advantage of both. • *Chapter 12* studies structures, unions, and enumerated types, including arrays of structures, using all of them in a simple data base program. • *Chapter 13* continues our study of structures by showing how to write insertion sort using linked lists and trees, and combining both in a C program cross-referencer. • *Chapter 14* explains external files, providing complete coverage of the standard I/O library, bringing together the ideas of the chapter in an indexed data base for names, addresses, and phone numbers.

Part V—Real-World Programming Issues • *Chapter 15* shows how Turbo C's memory models and pointer modifiers support writing programs that require large amounts of memory. Its case study describes how to write programs that work well under multiple memory models. • *Chapter 16* presents common portability problems and suggests some solutions, concluding with a set of functions for portably managing console displays. • *Chapter 17* examines efficiency, including techniques for making our programs run faster or take up less space. Its case study provides fast functions for allocating fixed-size blocks of memory and for reading in an array of integers. • *Chapter 18* is an in-depth discussion of Turbo C graphics programming that ends with a program to plot functions. • *Chapter 19* describes the debugger and uses it to debug several short programs. The book concludes with a complete set of appendices that discusses configuring Turbo C, presents the different command-line options, menu entries, and header files, and summarizes the Turbo C library functions.

ACKNOWLEDGMENTS

Contributions by several of our friends and colleagues have greatly improved the quality of this text. We're deeply in debt to Robert Quilici for painstakingly plowing through our prepublication drafts, unearthing plenty of problems with our programs and explanations. And we're grateful to Jake Richter for his careful proofreading, to David Smallberg for his always perceptive comments and criticisms, and to Dorab Patel for his invaluable wizardry with formatting.

We would like to thank the UCLA Computer Science Department and USC's Information Science Institute for the generous use of their resources and their allowing us the time to produce this work. We would also like to thank the people at John Wiley, especially our editors, Gene Davenport and Teri Zak, who as usual have been extremely helpful and made life pleasant for their authors.

And finally, we're grateful for all of the encouragement and support given to us by our families and friends—especially Rita Grant-Miller, Tammy Merriweather, Irene Borromeo, and Doris Perl.

Lawrence H. Miller
Alexander E. Quilici

Los Angeles, California

CONTENTS

1 INTRODUCING
TURBO C

Turbo C is a fast, efficient, easy-to-use C compiler. This makes Turbo C ideal not only for learning how to program in C, but also for writing complex programs once the language has been mastered. This chapter introduces C language programming and the Turbo C development environment. We start by examining an initial Turbo C program, one that computes the interest that accumulates in a bank account over time. We then show how to use the command-line and interactive versions of Turbo C to actually compile, load, and execute programs.

1.1   OUR FIRST TURBO C PROGRAM

Let's dive right into a Turbo C program. The program in Figure 1.1 calculates and prints the interest accumulating in a bank account over a 10-year period, assuming an initial deposit of $5000 and an interest rate of 7 percent. When we compile and run it, we obtain the output shown in Figure 1.2. This output includes the interest rate, and the account balance at the start of each year in the period. The program uses a simple interest rate compounding formula to do its calculations.

balance at year's end =
    balance at year's start + (balance at year's start * interest rate)

We'll now examine this program in detail.

Comments, File Inclusion, and Constants

The program's first few lines, beginning with a /* and ending with a */, are a *comment*. The compiler ignores comments; they are merely notes to the program's reader that help explain what the program does and how it works. We can place comments anywhere blank spaces can occur—at the end of a line, at the beginning, or even in the middle—but for readability we usually place them only at the end of lines or on lines by themselves.

The next group of lines, the ones that start with a #, are handled by the *preprocessor*, a special program that processes C programs before the compiler sees them. The first line,

1

```
/*
 * Generate a table showing interest accumulation.
 */
#include <stdio.h>

#define PRINCIPAL  5000.00        /* start with $5000 */
#define INTRATE       0.07        /* interest rate of 7% */
#define PERIOD       10           /* over 10-year period */

main()
{
  int     year;                   /* year of period */
  float   balance;                /* balance at end of year */

  balance = PRINCIPAL;
  year = 0;
  printf("Interest Rate: %5.2f%%\n\n", INTRATE * 100);
  printf("Year     Balance\n");
  while (year <= PERIOD)
  {
    printf("%4d   $ %7.2f\n", year, balance);
    balance = balance * INTRATE + balance;
    year = year + 1;
  }
  return 0;                       /* indicate program worked */
}
```

Figure 1.1 intrate.c—A program to calculate accumulated interest.

```
Interest Rate:  7.00%

Year     Balance
   0   $ 5000.00
   1   $ 5350.00
   2   $ 5724.50
   3   $ 6125.21
   4   $ 6553.98
   5   $ 7012.76
   6   $ 7503.65
   7   $ 8028.91
   8   $ 8590.93
   9   $ 9192.30
  10   $ 9835.76
```

Figure 1.2 The output when we run the interest accumulating program.

```
#include <stdio.h>
```

instructs the preprocessor to *include* the contents of the file stdio.h in the program it passes on to the compiler. That means the compiler sees only the contents of the included file and not the `#include` itself. Why include stdio.h at all? Simply because it contains some special information needed to perform input and output. Later, we'll examine `#include` in much more depth; for now, simply remember to include stdio.h in all your programs.

The other preprocessor statements, the `#define`'s, define three constants. PRIN-CIPAL is the initial balance (5000.00), INTRATE is the interest rate (0.07), and PERIOD is the number of years over which we compute the accumulating interest (10).

`#define` gives a name to a value. Its syntax—that is, the way the statement is constructed—is simple. The keyword `#define` starts in column one, and is followed by a *NAME* and a *VALUE*. (Italics such as *NAME* or *VALUE* indicate generic symbols; the programmer provides the actual name and its value).

```
#define NAME VALUE
```

`#defines` can occur anywhere in a program, but we usually place them at the beginning. We also usually use all uppercase names for constants to make them more noticeable.

`#define`'s semantics—that is, what the statement actually does—are more complex. When the preprocessor encounters a `#define`, it associates the value with the name. Then, whenever the name occurs later on in the program, the preprocessor replaces it with its corresponding value. After the preprocessor has finished its replacements, it passes the program to the compiler—which means the compiler never sees the names in the `#defines`. In our program, the preprocessor replaces each use of PRINCIPAL with its defined value, 5000.00, and performs a similar action for the other two defined constants.

We find that we use `#define` in almost every program we write. Why? Because by using it to give names to constant values, we make our programs easier to read and easier to change. In fact, later on we'll see that `#define` is more powerful than we have indicated here; it is actually a general mechanism for replacing a name with a string of characters.

The Main Program

The rest of the program is a single function named `main`. Because `main` is the first function *called* (or, in other words, executed) when a program begins, every program must have a function with this name.

Functions in C are analogous to procedures in Pascal and subroutines in FORTRAN and BASIC—they're simply a way to package together and name a collection of statements. Functions have two parts: a header and a body. The header provides the function's name and a description of its parameters. `main`'s header is simply:

```
main()
```

The parentheses following the word `main` indicate that it's a function that takes no parameters. The body consists of variable declarations and the statements to be executed when the function is called. We enclose them in braces (`{` and `}`) to group them with the function header.

Variable Declarations

In C, unlike some programming languages, we have to declare the type of every variable we use. These variable declarations appear at the beginning of a function. Our variable declarations are:

```
int     year;
float   balance;
```

The first tells the compiler that `year` is an `int`, an abbreviation for the word *integer*. The other specifies that `balance` is a `float`, a *floating point* or *real* number. We need these declarations because a variable's storage requirements and internal representation depends on its type. And by making them explicit (rather than relying on naming conventions) we make our program more readable.

We use integers when we need exact "whole" numbers, since their representation is exact within the range of integers that a given word size can represent. We also use them when speed of arithmetic operations is important, since most operations are faster with integers than with reals. In Turbo C, an `int` is 16 bits, with one bit used for the sign, which means that we can use an `int` to store values between -32.768 and 32.767 (that is, between -2^{15} and $+2^{15} - 1$). But on other compilers on other machines, an `int` is 32 bits, again with one bit used for the sign. A 32-bit integer can hold a much larger value, one between $-2.148.483.648$ and $+2.148.483.647$ (that is, between -2^{31} to $+2^{31} - 1$).

Floating point numbers, or reals, are numbers with a decimal point. Their accuracy depends on the machine's representation. Typically, a `float` represents about 7 significant digits, with exponents generally ranging from about -38 to $+38$. This means reals can hold values between 10^{-38} and 10^{38}.

Assignment Statements

We follow a function's variable declarations with its statements. Our `main` begins with two assignment statements.

```
balance = PRINCIPAL;
year = 0;
```

They work as one might expect. The first assigns the value defined for the constant `PRINCIPAL` (5000.00) to the variable `balance`; the second sets the variable `year` to 0.

The Printf Statement

The next two statements write the output headings.

```
printf("Interest Rate: %5.2f%%\n\n", INTRATE * 100);
printf("Year      Balance\n");
```

printf is a predefined function that performs formatted output. *Predefined* means that it has been written and compiled for you, and is linked together with your program after it compiles. In C, all input and output is done by predefined functions. Together, these functions comprise the standard input/output (I/O) library. *Formatted output* means that we provide the format in which printf writes a set of values.

We specify the format as printf's first parameter, the formatting control string. printf's then writes its other parameters to the standard output, according to the specification of the format string. The standard output is usually the console (to change this we have to do something special before we run the program, a topic discussed in the next chapter).

In general, printf writes anything in the formatting control string (between the quotation marks) as is. One exception is a %, which it takes as the start of a description of how to write a value. printf expects the % to be followed by a letter specifying the value's type. %d indicates a decimal integer, %f a floating point value. Of course, using % to indicate formatting codes causes a problem: How do we write a percent sign? It turns out to be easy; we simply use two of them, %%.

Normally, %d uses just enough space to print the entire value, and %f prints floating point values with exactly six digits after the decimal point and however many digits are necessary preceding it. We change these defaults by providing an optional field width. In the interest program, we specify a format of %5.2f for the interest rate, which tells the compiler that we want floating point output, with five places in all and two places to the right of the decimal point. The value of INTRATE * 100 is calculated and printed according to this formatting specification.

What happens when the field width is too small, as if we tried to use %3.2 to write an interest rate of 11.5? printf stretches the field so that it's just large enough to write the entire value. We get the same behavior if we leave off the field width entirely, as in %.2f. And what happens if the field width is too large? printf simply *right*-justifies the number within the field. Since we print our interest rate of 7.00 with the %5.2 format, it is preceded by a single space.

Perhaps you have noticed the \n at the end of the formatting string. The backslash indicates a special character. \n is the newline character; writing a \n causes further output to start on the next line. Without it, output continues on the same line. In our example, we write two of them in order to get a blank line between the interest rate and the header line that follows it.

These printfs have written only one value. But we can write any number of values, as long as we provide a formatting instruction for each of them. The final printf, which writes the year and its balance, provides an example.

```
printf("%4d   $ %7.2f\n", year, balance);
```

First, it prints year according to the %4d specification. Since a size is given, it right-justifies the number within the field allocated for it. Then, it writes several spaces, a dollar sign, and another space, before printing balance using the %7.2f format. Finally, it writes a single new line.

Warning: There should be a one-to-one correspondence between formatting instructions and values to print. Provide too few values or values of the wrong type and your program will terminate early or produce output consisting of bizarre values. Provide too many values and the extra values will be ignored.

printf is more powerful than we've let on, and we'll present more of its capabilities later. But because printf is so powerful, there are times when it is inefficient and there are better ways to produce output. We'll discuss these methods in Chapter 14, along with other functions in the standard I/O library. A complete description of printf can also be found in Appendix E.

The While Loop

After writing the headings, the program computes the ending balance for each of the years in the period. It does so with a single while loop.

```
while (year <= PERIOD)
{
  printf("%4d   $ %7.2f\n", year, balance);
  balance = balance * INTRATE + balance;
  year = year + 1;
}
```

while is a mechanism for repeating a statement or a group of statements. Its syntax is

```
while (expression)
  statement;
```

A while evaluates the *expression* in parenthesis and if the condition is true, executes *statement*. It repeats the process until the condition is false, when it skips to the statement that follows it.

Here, as long as year is less than or equal to PERIOD, we execute the three statements:

```
printf("%4d   $ %7.2f\n", year, balance);
balance = balance * INTRATE + balance;
year = year + 1;
```

Because while expects only a single statement, we have to group these statements together with { and }. The first statement in the group does the printing; the second updates balance, and the last updates year. Each time through the loop year increases by one, and the loop exits when year is finally greater than PERIOD.

This while loop uses one of C's relational operators, <=, which tests whether a value is less than or equal to another value (<=). There are also operators to test for inequality (!=), equality (==), less than (<), greater than (>), and greater than or equal to (>=).

C also has the usual arithmetic operators (+, -, *, /), along with several others, which we will introduce later. * and / have higher precedence than + and -, but as with most other programming languages, we can use parentheses to change the order of evaluation.

The Return Statement

In C, as in most programming languages, a function can return a value to the function that called it. `main` is no exception. Our interest rate program's final statement,

```
return 0;
```

causes `main` to return zero to its caller. But why zero? And who is `main`'s caller?

By convention, programs return zero when they succeed and some other value when they fail. This behavior may seem strange, but the rationale behind it is sensible. Usually there is only a single way to succeed and many different ways to fail (mistakes in the input, a full disk, and so on), so we use specific nonzero return values to indicate the cause of the program's failure, if any. Our program, however, assumes that nothing goes wrong, so it always returns zero.

It turns out that `main`'s value is returned to whatever program invoked it. When the invoking program is the normal DOS command interpreter, this value is simply ignored. But there are other programs that test this value to determine which action to take. It's good programming practice to have `main` return a value.

Program Layout

C is a free-format language—there are few restrictions on the format of C programs. This means we can lay out our programs any way we choose. There is nothing to prevent us from placing most of our example program on a single, lengthy line. But we didn't, for an obvious reason: The program would have been completely unreadable. Instead, because white space and consistent indentation make programs easier to understand, we took care to indent our statements carefully and to place spaces around operators. You don't have to mimic our formatting style, but try to ensure that whatever style you choose is consistent and readable.

1.2   COMPILING AND RUNNING TURBO C PROGRAMS

The previous section presented a simple C program. But how do we actually arrive at an executable program, one that when run produces our earlier output? In general, we have to go through several steps:

1. Enter the program into a source file, usually with an *interactive text editor*.

2. Run the source file through the *preprocessor*, which replaces defined names with their values.

3. Provide this expanded program to the compiler, which takes it and produces an *object module*

4. Give this object module to a *linking loader*, which produces an executable program.

The object module the compiler creates contains compiled code, along with references to any functions, such as `printf`, that the code uses but didn't define. These references are called *externals*. Before a program can be executed, the compiled versions of these external functions must be linked together with the object module. That's the job of the loader. It looks for definitions of these externals in a standard location that contains a library of precompiled standard functions, and links them together with the object module to produce a runnable program.

There are two ways to compile and run Turbo C programs: the command-line environment and the integrated development environment. The rest of the chapter describes them. It assumes that your system has been configured as discussed in Appendix A, so you might want to take a peek at that appendix before reading on.

1.3   USING THE TURBO C COMMAND-LINE ENVIRONMENT

Turbo C's command-line environment is similar to the command-line environments most of us have used for writing and running programs in other languages or on other machines. We use separate commands to edit, compile, and run our programs.

Compiling with tcc

We first use the editor of our choice to enter our program into a file. This file's name should end with .c. Doing so is not required but helps distinguish your C source files from other types of files. We then run the Turbo C compiler, tcc, which automatically invokes the preprocessor, compiler, and linker. Assuming that there are no errors, the result of running tcc is an executable program.

Suppose we've entered our interest rate program into a file named intrate.c. Then compiling it with

    tcc intrate.c

results in a runnable program named intrate.exe. Here's the output when we run tcc on our computer. We can then run our program by typing either intrate or intrate.exe, which results in the output shown in Figure 1.2.

Actually, we've made two assumptions here. The first is that intrate.c is on the currently active disk drive. If it isn't, we have to specify the disk drive the program is on, as in b:intrate.c. The other assumption is that tcc is in the current directory, or in some directory mentioned in the DOS search path (Appendix A discusses how to set the search path appropriately).

Dealing with Compile Errors

Unfortunately, things don't always go as smoothly as we may be leading you to believe. So far we've assumed that no errors occur. But C's syntax can be somewhat confusing, which makes it likely that your first few C programs will not compile successfully the first time. Figure 1.3 contains another version of our interest rate program, one that illustrates several of the most common mistakes. When we compile

```
/*
 * Generate a table showing interest accumulation.
 */
#include <stdio.h>

#define PRINCIPAL   5000.00       /* start with $5000 */
#define INTRATE        0.07       /* interest rate of 7% */
#define PERIOD        10          /* over 10-year period */

main()
{
  int     year;                   /* year of period */
  float   balance;                /* balance at end of year */

  year = 0;
  printf("Interest Rate: %5.2f%%\n\n", INTRATE * 100)
  printf("Year     Balance\n");
  while (year <= PERIOD)
  {
    printf("%4d   $ %7.2f\n", year, balance);
    balance = balance * INTRATE + balance;
    year := year + 1;
  }
  return 0;                       /* indicate program worked */
}
```

Figure 1.3   oops.c—A less-than-perfect version of our interest rate program.

this file, which we've named oops.c, the compiler produces the error messages shown in Figure 1.4.

These error messages include the type of error, the file and line number where the error occurred, and a description of the mistake made. There are two types of errors. The first type, Error, indicates a serious problem. So serious, in fact, that no object module will be created for a program with Errors. In our example, the serious errors are the missing semicolon after the first printf, and the incorrect assignment operator in the statement to update year. The other type of error, Warning, indicates a potential problem—but not one serious enough to terminate compilation early. As long as there are no Errors, the program will compile, even with warnings. The three warnings above were generated because we didn't initialize balance before we used it (which means that its initial value would be whatever value is in the memory location assigned to it). This occurred because we forgot the statement assigning PRINCIPAL to it.

Warning: Don't take warnings lightly. Inevitably they indicate some programming mistake or faulty assumption. Failing to take heed of them often leads to disastrous results. Fixing our syntax errors (the mistakes in lines 17 and 22) and running our program without fixing the source of the warning results in the following output:

```
Turbo C  Version 2.0  Copyright (c) 1988 Borland International
oops.c:
Error oops.c 17: Statement missing ; in function main
Warning oops.c 20: Possible use of 'balance' before definition ...
Warning oops.c 21: Possible use of 'balance' before definition ...
Warning oops.c 21: Possible use of 'balance' before definition ...
Error oops.c 22: Expression syntax in function main
*** 2 errors in Compile ***

        Available memory 392084
```

Figure 1.4 The output from compiling our erroneous program.

```
    Interest Rate:  7.00%

    Year      Balance
    Floating point error: Domain
```

The floating point exception arises because we didn't initialize balance before we tried to print its value.

We're done with our discussion of tcc. Sit down at the computer and do the following exercises before going on to the next section.

EXERCISES

1–1   Use the editor of your choice to enter the interest rate program shown in Figure 1.1. Use tcc to compile and run your program. Do you get the same results we did? You should!

1–2   Try different values for PRINCIPAL, INTRATE, and PERIOD. Start with a principal of $1000, an interest rate of 10%, and a period of 10 years. The final balance should be $2593.74.

1–3   Write a program to print the integers between M and N, where M and N are program constants. With an M of 1 and an N of 5, its output is 1, 2, 3, 4, and 5. Assume M is less than N.

1.4   USING THE INTERACTIVE TURBO C ENVIRONMENT

The command-line version of Turbo C is easy to learn, provides fast compilation, and lets us use our favorite editor to enter our source file. But it has several problems. The first is that incremental program development can be time-consuming. To compile our program, we have to save our file and leave the editor. And to make changes, we have to reenter the editor, and the editor has to reload our file. The other problem is that correcting errors is a potentially painful process. The compiler provides a list of error messages, which we need to record somewhere and then refer to as we work our way through the source file, trying to find and correct all of our mistakes.

The interactive Turbo C environment, tc, provides one solution to these problems. The editor, compiler, and linker are all integrated under a single easy-to-use interface. We can compile and execute our programs with a single keystroke—without ever leaving the editor. We can also more easily correct our errors. If the compiler detects any errors, we are placed in the editor at the location where the first error occurred, with a message on the bottom of the screen that describes our mistake. After fixing this error, a single keystroke takes us to the location of the next error, and another keystroke to the error after that, and so on.

It takes longer to learn how to use tc than tcc—but the extra time is well worth it.

Entering a Program in tc

To load tc, simply type

> tc *filename*

where *filename* is the name of the file that contains or is to contain your C source file. To enter our buggy interest rate program into a file called oops.c, we start up the Turbo C environment using the command:

> tc oops.c

As before, we assume that oops.c is on the currently active disk drive, and that tc is in the DOS search path.

Figure 1.5 shows what the screen looks like as a result of this command. The screen is divided into several sections. At the top there is a menu listing our available choices: FILE, EDIT, RUN, COMPILE, PROJECT, OPTIONS, DEBUG, and BREAK/WATCH. Underneath this menu is an editor window in which the source file is displayed. Its top line provides the current location within the file (the line number and column) and the active editor modes (insert, autoindent, and so on). The window's other lines normally contain the program, but because we haven't yet entered it, this part of the window is empty. Toward the bottom of the screen there is another window. This window is where compiler messages and watched variables are displayed. It, too, is empty, since we haven't yet tried to compile our program. Finally, at the very bottom of the screen, there is the *quick-ref* line, a description of several important keys and their functions. (Holding down the *ALT* key for about a second causes this line to display descriptions of the important *ALT*-key combinations.)

When we start tc, we are placed by default in the editor window at the first line of the file. We can then use the built-in editor to enter text. Appendix B provides a detailed description of the various editor commands.

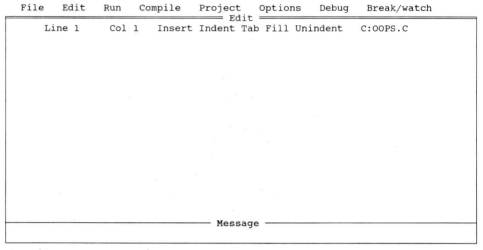

```
   File    Edit    Run    Compile    Project    Options    Debug    Break/watch
┌─────────────────────────────────────── Edit ═══════════════════════════════┐
│      Line 1       Col 1      Insert Indent Tab Fill Unindent     C:OOPS.C    │
│                                                                             │
│                                                                             │
│                                                                             │
│                                                                             │
│                                                                             │
│                                                                             │
│                                                                             │
│                                                                             │
│                                                                             │
│                                                                             │
│                                                                             │
│────────────────────────────────── Message ─────────────────────────────────│
│                                                                             │
└─────────────────────────────────────────────────────────────────────────────┘
 F1-Help   F5-Zoom   F6-Switch   F7-Trace   F8-Step   F9-Make   F10-Menu
```

Figure 1.5 The screen when we start up Turbo C.

Once we finish entering a program, we usually want to save it onto the disk and then compile and execute it. tc provides a set of keys for performing these kinds of actions. To perform the desired action, all we do is hit the appropriate key. Table 1.1 lists the special keys and their functions.

Obtaining Help

When first using tc, *F1* is probably the most important key. Hitting it places us inside a *help window* that provides information on whatever window we were in. So hitting *F1* while in the editor window provides help on using the editor, hitting it while in the help window provides a index of topics for which help is available, and so on. When we're all done with the help window, hitting *ESC* returns us to our previous window. Or we can hit *ALT-F1* to return the previous help window.

On-line help is a convenient feature that you'll frequently take advantage of when you're first using Turbo C.

KEY	FUNCTION
F1	Bring up a help window
F2	Save the file currently in the editor window
F3	Load a new file into the editor window
F4	Run program, stopping at line containing cursor
F5	Zoom and unzoom active window
F6	Switch active window
F7	Run next statement (trace into function)
F8	Run next statement (step over function)
F9	Compile and link program
F10	Invoke the main menu
CTRL-F1	Help on a particular library function
CTRL-F2	Reset the current debugging session
CTRL-F3	Display the call stack
CTRL-F4	Evaluate an expression
CTRL-F7	Add a watch expression
CTRL-F8	Toggle breakpoint
CTRL-F9	Run program
ALT-F1	Bring up the previous help window
ALT-F3	Load a previously loaded file
ALT-F5	Switch between tc screen and I/O screen
ALT-F6	Restore previous content of window
ALT-F7	Go to previous error
ALT-F8	Go to next error
ALT-F9	Compiles program being edited
ALT-X	Exit tc
SHIFT-F10	Identify version of Turbo C

Table 1.1   Turbo C's most important keys.

Saving and Loading Files

The changes we make in the editor window don't actually affect the file we're editing until we save it—that is, until we cause the editor window to be written onto the disk. Hitting *F2* saves whatever file you're currently editing. Get into the habit of saving your program whenever you make substantial changes to it. If you don't, you'll be sorry when the unthinkable happens and your computer crashes, forcing you to retype your latest changes.

Once we're done with a particular file, we don't have to leave the interactive environment to edit another file. All we have to do is hit *F3*, which loads a new file into the edit window. Hitting *F3* causes a new window to appear on the screen, as shown in Figure 1.6. We then type into this window the name of the file to load and

```
 File    Edit    Run    Compile    Project    Options    Debug    Break/watch
═══════════════════════════════════════════ Edit ═══════════════════════════════
┌────────────────┬─────────────────────────────────────────────────────────────
│   Load      F3 │Col 1   Insert Indent Tab Fill Unindent    C:OOPS.C
/│                └── Load File Name ────────────────────────────────
 │   ┌─ oops                                                    │ on.
 │   │
#│  Write to     │ >
 │  Directory    │
#│  Change dir   │ 5000.00        /* start with $5000 */
#│  OS shell     │    0.07        /* interest rate of 7% */
#│  Quit    Alt-X│   10           /* over 10-year period */
 └────────────────┘
main()
{
   int     year;                   /* year of period */
   float   balance;                /* balance at end of year */

   year = 0;
   printf("Interest Rate: %5.2f%%\n\n", INTRATE * 100)
   printf("Year      Balance\n");
   while (year <= PERIOD)
─────────────────────────────────── Message ──────────────────────────────
└──────────────────────────────────────────────────────────────────────────

 F1-Help   F5-Zoom   F6-Switch   F7-Trace   F8-Step   F9-Make   F10-Menu
```

Figure 1.6 The screen after hitting *F3*.

hit *ENTER*. Of course, it's a good idea to save the current file before loading a new file. Another way to load a file is to hit *ALT-F3*. This too causes a new window to appear on the screen. But we don't type into this window. Instead, it lists the last few files we've loaded into the editor window, and we can use the arrow keys to select the particular file we want to load again. Hitting *ENTER* then loads that file.

Compiling and Executing Programs

There are three different keys we can use to compile programs. *F9* compiles and links our program (and is smart enough to do nothing if we haven't changed the program since the last time we compiled and linked it). *CTRL-F9* is like *F9* except that it also runs the program. And *ALT-F9* is like *F9* except that it only compiles the program; it doesn't try to link it. *ALT-F9* also differs from the other two keys in that it will compile the program even if it's not really necessary.

Regardless of which of these keys we use to compile our program, if the compiler detects any errors, it places them in the message window and the cursor in the message window at the location of the first error. Figure 1.7 shows the result of trying to

```
   File    Edit    Run    Compile    Project   Options   Debug    Break/watch
 ┌─────────────────────────────── Edit ──────────────────────────────────┐
 │    Line 17      Col 9    Insert Indent Tab Fill Unindent    C:OOPS.C   │
 │{                                                                       │
 │  int     year;                 /* year of period */                    │
 │  float   balance;              /* balance at end of year */            │
 │                                                                        │
 │  year = 0;                                                             │
 │  printf("Interest Rate: %5.2f%%\n\n", INTRATE * 100)                   │
 │  printf("Year     Balance\n");                                         │
 │  while (year <= PERIOD)                                                 │
 │  {                                                                     │
 │    printf("%4d   $ %7.2f\n", year, balance);                           │
 │    balance = balance * INTRATE + balance;                              │
 │    year := year + 1;                                                   │
 │  }                                                                     │
 ├═══════════════════════════════ Message ═══════════════════════════════┤
 │Compiling C:\OOPS.C:                                                    │
 │Error C:\OOPS.C 17: Statement missing ; in function main                │
 │Warning C:\OOPS.C 20: Possible use of 'balance' before definition in function│
 │Warning C:\OOPS.C 21: Possible use of 'balance' before definition in function│
 │Warning C:\OOPS.C 21: Possible use of 'balance' before definition in function│
 │Error C:\OOPS.C 22: Expression syntax in function main                  │
 └────────────────────────────────────────────────────────────────────────┘
   F1-Help  F5-Zoom  F6-Switch  F7-Trace  F8-Step  F9-Make  F10-Menu
```

Figure 1.7 The Turbo C screen after compiling oops.c

compile Figure 1.3. To correct an error, place the cursor on the appropriate error message in the message window and hit *ENTER*. This places the cursor in the edit window, at the location of the corresponding error, where normal editor commands can be used to correct it.

There are several keys that help us correct subsequent errors. *F6* switches between the editor and error message windows. Once we've fixed a mistake, we can hit *F6* to place the cursor back in the message window, where we can select another error message. This is useful when we want to fix a specific error message. But it is awkward when we are correcting errors in sequence, since it forces us to switch back and forth between windows. Luckily, there is an alternative. *ALT-F8* places the cursor in the editor window at the start of the next error. *ALT-F7* is similar, except that it places the cursor at the start of the previous error. One other important key is *F5*, the *zoom* key. Hitting *F5* makes your current window take up the entire screen. This allows editing with a larger window, or easy viewing of more than just the first few error messages. Hitting *F5* in a full-screen window returns it to its normal size.

When we hit *CTRL-F9* and our program compiles successfully, it then starts running. This causes the message window to disappear, to be replaced with a *watch*

KEY	ENTRY	FUNCTION
ALT-F	FILE	Menu of file handling commands
ALT-E	EDIT	Places you in editor
ALT-R	RUN	Menu of execution commands
ALT-C	COMPILE	Menu of compile-oriented commands
ALT-P	PROJECT	Menu of project options
ALT-O	OPTIONS	Menu of various tc options
ALT-D	DEBUG	Menu of debugger commands
ALT-B	BREAK/WATCH	Menu of more debugger controls

Table 1.2   Turbo C main menu entries and their functions.

window. The watch window is used by the debugger (Chapter 19) to display various variables and expressions. We're not using the debugger yet, so this window remains empty. But now we've got a problem—Where does the program's output go? What happens is that tc manipulates two screens. One is the usual tc display, the edit screen that contains the editor, compiler, and debugger windows. The other is the I/O (or execution) screen, which contains the program's input and output. When the program is running, the I/O screen is displayed. When the program finishes or the debugger produces output, the edit screen is restored. At any time, however, we can use *ALT-F5* to display the contents of the I/O screen.

Finally, there's one other important key. That's *ALT-X*, which exits tc and returns to DOS. If we've changed the file in the editor window since we last saved it, we are asked whether we really want to exit without saving our work.

Using Menus

Because there are so many special keys, it can be difficult to remember what all of them do. The Turbo C main menu provides a helpful alternative. This menu contains the names of various commands and submenus. Table 1.2 lists its entries and their functions.

The easiest way to access these menu entries is to hit *ALT-?*, where *?* is the first letter of the desired menu. So hitting *ALT-F* selects the FILE menu. When we select an entry that happens to be the name of a menu, that menu pops up onto the screen, as shown in Figure 1.8.

Once a menu has popped up on the screen, we have to select a particular menu entry. There are two ways to do this. One is to move the arrow keys to the desired entry and hit *ENTER*. The alternative is to type the first character of the entry's name. So to save a file, which we do by selecting the SAVE entry on the FILE menu, we can either hit *S*, or we can move the cursor to the SAVE entry and hit *ENTER*. (These methods of selecting menu entries also work with the main menu, which we can select by hitting *F10*. Obviously, however, they're less frequently used since the *ALT*-keys

```
     File    Edit    Run    Compile   Project   Options   Debug   Break/watch
═══╤════════════════════════════════════ Edit ═════════════════════════════════
   │ Load       F3 │Col 1    Insert Indent Tab Fill Unindent    C:NONAME.C
   │ Pick   Alt-F3 │
   │ New           │
   │ Save       F2 │
   │ Write to      │
   │ Directory     │
   │ Change dir    │
   │ OS shell      │
   │ Quit    Alt-X │
   └───────────────┘




                            ──────────────── Message ────────────────


───────────────────────────────────────────────────────────────────────────────
 F1-Help   F5-Zoom   F6-Switch   F7-Trace   F8-Step   F9-Make   F10-Menu    NUM
```

Figure 1.8   The FILE menu.

are so much more convenient.)

The FILE menu has several entries besides SAVE that you are likely to use frequently. LOAD is equivalent to *F3*, loading in a new file. PICK is equivalent to *ALT-F3*, listing the files you've most recently loaded, and letting you select which of these files you want to load. WRITE is like SAVE, except that it allows you to save the file you're currently working on into the file of your choice. DIR prompts for a directory and then lists the files in it. Finally, OS-SHELL temporarily exits tc and returns you to DOS. This allows us to run DOS commands without ever leaving tc Once you're through running commands, typing exit returns you to tc. It's useful because we can compile and link a program using *F9*—without executing it—and then, at some later time, use this menu entry to access DOS and run the program.

For simple operations such as compiling, executing, and loading, we prefer to use the special keys. But there is no special key for listing the contents of a directory, and the menu system is a convenient alternative. We will discuss the various menus in detail later on. Appendix C provides a complete description of the Turbo C menu choices and their functions.

It's time for another exercise break. Do at least one of the programming exercises before going onto the next chapter.

EXERCISES

1-4 Use tc to enter our buggy interest rate program. Use the special keys to compile and execute it. Correct the errors and recompile and execute the program. Repeat the process using the menu system.

1-5 An earlier exercise asks for a program to print the values between M and N. Rewrite it to print the values in reverse order. That is, with an M of 1 and an N of 5, its output is 5, 4, 3, 2, and 1. Develop this program using tc.

1-6 Write a small program to print the sum of the integers between M and N, inclusively, where M and N are program constants. With an M of 1 and an N of 100, your program should print 5050.

1-7 Write a program to print a multiplication table for the integers 1 through 12. Hint: Use nested `while` loops and the `%3d` format of `printf`.

2 SOME EXAMPLE PROGRAMS

The best way to learn a programming language is to see example programs written using it. This chapter presents three simple Turbo C programs, each illustrating several new language features. The first program is a version of the interest rate accumulator that obtains its information from its input. The second prints its input in reverse order. And the third sorts its input using a technique known as insertion sort, tying together all of the language features discussed so far.

2.1   EXTENDING OUR FIRST C PROGRAM

Let's make our interest accumulation program more flexible. Rather than hard-wiring the initial balance (PRINCIPAL), the interest rate (INTRATE), and the number of years (PERIOD), we'll obtain these values from an interactive user. To do so we need another function from the standard I/O library, scanf, the input analog to printf. scanf reads formatted input from the standard input, which is usually the console keyboard (but we'll show how to change this later in the chapter). The new version of the program appears in Figure 2.1; its output in Figure 2.2

Using Scanf

As with printf, scanf's arguments are a formatting control string, enclosed in quotation marks, and a list of variables. The control string uses conventions similar to those of printf: %d indicates a decimal integer, %f a floating point, and so on. When reading a value, scanf ignores white space characters such as blanks, tabs, and line boundaries, and simply looks for the next appropriate character. It expects any characters that appear between the formatting codes to appear in its input.

The program in Figure 2.1 begins by using printf to write a prompt requesting the starting balance, interest rate, and period. It then uses scanf to obtain their values from the user.

```
printf("Enter interest rate, principal and period: ");
scanf("%f %f %d", &intrate, &balance, &period);
```

```
/*
 * A second version of our interest accumulator.  This version
 * uses scanf to get its input from the user.  It doesn't
 * run correctly unless it's given the input it expects.
 */
#include <stdio.h>

main()
{
  float    balance,                  /* balance at end of year */
           intrate;                  /* interest rate */
  int      period,                   /* length of period */
           year;                     /* year of period */


  printf("Enter interest rate, principal and period: ");
  scanf("%f %f %d", &intrate, &balance, &period);
  printf("Interest Rate: %5.2f%%\n\n", intrate * 100);
  printf("Year     Balance\n");
  year = 0;
  while (year <= period)
  {
    printf("%4d   $ %7.2f\n", year, balance);
    balance = balance * intrate + balance;
    year = year + 1;
  }
  return 0;
}
```

Figure 2.1   intrate2.c—The interest accumulator modified to obtain input from the user.

```
Enter interest rate, principal and period: .10 1000 10
Interest Rate: 10.00%

Year     Balance
   0   $ 1000.00
   1   $ 1100.00
   2   $ 1210.00
   3   $ 1331.00
   4   $ 1464.10
   5   $ 1610.51
   6   $ 1771.56
   7   $ 1948.72
   8   $ 2143.59
   9   $ 2357.95
  10   $ 2593.74
```

Figure 2.2   The input and output when we run our new interest rate program.

This `scanf` reads two floating point values and an integer from the program's input. Because `scanf` automatically ignores intervening white space, the input values can be widely separated and do not even have to be on the same line.

Actually, we don't simply provide `scanf` a list of variable names. It turns out that `scanf` expects to be passed a variable's address rather than its name. This forces us to precede each variable with a new operator, `&`, which returns the variable's address.

Warning: Remember to precede any variables passed to `scanf` *with an* `&`. Forgetting the address operator `&` causes strange and unforgiving behavior (we'll see why when we consider how parameters work in Chapter 7).

Handling Input Errors

Our current interest accumulator has one major flaw: It doesn't provide any indication if it isn't given the two floating point and one integer values it expects. In fact, it simply produces incorrect results. This is obviously undesirable, since the user could accidentally provide three floating point values instead of two, provide letters rather than numbers, or possibly provide no input at all. At the very least, invalid input should result in an error message.

Luckily, we can easily correct this problem. It turns out that `scanf` returns a useful value—either the number of values it correctly read from the input or the special value `EOF`, a predefined constant (usually −1, although its value is system-dependent) that indicates that the end of the input has been reached (the user has typed a control-Z at the beginning of the line and provided a carriage return).

We can determine whether an error has occurred by comparing the number of values correctly read (returned by `scanf`) with the expected number. Since we are reading three values, `scanf` should return three. Any other return value indicates an input error or the end of the input. In either case, the program prints a simple message and terminates. A version that does this is shown in Figure 2.3. For valid input, it produces the same output as the previous version.

The If Statement

We haven't yet explained how we test `scanf`'s return value. We do so with an `if` statement. The `if` statement has a simple form:

```
if (expression)
    true-statement
else
    false-statement
```

`if` evaluates the expression in parentheses and, if the condition is true, executes *true-statement*. If the condition is false, it executes *false-statement*. Like Pascal, the `else` *false-statement* is optional. If we omit it and the condition is false, *true-statement* is simply skipped. Unlike Pascal, there is no `then` keyword, and *expression* must be surrounded with parenthesis. As with the `while`, braces are used if we want a group of statements where C requires a single statement.

In Figure 2.3, we expect `scanf` to return three. We test `scanf`'s return value using the test-for-equality operator, the *double* equal sign (`==`). If the test is true, we

```
/*
 * The third version of our interest accumulating program.
 * Gets its input from the user and makes sure it's valid.
 */
#include <stdio.h>

main()
{
  float    balance,          /* balance at end of year */
           intrate;          /* interest rate */
  int      period,           /* length of period */
           year;             /* year of period */

  printf("Enter interest rate, principal and period: ");
  if (scanf("%f %f %d", &intrate, &balance, &period) == 3)
  {
      printf("Interest Rate: %5.2f%%\n\n", intrate * 100);
      printf("Year     Balance\n");
      year = 0;
      while (year <= period)
      {
        printf("%4d  $ %7.2f\n", year, balance);
        balance = balance * intrate + balance;
        year = year + 1;
      }
  }
  else
    printf("Invalid input - Program terminated\n");
  return 0;
}
```

Figure 2.3   intrate3.c—Yet another version of the interest accumulator.

execute the group of statements immediately following it, writing the heading and computing the balances for the various years—the body of our earlier interest rate program. If the test is false, it means that scanf did not return three, and we execute the else part, writing an appropriate error message.

scanf is a useful function, but less useful than it may at first appear. One problem is that we usually can use it only when we can assume that the input is correct, as when our input has been generated by another program. Why? Because scanf simply quits reading input at the first unexpected character, there is no easy way to use it to skip over illegal input. Another problem has to do with efficiency. Since scanf can read an arbitrary number of values with differing types, its underlying implementation is large and cumbersome.

In subsequent chapters we'll look at low-level input in detail and develop solutions to these problems. In fact, we'll end up writing our own special-purpose versions of scanf. The methods we use are brief and surprisingly simple, and they can reduce the running times of our programs and the size of our compiled code by one-third or more.

The For Loop

Let's make one final change to our interest accumulator before abandoning it forever. Our previous version used a `while` loop to update the balance.

```
year = 0;
while (year <= period)
{
  printf("%4d   $ %7.2f\n", year, balance);
  balance = balance * intrate + balance;
  year = year + 1;
}
```

We'll now replace it with another looping construct, the `for` loop.

```
for (year = 0; year <= period; year = year + 1)
{
  printf("%4d   $ %7.2f\n", year, balance);
  balance = balance * intrate + balance;
}
```

We do so because the `for` leads to a more concise program, even though both loops are appropriate.

Most other programming languages have a construct that allows us to initialize a loop index to some starting value, increment or decrement it each time through the loop, and terminate the loop when some stopping condition is met. C's `for` loop is similar but more general. Its basic form is:

> `for` (*Start ; Test ; Action*)
>   *Statement*

Start, *Test*, and *Action* can be any C expressions. As with the `while`, a loop body containing multiple statements must be surrounded by braces.

A `for` first evaluates *Start*, which usually initializes a counter. Then it evaluates *Test*, which usually tests whether the counter has not exceeded some value. It exits the loop if the condition is false. Otherwise, it executes the loop body, evaluates *Action*, and repeats the cycle. *Action* usually increments the counter controlling the loop.

The `for` loop above initializes `year` to 0, and then tests to see whether is it is less than or equal to the period. If it is, it executes the loop body (printing the current balance and computing the next balance), increments `year`, and does the test again. The loop exits when the year is greater than the period.

We've been talking about `for`, `if`, and `while` testing whether a condition is true or false. But that isn't exactly what happens. C's relational operators (`<=`, `==`, and so on) actually return 1 if the condition is *true* and 0 if it is *false*. So these statements really test whether the expression evaluates to zero. A zero value means the test is false. A nonzero value means the test is true. In later chapters we take advantage of this to make our code more concise.

We're finally done with the interest accumulator. The following exercises give you practice with `scanf`, `if`, and `for`. Do a few of them before moving on to the next section.

EXERCISES

2-1 Create intrate4.c, which should be intrate3.c modified to use the `for` loop we showed earlier instead of the `while`.

2-2 Write a short program to read two values with `scanf` and to print the sum of the values between them. If its input is 1 and 5, its output is 15.

2-3 Write a program that sums its input values and prints the total. If the program's input is 1.6, 5.1, and 6.9, its output should be 13.6.

2-4 Write a program that reads two values, `min` and `max`, and then reads the remainder of its input, counting the values less than `min` and those greater than `max`. When the program is done reading its input, it prints these two counts.

2-5 Extend Figure 2.3 to let the user provide more than one interest rate, principal, and period.

2.2   **A PROGRAM TO REVERSE ITS INPUT**

Our next program, rev, reverses its input. That is, it reads all of its input values and then writes them in reverse order; the last value read is the first one written. Although that doesn't sound like a useful thing to do, we can use this program, shown in Figure 2.4, to take values sorted in ascending order and print them in descending order. Figure 2.5 shows the output when this program is run. This program introduces the array, which is a convenient method for storing a large table of values.

Arrays

An array is a collection of values, all of which are of the same underlying type. C supports arrays of any of its data types. We declare an array by giving the type of its elements, its name, and the number of elements. The declaration

```
int table[MAXVALS];
```

declares `table` to be an array, consisting of MAXVALS ints (1000 in Figure 2.4).

We access an array element by following the array's name with an index enclosed in square brackets. The index can be any expression that can be interpreted as an integer. Arrays are indexed from 0, so in this example we can access `table[0]` through `table[999]`. There is no run-time array bounds checking, unlike languages such as Pascal, where an illegal array access terminates the program. In C, if we

```
/*
 * Read values and print them in reverse order.
 */
#include <stdio.h>

#define MAXVALS 1000            /* max values in array "table" */

main()
{
  int table[MAXVALS],           /* input array */
      i,                        /* index used in writing values */
      n;                        /* number of values in "table" */

  printf("Enter values:\n");

  n = 0;                                      /* read values */
  while (n < MAXVALS && scanf("%d", &table[n]) == 1)
    n = n + 1;

  printf("Values in reverse order:\n\n");   /* write values */
  for (i = n - 1; i >= 0; i = i - 1)
    printf("%d\n", table[i]);
  return 0;
}
```

Figure 2.4 rev.c—A program to print its input in reverse order.

```
Enter values:
10 20 18 24 68 1 19
^Z
Values in reverse order:

19
1
68
24
18
20
10
```

Figure 2.5 Some example input and output for our reversing program. The user types a control-Z to indicate the end of the input.

attempt to access a location such as `table[-10]`, neither the compiler nor the run-time environment will complain. *Warning: We are responsible for doing our own bounds checking during the running of our program.*

Figure 2.4 reverses its input by reading the input values into an array and then printing the array in reverse order. A single `while` controls the reading of the program's input values.

```
n = 0;
while (n < MAXVALS && scanf("%d", &table[n]) == 1)
    n = n + 1;
```

This `while`'s test is more complicated than any we've seen before. We want to keep reading values as long as there is room in the array (`n < MAXVALS`) and there are more values to read (`scanf` returns 1). This means we have to make two tests and leave the loop if either fails. To do so, we use the logical AND operator, `&&`, which returns true only if both conditions are true. But, perhaps surprisingly, `&&` doesn't always test both conditions. It first tests the condition on the left. Only if this condition is true (nonzero) does it test the next condition. We take advantage of this to try to read a value only if there is room in the array. We enter the loop body only if there is room in the array and we read a value successfully.

Logical OR, `||`, and , `!`, are also available. `||` takes two conditions and returns true if either condition is true. Like `&&`, it doesn't always test both conditions. It first tests the condition on the left and, only if it is false (nonzero), does it test the next condition. `!` is different. It takes only one condition and returns the negation of the condition's truth value.

We use `scanf` to read each value into an array element. As always, we are careful to pass `scanf` the variable's address, in this case, `&table[n]`.

The program concludes with a `for` loop that prints `table`'s elements in reverse order.

```
for (i = n - 1; i >= 0; i = i - 1)
    printf("%d\n", table[i]);
```

We use `i` to index through `table`'s elements, going backwards from its last element to its first. The loop is straightforward, with one subtlety. Even though `n` is the number of array elements, when we initialize `i` as the index of `table`'s last element, we initialize it to `n-1`, not `n`. We do this because arrays are indexed from 0, not 1. We want to ensure we access only `table[0]` through `table[n-1]`. In fact, `table[n]` is not a value we've read into the array.

Functions

Up to now, our programs have consisted of only the single function `main`. But when we write larger programs, we need to break them into smaller, more efficient, more manageable pieces. Functions are the mechanism that lets us do so. We can create common, single purpose routines and use them from the main program, without the main program having to know how they actually accomplish their task. In fact, we have already used functions that were prewritten and compiled for us, such as `printf` and `scanf`, without knowing what they look like internally.

A C program is simply a collection of one or more functions (including `main`), some predefined, others user-defined. To show how to create and use user-defined functions, we rewrite our input reversal program to use two new functions. The first reads data into an array and counts the number of elements read, the other prints an array in reverse order. Although simple, these functions demonstrate the different aspects of function use and will guide you in writing your own functions. Figure 2.6 contains the new input reversing program, showing where the functions are defined and how they are called.

This main program has the same task as before: read values into an array and print them in reverse order. But now it accomplishes this task by calling two functions, `get_data` and `print_reverse` The underscore (_) is part of the function name, which we use to make the name more readable. An alternative would be to use uppercase and lowercase, such as `GetData` or `PrintReverse`.

Unlike `scanf` and `printf`, `get_data` and `print_reverse` have not already been written for us and placed in a library, so we are forced to define them ourselves. To define a function, we have to specify the function's parameters, the type of value that the function returns, the function's local variables, and the code executed when the function is called.

> *return-type function-name* (*parm1*, *parm2*, ..., *parmN*)
> {
>   *local declarations*
>
>   *statements*
> }

We precede the function's name with the type of value it returns, such as `int` or `float`. By default all functions are assumed to return an `int`, and we've secretly been taking advantage of this feature by not bothering to declare `main`'s return value. But in general our code is more readable when we explicitly provide this declaration, as we have done with `get_data`. It turns out that there is also a special type, `void`, for functions such as `print_reverse` that never return a useful value. These functions behave like a procedure in languages like Pascal.

We follow the function's name with a parenthesized parameter list, a list of variable declarations that specify each parameter's name and type. When we have a function that takes no parameters, we can simply leave the list empty, as we've done with `main`, or we can specify a parameter list of `void`.

Finally, we follow the parameter list by the function's body. This is where we declare any variables local to the function (such as loop counters and array indexes). These *local variables* can be accessed only within the function where they are declared. The statements executed when the function is called follow these declarations. We must supply the braces surrounding the function's body, even if it contains no variable declarations or statements.

The Function `get_data`

`get_data` is a function that takes two parameters: the array where the input values are to go (`a`) and the maximum number of values to read (`max`). We declare these

```
/*
 * A second program to read values and print in reverse order.
 */
#include <stdio.h>

#define MAXVALS    1000    /* max values in array "table" */

main()
{
  int table[MAXVALS],     /* input array */
      n;                  /* number of values in "table" */
  int get_data(int a[], int max);
  void print_reverse(int a[], int max);

  printf("Enter values:\n");
  n = get_data(table, MAXVALS);
  printf("Values in reverse order:\n\n");
  print_reverse(table, n);
  return 0;
}

/*
 * Read up to "max" values into "a"
 */
int get_data(int a[], int max)
{
  int count;

  count = 0;
  while (count < max && scanf("%d", &a[count]) == 1)
    count = count + 1;
  return count;
}

/*
 * Print "a" in reverse order
 */
void print_reverse(int a[], int num)
{
  int i;

  for (i = num - 1; i >= 0; i = i - 1)
    printf("%d\n", a[i]);
}
```

Figure 2.6   newrev.c—A new version of our input reversal program.

parameters in the function header, a as an array of integers and max as an integer.

```
int get_data(int a[], int max)
{
   ...
}
```

get_data reads values into the array and returns the number of values read (count). When it returns, a contains values at a[0] through a[count-1]).

To actually execute get_data, we need to call it. A function calls another function by specifying its name and providing a list of values, the function's arguments.

```
n = get_data(table, MAXVALS);
```

These argument values are copied and supplied as the function's parameters—which means that changes to a function's parameters do *not* affect its arguments. In Figure 2.6, for example, get_data can change max without affecting MAXVALS, the value passed to it. This parameter-passing mechanism is known as *call by value* because the argument's *value* is copied to the function.

When we pass an array, however, we really only pass the address of its first element, not the entire array. This means we don't need to declare the size of a one-dimensional array parameter. And in get_data we don't specify the number of elements in a. *Warning: This also means that if we change an array element within a function, it changes the array passed to the function.* An assignment within get_data, such as

```
a[0] = 10;
```

changes the value of table[0]. In our case, we read values into a, which places the values into table.

We've seen how parameters allow functions to communicate. Functions can also communicate through return values. A function returns a value with the return statement.

```
return expression;
```

A return evaluates *expression*, exits the function, and returns its value to the function's caller. In Figure 2.6, we have get_data return the number of values read, which is stored in the local variable count.

```
return count;
```

After get_data executes this return statement, n is assigned the number of values read into a.

Just because a function returns a value, however, we're not obligated to do anything with it. If we didn't care how many values we read, we could simply ignore get_data's return value.

```
get_data(table, MAXVALS);
```

And in Figure 2.1 we simply ignored scanf's return value and assumed that the input was read successfully.

The Function `print_reverse`

`print_reverse` also takes two arguments, the array to print and the number of values in the array. `print_reverse` does not return a value, so we declare it to return `void`.

It prints the array elements in reverse order using a single `for` loop. Because we declare the loop index variable `i` within `print_reverse`, it is local to `print_reverse`, and we can't access it from the `main` program.

Since we don't specify the size of an array parameter when we define a function, we can pass the function any size array of the specified type. This makes `get_data` and `print_reverse` fairly general. We can use `get_data` to read in any size array of integers, and `print_reverse` to print any size array of integers in reverse order.

The Main Program

As usual, the `main` program begins with a set of declarations. Two of them are new.

```
int get_data(int a[], int max);
void print_reverse(int a[], int max);
```

Since these declarations look exactly like the function header, you should be wondering why we need them. Don't we provide the same information when we define the function?

Unfortunately, we often define functions after we define their callers, as we did here, defining `get_data` and `print_reverse` after `main`. The declarations tell the compiler how `get_data` and `print_reverse` are supposed to be used—describing the types of their return values and parameters. Without them, the compiler couldn't check whether we were passing the right arguments to the function or using its return value correctly. The compiler needs the above declaration to detect common mistakes such as accidentally reversing the order of `get_data`'s parameters, passing an incorrect number of arguments to `print_reverse`, or trying to use `print_reverse`'s return value.

When we call a function, the compiler need only know the types of the function's parameters, not their names. That means that we can omit the names entirely or include different names—the names we supply are *dummies*, so they need not correspond in any way to the names used as the function's parameters or function arguments when it is called. We take the trouble to provide names, since they help document what the function does.

Input/Output Redirection

Our input reversal program doesn't explicitly deal with files, so it may not appear to be too useful. After all, of what use is a program that simply reads the values we type and writes them on the console in reverse order? The program would be more useful if we could somehow make it read its input from a file, or write its output to a file.

To do so, we need to execute it as a DOS command, and to take advantage of DOS's ability to redirect a program's standard input and output. But we can only execute DOS commands directly when we're in something called the DOS shell—the place from which we originally invoked Turbo C by typing tc or tcc. In tc, we can get to the DOS shell by selecting the FILE/OS-SHELL entry. If we're using tcc, we're already there.

Suppose we've successfully compiled and linked newrev.c and obtained the executable program named newrev.exe. When we execute it, by typing

newrev

at the DOS prompt, DOS sets things up so that the program's standard input comes from the console keyboard and so that its standard output goes to the console monitor. But if we follow the command with a < and a file name, the program's standard input is the named file rather than the keyboard. That means that if numbers contains a list of integers, we can use

newrev < numbers

to display them in reverse order. This command executes newrev so that every time it reads a value with `scanf`, it is reading from numbers instead of the console.

Similarly, following a command with a > and a file name causes the program's standard output to be the named file rather than the console monitor. So instead of displaying the result of reversing numbers on the console, we can place them into a file reversed with

newrev < numbers > reversed

Figure 2.7 further illustrates what happens when we redirect a `newrev`'s input and output. We'll see many other useful examples of redirection throughout the text.

EXERCISES

2–6 Rewrite `get_data` to use a `for` rather than a `while` to read the input values.

2–7 Write a function, `init_array`, that sets every element of an array of integers to a particular value. The function takes three parameters, the array, its size, and the initial value.

2–8 Write a function, `print_array`, that prints an array's elements in order, one per line, starting with its first element and ending with its last. Write a slightly different version of this function that prints the array elements and their positions.

2–9 Write a program that reads values from its input and counts the occurrences of each unique value in the input. Assume the values are between 1 and 256. Once the input has been read, write each value and the number of its occurrences. Ignore values that didn't appear in the input. The functions written in the previous exercises provide a useful starting point.

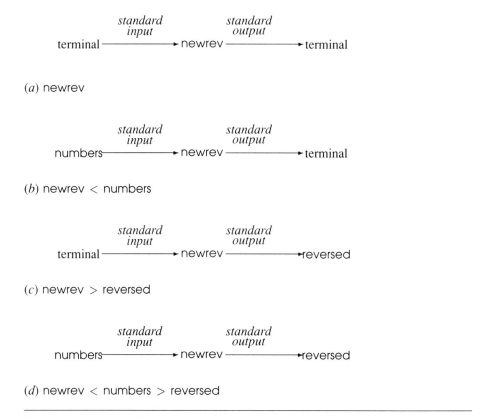

Figure 2.7 How input/output redirection works.

2-10 Write a function, sum, that computes and returns the sum of the first n elements in an array of ints. Test it with a small program that uses get_data to fill the array with values.

2-11 Write a function, search, that finds the location of a value in an array. The function takes three parameters: the value to search for, the array to be searched, and the number of array elements. The function returns an int, the index where the value is found. If the value is not in the array, the function should return −1.

2-12 How can we place the output of the latest version of our interest rate program into the file output? How can we enter numbers at the terminal and have them end up in reverse order in the file reversed?

2.3   CASE STUDY—INSERTION SORT

We tie together the ideas we have presented in this chapter in a program, named isort, that reads integers, keeps them sorted in an array, and prints the array when it is done reading. The program reads from its standard input and writes to its standard output, but we can use redirection to use it to sort a file. Assuming that we have a file called numbers containing the values we wish to sort, typing

        isort < numbers > sorted

in the DOS shell creates a file sorted containing the values in numbers in sorted order.

We use a sorting technique known as *insertion sort*; it is easy to understand and to program, and usually works with little debugging effort. Its drawback is that it is not the fastest sorting routine; the computing time increases as the *square* of the number of values to be sorted. Double the number of values and the computing time goes up by a factor of 4, triple the number and the computing time goes up by a factor of 9. Even so, insertion sort is suitable when we have to sort fewer than 50 to 100 values.

Insertion sort works by assuming that the array is already sorted and then trying to find the appropriate place to insert a new value. We compare the new value with the last, "largest" element in the array. If the new value is smaller than the largest, we shift the largest over one place in the array, and compare the new value with the next largest value. When the new number is finally larger than some value in the array, we have found the appropriate place to insert it. If the new value is smaller than every value in the array, it goes into the first position. The entire operation can be characterized as "compare, shift; compare, shift . . ." until we find the appropriate place. The technique is diagrammed in Figure 2.8.

Insertion sort is an enjoyable algorithm to implement because it is so natural. Give someone one suit from a deck of cards and ask them to sort it, and the person will usually do something resembling insertion sort—compare the next card with each in turn, until the right place is found and then insert the new card in its correct place. Our insertion sort program is shown in Figure 2.9.

Handling Input Errors

Our earlier programs didn't handle errors very well. In fact, if scanf did not read the expected number of values, they simply assumed that the end of file was reached successfully and ignored the possibility that an illegal value had been entered. We would prefer that our program print an appropriate message if an input error occurs.

Unfortunately, doing so complicates the input reading. Here's the loop that reads values, inserts them into their correct place in the array, and updates a count of the number of values read.

```
for (n = 0; n < MAX &&
            (res = scanf("%d", &next)) == 1; n = n + 1)
    insert(table, next, n);
if (res != EOF)         /* check for input errors */
    printf("Error while reading input.\n");
```

table

[0]	[1]	[2]	[3]	[4]	[5]		val	pos
2	7	9	18	21		· · ·	8	5

(*a*) value is smaller than `table[pos-1]`, shift, decrement pos

table

[0]	[1]	[2]	[3]	[4]	[5]		val	pos
2	7	9	18	21	21	· · ·	8	4

(*b*) value is smaller than `table[pos-1]`, shift, decrement pos

table

[0]	[1]	[2]	[3]	[4]	[5]		val	pos
2	7	9	18	18	21	· · ·	8	3

(*c*) value is smaller than `table[pos-1]`, shift, decrement pos.

table

[0]	[1]	[2]	[3]	[4]	[5]		val	pos
2	7	9	9	18	21	· · ·	8	2

(*d*) compare value with table[pos-1], value is bigger, install in array.

table

[0]	[1]	[2]	[3]	[4]	[5]	
2	7	8	9	18	21	· · ·

(*e*) final array.

Figure 2.8 *Stages in insertion sort. The new value is eventually put between the 7 and the 9.*

We want to keep reading values as long as two conditions hold. The first is that the array has space for the new values. We may eventually run out of room, since the array only has MAX elements (MAX is a program constant set to 100 using #define). We handle this condition with a simple comparison. The other condition is that we haven't had an error or hit the end of the input. One way to handle this condition is to test whether scanf's return value is one, the number of values we expect it to read. But this doesn't distinguish between errors and end of file.

```
/*
 * Read a table of values and sort them using "insertion sort."
 */
#include <stdio.h>

#define  MAX    100        /* maximum number of values to sort */

main()
{
  int n,                   /* number of values in table */
      res,                 /* value returned by scanf */
      table[MAX],          /* table of values */
      next;                /* current value */
  void insert(int a[], int val, int num);
  void print_table(int a[], int);

  for (n = 0; n < MAX &&
             (res = scanf("%d", &next)) == 1; n = n + 1)
    insert(table, next, n);
  if (res != EOF)          /* check for input errors */
    printf("Error while reading input.\n");
  print_table(table, n);
  return 0;
}

/*
 * Place value in correct place in array.
 */
void insert(int a[], int val, int num)
{
  int pos;

  for (pos = num; pos > 0 && val < a[pos - 1]; pos = pos - 1)
    a[pos] = a[pos - 1];
  a[pos] = val;
}

/*
 * Print array in sorted order.
 */
void print_table(int a[], int num)
{
  int i;

  for (i = 0; i < num; i = i + 1)
    printf("%d\n", a[i]);
}
```

Figure 2.9   isort.c—A program to sort integers using insertion sort.

What we need to do instead is record `scanf`'s return value inside the loop test, and then compare it against the special value EOF after we've left the loop.

```
n < MAX && (res = scanf("%d", &next)) == 1
```

`scanf` returns EOF only if it reaches the end of file when it tries to read a value. (EOF itself is a constant defined in stdio.h.) The above fragment works because assignment, =, is an operator; it assigns a value to a variable and then returns the value assigned. In this case, after `scanf` reads the value, its return value is assigned to `res`. After the assignment, this value is compared with one to determine whether the loop should exit.

Implementing Insertion Sort

We use two functions to implement insertion sort: `insert` places a value in its correct place in the array, `print_table` prints the array.

`insert` needs to determine where the new element should go and put it there. To insert a value in the array, we compare it with each array element, starting with the largest, or last, element and shifting values one place whenever it is smaller than the element we are comparing. Eventually, it will be greater than or equal to some array element, or we will have reached the start of the array. In either case we insert it into the newly created hole. Finding the place for the new element is accomplished with a single `for` loop, whose body consists of a single statement:

```
for (pos = num; pos > 0 && val < a[pos - 1]; pos = pos - 1)
    a[pos] = a[pos - 1];
```

A great deal is taking place within this `for` loop; we suggest trying to work through it by hand to see its effect.

`print_table` is almost identical to `print_reverse`; the only difference is in the order in which the table is printed. Notice that like `print_reverse`, `print_table` is passed the number of elements in the array it is printing, so it also works for any size array.

EXERCISES

2-13 How can we combine newrev and isort to sort a file's input values from high to low?

2-14 Write a version of insertion sort that works with floating point values.

2-15 Add additional code to the insertion sort program that counts the number of elements moved. After printing the entire sorted array, print this movement count. For a random set of n input values, it should be approximately $n(n + 1)/2$. Compare your result with this expected result.

2-16 Write a version of the insertion sort program that first finds the appropriate place to insert the new value, and then shifts everything after it one place before inserting the value.

2-17 Write a program that prints the ten smallest values in its input. Extend the program to print the ten largest values.

2-18 Write a program that prompts for a count of test scores, and then prompts and reads each of these scores into an array. Once it's read the scores, have it print the mean (the average score), median (the score that half the students are less than and the other half are better than), and mode (the score the most students had).

2-19 Extend the program in the previous exercise to print the scores in sorted order.

3 BASIC DATA TYPES

Every variable has a name and a type—the name identifies the variable, the type tells how we plan to use it. This chapter first presents the rules for composing C identifiers, and then delves into the details of C's basic data types, integer, real, and character. We study the range of values they can hold, how to read and print them, and when each is appropriate. As part of our discussion of characters, we introduce character-at-a-time input and output and Turbo C's special functions for unbuffered character-at-a-time input. The chapter concludes with a case study that builds a program to display its input, one screenfull at a time.

3.1 IDENTIFIERS AND NAMING CONVENTIONS

Variable and function names are known as *identifiers*. But not every combination of characters is a legal identifier. First, identifiers consist only of lowercase and uppercase letters, digits, and underscore (_) characters—no other characters are allowed. And second, the first character must be a letter or an underscore. Because some system functions begin with an underscore, however, always starting identifiers with a letter will prevent name conflicts.

Case is significant in identifiers: `get_data` refers to a different identifier than `Get_data`, which refers to a different identifier than `Get_Data`.

Turbo C reserves the identifiers listed in Figure 3.1 as keywords, so we can't use them as normal identifiers (the identifiers we've labeled with an asterisk are extensions to the standard C keywords; use the -A compiler option or a OPTIONS/COMPILER/SOURCE menu entry to allow these keywords to be used as identifiers). Turbo C also reserves a set of identifiers beginning with tc, so avoid starting names with this prefix. Finally, other compilers reserve `entry` and `fortran`, so avoid using them as well.

We can have identifiers of any length, but most compilers limit the number of significant characters. In the original definition of C only the first 8 characters were significant, implying that `var_name1` and `var_name2` referred to the same identifier. In Turbo C, as in most modern C compilers, the first 32 characters are sig-

asm*	auto	break	case	cdecl*	char
const	continue	default	do	double	else
enum	extern	far*	float	for	goto
huge*	if	int	interrupt*	long	near*
pascal*	register	return	short	signed	sizeof
static	struct	switch	typedef	union	unsigned
void	volatile	while			

Figure 3.1 Turbo C reserved words.

nificant, although to be portable to all current compilers, it may be necessary to restrict names to six, seven, or eight characters. You can use the -iX option or an OPTIONS/ENVIRONMENT menu entry to specify the desired number of significant characters. Setting X to 8, for example, helps disclose those identifiers that are similar in the first 8 characters.

3.2   DATA TYPES

Identifiers constitute only the first part of a variable declaration. The other part specifies the type of data the identifier is to hold. There are three basic data types in C: integers, reals, and characters.

Integers

Integers are whole numbers. C provides three classes of integer storage: short, int, and long, in both signed and unsigned forms. These classes vary in size and efficiency of use. Table 3.1 lists the sizes and ranges of these values for Turbo C. On most systems, a short is 16 bits, an int is either 16 or 32 bits, and a long 32 bits. But the only guarantee is that a short is not going to be larger than an int, which is not going to be larger than a long.

Why do we have all of these different classes? Because they all have different uses. ints occupy one word of storage and are generally the most efficient data type to use. But since the word size varies between machines, we use longs for values that require more than 16 bits. shorts allow us to save space when a variable's value always falls within a small range.

Integers can be either signed or unsigned. Signed integers use one bit for the sign of the number. A signed int (or just int, the default) uses one bit for the sign and 15 bits for the magnitude on 16-bit machines or 31 bits for the magnitude on 32-bit machines. Unsigned integers have no sign bit and use all the bits for the magnitude, which doubles the range of values they can represent. When a variable will only hold nonnegative values, as in a loop counter or an array index, making it unsigned increases the range of values it can hold. We declare unsigned

INTEGER TYPE	BITS	RANGE
short	16	−32768 to 32767
int	16	−32768 to 32767
long	32	−2147483648 to 2147483647
unsigned short	16	0 to 65535
unsigned int	16	0 to 65535
unsigned long	32	0 to 4294967295

Table 3.1   Sizes and values of Turbo C integers.

integers with `unsigned int` (or simply, `unsigned`), `unsigned short`, and `unsigned long`.

Integer constants are expressed as a string of digits, with a leading minus sign indicating a negative number. A number that is too large for an `int` is automatically treated as a `long`. To force a number to be treated as a `long` (that is, stored using 32 bits), place the letter 'l' or 'L' after it. `32767L` is a `long` constant. To force a number to be treated as `unsigned`, place the letter 'u' or 'U' after it. So, `32767U` is an `unsigned` constant. The suffixes can be combined to create `unsigned long` constants, as in `32767LU`. There are no short constants.

In addition to decimal (base 10) numbers, integers can be specified in either octal (base 8) or hexadecimal (base 16) (Appendix F describes the octal and hexadecimal numbers). A leading zero indicates an octal number; a leading '0x' or '0X' indicates a hexadecimal (hex for short). Regardless of how the value is specified, it is stored in its binary equivalent. For example, the decimal value 63, the octal value 077, and the hex value 0x3f are all stored as 0...0111111.

Table 3.2 shows how these various types are read with `scanf` and printed with `printf`.

Reals

Reals, or floating point numbers, are stored differently than integers. Internally, they are broken into a fraction and an exponent. The numbers of bits for each is machine-dependent, but a typical representation for a 32-bit real uses 23 bits for the fraction and 9 bits, including the sign, for the exponent, as shown below. Bit 0 is the sign of the fraction, bits 1 through 8 are the exponent, and bits 9 through 31 contain the fraction.

0	$1 \cdots 8$	$9 \cdots 31$
SIGN	EXPONENT	FRACTION

TYPE	READING WITH scanf	PRINTING WITH printf
short	%hd	%d
int	%d	%d
long	%ld	%ld
unsigned short	%hu	%u
unsigned int	%u	%u
unsigned long	%lu	%lu
octal short	%ho	%o
octal int	%o	%o
octal long	%lo	%lo
hex short	%hx	%x
hex int	%x	%x
hex long	%lx	%lx

Table 3.2 Formatting codes for reading and printing integers.

We normally write real numbers with a decimal point, as in 13.45 or -211.0, but we can also write them in 'e' notation, giving both a fraction and an exponent to base 10. 'e' notation is similar to scientific notation, except that the letter 'e' replaces the times sign and the base.

Floating Point	'e' notation	Scientific Notation
12.45	1.245e1	1.245×10^1
-211.0	-2.110e2	-2.110×10^2
0.0056	5.600e-3	5.600×10^{-3}
-0.000123	-1.230e-4	-1.230×10^{-4}
1000000.0	1e6	1.0×10^6

There are two types of real values, float and double. A float requires 32 bits of storage and provides around seven significant digits. A double requires 64 bits of storage and provides approximately 14 significant digits. There is a third type, long double, which is designed to provide even more significant digits, but in Turbo C a long double is no different from a double. doubles provide more significance and a wider range of values than floats, but require more space. Most compilers, however, including Turbo C, do all arithmetic in double precision, so we use double real variables unless saving space is crucial.

By default, any constant we define in either floating point or exponential notation is a double. To have float constants, we follow the number with an 'f' or 'F', as in 3.1415926F.

floats and doubles are read with scanf using the %f for floats and %lf for doubles. Both types are printed with printf using %f. If we need output in 'e' notation (1.3e5 instead of 1300000), we use %e in place of %f.

```
/*
 * Compute the area of a circle.
 */
#include <stdio.h>

#define  PI   3.1415926

main()
{
  double radius, area;

  printf("Enter radius: ");
  scanf("%lf", &radius);
  area = PI * radius * radius;
  printf("Area in floating point notation: %f\n", area);
  printf("Area in exponential notation:    %e\n", area);
  return 0;
}
```

Figure 3.2   area.c—A program to compute the area of a circle.

```
Enter radius: 34.5
Area in floating point notation: 3739.280592
Area in exponential notation:    3.739281e+03
```

Figure 3.3   Sample output when we run the area-computing program.

Figure 3.2 contains a simple program that uses the simple formula

$$area = \pi * radius^2$$

to compute the area of a circle, given its radius. It uses doubles for all of its calculations. Figure 3.3 shows the program's output.

Characters

We usually think of characters as letters of the alphabet, but they encompass more than that. There are characters for digits and punctuation, as well as to represent special actions such as ringing a bell or causing a form feed.

Internally, every character is represented by a small integer. What characters are available characters and how they are represented internally depends on the machine on which the program runs. The most common character sets are ASCII (American Standard Code for Information Interchange) and EBCDIC (Extended Binary Coded Decimal Interchange Code). ASCII is the character set used on most personal, micro, and minicomputers, as well as several large mainframes, while EBCDIC is used on large IBM mainframes. ASCII characters are seven bits, but are usually put into an 8-bit byte, while EBCDIC is an 8-bit set. There are 128 ASCII and 256 EBCDIC characters. Appendix G describes the ASCII character set.

We declare a character variable using the type identifier char:

```
char   c;
```

A variable declared in this way can hold the representation for one character, stored internally as an 8-bit integer, the size that is appropriate for most machines. We can also have character constants, just like we can have numeric constants, by placing a character between quotation marks, as in 'A', 'z', '7', or '?'. But strangely enough, they are stored as regular 16-bit integers, and when we assign a constant to a character variable, the extra bits are truncated.

We can read a value into a character with scanf using %c.

```
scanf("%c", &c);
```

We can write a character with printf in a similar way.

```
printf("%c", c);
```

Some characters perform special actions when printed. We represent these characters by an *escape sequence*: a backslash (\) followed by a code letter for the particular function. Table 3.3 provides a complete list of these escape sequences. We've already used the \n code to obtain a new line. As another example, note that we can produce a bell by writing a \a.

```
printf("Wake up!\a\n");
```

The last two codes in Table 3.3, \ddd and \xddd, don't look like characters at all. But they're provided because we need a flexible mechanism to specify all the available characters, including the ones that don't print. A backslash followed by one to three octal digits (0 through 7) specifies a single character based on its octal representation. If we are stuck with a compiler that doesn't know about \a, we can still write a bell using \007.

```
printf("Wake up!\007\n");
```

A backslash followed by an upper- or lowercase x, followed by one to three hexadecimal digits (0 through 9, A through F) specifies a single character based on its hexadecimal representation. We could make our code more obscure by writing a \x3F instead of a question mark, although we probably wouldn't want to.

```
printf("Are you awake yet\x3F ");
```

Figure 3.4 combines all of this into a single program that prints several bells to obtain the user's attention, asks a question, and then prints the response.

CODE	CHARACTER	HEX VALUE
\0	null character	0
\a	audible bell	0x07
\b	backspace	0x08
\f	form feed	0x0C
\n	new line	0x0A
\r	carriage return	0x0D
\t	horizontal tab	0x09
\v	vertical tab	0x0B
\'	single quote	0x2C
\"	double quote	0x22
\\	backslash	0x5C
\?	question mark	0x3F
\ddd	up to 3-digit octal value	
\xddd	up to 3-digit hexadecimal value	

Table 3.3 Characters available using the backslash quoting mechanism.

3.3   CHARACTERS AND INTEGERS

Because characters are stored in an integer representation, we're allowed to treat them as integers. We can write a character in its integer representation, for example, simply by writing it as an integer. Assuming an ASCII character set,

```
printf("%d", 'a');
```

prints the number 97. We can also assign integers to character variables and characters to integer variables. The following statements write the letter 'a'.

```
c = 97;
printf("%c", c);
```

Characters give us our first hint that C is not a strongly typed language, since we can use characters and integers interchangeably. In a strongly typed language such as Pascal, we need built-in functions to convert between the two. But in C we don't need any explicit conversions from one to the other. We simply think of `signed` characters as small integers, and `unsigned` characters as small `unsigned` integers.

Figure 3.5 is a program that takes advantage of this feature to print all the characters in a machine's character set (assuming a maximum of 128 characters), showing the decimal, octal, and character values. Caution is needed in running this program, though, because some of the nonprinting characters do strange things such as erasing the screen or causing a form feed. For this reason, we have chosen the inelegant method of placing each character on a separate line.

```
/*
 * Example program using the various character codes.
 */
#include <stdio.h>

#define MAXBEEP 10

main()
{
  int i;
  char c;

  for (i = 0; i < MAXBEEP; i = i + 1)    /* lots of beeps */
    printf("Wake up!\a\n");

  printf("Are you awake yet\x3F ");       /* query user */
  if (scanf("%c", &c) == 1)               /* obtain response */
  {
    printf("You responded with a '%c'\n", c);
    if (c == 'y' || c == 'Y')
      printf("We're glad you're awake!\n");
    else
      printf("Well, we tried!\n");
  }
  else
    printf("No Response found.\n");
  return 0;
}
```

Figure 3.4 wakeup.c—An example program using the various character codes.

```
/*
 * Print character set in decimal, octal, and character form.
 */
#include <stdio.h>

#define MAXCHAR  128    /* change to 256 for EBCDIC machines */

main()
{
  unsigned char c;

  for (c = 0; c < MAXCHAR; c = c + 1)
    printf("%4d\t%4o\t%c\n", c, c, c);
  return 0;
}
```

Figure 3.5 charset.c—A program to print the local character set.

When we convert an `int` to a `char`, the high-order byte of the integer is discarded and the low-order byte is assigned to the character. As long as the `int` represents a valid character, this conversion is perfectly safe. *Warning: If the* `int` *is larger than a valid character, we'll lose its high-order bits.*

Converting a `char` to an `int` can be trickier. The `int`'s low-order byte gets the `char`. But the contents of the `int`'s high-order byte depend on whether we have `signed` or `unsigned` characters. `signed` characters, the default, are automatically sign-extended. What that means is that if the character is larger than 127, the `int`s high-order byte is filled with ones. On the other hand, converting an `unsigned` character to an `int` always results in a zero-filled high-byte.

As a result, it is always always safe to convert a character within the standard ASCII character set, whose values range from 0 to 127, which means the sign bit is always zero. But non-ASCII characters cause problems. These characters have their high bit on, which means that they convert into negative integers unless they are declared as an `unsigned char`. In Figure 3.5, we declare c, the variable we use to index through the ASCII characters, as `unsigned char`, because we notice that we've completed the printing when c is `128`, which isn't an ASCII character.

These automatic conversions allow us to use `int` variables to store characters. In Figure 3.5, c could have been an `int` with no change in the program's behavior. This means that `char` variables are less useful than one might think, and we ordinarily use them only with arrays of characters, a topic discussed in Chapter 6.

EXERCISES

3–1 Write a program to read an `int` and print its octal, decimal, hexadecimal, and unsigned decimal equivalents. Modify your program to read a `long` instead.

3–2 Write a program to read in a number in binary and print its octal and decimal equivalents. There is no formatting code to indicate a binary number, so you'll have to read the number a digit at a time. (To read one digit at a time, use the formatting code `%1d`. Don't worry about blanks between digits within the number.)

3–3 Modify Chapter 2's input reversing program to work with `doubles` instead of `ints`.

3–4 Repeat the previous exercise for Chapter 2's insertion sort.

3–5 Write a program that reads a single character and prints its integer equivalent. Then write a program that reads an integer and prints its character equivalent. Be sure to do appropriate error/range checking.

3.4   CHARACTER INPUT AND OUTPUT

Just as there are prewritten routines for formatted input and output of numerical and string data, there are predefined functions for character input and output. The two character-equivalent functions of `scanf` and `printf` are `getchar` and `putchar`, respectively.

```
/*
 * Copy the input to the output.
 */
#include <stdio.h>

main()
{
  int c;                    /* next character */

  while ((c = getchar()) != EOF)
    putchar(c);
  return 0;
}
```

Figure 3.6 display.c—A program to copy input to its output.

Getchar and Putchar

getchar takes no arguments and returns as its value the integer representation of a single character—the next character in the input stream. Like scanf, getchar returns the special value EOF if the end-of-file character is entered. As we saw earlier, EOF is usually −1, a value that does not represent a legal character.

Similarly, putchar takes an integer that represents a legal character, and writes it as a character to the standard output. Anomalous results occur if the number does not represent a legal character, although most machines simply use the least significant bits (equivalent to the local character representation). It's your responsibility to provide a value that represents a legitimate character. putchar does not return a value and should not fail, although it can fail if the character is being written to a file. Handling input and output failures is discussed in detail in Chapter 14.

As a result of the need for an "extended" character set (that is, one that includes all of the machine's characters, plus EOF), we usually deal with variables declared as ints when reading character data. We can see this in Figure 3.6, a program, display, that echoes its input to its output, one character at a time. Figure 3.7 shows sample input and output for the program.

This is another program that at first glance seems almost useless. But with the DOS input and output redirection introduced in Chapter 2, we can use this program to display and copy files. In DOS,

> display < display.c

lists the program's source on the console. And

> display < display.c > olddisplay.c

creates a backup copy of it.

The program itself simply reads characters using getchar and writes them with putchar, stopping when getchar returns EOF. We have included stdio.h because

Now is the time
Now is the time
for all good men
for all good men
to come to the aid
to come to the aid
of their party
of their party
^Z

Figure 3.7 Sample input and output for character-copying program. The output is written only when an entire input line has been read.

getchar and putchar, as well as EOF, are defined there. Because of the need for the extended character set, the variable c, which holds the character being read or written, is declared as an int. Note that reading the character and assigning it to c occur within the loop's test, taking advantage of the assignment operator's ability to return the value that it has assigned.

When we examine the output shown in Figure 3.7, we notice something strange: The characters aren't printed until after an entire line has been read. How can this be when we're reading a character at a time?

It turns out that getchar is buffered (as is scanf). In other words, when we read from the keyboard, the operating system collects characters in a special location until we type a carriage return or hit the enter key. And it does something similar when we read from a file, except that it reads a larger chunk of characters each time. All getchar does is return the next character in the buffer. This buffering is also done when we do output to a file. The operating system collects characters in a different location and writes them to the file in large groups. Why buffer at all? Because it allows us to use backspace to edit our input, and because it makes input and output more efficient.

We can take advantage of this buffering to extend our character-copying program to perform more complex input transformations. The program in Figure 3.8 prints each line in its input preceded with a line number. Like Figure 3.6, this program reads one character at a time until it reaches the end of the input, writing each character onto its output. But this program also remembers the last character read. When a character is to be printed, if the preceding character was a newline (\n), it is the beginning of a new line, and a line number is printed. Figure 3.9 shows the output of running the line-numbering program on itself.

Unbuffered Character Input

Because getchar buffers its input, it is not well suited for interactive programs such as editors or menu-driven interfaces. These programs want to read a character as soon as the user types it—they don't want to wait for a carriage return. An interactive screen editor, for example, shouldn't make the user type a carriage return after entering

```
/*
 * Copy the input to the output, giving each line a number.
 */
#include <stdio.h>

main()
{
  int c,            /* current and */
      lastch,       /*    previous characters */
      lineno;       /* lines printed so far */

  lineno = 0;
  for (lastch = '\n'; (c = getchar()) != EOF; lastch = c)
  {
    if (lastch == '\n')
    {                               /* hit end of line */
      lineno = lineno + 1;
      printf("%6d ", lineno);
    }
    putchar(c);
  }
  return 0;
}
```

Figure 3.8 lineno.c—A program to line number its input.

an editor command. And an interactive data base interface shouldn't force the user to hit *ENTER* after making a menu selection. In fact, when we do console I/O (reading input from the keyboard or writing output to the display) we generally don't want buffering.

By default, console output is unbuffered. And luckily Turbo C provides two special functions, getche and getch, that let us do unbuffered input. To use these functions we include conio.h.

getche is identical to getchar except that it doesn't wait for a carriage return. That is, we get the character when the user types it. The "e" at the end of its name stands for *echo*; getche echos the character as it's typed (as does getchar). getch is like getche except that it does not echo the character.

We use getche in Figure 3.10, which contains a function yesorno that obtains a "yes" or "no" response. yesorno uses getche to read the next input character, and then determines whether it is a 'Y' or an 'N'. An invalid character makes yesorno print an error message and repeat the process; otherwise, it returns a 1 for a "yes" and a 0 for a "no". Because yesorno takes no parameters, we supply a parameter list of void.

We use getch in a second version of yesorno, shown in Figure 3.11. This one doesn't echo the character the user types, but instead rings a bell if the user types an inappropriate character.

```
 1 /*
 2  * Copy the input to the output, giving each line a number.
 3  */
 4 #include <stdio.h>
 5
 6 main()
 7 {
 8   int c,                /* current and */
 9       lastch,           /*    previous characters */
10       lineno;           /* lines printed so far */
11
12   lineno = 0;
13   for (lastch = '\n'; (c = getchar()) != EOF; lastch = c)
14   {
15     if (lastch == '\n')
16     {                                 /* hit end of line */
17       lineno = lineno + 1;
18       printf("%6d ", lineno);
19     }
20     putchar(c);
21   }
22   return 0;
23 }
```

Figure 3.9   The output of running the line-numbering program on itself.

How do we decide which input function to use? We use getchar when we don't care whether we obtain the character as soon as the user types it, or when our program's input is likely to be redirected. We use getche when we need the character as soon as the user types it and we want it echoed to the screen. And we use getch when we want the character right away but don't want it echoed.

Warning: Don't interweave calls to getchar *with calls to* getche *and* getch. Why not? Because all of these functions read from the standard input, and only getchar uses a buffer, following a getchar with a getch can cause any characters in that buffer to be ignored.

EXERCISES

3–6 What command did we use to obtain the example output of the line-numbering program?

3–7 Add page numbering to the line-numbering program. That is, place a line with "PAGE *N*" at the beginning of each page, with a blank line between the page-numbering line and the next line of the output. Assume that a page has a maximum of 66 lines (use a constant PAGE_LEN).

```
/*
 * A first version of a program and function to get
 * a yes or no answer from the user.
 */
#include <stdio.h>
#include <conio.h>

main()
{
  int answer;
  int yesorno(void);

  printf("Do you like Turbo C? ");
  if ((answer = yesorno()) != 0)
    printf("We received a YES!\n");
  else
    printf("We received a NO!\n");
  return answer;                        /* 1 for yes, 0 for no */
}

int yesorno(void)
{
  int c;

  while ((c = getche()) != 'Y' && c != 'N')
  {
    putchar('\n');  /* Go to next line */
    printf("Please enter a Y or N: ");
  }
  putchar('\n');
  return c == 'Y';
}
```

Figure 3.10 yesorno1.c—A function to get a yes-or-no answer from the user and an example of how it's used.

3–8 Write a program to count the number of lines in its input.

3–9 Write a program that eliminates all blank lines from its input.

3.5	**CHARACTER TESTING FUNCTIONS**

When we read a character we often need to know what type of character we have. Is it an uppercase letter—or lowercase? A digit? Is it printable—or is it a control character? And so on.

One way to find out this information is to check whether the character falls within a particular range of characters. For example, we can determine whether c is a

```
/*
 * A second version of our yesorno function.  This one
 * only displays the user's input if it's correct, and it
 * displays the entire YES or NO, not just its first letter.
 * The function beeps if given an incorrect answer.
 */
#include <stdio.h>
#include <conio.h>

main()
{
  int answer;
  int yesorno(void);

  printf("Do you like Turbo C? ");
  if ((answer = yesorno()) != 0)
    printf("yes\n");
  else
    printf("no\n");
  return answer;
}

int yesorno(void)
{
  int c;

  while ((c = getch()) != 'Y' && c != 'N')
    putchar('\a');          /* BEEP on incorrect character */
  return c == 'Y';
}
```

Figure 3.11 yesorno2.c—A new version of `yesorno` that beeps at invalid characters. The main program prints the answer the user gave.

lowercase letter with:

```
if (c >= 'a' && c <= 'z')
  printf("It is a lowercase letter\n");
```

This tests whether c's integer representation is between the integer representations of `'a'` and `'z'`. That works fine if the lowercase letters are contiguous within the local character set. Unfortunately, while this is true of ASCII, it is not true of EBCDIC. If we want our program to work regardless of the underlying character set, we need another method. Fortunately, C provides a set of functions (macros, actually) that we can use to perform these comparisons. These functions are listed in Table 3.4. To use them we include ctype.h.

Each of these functions takes a character and returns a nonzero value if it falls into the given class and zero if it doesn't. For example, we can use `islower` to rewrite the test above.

FUNCTION	CHARACTER TYPE
isalpha	a letter (a-z, A-Z)?
islower	a lowercase letter (a-z)?
isupper	an uppercase letter (A-Z)?
isalnum	a letter or digit (a-z, A-Z, 0-9)?
isdigit	a digit (0-9)?
isxdigit	a hexadecimal digit (0-9, a-f, A-F)?
isspace	a space, \t, \v, \f, \r, or \n?
iscntrl	a control (0x00-0x1F) or delete (0x7F) character?
ispunct	punctuation (isprint && !isalnum)?
isgraph	displayable (not including space) (0x21-0x7E)?
isascii	an ASCII character (0-0x7F)?
isprint	printable (0x20-0x7E)?

Table 3.4 Character testing functions.

```
if (islower(c) != 0)
  printf("It is a lowercase letter\n");
```

And we can verify that a character is not an uppercase letter in a similar way.

```
if (isupper(c) == 0)
  printf("It is not a uppercase letter\n");
```

Actually, we can write these tests even more concisely. Earlier we mentioned that C considers an expression that evaluates to zero to be false, and any other expression to be true. So

```
if (islower(c))
  printf("It is a lowercase letter\n");
```

and

```
if (!isupper(c))
  printf("It is not an uppercase letter\n");
```

are more compact versions of our earlier tests (remember that ! inverts the sense of a test).

We use several of these function in Figure 3.12, a program that writes its input onto its output, one word per line. A word is defined as a letter optionally followed by letters or digits. The input

```
Some sample input.  A9 is a word!  999 is not.
```

produces the output

```
/*
 * Break input into words (letter followed by letters + digits).
 */
#include <stdio.h>
#include <ctype.h>

#define   YES   1
#define   NO    0

main()
{
  int c,        /* next input character */
      word;     /* flag: are we dealing with a word */

  word = NO;
  while ((c = getchar()) != EOF)
    if (isalpha(c) || (word && isdigit(c)))    /* word */
    {
      putchar(c);         /* write it and note we're in word */
      word = YES;
    }
    else                  /* nonletter */
      if (word)           /* ignore it unless we're in word */
      {
        putchar('\n');
        word = NO;
      }
  return 0;
}
```

Figure 3.12 brkwd.c—A program to print its input onto its output, one word per line.

```
Some
sample
input
A9
is
a
word
is
not
```

Figure 3.12 is yet another extension to our earlier character-copying program. It reads its input one character at a time, writing any character that is part of a word, and writing a new line when the end of a word is reached. To test whether a character is part of a word, we use isalpha and isdigit. A letter is always part of a word, but a digit is part of a word only if we are already sure we have a word.

In addition to the functions for testing characters, there is also a small set of functions for converting characters. These functions are listed in Table 3.5. Each

FUNCTION	CONVERTS
tolower	uppercase to lowercase (others unchanged)
toupper	lowercase to uppercare (others unchanged)
_tolower	uppercase to lowercase (must be uppercase)
_toupper	lowercase to uppercase (must be lowercase)
toascii	character to ASCII (clear high-order bits)

Table 3.5   Character converting functions.

takes a character and returns a character. As before, we must include ctype.h.

We use one of them, toupper, to extend yesorno to handle either upper- or lowercase input. All we have to do is convert the character we read to uppercase before comparing it with "Y" or "N".

```
while ((c = toupper(getch())) != 'Y' && c != 'N')
    putchar('\a');    /* beep on incorrect character */
```

If the character isn't lowercase, toupper simply returns it unchanged.

We'll see many other uses of these functions throughout the text.

EXERCISES

3-10 Write a program to lowercase its input and convert all nonalphabetic characters to spaces.

3-11 Write a program that counts the number of unprintable characters in its input.

3-12 Write a function getletter that reads an upper- or lowercase letter between minimum and maximum letters provided as arguments.

3.6   CONVERTING CHARACTERS INTO NUMBERS

We often want to read characters and convert them into integers. Our first thought is to use scanf—but unfortunately it handles input errors poorly. An alternative is to read characters one at a time, and to convert them into a single integer ourselves.

getdigit, shown in Figure 3.13, is a variation of yesorno that obtains a single digit from the user and returns its numeric value. It takes two parameters: the smallest and largest acceptable values. So the call

```
getdigit(1,5)                    /* get user's entry */
```

indicates that the user must enter a digit between 1 and 5. If we've displayed a menu with several entries, `getdigit` is a convenient way to obtain the user's desired selection.

`getdigit` uses `getche` to read a character and `isdigit` to verify that it is indeed a digit. It then converts the character to its integer equivalent and verifies that the resulting value is acceptable. If it isn't, `getdigit` writes an error message and repeats the process until the character is one of the desired digits.

To perform the conversion, we need not know the character's internal representation. We can convert a digit character to an integer by subtracting the character `'0'` from it. (This assumes that all digits are represented by contiguous codes, which is the case with both ASCII and EBCDIC.) For example, in ASCII, the code for `'7'` is 55 and the code for `'0'` is 48; the subtraction yields the integer value 7.

`getdigit` is useful, but it's not very general; it only handles single-digit numbers. Figure 3.14 contains `getnumber`, an extension to `getdigit` that reads and converts a *sequence* of characters.

`getnumber` uses `getch` to read characters, and it uses `isdigit` and `isspace` to determine whether the character is a digit or white space. If it's a digit, `getnumber` updates a sum representing the value of the sequence. It updates the sum by multiplying the current sum by 10, and then adding the digit that the new character represents.

```
sum = 10 * sum + (c - '0');
```

If it's a white space character, `getnumber` returns the value of the sequence. Otherwise, `getnumber` ignores the character and beeps to notify the user of the error.

Reading numerical data one character at a time and doing our own conversions may seem wasteful when we already have `scanf`. But it isn't. `scanf` has several problems: it compiles into a large amount of runnable code, and it is slower than using our own conversions. More importantly, `scanf` makes error handling difficult by telling us only how many values it correctly converted, and providing no information about why a failure might have occurred. To provide suitable error messages or error recovery when a failure occurs, we still have to deal with the input one character at a time.

EXERCISES

3–13 Write a version of `getnumber` that reads binary numbers and turns them into integers.

3–14 Modify `getnumber` so that it reads and converts real numbers (that is, numbers containing a decimal point) instead of integers. Extend the function to handle numbers in scientific notation as well.

3–15 Write a new version of `getnumber` that takes an additional parameter: the base of the numbers it is to read, a number between 2 (binary) and 10 (decimal).

```
/*
 * Get a digit between "min" and "max" from the user.
 */
#include <stdio.h>
#include <conio.h>
#include <ctype.h>

#define MIN   1
#define MAX   5

main()
{
  int getdigit(int min, int max);

  printf("Select an entry: ");
  printf("You entered a %d!\n", getdigit(MIN, MAX));
  return 0;
}

int getdigit(int min, int max)
{
  int c, value;

  c = getche();          /* get a character */
  while (!isdigit(c) || ((value = c - '0') < min || value > max))
  {
    putchar('\n');        /* get to next line */
    printf("Please enter a value between %d and %d: ", min, max);
    c = getche();         /* get another character */
  }
  putchar('\n');
  return value;
}
```

Figure 3.13 getdig.c—A function to get a single digit from the console and a main program using it.

3-16 Write a function, getnumbers, that reads values from a single input line, stopping when a \n is read. It now takes two arguments. The first tells it how many values to read, the second is an array in which to place those values. This getnumber uses blanks or tabs to delimit numbers.

3-17 Write a function, getletter, that obtains a single character from the user, making sure that it's an upper- or lowercase letter.

```c
/*
 * Read characters, converting into number.  Beep at nondigits.
 */
#include <stdio.h>
#include <conio.h>
#include <ctype.h>

main()
{
  int age;
  int getnumber(int min, int max);

  printf("What's your age? ");
  if ((age = getnumber(1, 99)) >= 21)
    printf("%d is old enough to drink.\n", age);
  else
    printf("%d is too young to drink.\n", age);
  return 0;
}

int getnumber(int min, int max)  /* prompt for number */
{
  int value;               /* number's value */
  int readnumber(void);      /* actually read number */

  while ((value = readnumber()) < min || value > max)
  {
    putchar('\n');
    printf("Enter a value between %d and %d: ", min, max);
  }
  putchar('\n');
  return value;
}

int readnumber(void)         /* actually read a value */
{
  int c, sum;

  sum = 0;                 /* value so far */
  for (c = getch(); !isspace(c); c = getch())
    if (isdigit(c))
    {
      putchar(c);             /* update input */
      sum = 10 * sum + (c - '0');
    }
    else
      putchar('\a');          /* beep at nondigit/nonspace */
  return sum;
}
```

Figure 3.14   getnum.c—A program to read a group of characters and turn them into a single integer.

3.7 ## CASE STUDY—A FILE DISPLAY PROGRAM

Earlier in the chapter we wrote a program to copy its standard input to its standard output. We mentioned that by redirecting its standard input we could use it to display the contents of files. The problem with doing so is that files longer than a screenfull scroll by so fast that they are unreadable. It would be much nicer if the program would stop at the end of every page, wait for us to hit a key, and then continue. We will now write a program, page, that does just that. page even has an added feature: If we type a 'q' or a 'Q' (for quit), the program stops before finishing its entire input. We can use page to display its source file with

    page < page.c

The program, shown in Figure 3.15, uses a function showpage to do most of its work. showpage displays one screenfull of the file. It's basically our copying program modified to count new lines and to stop when it has read and displayed a certain number of lines. It returns the number of lines displayed.

The main program simply calls showpage to display a block of lines. Once showpage has displayed a full screen (its return value is equal to PAGESIZE lines), the program asks the user whether it should go on. We want the user's response right away, so we would think we could use getch or getche to read it. But we can't—getch does an unbuffered read from the *standard input*, which won't be the terminal when page is run. So now we have a problem: How can we get a character from the keyboard, even when the standard input has been redirected?

It turns out that we have to use a DOS system call, bioskey, that is provided as part of the Turbo C library (Appendix E provides a detailed description of some of these library functions). bioskey takes a single integer argument which tells it what to do. If this argument is 0, it does what we're looking for—it waits for the user to hit a key and then returns its value. Well, almost. Actually, it returns an integer with the character's integer representation in its low byte, and some additional information in the high byte. But we can easily get rid of this extra information by converting bioskey's return value into an unsigned char.

Our paging program uses a function getkey, written using bioskey, to read the user's response. getkey simply reads a character typed at the keyboard and returns its integer representation. Figure 3.16 contains a useful companion function, getkeye, that is similar to getkey but also echos the character. page stops if the user enters a 'q' or a 'Q'; any other key causes the process to repeat.

EXERCISES

3-18 Modify page to display only the next line if the user hits a carriage return.

3-19 Modify page to allow the user to type a 'g', followed by a number, to specify which line should be displayed next (this feature allows skipping ahead in the file). Make sure your program behaves reasonably if the user requests a line previously displayed, or one past the input's end.

```
/*
 * Program to print its input, a screenfull at a time.
 */
#include <stdio.h>
#include <ctype.h>
#include <conio.h>
#include <bios.h>

#define PAGESIZE 22              /* assume 22 lines on screen */

main()
{
  int resp;                     /* holds user's response */
  int showpage(int maxlines);
  int getkey(void);

  resp = ' ';
  while (resp != 'Q' && showpage(PAGESIZE) == PAGESIZE)
  {
    printf("--Go on?--");
    resp = toupper(getkey());
    printf("\r          \r");  /* overwrite prompt */
  }
  return 0;
}

int showpage(int maxlines)      /* print up to maxlines */
{
  int c, lines;                 /* next input char, line count */

  lines = 0;
  while (lines < maxlines && (c = getchar()) != EOF)
  {
    if (c == '\n')
      lines++;
    putchar(c);
  }
  return lines;
}

int getkey(void)                          /* read from keyboard */
{
  unsigned char key;

  key = bioskey(0);
  return key;
}
```

Figure 3.15   page.c—A program to display its standard input on the console, one screenfull at a time.

```
/*
 * Read character from keyboard (with echo).
 */
#include <stdio.h>
#include <bios.h>

int getkeye(void)
{
  unsigned char key;

  key = bioskey(0);
  putchar(key);
  return key;
}
```

Figure 3.16   A function to read a character from the keyboard, echo it, and then return it.

3-20 Modify page to line number its output.

4 OPERATORS
AND
CONVERSIONS

C provides an especially rich set of operators. This chapter examines more closely the operators we've already introduced and introduces the operators we previously ignored. And it carefully considers the conversions that happen when an operator's operands have differing data types. Because so many of C's operators are just similar enough to those of other programming languages to cause problems, we emphasize their caveats and quirks. We also pay special attention to the operators that have no analog in most other programming languages, such as the shorthand assignment and bit-manipulation operators. The chapter concludes with a case study—a pair of programs that compress and uncompress their input.

4.1   OPERATORS, OPERANDS, AND PRECEDENCE

Much of a programming language's power derives from the operators it provides. And C possesses a wide selection of operators. Table 4.1 summarizes these operators, the operations they perform, and their relative precedence. The table is organized in order of decreasing precedence. As in most programming languages, we can use parentheses to override the default order of evaluation—but not in all cases. *Warning: The compiler is free to arbitrarily rearrange expressions involving a single commutative operator (+, *, &, |, or ^), even if we use parentheses.* So even if we write

```
a * (b * c)
```

the compiler may evaluate it as

```
(a * b) * c
```

If we absolutely demand a particular order of evaluation for expressions involving these operators, we have to use temporary variables.

Most operators expect their operands to agree in type. When they don't, fairly straightforward automatic conversions occur (to be discussed later in the chapter). In addition, some operators expect operands of a certain type. The operation may still

LEVEL	OPERATOR	DESCRIPTION
1	`x[i]`	Array subscripting
1	`f(x)`	Function call
1	`.`	Structure field selection
1	`->`	Indirect structure field selection
2	`++, --`	Postfix/Prefix increment and decrement
2	`sizeof`	Size of a variable or type (in bytes)
2	`(type)`	Cast to *type*
2	`~`	Bitwise negation
2	`!`	Logical NOT
2	`-`	Unary minus
2	`&`	Address of
2	`*`	Indirection (dereferencing)
3	`*, /, %`	Multiply, divide, modulus
4	`+, -`	Addition, subtraction
5	`>>, <<`	Left, right shift
6	`<, >, <=, >=`	Test for inequality
7	`==, !=`	Test for equality, inequality
8	`&`	Bitwise AND
9	`^`	Bitwise XOR (exclusive OR)
10	`|`	Bitwise OR
11	`&&`	Logical AND
12	`||`	Logical OR
13	`? :`	Conditional operator
14	`=`	Assignment
14	`+=, -=, *=, /=, %=`	Add, subtract, multiply, divide, mod
14	`>>=, <<=`	Shift right and left
14	`^=, &=, |=`	Bitwise XOR, AND, OR
15	`,`	The comma operator—sequential evaluation of expressions.

Table 4.1　C's operators and their precedence.

be performed if we provide an operand of an incorrect type—with strange and unanticipated results. *Warning: It is your responsibility to guarantee that operands are the correct type, in range, and that the result has not produced overflow or underflow.* The alternative is for the compiler or run-time environment to capture incorrect operand types, as with languages such as Pascal. But doing so requires longer compilations or time-consuming run-time type checking. The benefit with C is that *if* our programs run, they run more efficiently.

The remainder of this chapter examines the operators in this table in more detail.

4.2   ARITHMETIC OPERATORS

The arithmetic operators are + (addition), – (subtraction when between two operands, sign change when it precedes a single operand), * (multiplication), / (division), and % (remaindering). As expected, all except % operate on integer, character, and real operands. The arithmetic operators associate (are evaluated) left to right, following the precedence rules in Table 4.1. *, /, and % have higher precedence than either + or –. That means that

```
balance = balance + balance * INTRATE;
```

is evaluated as though it were written as

```
balance = balance + (balance * INTRATE);
```

Integer Arithmetic

Integer arithmetic is always exact within the limits of the number of values that can be represented within the particular integral data type used—so you don't have to worry about precision problems. But you do have to worry about overflow. *Warning: C provides no run-time indication that an integer overflow has occurred—it simply carries out the arithmetic and gives an incorrect result.* On most machines (including the PC), for example, adding one to the largest positive number yields the largest negative value, and conversely, subtracting one from the largest negative value yields the largest positive value (both operations cause the sign bit to change). Overflow can also be caused by multiplying two large numbers together, regardless of their signs. While it is possible to detect overflow after the fact—perhaps by noting that adding two positive numbers produced a negative result—it is better to try and avoid any overflow in the first place. Simply make sure to use data types appropriate to the range of values the result might cover. If you are adding two ints and their result might not fit in an int, use longs instead.

Integer division (both operands are integers) produces a *truncated* result. That is, it simply throws away the real part of the result. This means that "fractional" division of integers always returns zero. 1/3, for example, evaluates to 0, and 5/3 evaluates to 1.

The remaindering operator, %, takes two integer operands and returns the remainder when the first is divided by the second. 5%3, for example, is 2, and 1%3 is 1. For positive integers, this is the familiar modulus operation. The result is normally the sign of the dividend (the value "upstairs"), but is machine dependent if the divisor is negative. For this reason, `%` is best used only with positive values. Regardless of the sign of `a` and `b`, however, `a/b * b + a % b` will always equal `a`.

Floating Point Arithmetic

Floating point arithmetic is an approximation of the correct result, since floating point values are rounded to the number of significant digits allowable in the representation. Typically, this is 7 digits for `float`s and 14 digits for `double`s. Both overflow and underflow can occur with real arithmetic; the action taken is machine dependent. For example, adding to the largest possible `float` will produce overflow, and dividing the smallest possible `float` by a large value will cause underflow. The hardware of most machines traps floating point overflow and underflow, causing a run-time error and termination of the program. We can avoid some floating point overflows by using a `double` instead of `float`.

Floating point division differs from integer division in that the real part of the result is not thrown away. As long as either operand of `/` is real, floating point division is used. That means, $1.0/3.0$, $1/3.0$, and $1.0/3$ all give the result 0.333333.

Unsigned Arithmetic

Unsigned arithmetic is similar to integer arithmetic, except that there are no negative results and no overflow. Instead, all unsigned arithmetic takes place modulo 2^n, where n is the number of bits in the unsigned operands. This means that adding one to the largest unsigned value gives zero, and conversely, subtracting one from zero gives the largest unsigned value. Figure 4.1 contains a program to illustrate unsigned arithmetic, Figure 4.2 contains its output. We've hard-coded the largest unsigned integer in our program; later in the chapter we will see how to determine its value automatically.

EXERCISES

4-1 Another way to avoid overflow is to use an array to represent the numbers, with one integer in the array corresponding to one digit in the number. Write a function, `add_bignum`, that adds two numbers represented by digit arrays, and fills in a third digit array with the result. Also write its counterpart, `sub_bignum`, that subtracts two numbers represented by digit arrays.

4-2 Extend your solution to the previous exercise to include two additional functions, `mult_bignum` and `div_bignum`, which multiply and divide two numbers represented by digit arrays.

4-3 Write a program to determine whether a particular year is a leap year. Assume that a year is a leap year if it's divisible evenly by 4 or 400, but not by 100.

```
/*
 * Display largest unsigned int, and the numbers following it.
 */
#include <stdio.h>

main()
{
  unsigned int i;

  i = 65535u;        /* (2^16)-1, the largest unsigned int */
  printf("i: %u\ni+1: %u\ni+2: %u\n", i, i + 1, i + 2);
  return 0;
}
```

Figure 4.1   unsign.c—A program to illustrate unsigned arithmetic.

```
i: 65535
i+1: 0
i+2: 1
```

Figure 4.2   The program's output on a machine with 16 bit `ints`.

4.3   RELATIONAL AND LOGICAL OPERATORS

We use relational operators to test whether a particular relationship holds between two values. C has relational operators to compare values for equality (==), inequality (!=), greater than (>), less than (<), greater than or equal (>=), and less than or equal (<=). A relational operator returns either one (true) if the specified relation between the operands holds or zero (false) if it doesn't.

The operators >, <, >=, and <= have the same precedence, which is higher than the precedence of == and !=. But all of these operators have precedence higher than assignment, so we often have to use parentheses to guarantee that comparisons are done after any assignments, as in

```
while ((c = getchar()) != EOF)
  putchar(c);
```

The same statement written without the parenthesis,

```
while (c = getchar() != EOF)    /* OOPS! */
  putchar(c);
```

is evaluated as if it were

```
while (c = (getchar() != EOF))  /* YUCKO! */
  putchar(c);
```

OPERANDS		RESULT	
OP1	OP2	&&	||
Nonzero	Nonzero	1	1
Nonzero	Zero	0	1
Zero	Nonzero	0	1
Zero	Zero	0	0

Table 4.2 Results of using the logical operators.

That is, as though we were assigning the result of comparing the newly read character with EOF. In general, it's a good idea to parenthesize relational operators, since they are in the middle of the precedence hierarchy.

We often need to combine relational tests in a single expression. For example, to verify that a value falls between two other values, we need to test whether it is less than the first value and greater than the second. We do so using the logical operators, logical AND (&&), logical OR (||), and logical negation (!). These return one (true) or zero (false) according to Table 4.2. Logical AND and OR interpret nonzero operands as true and zero operands as false. Negation returns one if its operand is zero, and zero otherwise.

The logical operators associate left to right, and their precedence is low, so we rarely need to parenthesize when we combine them with the relational operators. The expression

```
x < min || x > max
```

is evaluated as though written as

```
(x < min) || (x > max)
```

Normally both operands of an operator are evaluated and then the operator applied to the resulting values. But it's possible that one of the operands of a logical operator might never be evaluated. The reason is that the operator's value can often be determined only after its first operand has been evaluated—eliminating the need to evaluate the other operand. When evaluating the logical AND in the statement

```
while (i < MAX && scanf("%d", &value) != EOF)
    a[i] = value;
```

the clause i < MAX is evaluated first. If it is false, the value of the entire logical expression is false, regardless of how the second clause would evaluate, so the second clause is *not* evaluated. More to the point, the call to scanf does not occur; no reading or assignment to value occurs. If there are multiple clauses connected by logical AND, the first false one terminates the evaluation. In this example, only when i < MAX evaluates to true is the second clause, the scanf, evaluated.

In logical OR the first true clause terminates evaluation of all succeeding clauses. In the following statement, x is not compared with max when count is zero.

```
if (count == 0 || x > max)
    max = x;
```

4.4   BITWISE OPERATORS

The operators we've seen so far are common to most higher-level programming languages. C also provides less common operators for shifting bits left (<<) or right (>>); for bitwise AND (&), OR (|), and XOR (^); and for bitwise inversion (~). These operations allow us to deal with the details of the machine. We need them because some hardware operations require that individual bits be set and then other bits read to determine whether the operation succeeded. We can also use them to provide faster versions of some numerical operations, and to optimize our use of storage.

Bit Shifts

The left (<<) and right (>>) shifts take an operand and return its value shifted left or right by a specified number of bits. The operand itself is not affected. The form of the operators is *op >> n* and *op << n*. As an example,

```
a = val << 1;
```

assigns val, shifted one bit to the left, to a. The result is to assign val times two to a. Similarly,

```
a = val >> 1;
```

assigns val, shifted one bit to the right, to a, in effect assigning val divided by two to a. Assuming val is 6, here is what val looks like, shifted left by one bit and right by one bit.

val	val << 1	val >> 1
0...00110	0...01100	0...00011
6	12	3

The number of bits to shift should be a positive integer, less than or equal to the number of bits in the variable being shifted. Negative or excessive shifts produce machine-dependent results. On *left* shifts, zeros are always shifted into the vacated bits on the right. On *right* shifts, the bit shifted in depends on the variable's type. If the variable is unsigned, zeros are shifted in; if the variable is signed, *usually* the sign bit is extended, but this operation is machine dependent. It is possible that on some machines zeros are shifted in for signed values, which would have the (most likely undesired) effect of changing the sign of the value. *Warning: Avoid right shifts on signed values.*

OPERANDS		RESULT		
OP1	OP2	&	|	^
1	1	1	1	0
1	0	0	1	1
0	1	0	1	1
0	0	0	0	0

Table 4.3   Results of using the bitwise operators.

Bitwise Logical Operators

There are three bitwise logical operators: bitwise AND (&), bitwise OR (|), and bitwise XOR (^). These operators work on their operands bit by bit, setting each bit in the result, as shown in Table 4.3. Bitwise AND is one only when both bits are one. Bitwise OR is one if either operand is one. And bitwise XOR (exclusive OR) is one if exactly one of the bits is one. AND is sometimes called the "both" or "all" function, OR the "either" or "any" function, and XOR the "odd" or "only one" function.

As an example of the results of these bitwise operations, here is the result of AND, OR, and exclusive OR on two 16-bit ints.

```
A:       10010110 11100001
B:       00011010 11011001
A & B:   00010010 11000001
A | B:   10011110 11111001
A ^ B:   10001100 00111000
```

We can use these bit operations to test or set the value of individual bits or groups of bits in a word. This ability is often needed to manipulate devices that use individual bits as controlling signals or status indications. When manipulating bits, we generally create a *mask* that selects particular bits. A mask is simply an integer with only those bits we are interested in turned on, as in

```
#define ERRORBIT  0x80      /* Bit 7 on (10000000) if error */
```

Given this mask, we can turn on the desired bit in an integer status with

```
status = status | ERRORBIT; /* turn on ERROR INDICATING bit */
```

And we can test it with

```
if ((status & ERRORBIT) != 0)  /* test if ERROR BIT IS ON */
    printf("Error bit was set\n");
```

We need parentheses here because bitwise & has lower precedence than the test-for-inequality operator !=. Notice that the meaning and use of the bitwise operators & and | are much different than those of the logical operators && and ||.

The last bitwise operator, negation (~), inverts each bit in its operand; that is, each one bit becomes zero, each zero becomes one. If x is represented with 16 bits, here is ~x.

```
x:      00000000 10011001
~x:     11111111 01100110
```

Note that ~ doesn't produce the negative of a value. ~0, for example, is a word of all 1's, the largest unsigned integer.

Getting and Setting Bits

Sometimes it seems as though C has an operator for everything. There are, however, many desired operations for which no built-in operator exists. One important example is accessing a bit or group of bits within a word. Although we can create our own mask and then do a bitwise AND or OR to access them, what we really want is a set of functions that build the mask for us and then access the appropriate bits.

We've implemented these functions in Figure 4.3, which also contains a main program that uses them to store several integers—representing an employee's sex, age, marital status, and years employed—into a single unsigned int, as shown below.

0 ··· 1	2 ··· 8	9	10 ··· 15
STATUS	AGE	SEX	YEARS

Why go to this extra trouble when we could more easily store these values in four separate ints? The main reason is that it saves storage. We really only need 1 bit to represent a person's sex, 7 bits to represent a person's age, and so on. By compressing this information into a single word we make the most efficient use of our available memory.

We've written four functions: getbit and setbit get or set the value of the nth bit within a word, getbits and setbits are similar, but work with a group of k bits, starting at position n within a word. All assume the *rightmost* bit in the word is bit number zero. Table 4.4 shows the results of some example calls, given a variable word whose value is 181 (0...10110101). And Figure 4.4 shows how some of these results are computed.

getbit works by shifting word *right* n places, so that its bit 0 holds the desired bit value. It then ANDs the entire word with a mask containing a single 1 in its rightmost bit, effectively turning off all of word's other bits.

setbit works differently depending on whether it is turning on or turning off the desired bit. To turn on the nth bit, setbit ORs the word with a mask containing a single 1 in the nth position. It is easy to create this mask: setbit simply shifts a 1 *left* n places. To turn off the nth bit, setbit ANDs the word with a mask containing a single 0 in the nth position, the negation of the mask above.

We could write getbits and setbits on top of repeated calls to getbit or setbit—which is acceptable if we don't care how quickly our program runs. We care, so instead both functions work by creating a mask that somehow isolates the desired group of bits. They do so by taking a word of all 1's (~0), shifting it left k

```c
/*
 * Program to pack employee information into a single word.
 * Assumes information has been entered correctly.
 */
#include <stdio.h>

#define SINGLE    0          /* marital status flags */
#define MARRIED   1
#define SEPARATED 2
#define DIVORCED  3

#define MALE      1          /* sex */
#define FEMALE    0

#define MSBIT     0          /* marital status: bits 0-1 */
#define MSBITS    2
#define AGEBIT    2          /* age: bits 2-8 */
#define AGEBITS   7
#define SEXBIT    9          /* sex: bit 9 */
#define YRSBIT    10         /* year: bits 10-15 */
#define YRSBITS   6

main()
{
    unsigned int mstat, sex, age, years;
    unsigned int info;          /* holds info on one person */

    unsigned int
        getbit(unsigned int word, int n),
        setbit(unsigned int word, int n, unsigned int v),
        getbits(unsigned int word, int n, int k),
        setbits(unsigned int word, int n, int k, unsigned int v);

    info = 0;                   /* all bits off initially */

    printf("male=%d, female=%d? ", MALE, FEMALE);
    scanf("%d", &sex);
    info = setbit(info, SEXBIT, sex);

    printf("age? ");
    scanf("%d", &age);
    info = setbits(info, AGEBIT, AGEBITS, age);

    printf("single=%d, married=%d, separated=%d, divorced=%d? ",
            SINGLE, MARRIED, SEPARATED, DIVORCED);
    scanf("%d", &mstat);
    info = setbits(info, MSBIT, MSBITS, mstat);

    printf("years employed? ");
    scanf("%d", &years);
    info = setbits(info, YRSBIT, YRSBITS, years);
```

```
    printf("Here's the info: 0x%04x\n", info);
    printf("Sex: %d\n", getbit(info, SEXBIT));
    printf("Age: %d\n", getbits(info, AGEBIT, AGEBITS));
    printf("Marital status: %d\n", getbits(info, MSBIT, MSBITS));
    printf("Years employed: %d\n", getbits(info, YRSBIT, YRSBITS));
    return 0;
}


/*
 * Functions to get and set bit values.
 *     getbit:  gets the value of bit "n" in "word"
 *     setbit:  returns word with bit "n" assigned "v"
 *     getbits: gets the value of "k" bits at position "n"
 *     setbits: returns word with "k" bits at position "n"
 *              assigned "v"
 * All assume reasonable values for "k", "n" and "v".
 */

unsigned int getbit(unsigned int word, int n)
{
    return (word >> n) & 01;
}

unsigned int setbit(unsigned int word, int n, unsigned int v)
{
    unsigned int new_word;

    if (v != 0)                        /* turn on the bit */
        new_word = word |  (01 << n);
    else
        new_word = word & ~(01 << n); /* turn off the bit */
    return new_word;
}

unsigned int getbits(unsigned int word, int n, int k)
{
    return (word & (~(~0 << k) << n)) >> n;
}

unsigned int
  setbits(unsigned int word, int n, int k, unsigned int v)
{
    return (word & ~(~(~0 << k) << n)) | (v << n);
}
```

Figure 4.3 bits.c—Functions to determine and set the value of bits in a word, and a main program that uses them to compress information.

CALL	RETURN VALUE	BIT PATTERN
`getbit(word, 1)`	0	0...00000000
`getbit(word, 2)`	1	0...00000001
`setbit(word, 3, 1)`	189	0...10111101
`setbit(word, 4, 0)`	165	0...10100101
`getbits(word, 3, 2)`	2	0...00000010
`getbits(word, 0, 4)`	5	0...00000101
`setbits(word, 2, 5, 16)`	193	0...11000001
`setbits(word, 0, 4, 7)`	183	0...10110111

Table 4.4 The results of some example calls of our bit-manipuating functions.

places, and negating it. This gives us a group of 1-bits in the k rightmost bits of the mask. They then shift this group left n places, which puts them in the correct place.

getbits simply ANDs this mask with the word and shifts the result right n places, returning the desired bits. setbits is more complex. It ANDs the *negation* of the mask to turn off the relevant bits, and then ORs the word with the new value shifted left n places.

Using Exclusive OR

We have used all of the bitwise operators except exclusive OR. One use for it is in data encryption. Encrypting a file makes its contents unreadable while preserving the information it contains. And one of the simplest ways to encrypt text is to exclusive OR the text with a lengthy key. If the text is larger than the key (which is usually the case), just cycle through the key repeatedly until the entire file has been encrypted. The nice aspect of this scheme is that we use the same method and the same key to decrypt the encrypted version of the file: we just take the exclusive OR with the key one more time.

As an example, suppose we have an 8-bit piece of data to be encrypted and an 8-bit key. Taking the exclusive OR with the key produces the encrypted data.

```
DATA (ASCII 'P')   01010000
KEY                00010010
DATA xor KEY       01000010 (encrypted data)
```

Taking the exclusive OR with the key again produces the original data.

Figure 4.5 contains a program that encrypts (or decrypts) its input. We can use it to encrypt itself with

encrypt < encrypt.c > encrypted

and then decrypt it with

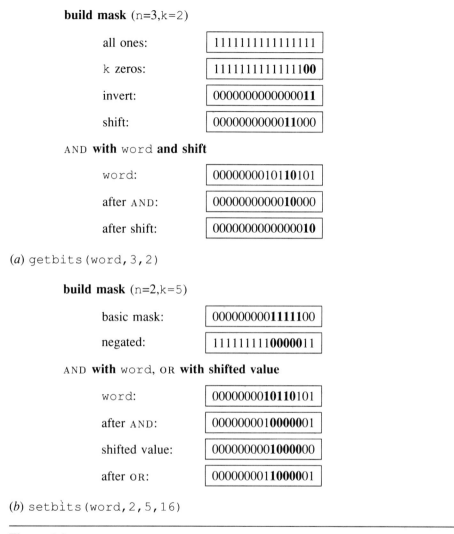

build mask (n=3,k=2)

all ones:	1111111111111111
k zeros:	11111111111111**00**
invert:	0000000000000**11**
shift:	00000000000**11**000

AND **with** word **and shift**

word:	00000000**10110**101
after AND:	0000000000**1**0000
after shift:	00000000000000**10**

(*a*) getbits(word,3,2)

build mask (n=2,k=5)

basic mask:	00000000**011111**00
negated:	11111111**10000001**1

AND **with** word, OR **with shifted value**

word:	00000000**10110**101
after AND:	00000000**1**0000**001**
shifted value:	0000000001**000000**
after OR:	0000000001**1000001**

(*b*) setbìts(word,2,5,16)

Figure 4.4   How to build and use a mask to get and set a group of bits within a word.

encrypt < encrypted > encrypt.c

encrypt is virtually identical to our earlier character-copying program, display, except that instead of copying each character directly to the output (via putchar), we take the exclusive OR of the current character with the next character of the key. Actually, we turn on the high bit in the key character before we do the exclusive OR. Why? Because it turns out that DOS uses a control-Z (00011010) to indicate the end of the file, and this pattern can result from doing an exclusive OR with a key character—but only if its high bit is off. Turning it on prevents a potentially nasty

```
/*
 *    Encrypt the standard input using a built-in encryption key.
 *    The encryption key is "The encryption key."
 */
#include <stdio.h>

#define MAXKEY     19L      /* length of the key */
#define HIGHBIT  0x80      /* mask to access high bit only */

main()
{
  char key[MAXKEY];
  int  c;                   /* next character */
  unsigned long j;          /* character count */

  key[0]  = 'T';  key[1]  = 'h';  key[2]  = 'e';  key[3]  = ' ';
  key[4]  = 'e';  key[5]  = 'n';  key[6]  = 'c';  key[7]  = 'r';
  key[8]  = 'y';  key[9]  = 'p';  key[10] = 't';  key[11] = 'i';
  key[12] = 'o';  key[13] = 'n';  key[14] = ' ';  key[15] = 'k';
  key[16] = 'e';  key[17] = 'y';  key[18] = '.';

  for (j = 0L; (c = getchar()) != EOF; j = j + 1)
    putchar(c ^ (key[j % MAXKEY] | HIGHBIT));
  return 0;
}
```

Figure 4.5 encrypt.c—A program to encrypt a file, using exclusive OR with a built-in key.

problem.

   To simplify the structure of the program, we've built the key into the program. But in a truly secure encryption program, the key would be provided independently by the user of the program.

EXERCISES

4-4 Write a portable function, wordlength, that returns the number of bits in an int on a machine.

4-5 Write a function, invbits, that inverts a group of bits within a word. invbits should be passed a word, the position (from the right) of a group of bits within the word, and the number of bits to invert.

4-6 Write a function that takes an integer and prints its binary representation.

4-7 Write a function that uses exclusive OR to exchange the values in two unsigned int variables.

4.5   ASSIGNMENT OPERATORS

We have seen that in C, unlike most other programming languages, assignment not only assigns the result of an expression to a variable but also returns this value. One benefit is that we can use assignment operators more than once in a single statement. We can initialize more than one variable to some initial value (say, 0) with

```
a = b = c = 0;
```

The assignment operator is evaluated right to left, so this multiple assignment is equivalent to

```
a = (b = (c = 0));
```

Shorthand Assignment Operators

C doesn't just provide a single assignment operator, but an entire collection, including a set of operators of the form

lhs op= rhs

where *lhs* is the left-hand side of the assignment, *rhs* is an expression, and *op* is any one of C's arithmetic or bit-shift operators (so the shorthand operators are +=, -=, *=, /=, %=, >>=, <<=, &=, |=, and ^=). The shorthand form is equivalent to

lhs = lhs op (rhs)

with *lhs* evaluated once. Like =, the shorthand assignment operators return the value assigned and can be used in other expressions.

The shorthand operators are so convenient that after using them for just a little while, you'll find it hard to program in any language that doesn't have them. If nothing else, they save a large amount of typing. With the shorthand operators, we can easily divide `val` by two with

```
val /= 2
```

a terse equivalent of

```
val = val / 2
```

Actually, assuming `val` is nonnegative, we could also do this division by shifting right one bit, using

```
val >>= 1
```

the shorthand for

```
val = val >> 1
```

These operators lead to more concise, more efficient, and perhaps surprisingly, more readable code. To see why, consider the assignment

```
table[2 * i * j] = table[2 * i * j] + newval;
```

We use the assignment operator += to write this assignment more concisely.

```
table[2 * i * j] += newval;
```

The latter is more efficient because the subscripting expression is evaluated only once. It is more likely to be correct because we have to enter the subscripting expression only once. And it is more readable because it makes it clear that only one array element is involved in the computation.

Postfix and Prefix Assignment

C even provides two special sets of shorthand operators for the common operations of incrementing and decrementing by one: ++ add one to its operand, -- subtracts one from its operand. There are two forms of these operators, *prefix* (preceding its operand) and *postfix* (following its operand). As either a prefix or a postfix operator, ++ adds one to its operand. But when we use it as a postfix operator, ++ first evaluates the operand, providing its value to the rest of the statement or expression, and then adds one to it. And when we use it as a prefix operator, it does the additions first and makes the new value of the variable available to the expression. Prefix and postfix -- behave similarly to ++, except that they decrement their operand.

As an example, if n is 5, the postfix assignment

```
a = n++;
```

assigns 5 to a and then increments n. The corresponding prefix assignment

```
a = ++n;
```

first increments n and then makes the assignment. After the assignment, both a and n are 6.

We often use one form or the other when going through an array. Because an assignment using the ++ or -- operator causes two assignments to occur, we can often save an instruction and produce more efficient code. The assignment

```
max = a[i++];
```

assigns the current a[i] to max and then increments i, equivalent to the two statements

```
max = a[i];    i++;
```

Similarly,

```
max = a[++i];
```

first increments i, then makes the assignment, which is equivalent to the two statements

```
i++;    max = a[i];
```

Notice that as a statement not involving other side effects

```
i++;
```

is the same as

```
++i;
```

Using either form can make our loops more compact, as in the following loop to print an array in reverse order.

```
while (n > 0)
    printf("%d\n", a[--n]);
```

EXERCISES

4-8   Write a pair of functions, `bits_on` and `bits_off`, that return the number of bits that are on and off in word. Use the shorthand bit-manipulating operators.

4-9   Write a program that reads the values in its input into an array, prints the sum and average of these values, and then prints the number of values above, below, and exactly equal to the average. Use shorthand operators wherever possible.

4-10   Rewrite Chapter 2's insertion sort program to take advantage of the shorthand operators. Is the more concise version of the program more or less readable?

4-11   Repeat the previous exercise for the Chapter 2 program to reverse its input.

4-12   Rewrite Chapter 3's `getnumber` function to take advantage of the shorthand operators.

4.6   **OTHER OPERATORS**

There are three other operators of interest, the comma operator, the `sizeof` operator, and the conditional operator. None of these have analogs in other high-level languages like Pascal or BASIC.

The Comma Operator

We use the *comma operator* to link related expressions together, making our programs more compact. A comma-separated list of expressions is treated as a single expression and evaluated left to right, with the value of the rightmost expression returned as the expression's value.

We can use the comma operator to rewrite a program fragment to exchange the values of two variables x and y

```
temp = x;                          /* swap x and y */
x = y;
y = temp;
```

more concisely as

```
temp = x, x = y, y = temp;    /* swap x and y */
```

We can also use the comma operator to eliminate embedded assignments from tests. For example, we can rewrite

```
while ((c=getchar()) != EOF)
    putchar(c);
```

as

```
while (c = getchar(), c != EOF)
    putchar(c);
```

```
/*
 * Print the sizes of various types.
 */
#include <stdio.h>

main()
{
  int a[100];

  printf("Size of array a:\t %d\n", sizeof a);
  printf("Size of short:  \t %d\n", sizeof(short));
  printf("Size of int:    \t %d\n", sizeof(int));
  printf("Size of long:   \t %d\n", sizeof(long));
  printf("Size of float:  \t %d\n", sizeof(float));
  printf("Size of double: \t %d\n", sizeof(double));
  return 0;
}
```

Figure 4.6   sizeof.c—A program that prints the size of the basic data types.

separating reading the character from testing for end of file. Because the comma operator evaluates left to right, the rightmost expression's value (here, the test for end of file) controls the `while`'s execution. Either method is acceptable and we find ourselves using them interchangeably; use the one you find easiest to read.

The comma operator has the lowest precedence of any of C's operators, so we can safely use it to turn any list of expressions into a single statement. *Warning: The comma used to separate the parameters in function calls is not a comma operator and does not guarantee left-to-right evaluation.*

The Sizeof Operator

The `sizeof` operator returns the number of bytes in its operand, which may be a constant, a variable, or a data type. `sizeof` requires parentheses around a type but not around a variable.

What exactly is a byte? `sizeof` loosely defines it as the size of a character, which is eight bits on most but not all machines. If the variable is an array or another constructed type (Chapter 13), `sizeof` returns the total number of bytes needed. For arrays, `sizeof` returns the size of the base type times the declared size of the array. If `a` is an array of 100 `int`s, `sizeof(a)` is 200, assuming 2-byte (16-bit) `int`s (as on the PC). The `sizeof` operator is unique because it is evaluated at compile time instead of run time. The compiler replaces the call with a constant.

The program in Figure 4.6 prints the size of several different data types, including the standard types `short`, `int`, `long`, and so on. We didn't bother to print the size of a `char`, since by definition that is one byte. Figure 4.7 shows its output.

```
Size of array a: 200
Size of short:    2
Size of int:      2
Size of long:     4
Size of float:    4
Size of double:   8
```

Figure 4.7 The output when we run the sizeof program.

The Conditional Operator

The *conditional operator* is an `if` statement in disguise.

> *expression* ? *true-expression* : *false-expression*

It first evaluates *expression*, and if it is nonzero, then evaluates and returns *true-expression*. Otherwise, it evaluates and returns *false-expression*. At most, one of *true-expression* and *false-expression* is evaluated.

The conditional operator provides a convenient shorthand for `if` statements that decide which of two values a particular variable should be assigned. We can use `?:` to rewrite the following `if` that decides which of two values is smaller

```
if (x < y)
    min = x;
else
    min = y;
```

as

```
min = (x < y) ? x : y;
```

We don't have to parenthesize the test, but doing so is a good idea; the parentheses help distinguish the test from the values returned.

We can nest conditional operators, which allows us to rewrite more complex decisions. The following messy expression returns the middle value in a set of three values, x, y, and z.

```
(x > y) ? (y > z ? y : ((x > z) ? z : x))
        : (y < z ? y : ((x < z) ? z : x));
```

In addition to parenthesizing the expressions tested by the conditional operators, we parenthesized the nested conditional operators. Again, although not strictly necessary, this is a good habit to get into since it protects against possible precedence problems.

In their neverending quest for compact code most programmers have a tendency to go overboard with conditional operators. Using them leads to more concise, possibly more efficient, and definitely less readable code. Anything with more than a single nested conditional operator is better written using `if`s.

EXERCISES

4-13 Write an expression that returns the larger of two values.

4-14 Write expressions that return the smallest and largest of three values.

4.7   TYPE CONVERSIONS

Our discussion of operators has ignored an important question: What happens when an operator's operands are not both the same type? This happens, for example, when we multiply a `long` and a `double`, or assign a `long` to a `short`. In these cases, automatic type conversions occur. There are two types of conversions: assignment and arithmetic.

Automatic Type Conversions

Whenever we assign one value to another, C automatically converts the assigned value to the type on the right-hand side of the assignment, if possible. Sometimes this involves truncating a value or changing its internal representation, as when we assign a `float` to an `int`.

These automatic assignment conversions are convenient, but can cause problems when we assign a value of one type to a value with a shorter type. Consider the program shown in Figure 4.8 It first multiplies two `long`s together, assigns them to an `int`, and prints the result. And then it assigns a large negative `long` to the same `int`, and prints the result. Here's its strange output.

```
First answer: -7936
Second answer: 1980
```

How did multiplying two positive values give a negative result? And how did assigning a negative value give a positive result? When we multiply the two `long`s, we obtain the correct result, 100,000,000 in this case. But when we assign this value to an `int`, only its least significant bits were actually assigned. And the same thing happens when we assign the negative `long` to the `int`, as illustrated below.

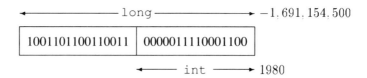

The sign bit (the leftmost bit) is on in the `long` and off in the `int`. *Warning: Conversion from a longer type to a shorter type leads to loss of significance, or worse, meaningless results, and is best avoided.*

```
/*
 * Example of automatic conversions.
 */
#include <stdio.h>

main()
{
  int answer;
  long i, j;

  i = j = 10000;
  answer = i * j;
  printf("First answer: %d\n", answer);
  answer = -1691154500L;
  printf("Second answer: %d\n", answer);
  return 0;
}
```

Figure 4.8 conex.c—A program illustrating potential problems with automatic conversions.

In addition to assignment conversions, C performs the following conversions whenever it does arithmetic (most of these are intuitive, except those dealing with conversions involving chars and unsigned ints):

1. Any char or short operands are converted to int. Any float operands are converted to double. Then if both operands are the same type, no other conversions are performed.

2. Otherwise, if one operand is a double, the other is converted to a double.

3. Otherwise, if one operand is an unsigned long, the other is converted to an unsigned long.

4. Otherwise, if one operand is a long, the other is converted to a long.

5. Otherwise, if one operand is an unsigned int, the other will be converted to one as well.

6. Otherwise, both operands are of type int: no additional conversion takes place.

There are two important points to be made about these conversions. First, they cause all real arithmetic to be done in double precision. To avoid unnecessary conversions, real variables should be double rather than float. Second, they cause all integer arithmetic to be done with ints or longs, which means that arithmetic operations involving chars can be expensive. Table 4.5 provides a better idea of what happens during all these conversions.

Casts

As we've just discovered, C performs some type conversions automatically. There are times, however, when we want to force a type conversion in a way that is different from the automatic conversion. We call such a process *casting* a value. We specify a cast by giving a type in parentheses followed by the expression to be cast:

(*type*) *expression*

The cast causes the result of the expression to be converted to the specified type.

As an example, we can use a cast to force the floating point number 17.7 to be treated as an int.

```
a = (int) 17.7 * 2;
```

This casts 17.7 (and only 17.7, not the entire expression) to an int by truncation. The result of this assignment is that a receives the value 34. Here 17.7 is cast to an int, 17, rather than the entire product, since the precedence of the cast operator is higher than that of most other operators.

We normally cast a variable to ensure that the arithmetic is carried out with the type on the left-hand side. We can round (rather than truncate) a variable to an integer by adding 0.5 to it and then casting to an int.

```
a = (int) (val + 0.5);
```

If val is 37.8, adding 0.5 to it yields 38.3; casting this to an int truncates the result to 38, the value that is then assigned to a. Of course, the variable or expression being cast is not changed; a cast simply returns a value of the cast type. Because of the high precedence of the cast operator, we had to parenthesize the expression to be cast, as we did above. Contrast this to the effect of writing

```
a = (int) val + 0.5;
```

Another typical use of a cast is in to force division to return a real number when both operands are ints. For example, a program to average a series of integers might accumulate a total in an integer variable sum, and a count of the number of values read in the integer n. We compute the average with:

```
ave = (double) sum / n;
```

Casting sum to a double causes the division to be carried out as floating point division. Without the cast, truncated integer division is performed, since both sum and n are integers.

EXERCISES

4–15   When we compile our earlier encryption program, we get a warning that a conversion may lose significance in the line that produces output. That's because we're using unsigned long arithmetic and using the result as an int array subscript. How can we use a cast to make this warning go away?

4–16   Our earlier function getkey (Chapter 3) gets rid of the high byte of the key it reads by using an unsigned char variable and an assignment conversion. It can be written more readably and more compactly using a cast. Do so.

FROM	TO	REPRESENTATION CHANGE
signed char	int	sign-extended high byte
unsigned char	int	zero-padded high byte
short	int	none
float	double	pads mantissa with 0's
signed int	signed long	sign-extended high byte
unsigned int	unsigned long	zero-filled high byte
long	int	truncated high byte
signed long	unsigned long	none
signed int	unsigned int	none
unsigned int	signed int	none

Table 4.5   What happens when we convert one type to another.

<table>
<tr><td>**4.8**</td><td>## CASE STUDY—DATA COMPRESSION</td></tr>
</table>

We conclude this chapter with a pair of programs to compress and uncompress their input. Data compression reduces the amount of storage needed to hold a particular piece of information, such as a file.

Compressing files is useful because it saves disk space and lessens the time required to copy or move them. A straightforward way to compress a file replaces any sequence of identical bytes (or characters) with two bytes, one containing the repeated byte, and the other containing the length of the sequence. With this method, for example, a group of eight blanks becomes a single blank followed by an 8. Since many files, especially programs, have frequent runs of duplicated characters, this encoding scheme can provide substantial savings.

Unfortunately, this scheme also has a problem: What do we do with a single byte surrounded by different characters? We certainly don't want to replace it with two bytes (the character and a count of one), as the file would grow rather than shrink. Ideally, in fact, we would like to simply leave it alone. But then how do we tell whether a particular byte is a character or a count? One possibility is to precede the count by a special character that means "here comes a character/count pair," an approach that takes one *byte* per sequence. We can do better, however, if we assume that our input is ASCII characters. Then there is an alternative that takes a single *bit* per sequence. ASCII characters take seven bits and C characters are stored in 8-bit bytes, so we can use the extra (high order) bit to identify groups. Of course, this means our compression program only works with text files and cannot be used to compress binary files, such as object modules.

Figure 4.9 contains compress, a program that implements the latter compression scheme. It reads groups of identical characters, a character at a time, counting the characters in the group. As long as the group is larger than some minimum that makes

```c
/*
 * Simple data-compression program (assumes ASCII characters).
 */
#include <stdio.h>

#define MINSIZE    3    /* smallest group to actually compress */
#define MAXSIZE  255    /* longest group */
#define HIGHBIT 0x80    /* high bit indicates compressed char */

main()
{
  int c,              /* last character read */
      newc,           /* new character read */
      cntc;           /* count of last character */

  for (c = getchar(); c != EOF; c = newc)
  {
    cntc = 1;              /* count occurrences of c */
    while (cntc < MAXSIZE && (newc = getchar()) == c)
      cntc++;
    if (cntc >= MINSIZE)
    {                      /* write count (high bit on) */
      putchar(c | HIGHBIT);
      putchar(cntc);
    }
    else                   /* write chars (high bit off) */
      while (cntc-- > 0)
        putchar(c & ~HIGHBIT);
  }
  return 0;
}
```

Figure 4.9 compress.c—A program to compress its input.

it worthwhile to compress (in our case, three or more characters), the program writes the repeated character once, first turning its high-order bit on, and follows it with the count. Shorter groups are simply written directly.

We run compress with its standard input redirected to the file to be compressed, and its standard output redirected into some other file. For example, we compress our compression program with:

compress < compress.c > compress.cc

We use the pc suffix to flag a compressed C file.

We have to uncompress a compressed file to access its original contents. Figure 4.10 contains uncmprss, a program to accomplish this task. It reads a character at a time and examines the character's high-order bit. If the bit is off, it simply writes the character. Otherwise, the bit is on, and the next byte must be the count. It reads the count, and then writes that many characters (with their high bit turned off).

```
/*
 * Simple uncompress program.
 */
#include <stdio.h>

#define HIGHBIT   0x80     /* indicates compressed char */

main()
{
  int c,                   /* new character read */
      cntc;                /* count of times appeared */
  int getcount(int c);

  while ((c = getchar()) != EOF && (cntc = getcount(c)) != 0)
    while (cntc-- > 0)
      putchar(c & ~HIGHBIT);
  return 0;
}

/*
 * Determine number of times to write the character:
 *    1 (high bit off), next char (if not EOF), 0 (if EOF)
 */
int getcount(int c)
{
  return (c & HIGHBIT) ? ((c = getchar()) == EOF ? 0 : c) : 1;
}
```

Figure 4.10   uncmprss.c—A program to uncompress its input.

We ran compress on a collection of source programs and achieved space savings ranging from 10 to 20 percent. While this is commendable—we now have more available disk space and our files transmit faster over phone lines—other, more complex methods do much better. Most of these work by creating a frequency distribution of characters in the file, and using varying length bit strings to encode the different characters.

EXERCISES

4-17 Our compression scheme works only on ASCII files. Running it on a non-ASCII file could lead to disaster. Write a program that verifies that every character in its input is an ASCII character. A non-ASCII character (a character with its high-order bit set) causes an error message containing its octal code and position in the file (line number and character).

4-18 Our compress is restricted to ASCII characters because we use the high-bit to indicate compressed strings. Write a new version of compress that instead indicates sequences by preceding them with an extra byte, one that contains a null character. Your program should work on any input, even one with null characters. Of course, you have to modify uncompress to understand this new scheme.

4-19 Modify the data-packing program in Figure 4.3 to read a series of values, computing the average age and average length of employment. Then modify it to print all female employees before any male employees. Finally, modify it to print only the unmarried employees.

5 STATEMENTS

We've been concentrating on constants and variables, and the operators with which we combine them into expressions. Now we turn our attention to C's rather small set of statements. In this chapter we present the fine points of the statements we have already used, and describe in detail those we have so far overlooked. While doing so, we produce a collection of useful functions for manipulating arrays of integers, and we write programs to simulate a simple calculator, and to print various breakdowns of their input characters. The chapter concludes by tying its topics together in a program that prints an octal dump of its input.

5.1   EXPRESSION AND COMPOUND STATEMENTS

C's simplest statement is the *expression statement*, an expression followed by a semicolon. We can use an expression statement anywhere C's syntax requires a statement. Both assignment statements and function calls, such as

```
sum += value;
```

and

```
printf("sum is %d\n", sum);
```

are merely expression statements and not special statement types, as in FORTRAN or BASIC.

An expression statement executes by evaluating the expression and discarding its result. That means that to be useful, an expression statement must have a side effect, such as invoking a function or changing a variable's value. Unfortunately, it's easy to accidentally write a syntactically legal expression statement that accomplishes nothing. The legal but useless expression statement

```
sum / entries;
```

divides sum by entries but does nothing with the result. Luckily, Turbo C often warns you about such statements.

A *compound statement* or *block* is a group of statements surrounded by braces. Like expression statements, we can place compound statements anywhere C's syntax requires a statement. But unlike expression statements, we don't follow them with a semicolon.

When we have a compound statement composed entirely of expression statements, we can use the comma operator to turn it into a single, more compact expression statement. For example, we can replace

```
    { temp = x; x = y; y = temp; }
```
with
```
    temp = x, x = y, y = temp;
```

Transformations like this one lead to more compact but less readable programs. They also make our programs harder to modify and debug. To see why, just imagine that we wanted to print the values of the variables after the exchange. In general, leave compound statements alone unless they consist of closely related expression statements, or unless the lines saved make the function fit on a single page, aiding readability.

5.2   SIMPLE DECISIONS—IF

We've already seen the if statement. One common combination of ifs is the *nested if*, one if inside another, as in this if that converts military time (mhour), a twenty four hour clock, to standard time (stdhour).

```
    if (mhour <= 12)
      if (mhour == 0)
        stdhour = 12;            /* midnight */
      else
        stdhour = mhour;         /* AM */
    else
      stdhour = mhour - 12;      /* PM */
```

These nested ifs aren't a big deal unless the inner if doesn't have an else. Consider this mistaken alternative to the previous if:

```
    stdhour = mhour;             /* assume AM */
    if (mhour <= 12)
      if (mhour == 0)
        stdhour = 12;            /* midnight */
    else
      stdhour = mhour - 12;      /* PM */
```

To which if does the else belong? From the indentation, we might assume the outer. But the compiler ignores the indentation and simply assumes that any else attaches to the closest nonterminated if. So, despite this program's misleading indentation, the else associates with the *inner* if and the program does the time conversion incorrectly. We avoid the problem by placing the inner if in braces, as we've done in Figure 5.1, a short program that uses this fragment.

EXERCISES

5–1 Using nested ifs, write a function min3 that returns the smallest of three int values passed to it as parameters.

5–2 Rewrite Figure 5.1 so that is uses the conditional operator.

```
/*
 * Convert military time to standard time.
 */
#include <stdio.h>

main()
{
  int mhour, min;   /* military hours and minutes */
  int stdhour;      /* standard hour */

  printf("Enter military time (xx:xx) ");
  if (scanf("%d:%d", &mhour, &min) == 2)
  {
    stdhour = mhour;            /* assume AM */
    if (mhour <= 12)
    {
      if (mhour == 0)
        stdhour = 12;          /* midnight */
    }
    else
      stdhour = mhour - 12;  /* PM */
    printf("Standard time: %d:%02d\n", stdhour, min);
  }
  else
    printf("Confused input\n");
  return 0;
}
```

Figure 5.1   mtime.c—A program that converts military time to standard time.

5.3   MULTIWAY DECISIONS—ELSE-IF

So far we've used `if`s to select one of two alternatives But we often have to decide between one of many alternatives. We can make those decisions with an `else-if`, a chain of `if`s in which the statement associated with each `else` happens to be another `if`:

```
if (first-expression)
   first-statement
else if (second-expression)
   second-statement

      . . .
else if (final-expression)
   final-statement
else
   default-statement
```

The final `else` and *default-statement* are optional.

An `else-if` evaluates each expression in turn until one evaluates to something other than zero, and then executes the single statement associated with it. If all the expressions evaluate to zero, the `else-if` executes the *default-statement*, if any. In either case, control then passes to the statement following the `else-if`.

The program `countem` shown in Figure 5.2 provides an example. It counts the number of characters in its input that fall into different classes such as white space, letters, digits, punctuation, and so on. When we run the program on its source file

   countem < countem.c

we obtain the following output:

```
Total       1147

spaces       362 31.6%
letters      549 47.9%
digits        39  3.4%
puncts       197 17.2%
others         0  0.0%
```

From running this program on our files, we've discovered that typically C programs are about 50% letters, 25-30% spaces, and 15-20% punctuation; executables are 75% control characters; and input files to text formatting programs are 70% letters, 10% punctuation. But what is `countem` useful for—other than perhaps satisfying a bored statistician's curiosity? We use an extended version of it to make educated guesses about the contents of files, based on the percentage breakdown of their input characters.

`countem` reads its input one character at a time, and uses a single `else-if` to determine which type of character we have and to update the appropriate counter. The `else-if` checks whether the character is white space, a letter, a digit, or a punctuation character, stopping as soon as it falls into one of those classes. Then it updates the appropriate counter and exits. If the character doesn't fall into one of these classes, it updates the default counter, `others`.

EXERCISES

5-3 Modify `countem` to print the number of upper and lower case characters in its input, and to print the number of vowels and the number of consonants.

5-4 Write a simple program to aid in balancing a checkbook. The program's input is single-letter commands followed by an amount. The legal commands are `d` (deposit), `c` (check), `s` (service charge), `w` (withdrawal), and `b` (set starting balance). The program should print the balance after each transaction. Make sure your program is well behaved even when the input is in error.

```c
/*
 * Print counts of various types of characters (spaces,
 * digits, letters, punctuation, and so on).
 */
#include <stdio.h>
#include <ctype.h>

main()
{
  int c;
  long spaces, letters, digits, puncts, others, tot;

  spaces = letters = digits = puncts = others = 0L;
  while ((c = getchar()) != EOF)
    if (isspace(c))
      spaces++;                  /* whitespace */
    else if (isalpha(c))
      letters++;                 /* upper- or lowercase letter */
    else if (isdigit(c))
      digits++;                  /* digit */
    else if (ispunct(c))
      puncts++;                  /* punctuation */
    else
      others++;
  tot = spaces + letters + digits + puncts + others;
  printf("Total   %7d\n\n", tot);
  if (tot != 0)
  {
    printf("spaces %7ld %4.1f%%\n",
            spaces, spaces * 100.0 / tot);
    printf("letters %7ld %4.1f%%\n",
            letters, letters * 100.0 / tot);
    printf("digits  %7ld %4.1f%%\n",
            digits, digits * 100.0 / tot);
    printf("puncts  %7ld %4.1f%%\n",
            puncts, puncts * 100.0 / tot);
    printf("others  %7ld %4.1f%%\n",
            others, others * 100.0 / tot);
  }
  return 0;
}
```

Figure 5.2   countem.c—A program to print a breakdown of the different types of characters in its input.

5.4   **MULTIWAY DECISIONS—SWITCH**

There is an alternative to an `else-if` that tests for different values of the same expression, such as an `else-if` that compares a single-letter, user-entered command with the program's legal commands to determine which action to take. The `switch` statement is a more convenient, more efficient, and more readable way to make such decisions.

```
switch( expression )
{
  case case-label-1 :
    statement-list
  case case-label-2 :
    statement-list
       . . .
  case case-label-3 :
    statement-list
  default:
    statement-list

}
```

`switch` is similar to the case and computed goto statements found in other languages.

A `switch` contains zero or more labeled cases and an optional `default` case. There are several restrictions on the labels. They have to be expressions that the compiler can evaluate to an integer constant, and all of the labels within a single `switch` must be unique, although they can appear in any order. A *statement-list* can contain zero or more statements; there is no need to put braces around them.

A `switch` executes by evaluating *expression* and passing control to the case labeled with its value (or to the `default` if there is no such case). After executing the case's statement list, control falls through to the next case label. Since this is almost always undesirable, we usually place a `break` statement at the end of each `case`'s statement list; a `break` exits the enclosing `switch`.

The simple calculator program shown in Figure 5.3 illustrates `switch`. The calculator's input is a series of triplets containing a floating point operand, a single-character operator (such as +, −, *, or /), and another floating point operand. The calculator prints the result of applying the operator to its operands. Here's some sample input and the calculator's output:

```
35.6+23.9
59.500000
67/69
0.971014
87.12-56.11
31.010000
10*15
150.000000
1/0
Warning: division by zero.
0.000000
```

We use `scanf` to read the operand-operator-operand triplets. Because `scanf` doesn't skip white space before single characters, there can be no spaces between

```c
/*
 * Simple calculator program.
 */
#include <stdio.h>

main()
{
  int vals;                    /* scanf return value */
  double op1, op2;             /* operands */
  char operator;               /* operator */
  double result;               /* result */

  while ((vals = scanf("%lf%c%lf", &op1, &operator, &op2)) == 3)
  {
    switch(operator)
    {
      case '+': result = op1 + op2;
                break;
      case '-': result = op1 - op2;
                break;
      case '*': result = op1 * op2;
                break;
      case '/': if (op2 != 0.0)
                   result = op1 / op2;
                else
                {
                   printf("Warning: division by zero.\n");
                   result = 0.0;
                }
                break;
      default:  printf("Unknown operator: %c\n", operator);
                result = 0.0;
                break;
    }
    printf("%f\n", result);
  }
  if (vals != EOF)
    printf("Program terminated by illegal input value.\n");
  return vals == EOF;
}
```

Figure 5.3   calc.c—A simple calculator program that illustrates switch.

the operator and its operands (eliminating this restriction is left as an exercise). The program simply quits if the user enters any inappropriate input.

Most of the program is a `switch` that selects the appropriate action for the user-entered operator. There is one case for each legal operator, along with a default case that prints an error message for any invalid operator. We end the actions for each case with a `break` statement; without it, control would automatically pass to the following case. We don't need the `break` after the `default`, and have used it solely as a defensive measure, preventing an accidental fall-through if we add more case labels later.

Warning: Falling through cases automatically can lead to serious problems when we forget the `break`. But it's useful when we want numerous cases to select the same action. We take advantage of it in Figure 5.4, a program to provide a breakdown by group (quotes, brackets, and the usual delimiters) of the punctuation characters in its input. There is one counter for each group, and a `switch` that selects the counter to be updated. Each character within a group has a case label, with all labels for a group placed above the single statement that increments its counter. When control passes to the label for any character in the group, it falls through to the statement updating the group's counter.

Falling through is appropriate only when the same action occurs for many different constants. Don't use it to execute statements in one case followed by statements in another. The rare times when doing so simplifies code should be well commented.

EXERCISES

5–5 Modify the calculator program to include various synonyms for the existing operators (such as a for +, s for –, m for *, and d for /), along with two additional operators, % (remainder) and ^ (exponentiation).

5–6 Rewrite the calculator to use a multiway `if` instead of a `switch`. Which version is more readable? Which version makes it easier to add synonyms for operators?

5–7 Rewrite the earlier checkbook-balancing exercise using a `switch`.

5–8 Modify the calculator to allow the operands to to be preceded and followed by an arbitrary amount of white space.

5.5   **LOOPS**

C's provides three looping mechanisms: the `while`, the `do-while`, and the `for`. We're already well acquainted with `while`, and we've been introduced to the `for`. `do-while` is similar to `while`, except that it's guaranteed to execute its body at least once.

```
/*
 * Counts various types of punctuation characters.
 */
#include <stdio.h>
#include <ctype.h>

main()
{
  int c;
  long quotes, brackets, delims, others;

  quotes = brackets = delims = others = 0;
  while ((c = getchar()) != EOF)
    if (ispunct(c))
      switch (c)
      {
        case '\'':
        case '"':
        case '`':
                    quotes++;    /* single & double quotes */
                    break;
        case '(':
        case ')':
        case '[':
        case ']':
                    brackets++; /* punctuation brackets */
                    break;
        case ',':
        case '.':
        case ';':
        case ':':
        case '!':
        case '?':
                    delims++;    /* normal punctuation marks */
                    break;
        default:                 /* other punctuation chars */
                    others++;
                    break;
      }
  printf("Quotes %ld\nBrackets %ld\nDelimiters %ld\nOthers %ld\n",
         quotes, brackets, delims, others);
  return 0;
}
```

Figure 5.4 countpct.c—A program to count quotation, bracket, and punctuation characters in its input.

The Do-While Statement

Unlike the `while`, which tests before it executes its body, the `do-while` tests afterward.

```
do
  statement
while (expression);
```

A `do-while` executes by repeatedly executing *statement* and evaluating *expression*. As with the `while`, the cycle ends when *expression* evaluates to zero. But unlike the `while`, `statement` is always executed at least once. As you might have guessed, we use `do-while` much less often than we do `while`.

Figure 5.5 uses `do-while` in a new version of `getdigit` (Chapter 3), a function that asks the user for a one-digit integer and ensures that it falls within a specified range. This version differs from the previous version in that its prompts for the desired values.

The heart of `getdigit` is a single `do-while` that prompts the user, reads a character with `getche`, and then makes sure that this digit falls between the minimum and maximum values provided as `getdigit`'s parameters. An illegal value causes the user to be queried again. We use a `do-while` because we prompt the user at least once and we want to loop until we get a correct response.

The For Statement

The final looping construct is the `for` statement:

```
for (Start ; Test ; Action )
  statement
```

We've seen that a `for` executes by evaluating *Start*, and then entering a cycle of evaluating *Test*, executing *statement*, and evaluating *Action*. The cycle terminates when *Test* evaluates to zero.

Usually, *Start* and *Test* are assignments or function calls and *Action* is a relational test—but both expressions are both arbitrary and optional. We omit *Start* when we've already done any needed initializations, as in `print_tab`, shown in Figure 5.6. `print_tab` is passed a `table` of integers and the subscripts of the `first` and `last` elements to print. We use `first` to traverse `table`, but initialize it when the function is called, rather than within the loop.

A missing *Test* is assumed to be nonzero, which means that such a loop is infinite and is normally to be exited by a `return` or other control-flow altering statement (discussed in subsequent sections). For example,

```
for (;;)
  printf("Reflex test - hit the terminal interrupt key.");
```

keeps writing the same message until someone hits the terminal interrupt key. Notice that the semicolons remain even when the expressions are left out.

Because the `for`'s expressions are arbitrary, we can have multiple index variables. We do so in `reverse_tab`, shown in Figure 5.7, a function that reverses an array

```
/*
 * A new version of the "getdigit" program (Chapter 3).
 * This version prompts before reading the desired digits.
 */
#include <stdio.h>
#include <conio.h>
#include <ctype.h>

#define MIN 1
#define MAX 5

main()
{
  int getdigit(int min, int max);

  printf("You entered a %d!\n", getdigit(MIN,MAX));
  return 0;
}

int getdigit(int min, int max)
{
  int c;                            /* input character */
  int value;                        /* digits value */

  do
  {
    printf("Enter value between %d and %d: ", min, max);
    c = getche();
    putchar('\n');
  }
  while (!isdigit(c) || (value = c - '0') < min || value > max);
  return value;
}
```

Figure 5.5   getdig2.c—A function that reads and validates a single input value.

in place. That is, it exchanges the array's first and last elements, its second and next-to-last elements, and so on. We can use reverse_tab to turn an array sorted in ascending order into one sorted in descending order.

reverse_tab works by exchanging the array's first and last elements, incrementing first, decrementing last, and then repeating the entire process until first and last cross. Two tricks make our code more concise. We use the comma operator to turn the separate expressions updating first and last into the single expression used as the for's *Action* component. And, as in print_tab, we don't initialize first or last within the for, since their initial values are provided when the function is called.

Since the for is more general than the while, you may be wondering when each is appropriate. Use for when the loop control statements are simple and related, and

```
/*
 * Print table given subscripts to first and last table elements.
 */
#include <stdio.h>


#define MAX   20

main()
{
  int table[MAX], i;
  void print_tab(int a[], int first, int last);

  for (i = 0; i < MAX; i++)   /* place some values in the array */
    table[i] = i;
  print_tab(table, 0, MAX - 1);
  return 0;
}


void print_tab(int a[], int first, int last)
{
   for (; first <= last; first++)
     printf("%d\n", a[first]);
}
```

Figure 5.6   printtab.c—A function to print part of an array and a main program to test it.

the same values are updated each time the loop is executed. Use `while` when an equivalent `for` would contain unrelated computations or would omit both *Start* and *Action*. When in doubt, write the code for both and use the one that appears to be more readable.

Concise Control Expressions

We've seen that `for`, `while`, `do-while`, and `if` all work by evaluating an expression and comparing its result with zero. That means that we don't ever need to have explicit comparisons with zero. So far, we've only taken advantage of this feature in our use of the `ctype` functions, as in

```
    if (isdigit(c))
      digits++;
```

But we can also use it to make many of our loops more concise. For example, consider this loop from compress that repeatedly prints a character.

```
    while (cntc-- != 0)    /* print character c, cntc times */
      putchar(c & ~HIGHBIT);
```

```
/*
 * Reverse an array in place and then print it.
 */
#include <stdio.h>

#define MAX   20

main()
{
  int table[MAX], i;
  void reverse_tab(int a[], int first, int last);
  void print_tab(int a[], int first, int last);

  for (i = 0; i < MAX; i++)    /* place some values in the array */
     table[i] = i;
  reverse_tab(table, 0, MAX - 1); /* reverse the array */
  print_tab(table, 0, MAX - 1);   /* print the reversed array */
  return 0;
}


void reverse_tab(int a[], int first, int last)
{
  int temp;

  for (; first < last; first++, last--)
  {
    temp = a[first];
    a[first] = a[last];
    a[last] = temp;
  }
}

void print_tab(int a[], int first, int last)  /* same as before */
{
   for (; first <= last; first++)
     printf("%d\n", a[first]);
}
```

Figure 5.7   revtab.c—A function to reverse an array in place and a main program that uses it.

The test that cnt-- is not equal to zero is redundant, so we can remove it.

```
while (cntc--)          /* print character c, cntc times */
    putchar(c & ~HIGHBIT);
```

Implicit comparisons with zero is a nice feature, but can lead to disaster when we use = (assignment) when we meant to use == (test for equality). When

```
while (done = 0)
{
    printf("going through loop\n");
    done = 1;
}
```

is executed, the printf will never be executed, regardless of done's value. This happens because every time the while is executed, done is set to zero, causing the implicit test to fail. Most likely, the correct form is

```
while (done == 0)
{
    printf("went through loop\n");
    done = 1;
}
```

Warning: A control expression that consists of a single variable assignment is probably an accident.

EXERCISES

5-9 Write a program that prints all the prime numbers between 1 and 1000. A prime number is one that is exactly divisible only by one and itself.

5-10 Rewrite getdigit (Chapter 3) using do-while and using while. Which is the most compact? Which is the most readable?

5-11 Write a function to determine whether an array of ints is symmetrical. That is, its first element is the same as its last element, its second element is the same as its next-to-last element, and so on.

5.6   ### THE NULL STATEMENT

A lone semicolon with no preceding expression is a *null statement*, a statement that does nothing. The null statement is merely a placeholder used when C's syntax requires a statement but we don't desire any action. This situation occurs most frequently when side effects in a loop's control expression obviates the need for the loop body.

As an example, Figure 5.8 contains search, a simple function to search an array. search takes an array, the number of elements in the array, and a target value. It returns the target's position in the array or −1 if the target cannot be found. Because

```
/*
 * Search table for the target value, returning its position.
 */
#include <stdio.h>

#define MAX     10
#define TARGET   5

main()
{
  int table[MAX];                    /* array */
  int i;                             /* array index */
  int found;                         /* target position */
  int search(int a[], int n, int target);

  for (i = 0; i < MAX; i++)          /* initialize table with */
    table[i] = i;                    /*   0,1,2,3,... */
  if ((found = search(table, MAX, TARGET)) != -1)
    printf("Found %d as element %d.\n", TARGET, found);
  else
    printf("Didn't find %d.\n", TARGET);
  return 0;
}

int search(int a[], int n, int target)
{
  int i;

  for (i = 0; i < n && a[i] != target; i++)
    ;       /* search for matching value */
  return i != n ? i : -1;
}
```

Figure 5.8 search.c—A function to search an array for a desired value and a short program that uses it.

the two actions needed to search an array—testing for a matching value and updating the array index—occur within the for itself, we are forced to use a null statement as the loop's body.

Don't place a null statement on the same line as a for or a while. Although it's legal, and it makes the program more compact, it also makes the program more difficult to decipher. It's far too easy for the program's reader to ignore the semicolon at the end of the line and mistake the following lines for the loop's body. Place the null statement on a line by itself, indented slightly and followed by a comment, as we have done in our examples.

Warning: Watch out for accidentally inserting a null statement following the head of a loop. This fragment

```
for (sum = i = 0; i < n; i++); /* total first "n" elements */
sum += table[i];               /* (accidental null body) */
```

was probably meant to place the total of the first n array elements in the variable sum. But the semicolon on the line containing the for is a null statement that forms the loop's body. What was meant to be the loop body

```
sum += table[i];
```

executes only after the loop exits, when i is n+1 and is probably no longer a legal subscript.

EXERCISES

5–12 Rewrite search to use a while loop instead of a for loop. Which version do you find more readable? Which version is more efficient? (One way to measure efficiency is to examine the machine code the compiler generates. Specifying the -S option to tcc produces a file containing this assembly language code.)

5–13 Modify search to assume its table is in sorted order and to terminate the search as quickly as possible.

5.7   **ALTERING CONTROL FLOW**

Statements are ordinarily executed sequentially. C, however, provides several statements that alter this normal flow of control: break, continue, and goto. Although these statements violate some of the basic principles of structured programming, they can occasionally simplify otherwise complex code. Keep in mind, though, that their use is never unavoidable, and that their abuse leads to impenetrable programs.

The Break Statement

We've already used break to exit a switch. We can also use it to exit the nearest enclosing for, while, or do-while. As an example, we'll rewrite this loop from our earlier file display program, page.

```
resp = ' ';
while (resp != 'Q' && showpage(PAGESIZE) == PAGESIZE)
{
  printf("--Go on?--");
  resp = toupper(getkey());
  printf("\r          \r");   /* overwrite prompt */
}
```

to use break.

```
while (showpage(PAGESIZE) == PAGESIZE)
{
  printf("--Go on?--");
  resp = toupper(getkey());
  printf("\r          \r");   /* overwrite prompt */
  if (resp == 'Q')            /* leave early */
    break;
}
```

The break exits the while and passes control to the next statement. Using break simplifies the loop's control expression and highlights that the user's entering 'Q' or 'q' as a special case. In general, we can use break to simplify a loop's control expression by separating tests for special cases or errors.

The Continue Statement

A continue skips the rest of the loop body. In a while or do-while, continue causes the loop test to be immediately evaluated. In a for, *Action* is evaluated first. We use continue to help prevent excessive nesting within a loop.

In Figure 5.9, count_legal counts the number of array elements that fall into a particular range. Whenever count_legal encounters an out-of-range element, it writes an error message and uses a continue to skip further processing of the element. Since the continue occurs within a for, the loop's action (incrementing i) is executed before the loop test occurs.

This continue is actually somewhat silly, since we can eliminate it by reversing the sense of the range test. And, in fact, we can always avoid using a continue by making the code to be skipped a separate function. We use it only when we check for errors at the beginning of a loop, and find it convenient to leap over the rest of the loop if an error occurs.

The Goto Statement

The goto is the final control-flow altering command. It simply transfers control to a labeled statement.

> goto *label*
>   . . .
> *label*: *statement*

A label has the same syntax as an identifier and must be in the same block as the goto. A null statement must follow any label located at the end of a function.

One reasonable use of a goto is to rapidly bail out of nested loops when an error occurs.

```
for (...)
  for (...)
  {
    ...
    if (error condition)
      goto error;
/*
 * Count array elements falling within range.
 */
#include <stdio.h>

#define MAX 100

main()
{
  int n;                         /* number of items read */
  int table[MAX];                /* array to hold items */
  int get_data(int a[], int max);
  int count_legal(int a[], int n, int min, int max);

  n = get_data(table, MAX);
  printf("%d out of %d values are one-digit numbers.\n",
         count_legal(table, n, 0, 9), n);
  return 0;
}

int get_data(int a[], int max)
{
  int cnt;

  for (cnt = 0; cnt < max && scanf("%d", &a[cnt]) == 1; cnt++)
    ;
  return cnt;
}

int count_legal(int a[], int n, int min, int max)
{
  int i, cnt;

  for (cnt = i = 0; i < n; i++)
  {
    if (a[i] < min || a[i] > max)
      continue;   /* bad value, skip further processing */
    cnt++;
  }
  return cnt;
}
```

Figure 5.9 continue.c—A function to count array elements within a specific range and a main program that uses it.

```
          ...
     }
     ...
   error:
     printf("Serious error detected -- bailing out\n");
     ...
```

When the error condition occurs, control transfers to the label *error* and the error message is printed. To see why `goto` is useful in this situation, consider trying to avoid it. We can't use `break` because it exits only a single loop. We could let a Boolean variable note the error condition and add loop tests of its value, or make the code fragment containing the loops a function that returns a special value when an error condition occurs—but these alternatives seem to be more work than they're worth.

Although the above `goto` is reasonable, avoid them whenever possible. Most compilers generate less efficient code for loops implemented with `goto` instead of the structured loop constructs. In addition, rampant `goto`s render a program unreadable. `goto`s are scarce in well-written programs, and we haven't needed any in the programs in this book.

EXERCISES

5-14 Rewrite our `continue` example without using a `continue`.

5-15 Rewrite a `while`, a `do-while` and a `for` using only `if`s and `goto`s. Are the `goto` versions more or less readable than the standard loop constructs? You better say less readable!

5.8   CASE STUDY—OCTAL DUMP

We end this chapter with a program, octdump, shown in Figure 5.10, that prints an octal dump of its input. The input

```
   this is      a test
```

(which has two invisible tab characters between the "is" and the "a") produces

```
   000000   164 150 151 163 040 151 163 011
             t   h   i   s       i   s  \t
   000008   011 141 040 164 145 163 164 012
            \t   a       t   e   s   t  \n
```

octdump writes each input character on the output in octal and as a character if the character is printable. It displays special characters, such as tabs and form feeds, as escape sequences. An octal dump is useful for displaying binary files and text files containing strange characters.

The main program reads the input one character at a time, and places groups of these characters into an array. When the array is full, it calls print_group to print the octal and text representations for the characters. `print_group` writes the octal representation and, if the character is a special whitespace character, it calls `print_space` to print the escape sequence.

EXERCISES

5-16 Most PC programmers usually work in hex rather than octal. Modify `octdump` to produce a hex dump instead.

5-17 Modify `octdump` to print control characters in the form ^*X*. For example, a control G would print as ^G.

5-18 Write a program that prints the line numbers of those lines in its input that are over 80 characters long (those lines that are too big to fit on the typical terminal screen). Modify the program so that it also prints the length of those lines.

5-19 Write a program that prints the line numbers of those lines that contain only white space characters. Modify this program so that it also prints the line numbers of any line containing control characters, along with any control characters that lines contains.

```c
/*
 * Dump input in octal (and character if printable).
 */
#include <stdio.h>
#include <ctype.h>

#define MAXCHARS  8     /* number of chars on a line */

main()
{
  int c;                /* next character */
  int chars[MAXCHARS];  /* chars for current output line */
  int ingroup;          /* chars in current group */
  long cnt;             /* chars in input */
  void print_group(int t[], int n, long final);

  for (cnt = 0L, ingroup = 0; (c = getchar()) != EOF; cnt++)
  {
    chars[ingroup++] = c;
    if (ingroup == MAXCHARS)
    {
      print_group(chars, ingroup, cnt);
      ingroup = 0;
    }
  }
  if (ingroup)
    print_group(chars, ingroup, cnt);
  return 0;
}

void print_group(int t[], int n, long final)
{
  int i;
  void print_space(int);

  printf("%06ld  ", final - n + 1);
  for (i = 0; i < n; i++)    /* print octal codes */
    printf(" %03o", t[i]);
  printf("\n          ");
  for (i = 0; i < n; i++)
  {
    putchar(' ');            /* space */
    if (isspace(t[i]))
      print_space(t[i]);     /* whitespace */
    else if (isprint(t[i]))
      printf("  %c", t[i]);  /* printable */
    else
      printf("   ");         /* other chars */
  }
  putchar('\n');
}
```

```
void print_space(int c)
{
  int label;

  if (c == ' ')
    printf("    ");
  else
  {
    switch(c)
    {
      case '\b' :  label = 'b';
                   break;
      case '\f' :  label = 'f';
                   break;
      case '\n' :  label = 'n';
                   break;
      case '\r' :  label = 'r';
                   break;
      case '\t' :  label = 't';
                   break;
      case '\v' :  label = 'v';
                   break;
      default   :  label = '?';
                   break;
    }
    printf(" \\%c", label);
  }
}
```

Figure 5.10   octdump.c—An octal dump program.

6 ARRAYS
POINTERS
AND STRINGS

We can use arrays in C in the same way we use arrays in other languages. But doing so ignores some of their most important features and leads to slower, less powerful programs. This chapter shows how to take full advantage of C arrays. We introduce pointers, a data type that can hold addresses, and study how to use them to traverse arrays efficiently. We also introduce strings, a special type of array of characters, and present the standard library functions for manipulating them. Finally, we introduce dynamically allocated arrays, arrays whose space is allocated at run time rather than compile time. The chapter concludes with a program to eliminate duplicate lines from its input, building a useful new program from small existing functions.

6.1   POINTERS

A *pointer* is the address of a memory location. Whenever we declare a variable, as in

```
int  i;
```

the compiler reserves a memory location for it. The compiler might, for example, set aside memory location 10000 for i. When we subsequently refer to i, we are really referring to this location. Assigning zero to i with

```
i = 0;
```

places a 0 in memory location 10000. We say that 10000 is i's address or, in other words, a *pointer* to i. In C, we can access a value directly by providing its name, or indirectly through a pointer. We will soon see how this indirect pointer access allows us to traverse arrays more efficiently and lets us manipulate dynamically allocated arrays. In the next chapter, we'll see how we can use them to simulate call-by-reference parameter passing and to write functions that work with many different data types.

Declaring and Obtaining Pointers

Pointers are a basic data type in C. That means that we can declare pointer variables; that is, variables that contain addresses (or pointers to) other values. Like any other variable, a pointer must have a type—but unfortunately C has no single type `pointer`. Instead, we have to declare a pointer as pointing to a value of a particular type, such as an `int`, a `float`, a `char`, and so on. We must do so because when we access a value through a pointer, the compiler needs to know the value's type.

We declare a variable as a pointer to a given type with

> *type* *name

This declares *name* as a pointer to *type*. The following declares `iptr` as a "pointer to `int`," `fptr` as a "pointer to `float`," `cptr` as a "pointer to `char`," and `dptr` as a "pointer to `double`."

```
int    *iptr;        /* iptr is "pointer to int" */
float  *fptr;        /* fptr is "pointer to float" */
char   *cptr;        /* cptr is "pointer to char" */
double *dptr;        /* dptr is "pointer to double" */
```

Each of these declarations allocates space for the named pointer variable. Once we have declared a pointer variable, however, we still have to make it point to something. To do this, we use a new operator, `&` which returns the address of its operand. In the example above, `&i` is 10000. We can initialize `iptr` to point to `i` with the assignment

```
iptr = &i;
```

After this assignment `iptr` contains the address 10000, a pointer to `i`.

Dereferencing Pointer Variables

Once we have made a pointer point to something, we can access the value to which it points, a process called *dereferencing*. Dereferencing is done with the indirection operator `*`, which, when executed, follows the pointer and returns the value at that address. In the example above, `*iptr` is 0, the value of `i`.

Because `iptr` is of type "pointer to `int`," we can use `*iptr` anywhere a variable can occur, such as in assignments. The assignment

```
n = *iptr;
```

assigns to n whatever `iptr` points to, zero in this example. Similarly, the assignment

```
*iptr = j;
```

assigns the `j`'s current value to whatever `iptr` points to, `i` in this case. Similarly, the assignment

```
*iptr = *iptr + 10;
```

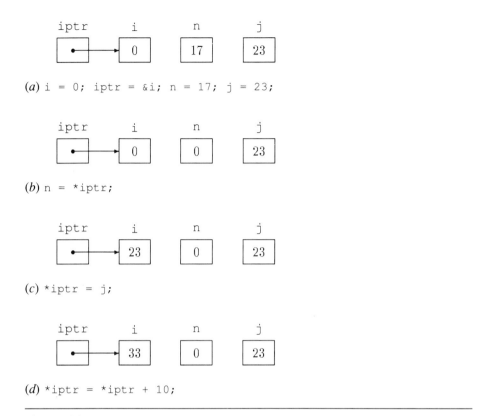

(*a*) i = 0; iptr = &i; n = 17; j = 23;

(*b*) n = *iptr;

(*c*) *iptr = j;

(*d*) *iptr = *iptr + 10;

Figure 6.1 Examples of indirectly accessing values through a pointer.

adds 10 to whatever `*iptr` points to. Figure 6.1 illustrates what's going on with these assignments.

Pointer variables, like other C variables, are *not* automatically initialized. In fact a pointer variable starts off with a random value—whatever happens to be in the memory location reserved for the pointer—and could therefore point anywhere. That means that `*iptr` is meaningless until `iptr` has been made to point to something. *Warning: Don't dereference a pointer variable until you've assigned it an address.*

One way to prevent problems with using uninitialized pointer variables is to initialize all of them to `NULL`, a special pointer that points to nowhere. `NULL` is equivalent to the constant 0. In C, it is illegal to dereference 0, and in most environments doing so causes a run-time error that terminates the program. This makes accidentally dereferencing `NULL` cause less harm than dereferencing a random pointer.

`NULL` is defined in stddef.h, so any program that uses the `NULL` pointer should have the preprocessor directive

```
#include <stddef.h>
```

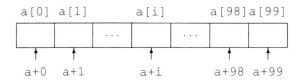

Figure 6.2 What happens when we declare an array. Here we declared a as an array containing 100 ints.

As an alternative, the program can simply use zero in place of NULL, or can precede its use with the statement

```
#define NULL 0
```

We will see additional uses of the null pointer throughout the book.

EXERCISES

6-1 We had to pass scanf the addresses of the variables it was to read. Write a function readint that takes a pointer to an integer and uses scanf to fill in the pointed-to integer.

6-2 Write a similar function printint that takes a pointer to an integer and uses printf to print the pointed-to integer. Write a main program to test it.

6.2   TRAVERSING ARRAYS USING POINTERS

In C, arrays and pointers are intimately intertwined. When we declare an array the compiler not only allocates a block of storage large enough to hold the array, but also defines the array's name as a constant pointer to its first (zeroth) element.

Figure 6.2 shows what happens when we declare a to be an array of 100 ints with

```
int a[100];
```

The compiler first allocates 100 contiguous storage locations, each holding a single int. It then defines a as the address of its zeroth element. Since array indexing begins with 0, a is equivalent to &a[0]. Here, a is the constant 1000, the location where a[0] is stored. Because a is a constant address, taking its address with &a does not make sense and is therefore illegal.

In C, there are two ways to access array elements. One is through direct array indexing. To access an array element, we provide the array name and a bracket-enclosed index. Arrays are indexed beginning at zero, so in a we can legally access

```
/*
 * Print first "n" elements using array subscripting.
 */
#include <stdio.h>

#define MAX   20

main()
{
  int table[MAX];
  int i;
  void print_table(int a[], int n);

  for (i = 0; i < MAX; i++)    /* provide some initial values */
    table[i] = i;
  print_table(table, MAX);     /* print the array */
  return 0;
}

void print_table(int a[], int n)
{
  int i;

  for (i = 0; i < n; i++)
    printf("%d\n", a[i]);
}
```

Figure 6.3   prtab1.c—A program that uses array subscripting to print the first n elements of an array.

elements between a[0] to a[99]. To traverse the array, we can use an index variable that runs through the possible index values, as we have done with print_table, shown in Figure 6.3.

Traditional array indexing is simple to use, easy to understand, and is similar to the way we process arrays in other languages. But we can traverse arrays more efficiently using another method: accessing array elements indirectly through pointers. We can do so because C provides pointer arithmetic—the ability to add integers to or subtract integers from a pointer.

Pointer Arithmetic

In C, pointer arithmetic is automatically done in units of the pointer's underlying base type. That is, adding 1 to a pointer to an array element gives a pointer to the next element—regardless of whether we have an array of ints, an array of doubles, or an array of any other type. In the declaration above, a is a pointer to its first element (&a[0]). That means that a + 1 is a pointer to its second element (&a[1]), a + 2 is a pointer to its third element (&a[2]), and so on. In general, a + i is the address of element a[i].

Since a + i is the address of a[i], *(a + i) is equivalent to a[i]. We can initialize a[3] to 0 with array indexing

```
a[3] = 0;
```

or with pointer indexing:

```
*(a + 3) = 0;
```

In fact, the compiler converts array subscripts into pointer dereferences—a[i] *becomes* *(a + i). These are equivalent because in the pointer dereference, *(a + i) the addition a + i is carried out in sizeof(int) increments. Selecting the *i*th element of an array involves calculating its address, given the array's base address (the location of a[0]). When we write a[3], C multiplies the index (3) by the size of an int (2 on the PC), and adds the result to the base address of the array. In our example, assuming a is 1000, the computation results in an address of 1006, which is where we find a[3].

So far it may seem that we haven't really gained anything other than a more complicated way to access array elements. But consider the new version of print_table shown in Figure 6.4. It uses a pointer, ptr, to traverse the array rather than an array index. We traverse the array by simply adding one to ptr each time we go through the loop. This works because incrementing a pointer makes it point to the next array element.

Why is this pointer-accessing method faster? The main reason is that we eliminate an address computation. When we write a[i], the compiler turns it into *(a + i), which requires an addition (and possibly a multiplication) to locate the desired element. In the pointer version, the pointer is incremented each time we go through the loop—which can often be done as part of the machine instruction that dereferences the pointer—and no other calculation is necessary. Surprisingly, we'll be able to improve this loop even further in the next section.

We can use pointer indexing to traverse any kind of array, not just an array of ints. Pointer arithmetic for references to an element in an array of doubles is done in terms of doubles, units of eight bytes (assuming 8-byte doubles). Suppose we have an array d declared as an array of doubles.

```
double  d[100];
```

The compiler converts a reference to d[i] to *(d + i). If d[0] is stored at location 2000 (equivalently, &d[0] is 2000, or equivalently, d is the constant value 2000), d[i] refers to the value in the location $2000 + 8i$. As with a earlier, we can print an element of d directly using d[i] or indirectly using a pointer. If we want dptr to be a pointer to a double (that is, to point to an element in array d), we can declare and use it as in the function print_dtable, shown in Figure 6.5, which prints the first n elements of d.

There is one final form of pointer arithmetic: subtracting one pointer from another. The result of subtracting a pointer q from a pointer p is j such that $p + j$ gives q. So if p is &a[0] and q is &a[3], q - p is 3. This operation gives a portable result only if both operands point to the same array.

```
/*
 * Print first "n" elements using pointer indexing.
 */
#include <stdio.h>

#define MAX   20

main()
{
  int table[MAX];
  int i;
  void print_table(int a[], int n);

  for (i = 0; i < MAX; i++)    /* provide some initial values */
    table[i] = i;
  print_table(table, MAX);     /* print the array */
  return 0;
}

void print_table(int a[], int n)
{
  int i;
  int *ptr;

  for (ptr = a, i = 0; i < n; ptr++, i++)
    printf("%d\n", *ptr);
}
```

Figure 6.4   prtab2.c—A pointer version of `print_table`. The main program is identical to the one we used before.

No other arithmetic operations are allowed on pointers. *Warning: We can't add, multiply, or divide two pointers.* This restriction is occasionally irritating. Suppose we need to find the middle element of part of an array; that is, we have an array a and we want the element halfway between a[L] and a[H]. We can easily find it using array indexing: it's a[(H + L) / 2]. But if lp is a pointer to a[L] and hp is a pointer to a[H], we cannot find the middle element at (ip + lp) / 2, since it is illegal to *add* pointers. We can legally *subtract* pointers, however, so we use an equivalent method, lp + (hp - lp) / 2. This may look like pointer addition, but it is not. Subtracting two pointers yields an integer, as does dividing an integer by two, and adding an integer to a pointer gives a pointer. So, assuming a is our array, we can find its middle element with either

```
    int  value;
       . . .
    value = a[(H - L) / 2];
```

or the equivalent

```
        int   value;
/*
 * Print an array of doubles using pointer indexing.
 */
#include <stdio.h>

#define MAX 20

main()
{
  double table[MAX];
  int i;
  void print_dtable(double d[], int);

  for (i = 0; i < MAX; i++)      /* some initial values */
    table[i] = i;
  print_dtable(table, MAX);
  return 0;
}

void print_dtable(double d[], int n)
{
  double *dptr;
  int i;

  for (i = 0, dptr = d; i < n; i++, dptr++)
    printf("%f\n", *dptr);
}
```

Figure 6.5   prdtab.c—A program using pointer arithmetic to print an array of `doubles`.

```
    int   *lp, *hp;
        .  .  .
    lp = &a[L];
    hp = &a[H];
        .  .  .
    value = *(lp + (hp - lp) / 2);
```

Pointer Comparisons

Not only can we do arithmetic with pointers, but we can also use the relational operators to compare them. We can test whether a pointer is equal (==), not equal (!=), less than (<), less than or equal (<=), greater than (>), or greater than or equal (>=) to another.

Two pointers are equal only if they point to the same location, and are not equal if they don't. One pointer is less than another if it points to a lower location in memory, so &a[3] is less than &a[5]. *Warning: Comparisons other than equality are portable only if the compared pointers access the same array.* It makes no sense

```
/*
 * Print first "n" elements using pointer indexing and comparison.
 */
#include <stdio.h>


#define MAX   20

main()
{
  int table[MAX];
  int i;  .
  void print_table(int a[], int n);

  for (i = 0; i < MAX; i++)    /* provide some initial values */
    table[i] = i;
  print_table(table, MAX);     /* print the array */
  return 0;
}

void print_table(int a[], int n)
{
  int *ptr, *endptr;

  endptr = a + n - 1;
  for (ptr = a; ptr <= endptr; ptr++)
    printf("%d\n", *ptr);
}
```

Figure 6.6 prtab3.c—A more concise version of print_table. Once again, the main program is the same as before.

to compare &a[3] with &d[7].

We can use pointer comparisons to write print_table more efficiently, and we have done so in Figure 6.6. This loop is more efficient because it no longer tests a counter to determine when the array has been traversed. Instead, we compare the indexing pointer with the address of the array's last element.

In fact, we can write the loop to print table's values even more compactly.

```
    endptr = (ptr = table) + n - 1;
    while (ptr <= endptr)
      printf("%d\n", *ptr++);
```

Because of the precedence and evaluation order of * and ++, *ptr++ means "obtain the value that ptr points to (i.e., *ptr), return the value, and then increment the pointer." This differs from (*ptr)++, which simply increments the value to which ptr points, after returning its original value. Similarly, *ptr-- decrements the pointer after returning the pointed-to value. The prefix forms increment (*++ptr)

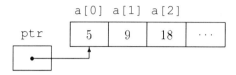

(*a*) initially assume `ptr = &a[0]`.

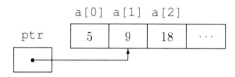

(*b*) `*ptr++` increments `ptr` and returns 5.

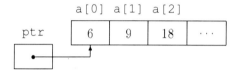

(*c*) `(*ptr)++` increments `a[0]` and returns 5.

Figure 6.7 The difference between `*ptr++` and `(*ptr)++`.

or decrement (`*--ptr`) the pointer and return whatever value it then points to. Figure 6.7 illustrates how these expressions differ.

EXERCISES

6–3 Write a function that sums the elements in an array, using only pointers (no extra array indexing).

6–4 Rewrite Chapter 2's program to reverse its input using pointers rather than array indexes. To do this you'll need to rewrite both `get_data` and `print_reverse`.

6–5 Write a function to search an array of `ints` for a particular value, again using only pointers. Your function should return the array subscript of the first matching value.

6–6 Rewrite the search function from the previous exercise to search backwards from the end of the array.

6–7 Write a function that deletes all occurrences of a particular item from an array. It does the delete by shifting array elements. Use pointers.

6.3   ARRAY PARAMETERS AND POINTERS

We saw earlier that when we pass an array parameter, we really only pass the address of its first element—or, in other words, a pointer. This means that

```
void print_table(int a[], int n)
{
    . . .
}
```

is equivalent to

```
void print_table(int *a, int n)
{
    . . .
}
```

When we call `print_table(table, MAX)`, the address of `table[0]` is copied into a. Because we only pass a pointer, we don't indicate bounds on `table`. Within `print_table`, we can access elements of a using either the array form (`a[i]`) or the pointer form (`*(a + i)`). Pick your favorite, although it's customary to use the form corresponding to the way the object was defined.

Since C's parameters are passed by value (copied), we can use the passed pointer to traverse the array instead of declaring an additional local variable. We do this in one final version of `print_table`, shown in Figure 6.8. When `print_table` is called, `ptr` is initialized with the address of the array's first element. We then use it to traverse the array, incrementing it after each element is printed (as before). `table` is a constant and is not affected by the call to `print_table`.

As we do not explicitly declare an array parameter's size, functions that process arrays need to know how many array elements to process. That means that when we pass an array, we usually also pass the number of elements in the array, n in `print_table`. We cannot use `sizeof` in `print_table` because `sizeof(ptr)` returns the size of a pointer, not of the entire array, which is not necessarily known at compile time.

One nice benefit of an array being passed as a pointer is that we can pass the address of any array element. This effectively allows us to pass only part of an array. We can print k elements of `table`, starting with `table[i]`, with either

```
print_table(&table[i], k);
```

or the equivalent

```
print_table(table + i, k);
```

In both cases we pass `table[i]`'s address. Figure 6.9 shows how `print_table` can still access any element of `table` through appropriate negative or positive offsets of `ptr`.

Don't make the common mistake of passing an array element to a function expecting an array parameter. The call

```
/*
 * Print first "n" elements using pointer indexing and comparison
 * (most concise version).
 */
#include <stdio.h>


#define MAX   20

main()
{
  int table[MAX];
  int i;
  void print_table(int *ptr, int n);

  for (i = 0; i < MAX; i++)    /* provide some initial values */
    table[i] = i;
  print_table(table, MAX);     /* print the array */
  return 0;
}

void print_table(int *ptr, int n)
{
  int *endptr;        /* pointer to last element */

  for (endptr = ptr + n - 1; ptr <= endptr; ptr++)
    printf("%d\n", *ptr);
}
```

Figure 6.8 prtab4.c—Printing an array's elements using the parameter to traverse the array.

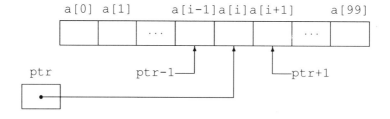

Figure 6.9 Passing part of an array. We can still access the entire array.

```
print_table(table[i], k);   /* wrong: pointer not passed! */
```

is a serious mistake, since print_table expects a pointer and instead receives an int. *Warning: A function expecting an array must be passed an array name or an element's address.*

EXERCISES

6-8 Write a function, insert, that takes a sorted array of longs and a long value and inserts the value in its correct place in the table. Write both pointer and array versions. Which is more efficient? Which is more compact?

6-9 Write a function, search, to search an array of integers. It takes three parameters: an address within the array where the search should start, an address within the array where the search should end, and a value to search for. It should return the element's relative subscript within the array, or −1 if the values cannot be found. What should search do if the starting address is greater than the ending address?

6.4 CHARACTER ARRAYS—STRINGS

Pointers are also closely coupled with strings. A string is an array of characters, terminated with an extra character, the null character, '\0'. To create a constant string, enclose a group of characters in double quotation marks; for example,

```
"by the light of the silvery moon."
```

Turbo C folds consecutive constant strings into a single string. So

```
"by " "the " "light " "of " "the " "silvery " "moon."
```

is equivalent to the string above. We make use of this most often when specifying lengthy printf control strings.

To place a double quotation mark in a string, we have to precede it with a back-slash:

```
"She said, \"Hello, stranger\"."
```

When the compiler sees a constant string, it terminates it with an additional null character, allocates space for it, and returns a pointer to its first character. Thus, we make s contain a string by declaring it as a pointer and assigning the string to it.

```
char  *s;
    . . .
s = "by the light of the silvery moon.";
```

s now points to a string containing 34 characters: the 33 between the double quotation marks, and the additional null character inserted by the compiler.

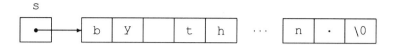

Even though the string is constant, the pointer to it is not. But it's bad practice to change the assignment, such as

```
s = "I love rock and roll.";
```

since that leaves the space occupied by the old string dangling in memory. It's also bad practice to change a character within the string, as the string is intended to be a constant. In fact, to save space, many compilers merge duplicated constant strings, so changing a constant string can have unintended side effects.

We can also create strings by providing the individual characters.

```
char   s[34];
       . . .
s[0]   = 'b';
s[1]   = 'y';
s[2]   = ' ';
       . . .
s[32]  = 'n';
s[33]  = '.';
s[34]  = '\0';
```

When we build string ourselves, we have to supply the trailing null ('\0'). When the compiler initializes a string constant, it supplies the trailing null for us. The reason for the terminating null is to make it easier to pass strings to functions; we don't have to pass their length. C also has a library of useful string functions, all of which expect a string to be null terminated. We can, for example, print a string using `printf`'s `%s` format, without supplying its length.

Building Strings from the Input

We often want to build strings from a program's input instead of creating them at compile time. `getline`, shown in Figure 6.10, is a short function that reads a line of input (with a maximum length of `max` characters) into a string `line`. The string passed to `getline` must be large enough to hold $max + 1$ characters (the characters on the line, plus the trailing null). The remainder of Figure 6.10 is a new version of our line-numbering program (from Chapter 3) that uses it to process the input one line at a time.

`getline` works by repeatedly reading characters and placing them into the array `line` until it encounters the end of the input line (a \n) or finds that the array is full. It doesn't place the new line in the string.

`getline` terminates the string with a null. Since there must be room for this extra null character, `getline` stops filling the array after it has read `max` characters—but it continues reading until it hits the end-of-line character, effectively ignoring any other characters on the line. This guarantees that the next time the function is called, it begins reading characters from the start of a new line. `getline` returns the number of characters placed in the string, not counting the added null character, or −1 when the end of file is reached.

```
/*
 * Line number its input, one line at a time.
 */
#include <stdio.h>

#define MAXLEN  80              /* longest line */

main()
{
  char line[MAXLEN + 1];      /* input line (plus NULL) */
  unsigned long lines;        /* line count */
  int getline(char *buf, int bufsize);

  lines = 0L;
  while (getline(line, MAXLEN) != -1)
    printf("%6lu %s\n", ++lines, line);
  return 0;
}

int getline(char line[], int max)
{
  int c,                        /* current character */
      i;                        /* character count */

  i = 0;
  while ((c = getchar()) != '\n' && c != EOF)
    if (i < max)
      line[i++] = c;
  line[i] = '\0';               /* terminate with null */
  return (c == EOF) ? -1 : i;
}
```

Figure 6.10 linenum.c—A new version of our line numbering program, uses `getline` to read an input line into a string.

String Functions from the Standard Library

C doesn't provide operators that work on strings directly. *Warning: We can't simply assign one string to another; we have to do the assignment one character at a time.* Although it seems as if the following set of declarations and assignments should work, they don't.

```
char  *s = "Hi Mom.  Hi Dad.";
char  t[100];
       . . .
t = s;
```

The reason is that even though `t` is indeed a pointer to the first character location in the array, it is a *constant*. Its value, the address of `t[0]`, may not change. If we really want to copy the characters in `s` into `t`, we have to do so one at a time.

Luckily, there is a function called `strcpy` (for *string copy*) provided in the standard string library that does the string copying task for us. There are other functions in this library that compute a string's length, concatenate two strings, compare two strings, and so on.

`strcpy` takes two arguments, both strings, and copies the second to the first. It assumes that the second string is null terminated and that the first string is large enough. To copy string `s` to string `t`, as we tried to do above, we use

```
strcpy(t, s);
```

Notice that the order of the parameters mimics that of the assignment `t = s`.

It is instructive to see how a function such as `strcpy` is written. Figure 6.11 shows one way, but the actual code differs from one machine to another. In fact, we'll provide a more compact example later in the chapter. These versions are also a slight simplification. Most versions of `strcpy` return a value, a pointer to the destination string. (The details of the returned values of functions in the standard string library are shown in Appendix E.) The advantage of having the string functions provided for us is not that they implement hard-to-code routines—`strcpy` is short and straightforward—but instead that they implement frequently used routines and therefore simplify our job of program construction.

The string-handling functions provided with most C compilers are shown in Table 6.1. To use the string library functions, we need to include the file string.h, which provides their type information. On some systems the file is named strings.h; other systems do not have the header file available at all. If the file is not available, we must declare the types of the functions before they are used.

We use another one of these functions, `strcmp`, in the case study at the end of the chapter. `strcmp` takes two strings, `s1` and `s2`, and returns a negative value if `s1` is alphabetically less than `s2`, zero if they are equal, and a positive value if `s1` is alphabetically greater than `s2`. As with `strcpy`, the function is short and simple to write. But because it is used so often, we see the value of having it provided in a standard library.

Figure 6.12 shows `strcmp`. It works by walking through the two strings and comparing corresponding characters (`s1[i]` and `s2[i]`). It stops if the characters differ, because that means one of the strings is alphabetically less than the other, or if the characters are the same but null, because that means the strings are the same. `strcmp` returns the difference between the characters. Subtracting two characters yields zero if they are the same, a negative value when the first is alphabetically less than the second, and a positive value when it is greater.

Despite their usefulness, the standard string functions are not part of the language definition. They are considered part of the entire environment, but are *not* guaranteed to be provided with every C compiler; some compilers provide only a few of these routines, and others provide them with slightly different names. If your compiler does not have them, they should be written and used whenever their capabilities are needed. Turbo C happens to includes a set of additional functions; these are listed in Appendix E.

```
/*
 * A program and a function to copy one string to another.
 */
#include <stdio.h>

#define MAXLEN  80

main()
{
  char *from;
  char to[MAXLEN + 1];
  void strcpy(char *dest, char *src);

  from = "copied string";
  to[0] = '\0';
  printf("Before copy: from=\"%s\", to=\"%s\"\n", from, to);
  strcpy(to, from);
  printf("After copy:  from=\"%s\", to=\"%s\"\n", from, to);
  return 0;
}

void strcpy(char dest[], char source[])
{
  int i;

  for (i = 0; (dest[i] = source[i]) != '\0'; i++)
    ;
}
```

Figure 6.11   An implementation of the `strcpy` library function and a program that uses it.

Additional String Functions

The standard I/O library provides two functions, extensions to `printf` and `scanf`, that allow output to and input from a string. These functions are `sprintf` and `sscanf`, respectively. Each of these functions takes a string for input or output, a control string, and a list of variables. As with `scanf`, `sscanf` returns the number of values correctly converted.

We can use `sscanf` together with `getline` to avoid some of the problems associated with illegal input using `scanf`. We can read an entire input line using `getline` and then use `sscanf` to extract the values of the variables: Figure 6.13 is a new version of the calculator program from Chapter 5 that reads the operands and operators using this technique. This method automatically ignores input lines containing invalid or missing data items, so we no longer have to quit the first time we encounter bad data.

NAME	WHAT IT DOES
`strcat(s1,s2)`	Concatenates `s2` to the end of `s1`
`strncat(s1,s2,n)`	Concatenates at most *n* characters from `s2` to the end of `s1`
`strcpy(s1,s2)`	Copies `s2` to `s1`
`strncpy(s1,s2,n)`	Copies *n* characters from `s2` to `s1`
`strcmp(s1,s2)`	Compares `s1` and `s2`, returning less than zero, zero, or greater than zero, depending on whether `s1` is less than, equal to, or greater than `s2`, respectively
`strncmp(s1,s2,n)`	Compares at most *n* characters; returns the same as `strcmp`
`strlen(s)`	Returns the number of characters in `s`, *not* counting the trailing null
`strchr(s,c)`	Returns a pointer to the first occurrence of `c` in `s`, or `NULL` (sometimes called `index`)
`strrchr(s,c)`	Returns a pointer to the last occurrence of `c` in `s`, or `NULL` (sometimes called `rindex`)

Table 6.1 Standard string functions.

Using Pointers to Traverse Strings

Strings are arrays, so we can process them using pointers. In Figure 6.13 we used a new version of `getline` that uses a pointer, `ptr`, to traverse the string. As it reads each character, it places the character into the location pointed to by `ptr`, and then increments `ptr`. This version of `getline` also makes use of two other pointers, `startptr`, which points to the first character in the array, and `endptr`, which points to the last. We compare `ptr` with `endptr` to determine whether there is still room in the array. When we've read a line, we subtract `startptr` from `ptr` to determine how many characters we read. Figure 6.14 shows the relationship between all of these pointers.

We can also rewrite our earlier version of `strcpy`, the string-copying function, to use pointers. The first version used an array index `i` to walk through the strings `source` and `dest`. Another way to write the function is to treat `source` and `dest` as pointers (initialized to the first element of the respective arrays) rather than as arrays. When we do this, we access the elements indirectly through pointers rather than directly through array indexes. This version is shown in Figure 6.15.

`dest` and `source` are used to traverse the destination and source strings, respectively. Each pass through the loop begins by assigning the character to which `source` points to the address to which `dest` points. This character is then compared with the null character to see if the end of the string has been reached. If it has not, both pointers are incremented and the loop continues. Notice that even though the

```
/*
 * A program and a function to compare one string to another.
 */
#include <stdio.h>

#define MAXLEN   80

main()
{
  char *str1;
  char *str2;
  int strcmp(char *s1, char *s2);

  str1 = "alex"; str2 = "tony";
  printf("Comparing %s with %s, result %d.\n",
         str1, str2, strcmp(str1, str2));
  printf("Comparing %s with %s, result %d.\n",
         str2, str1, strcmp(str2, str1));
  printf("Comparing %s with %s, result %d.\n",
         str1, str1, strcmp(str1, str1));
  return 0;
}

/*
 * Compare two strings, returning:
 *    0 if they are the same
 *    negative value if s1 < s2
 *    positive value if s1 > s2
 */
int strcmp(char s1[], char s2[])
{
  int i;

  for (i = 0; s1[i] == s2[i] && s1[i] != '\0'; i++)
    ;
  return s1[i] - s2[i];  /* return difference between chars */
}
```

Figure 6.12 An implementation of the strcmp library function and a program that uses it.

parameters dest and source are modified as the copy is performed, the pointers passed to strcpy remain unchanged. But the character string that dest points to is modified, becoming a copy of the character string pointed to by source.

What advantage do we gain by accessing storage through pointers rather than through array indexing? The answer, in most computers, is speed. We ran both the original array version and the pointer version of strcpy on several different computers, copying a string of 15,000 characters. On the average, the pointer version was about 50 percent faster!

```c
/*
 * Simple calculator program (uses getline) to read its input.
 */
#include <stdio.h>

#define MAXLEN 80

main()
{
  double op1, op2;              /* operands */
  char operator;               /* operator */
  double result;               /* result */
  char inpline[MAXLEN + 1];    /* to hold input line */
  int getline(char line[], int max);

  while (getline(inpline, MAXLEN) != -1)
  {
    if (sscanf(inpline, "%lf%c%lf", &op1, &operator, &op2) != 3)
    {
      printf("Input line in error.\n");
      continue;
    }
    switch(operator)
    {
      case '+': result = op1 + op2;
                break;
      case '-': result = op1 - op2;
                break;
      case '*': result = op1 * op2;
                break;
      case '/': if (op2 != 0)
                    result = op1 / op2;
                else
                {
                  printf("Warning: division by zero.\n");
                  result = 0;
                }
                break;
      default:  printf("Unknown operator: %c\n", operator);
                continue;
    }
    printf("%f\n", result);
  }
  return 0;
}
```

```
/*
 * Pointer version of getline.
 */
int getline(char *ptr, int max)
{
  int c;             /* current character */
  char *endptr,      /* pointer to last possible character */
       *startptr;    /* pointer to first character */

  startptr = ptr;
  endptr = ptr + max;
  while ((c = getchar ()) != '\n' && c != EOF)
    if (ptr < endptr)
      *ptr++ = c;
  *ptr = '\0';                   /* terminate with null */
  return (c == EOF) ? -1 : ptr - startptr;
}
```

Figure 6.13 newcalc.c—A new version of the calculator program that reads one line of input at a time. It makes use of a pointer version of `getline`.

EXERCISES

6-10 Write a function, `stoi` (for string to integer), that takes a null terminated string (array of `char`) and converts the characters to an integer. Use a method similar to that in Chapter 3.

6-11 Write a function, `itos`, that takes two parameters. The first is an integer and the second is a character array. The function converts the integer into characters (null terminated) and places them into the array parameter. Assume that the array is large enough to hold the necessary characters.

6-12 `strlen` is another useful string function from the standard library. It takes a string and returns its length in characters, not counting the null. Write `strlen`. Assume `s` is null terminated and that the length of a string consisting of just a null is zero. Test your function on a program using strings of various lengths.

6-13 Modify the insertion sort program in Chapter 2 to read its input with `getline` and `sscanf`.

6-14 Implement `strchr` and `strrchr`.

6-15 Using pointers and avoiding unnecessary local variables, write a function, `rmchr`, that takes a string and a character as arguments, removing all occurrences of the character from the string. `rmchr` should not leave holes in the string. What should `rmchr` return?

6-16 Write a function, `rmstr`, that takes two strings as arguments, removing all occurrences of any characters in the second string from the first string. Like `rmchr`,

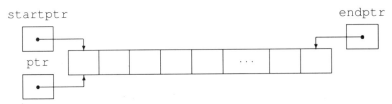

(a) The pointers when getline starts up.

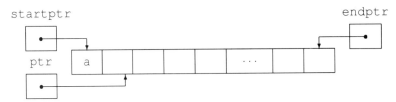

(b) The pointers after reading one character.

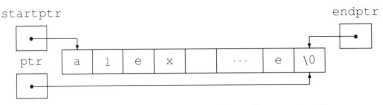

(c) The pointers after reading the input line "alex was here".

Figure 6.14   Pointers used in getline.

rmstr should not leave holes in the string. What should rmstr return?

6–17 Write compact pointer versions of the standard string library functions. Are these more efficient than straightforward array versions?

6.5   **DYNAMICALLY ALLOCATING ARRAYS**

Many languages allow us to specify an array's size at run time. This feature is convenient, since we don't always know at compile time exactly how many elements an array should have. The arrays we allocate at compile time often turn out to be much too big, which wastes space, or much too small, which makes our programs fail. What we would really like to be able to do is declare an array whose size is a

```
/*
 * A program and a function to copy one string to another.
 */
#include <stdio.h>

#define MAXLEN   80

main()
{
  char *from;
  char to[MAXLEN + 1];
  void strcpy(char *dest, char *src);

  from = "copied string";
  to[0] = '\0';
  printf("Before copy: from=\"%s\", to=\"%s\"\n", from, to);
  strcpy(to, from);
  printf("After copy:  from=\"%s\", to=\"%s\"\n", from, to);
  return 0;
}

void strcpy(char *dest, char *source)
{
  for (; (*dest = *source) != '\0'; dest++, source++)
    ;
}
```

Figure 6.15 Copying two strings using the passed pointers to traverse them.

variable.

```
func(int n)
{
  int a[n];  /* declare array of "n" elements (illegal) */
  ...
}
```

That way we could ask the user how large various arrays should be.

Unfortunately, C requires that the number of items in an array be known at compile time—which makes the above fragment illegal. Luckily, there are two library functions we can use to get around this restriction. The first, malloc, allocates storage space from an operating-system-maintained pool of memory. The other, free, allows us to return the space allocated by malloc to this pool so it can be reused. The idea is that we can use malloc to allocate space for an array and free to return it. These functions are defined in alloc.h, which must be included to use them.

We use both of these in a new version of our input reversing program, shown in Figure 6.16. This version expects its input to be broken into groups, with each group preceded by a count of the items in it. The program reads and reverses each of these groups. Like the previous version, it uses scanf for all input, so its input must be correct (the exercises examine removing this restriction).

To reverse a group, the program needs an array large enough to hold it. To do so, after the program reads the group's size, it uses malloc to allocate a large enough array. It then uses get_data to fill it and print_reverse to print it in reverse order, just like before. Once it's done with a group, it uses free to release the storage it occupies, so it can be reused for the next group.

Allocating Storage with Malloc

malloc is passed a single unsigned int argument specifying the number of bytes to allocate. It allocates a block of bytes of the desired size, and returns a pointer to it, or NULL if a large enough chunk could not be found. We can allocate an array large enough for size integers with:

```
int *table;    /* to hold array of SIZE integers */
    . . .
if ((table = (int *) malloc(size * sizeof(int))) == NULL)
  printf("Couldn't allocate space for that many elements\n");
```

malloc allocates bytes, not integers. If we want to allocate an array of 100 integers, we can't simply pass it 100. Instead, we must pass it the number of bytes an array of 100 integers requires, the size of an int times 100.

We can use malloc to allocate space for an array of any type, ints, chars, floats, and so on. malloc simply returns a pointer to the first byte in a block of bytes, and guarantees that the returned block satisfies the alignment considerations for all C data types. There is a special pointer type, pointer to void, for pointers to a block of bytes of no particular type. malloc is defined to return a pointer of this type; its header is:

```
void *malloc(unsigned int)
```

We can't directly dereference a pointer to void. Instead, we have to cast it into the appropriate type for the object in the block of bytes to which it points. In our case, the block is to contain ints, so we cast the pointer returned by malloc into a pointer to an int.

malloc can fail if there isn't sufficient storage remaining in the free storage pool. If it fails, it returns NULL instead of a legitimate pointer. We are careful to check whether this returned pointer is NULL before attempting to use it.

Treat the pointer malloc returns as a constant. Use a separate pointer to traverse the allocated array, as we have done in the following loop that initializes all of table's elements to zero (it assumes that p has been declared as a pointer to an int, and that size is the total number of bytes in the table).

```
for (p = table; p < table + size; *p++ = 0)
  ;      /* initialize all elements to zero */
```

This is actually a useful piece of code, since the bytes malloc returns are not guaranteed to be zero, and in fact, may contain garbage.

```
/*
 * Modified version of Chapter 2's reverse program.
 */
#include <stdio.h>
#include <stddef.h>        /* def of NULL */
#include <alloc.h>         /* defs of malloc and free */

main()
{
  int *table;              /* holds input array */
  int size, n;             /* elements in group, table */
  int res;                 /* scanf result */
  int get_data(int *ptr, int max);
  void print_reverse(int *ptr, int n);

  while ((res = scanf("%d", &size)) == 1)
  {
    if ((table = (int *) malloc(size * sizeof(int))) == NULL)
    {
      printf("Couldn't allocate %d elements\n", size);
      return 1;   /* out of memory error */
    }
    n = get_data(table, size);
    printf("Values in reverse order:\n\n");
    print_reverse(table, n);
    free((void *) table);
  }
  if (res != EOF)
    printf("Couldn't read number of elements to read\n");
  return res == EOF;
}

int get_data(int *ptr, int max)
{                   /* read input values (pointer version) */
  int *startptr, *endptr;

  endptr = (startptr = ptr) + max - 1;
  for (; ptr <= endptr && scanf("%d", ptr) == 1; ptr++)
    ;
  return ptr - startptr;
}

void print_reverse(int *table, int n)
{                   /* print in reverse order (pointer version) */
  int *ptr;

  for (ptr = table + n - 1; ptr >= table; ptr--)
    printf("%d\n", *ptr);
}
```

Figure 6.16   grprev.c—A program to reverse groups of values in its input.

Deallocating Storage with Free

`free` takes a pointer to an array of bytes allocated by `malloc`, and makes that storage available to be reallocated. We can return the array `table` allocated above with:

```
free((void *) table);
```

Since `free` can be used to free any block of bytes allocated by `malloc`, its argument is declared as a pointer to `void`. This forces us to cast `table`, since it is a pointer to an `int`, not a generic pointer.

EXERCISES

6-18 The program in Figure 6.16 uses `scanf` to read its input, which means its input must be correct. Make the program more robust by using `getline` and `sscanf` to read the input. Assume that there is one value on each input line. Terminate the program on an invalid count. If a group has a bad line of input, ignore the group.

6-19 Modify the program to allocate more space only if the existing array is too small.

6.6 CASE STUDY—ELIMINATING DUPLICATE LINES

To illustrate the use of arrays and string functions from the standard string library, we will write a program (called uniq) that takes text as input and copies it to its output, minus any lines that are the same as the line they follow. For example, if the input consists of the lines

```
Turbo C
Turbo C
Turbo C
is
really
really
wonderful
wonderful
wonderful
```

we want the output to be

```
Turbo C
is
really
wonderful
```

The program has a number of uses. We used a variation, suggested in the exercises, to create a list of the number of different words that appear in this book. We first ran a program over the text that breaks the input into individual words, one per line (which we wrote in Chapter 3) and then a program to sort its input (which we'll see in a later chapter), and finally uniq.

uniq is a useful program created from small, already existing pieces. It uses getline, strcmp, and strcpy, each of which we have already written, or is provided for us as a library function. It processes its input a line at a time, using strcmp to compare the current and previous input lines. If they differ, it prints the current line and copies the current line into the previous one using strcpy. The process ends when the end of the input is reached (getline returns -1). The main program is shown in Figure 6.17. Note that we include two files, stdio.h and string.h, to declare the types and parameters of the various library functions.

EXERCISES

6–20 Write a variation of uniq that prints only duplicated lines, and then only the first occurrence of each repetition.

6–21 Write a variation of uniq that prints one instance of each line, preceded by a count of the number of times the line is repeated.

6–22 Write a program that reads the input and breaks it up into individual words, which are then printed one per line. Words are strings of alphabetic or numeric characters separated by nonalphanumerics.

6–23 Write a function, putline, that takes a string and writes it and a trailing new line. Use putchar rather than printf. putline is identical to the standard I/O library function puts. Compare the size and running time of program that uses your own putline rather than printf.

```
/*
 * uniq -- A program to strip duplicate lines.
 */
#include <stdio.h>
#include <string.h>

#define MAXLEN      80     /* longest line program can handle */
#define FALSE        0
#define TRUE         1

main()
{
  char curr[MAXLEN + 1],         /* current line */
       prev[MAXLEN + 1];         /* previous line */
  int first;                     /* first time through? */
  int getline(char *buf, int bufsize);

  first = TRUE;
  while (getline(curr, MAXLEN) != -1)
  {
    if (first || strcmp(prev, curr) != 0)
    {
      printf("%s\n", curr);
      first = FALSE;
    }
    strcpy(prev, curr);
  }
  return 0;
}

int getline(char *ptr, int max)
{
  int c;                     /* current character */
  char *endptr, *startptr; /* ptr to first, last chars */

  endptr = (startptr = ptr) + max;
  while ((c = getchar ()) != '\n' && c != EOF)
    if (ptr < endptr)
      *ptr++ = c;
  *ptr = '\0';                 /* terminate with null */
  return (c == EOF) ? -1 : ptr - startptr;
}
```

Figure 6.17 uniq.c—A program to remove duplicate lines from its input.

7 FUNCTIONS

One of C's strengths is that functions are easy to define and use. This chapter discusses functions in great detail, concentrating on the aspects of parameter passing we have so far ignored. We show how Turbo C's function prototypes support enhanced type checking and automatic type conversions, and contrast them with C's old-style function declarations. We also show how to simulate call-by-reference parameter passing, how to write functions that can take a variable number of arguments, and how to pass functions as parameters. The chapter concludes with a discussion of recursive functions and a case study that implements an interesting and useful recursive algorithm, binary search.

7.1 FUNCTION PROTOTYPES

We've seen that we have to declare the types of a function's parameters and return value in any function that calls it. That declaration is called a *function prototype*. One reason for function prototypes is that they let the compiler check whether we are calling functions with the correct number of arguments, and that these arguments are of the right type. But this isn't their only use—they also help the compiler perform automatic type conversions on function parameters, and they specify the type of the function's return value.

Automatic Parameter Type Conversions

When we assign one value to another, C converts the value on the left to the type of the value on the right. Similarly, when we call a function, Turbo C converts each argument to the type of its corresponding parameter, using the same rules we saw for assignment conversion. The function prototypes specify the expected parameter types.

Figure 7.1 is an example. It contains `inrange`, a function to verify that one floating point value falls between two others, a simple range check. When we call `inrange` with three integer arguments, these arguments are automatically converted to `doubles` before being copied into `inrange`'s parameters.

Specifying the Types of Return Values

A function prototype not only specifies the types of the parameters but also the type of value the function returns. We provide the return type so the compiler can ensure

```
/*
 * Check if one value is between two others.
 */
#include <stdio.h>

main()
{
  int  inpval;
  int  inrange(double min, double max, double value);

  printf("Enter a value: ");
  scanf("%d", &inpval);          /* note: no error checking */
  printf("%d is %s range!\n", inpval,
         inrange(1,100,inpval) ? "in" : "out of");
  return 0;
}

int inrange(double min, double max, double value)
{
  return value >= min && value <= max;
}
```

Figure 7.1 inrange1.c—An example of the automatic conversions when function prototypes are used.

that we've used the function correctly and generate code that uses its return value appropriately.

Figure 7.2 illustrates how prototypes help ensure we use function return values correctly. It contains a new version of `reverse_tab`, our function to reverse an array of `int`s in place. But this version uses pointers rather than array subscripting: `ptr` starts at the beginning of the array and moves forward; `endptr` starts at the end of the array and moves backwards. Like the previous version, it returns `void`, since the function doesn't return a value. If we provide a prototype and accidentally try to use the function's return value, as in

```
void reverse_tab(int *ptr, int first, int last);
      . . .
printf("%d\n", reverse_tab(table, 0, MAX - 1));  /* OOPS! */
```

the Turbo C compiler reports an error.

We just saw that it is a mistake to try and access the value returned by a function that returns `void`. But it's alright to simply ignore the value of a function that doesn't return `void`. In Figure 7.1, for example, we just didn't bother to use `scanf`'s return value.

```
scanf("%d", &inpval);
```

But it's better style to cast `scanf`'s return value to `void`.

```
(void) scanf("%d", &inpval);
```

```
/*
 * A new version of the Chapter 5 program to reverse an
 * array in place.  This version uses pointers.
 */
#include <stdio.h>

#define MAX   20

main()
{
  int table[MAX], i;
  void reverse_tab(int a[], int first, int last);
  void print_tab(int a[], int first, int last);

  for (i = 0; i < MAX; i++)    /* place some values in the array */
     table[i] = i;
  reverse_tab(table, 0, MAX - 1); /* reverse the array */
  print_tab(table, 0, MAX - 1);   /* print the reversed array */
  return 0;
}


void reverse_tab(int *ptr, int first, int last)
{
  int *endptr;
  int temp;

  endptr = ptr + last;
  for (ptr += first; ptr <= endptr; ptr++, endptr--)
  {
    temp = *ptr;
    *ptr = *endptr;
    *endptr = temp;
  }
}

void print_tab(int *ptr, int first, int last)
{
  int *endptr;

  endptr = ptr + last;
  for (ptr += first; ptr <= endptr; ptr++)
     printf("%d\n", *ptr);
}
```

Figure 7.2   revtab.c—A pointer version of a function to reverse an array in place.

```
/*
 * Compute x to the y, for integers x and y.
 */
#include <stdio.h>

main()
{
  int     x, y;                   /* user inputs */
  double power(int x, int y); /* computes x to the y */

  while (printf("Enter x,y: "), scanf("%d,%d", &x, &y) == 2)
    printf("%d to the %d is %g\n", x, y, power(x,y));
  return 0;
}

/*
 * Return x to the y, works best for small integers.
 */
double power(int x, int y)
{
  double  p;                /* start with x to the 0 */

  p = 1.0;
  if (y >= 0)
    while (y--)             /* positive powers */
      p *= x;
  else
    while (y++)             /* negative powers */
      p /= x;
  return p;
}
```

Figure 7.3 power.c—A program that computes x^y for integers x and y.

The cast emphasizes that we're consciously ignoring the value and not simply over-looking it by mistake.

Our previous functions have returned only a single integer (int) or nothing at all (void). But a function can actually return any of C's other basic data types: short, long, char, float, double, or pointer. So in addition to stating whether or not the function returns a value, the prototype also tells the compiler how this return value is to be used. We illustrate the use of a non-int return value in Figure 7.3, a program to compute x^y for integers x and y. Since the result can be fractional if y is negative, or large for small values of x and y, we define power to return a double.

The main program precedes its call to power with the declaration

```
double power(int x, int y); /* computes x to the y */
```

This prototype ensures that power's return value is treated as a double. Without it, the compiler incorrectly assumes that power returns an int and generates incorrect code to handle its return value. This assumption is contradicted when `power`'s later definition occurs, causing the Turbo C compiler to report an error. Not all compilers detect this inconsistency, however, particularly when separate compilation (which we will discuss in the next chapter) allows the function to be defined in another file.

EXERCISES

7-1 Write a function to compute and return a percentage. It should take two `int`s `x` and `y`, and return a `double`, $x/y * 100$. Modify the character-counting program in Chapter 5 to use it.

7-2 Write a function that takes an array of `int`s and the number of elements in the array, and returns its average value. The function should return a `double`.

7-3 Write a function `lastchar` that returns the last character in a character string, the one preceding the null. Return the null character if the string is empty.

7-4 Write a function, `maxdouble`, that returns the largest value in an array of `double`s.

7.2   OLD-STYLE DECLARATIONS AND DEFINITIONS

Turbo C's function prototypes are a recent addition to C that resulted from a recent ANSI attempt to standardize the language. Previously we couldn't specify complete prototypes when declaring functions, only their return values. This was problematic, since the compiler can't do type checking or automatic conversions without full prototypes. Earlier versions of C also had a slightly different syntax for defining functions. Turbo C still allows these *old style* declarations and definitions—after all, there was more than a decade of C development without prototypes—but discourages their use.

Figure 7.4 shows an old-style definition of `inrange`. In the parameter list, we provide only the parameter names, and not their types. On subsequent lines we provide variable declarations for each of the parameters.

```
return-type func-name (name-1, name-2, ..., name-n)
   parm-decl-1;
   parm-decl-2;
      . . .
   parm-decl-n;
```

Turbo C's syntax is more compact—we don't have to list the parameter names and then provide declarations for them—but leaves no obvious place to comment on what each of the parameters do.

Figure 7.4 shows an old-style function prototype. We provide the function's return type, its name, and parentheses, but we don't list the parameter types.

```
return-type func-name ()
```

We need the parentheses, even if the function has no parameters, since they indicate that we are declaring a function.

```
/*
 * A program that's supposed to check if one value is between
 * two others (using old-style declarations).  But it doesn't
 * work correctly.
 */
#include <stdio.h>

main()
{
  int  inpval;
  int  inrange();                       /* old style */

  printf("Enter a value: ");
  scanf("%d", &inpval);
  printf("%d is %s range!\n", inpval,
         inrange(1, 100, inpval) ? "in" : "out of");
  return 0;
}

int inrange(min, max, value)
double min, max, value;                 /* old style */
{
  return value >= min && value <= max;
}
```

Figure 7.4 inrange2.c—An example of C's old style declarations. This program doesn't work because inrange's arguments aren't automatically converted.

Type Checking Problems

When we use an old-style prototype, we don't supply information about the types of the function's parameters. This means that Turbo C's parameter-passing mechanism works correctly only when there are no type mismatches—each argument must be the same type as its corresponding parameter. To avoid errors resulting from type mismatches, we must do any needed conversions ourselves.

Unfortunately, these type mismatches are not always detected at compile time and can cause strange run-time behavior. Consider what happens when we call inrange as shown in Figure 7.4. Surprisingly, the "out of range" message is never printed, regardless of the value of inpval we pass to inrange. This occurs because inrange expects its parameters to be doubles (four words in floating point representation), and instead receives ints (one word in two's complement representation). As a result, on the PC, regardless of the values passed, min and max are always zero—clearly, not what we intended. Because there is no information about the function's parameters, no automatic conversions can take place. Luckily, we can correct things by making sure that all the arguments are doubles:

```
    if (!inrange(1.0, 100.0, (double) inpval))
```

```
/*
 * Another version of our range-checking program that uses
 * old-style declarations.  But this one works correctly.
 */
#include <stdio.h>

main()
{
  float inpval;
  float lowval;
  float highval;
  int  inrange();          /* old style */

  lowval = 0.0;
  highval = 100.0;
  printf("Enter a value: ");
  scanf("%f", &inpval);
  printf("%f is %s range!\n", inpval,
         inrange(lowval, highval, inpval) ? "in" : "out of");
  return 0;
}

int inrange(min, max, value)
double min, max, value;    /* old style */
{
  return value >= min && value <= max;
}
```

Figure 7.5 inrange3.c—Another call of inrange with a parameter type mismatch.

All floating point constants are doubles, and the cast converts inpval's value to a double before it is passed as a parameter.

Actually, we just lied—we don't have to do *all* the conversions ourselves. When we don't supply a function prototype, C automatically converts any char or short argument to an int, and any float argument to a double. Even though we supplied no prototype in Figure 7.5, we don't have to explicitly cast lowval, highval or inpval. The necessary conversions are done automatically when they are passed. In the absence of a function prototype, the compiler automatically treats any short or char parameters as ints, and any float parameters as doubles. That's why printf has only a single formatting control code for printing real values. When we pass a float, it's automatically converted to a double.

Parameters and Portability

Old style declarations and sloppy programming can lead to all sorts of problems, including programs that work on one machine but fail on another. Consider the version of inrange shown and invoked in Figure 7.6. This version expects long

```
/*
 * A final version of our range-checking program.
 * This one works, sometimes, but isn't portable.
 */
#include <stdio.h>

main()
{
  int inpval;
  int inrange();                         /* old style */

  printf("Enter a value: ");
  scanf("%d", &inpval);
  printf("%d is %s range!\n", inpval,
         inrange(1, 100, inpval) ? "in" : "out of");
  return 0;
}

int inrange(min, max, value)
long min, max, value;
{
  return value >= min && value <= max;
}
```

Figure 7.6 inrange4.c—Yet another version of our range-checking function. This program isn't portable because it assumes that longs and ints are the same size.

arguments. On 32-bit machines, int and long are usually the same size (32 bits), and the code works as expected. But we get strange results on the PC, where int is one word and long is two. It's easy to make this program work correctly on all machines; we simply use long constants or cast the arguments appropriately.

```
    if (!inrange(1L, 100L, (long) inpval))
```

There is another area where portability problems are likely to occur: passing NULL to a function expecting a pointer. We might do so to indicate that some default address should be used. If we aren't using function prototypes, we have to cast NULL to the appropriate pointer type. If we don't, our program will only work on machines where pointers and integers are the same size, and not on machines where pointers are either one or two words, like the PC. Suppose we have a function func that takes a single parameter, a pointer to a char. To see why the call

```
    func(NULL)
```

is *not* portable if we don't supply a cast or a prototype, consider an architecture that has two-word pointers and one-word ints. Since NULL is defined as the constant zero, we are passing a one-word integer when a two-word pointer is expected. It is easy to prevent this mistake by casting NULL appropriately. The call

```
f((char *) NULL)
```

is portable.

Problems with Mixing Styles

Supporting two distinct styles of parameter declarations cause several problems. The first deals with what happens when we fail to supply parameter information in a declaration. Should the compiler assume that function takes no parameters? Or should it simply assume that the function may take parameters, but we're not supplying any information about them? It turns out the compiler does the latter. That's because there is a special way to indicate that a function takes no parameters; we provide a parameter list of void, as did in Chapter 3 in the function yesorno. void explicitly indicates that the function takes no parameters. That means that the compiler can now catch errors such as supplying a parameter when none is expected, as in

```
int yesorno(void);

yesorno("Do you like Turbo C? ");
```

The second problem is more subtle. What happens when we define a function using one style, and declare it using another? We could, for example, provide a complete prototype

```
double val1, val2, result;
int inrange(float x, float y, float z);
    ...
inrange(val1, val2, result)
```

and then define the function in the old style.

```
inrange(x, y, z)
float x, y, z;
{
    . . .
}
```

Warning: Mixing styles of parameter declarations can lead to serious problems. To see why, consider the example above. Since we provide a full prototype, when we call inrange C will pass floats. But since we declare inrange using the old style, it's going to expect to be passed doubles, which it will then convert to floats. This means the program won't work. We get into similar problems when we do the reverse. The simple solution: Don't mix styles, just stick to function prototypes.

Prototypes versus Old-Style Declarations

Function prototypes help the compiler catch type mismatches and incorrect numbers of parameters. When we've taken programs that were running fine on other machines, supplied prototypes for all their functions, and then compiled them with Turbo C, the compiler detected an amazing number of errors—any of which could have led to serious bugs. Prototypes also have several other benefits. They help document a function's arguments, making programs that use them easier to read. And they make programs run more efficiently, since they prevent automatic conversions of `float` arguments to `double` and `char` arguments to `int`.

But there is one big problem with function prototypes: What do we do if we have to port programs written in Turbo C to compilers that don't allow them? It is easy to remove all of the prototypes—but it is much more difficult to find all the places where successful parameter passing relies on the automatic conversions prototypes make possible. When a program has to work with Turbo C as well as other, less sophisticated compilers, use explicit casting to ensure that the types of parameters match the function definition.

EXERCISES

7-5 Run the various versions of `inrange`. Can you explain their output by examining the relative sizes of the data types on the PC? Which version produces the smallest amount of code? The largest?

7-6 Write a function, `isvalid`, that is similar to `inrange`, except that it verifies whether a pointed-to value is between two other pointed-to values. Assume the pointers passed to `isvalid` are pointers to `long`. A null pointer for either range should disable the range check.

7-7 What happens when we pass an integer when a pointer is expected? Assume that we haven't provided a prototype. (Hint: Think about what would happen if you passed `scanf` integers by mistake.)

7.3   THE RETURN STATEMENT

Parameters are one way functions can communicate; return values are another. We've used `return` to terminate a function and return a value to its caller.

        `return` *expression*;

But we can also use `return` to exit a function without returning a value.

        `return`;

`return` without an expression is similar to simply dropping off the function's end. Of course, we only use this form in functions that return `void`.

`return` is a full-fledged C statement that can appear anywhere within a function body. A function can also have more than one `return`—although it is generally considered better style for a function to have a single entrance and a single exit. But sometimes multiple `returns` simplify our code, as in Figure 7.7, which contains a little function, `search`, that uses a *linear* search to look up a value in an array. The function returns a pointer to the value's location in the array, or `NULL` if it can't be found.

```
/*
 * A program that uses sequential search to locate a target
 * value within a table.
 */
#include <stdio.h>
#include <stddef.h>                        /* to obtain NULL */

#define MAX    10

main()
{
  int table[MAX];                    /* table to search */
  int *fndptr;                       /* ptr to an item */
  int i;                             /* array index */
  int target;                        /* value looking for */
  int *search(int *ptr, int n, int v); /* search function */

  for (i = 0; i < MAX; i++)          /* initialize table with */
    table[i] = i;                    /*        0,1,2,3,... */


  while (scanf("%d", &target) == 1)     /* obtain targets */
    if ((fndptr = search(table, MAX, target)) != NULL)
      printf("Found %d as element %d.\n", target, fndptr - table);
    else
      printf("Didn't find %d.\n", target);
  return 0;
}


int *search(int *ptr, int num, int value)
{
  int *endptr;

  for (endptr = ptr + num - 1; ptr <= endptr; ptr++)
    if (*ptr == value)
      return ptr;            /* found, return pointer to it */
  return NULL;               /* failure, return null */
}
```

Figure 7.7   ssearch.c—A program that uses pointers in a sequential search of an array.

In searching an array this way there are two stopping conditions: either we find the value in the array or we reach the end of the table. If we find the value, it is convenient to simply exit the loop—and the function—with a `return`. Not doing so would require a test outside of the loop to determine which value to return.

The `return` at the function's end returns a null pointer if we don't find the desired value in the array. When a value is returned, it is automatically cast to the function's type (when such a cast makes sense), again using the rules for assignment conversions. This automatic return value conversion is often useful; in `search` it means that we do not have to cast the returned `NULL` to a pointer. In functions that do computations using `doubles`, yet return `ints`, the returned `double` is truncated into an `int` before being given to the caller.

EXERCISES

7–8 Write the function `index`, which takes a string and a character and returns a pointer to the character's first occurrence within the string. Here's the function header.

```
char *index(char *s, char c)
```

What should the function return if the character is not in the string?

7–9 Write the function `rindex`, which is similar to `index`, except that it returns a pointer to the character's *last* occurrence within the string.

7–10 Modify the function `insert` (Chapter 2) to return a pointer to the place in the table where the value was entered, or `NULL` if the table was full. Rewrite insertion sort using this version of `insert`.

7–11 Improve the sequential search shown in Figure 7.7 by assuming a *sorted* table.

7–12 Rewrite `search` to use only one `return` statement.

7.4   ## SIMULATING CALL-BY-REFERENCE

We have seen that C passes parameters by value. When we call a function, C allocates space for its parameters and copies the values passed as the function's arguments. When the function returns, this space is deallocated. This means that *a function cannot change the values of its arguments.* In fact, we can treat parameters as though they are local variables, conveniently initialized by the calling function. This allows us to pass arbitrary expressions and prevents us from accidentally modifying a functions' arguments.

But what do we do when we have a function like `scanf` that needs to modify a variable in its caller? Simply changing the value of a parameter doesn't work, since such changes are local. Instead, we must use `&` to pass a pointer to the variable. The function then dereferences the pointer with `*` to access or modify the variable's value.

We illustrate this technique with a function `swap` that exchanges the values of two integer variables. Because of *call by value*, the version of `swap` shown in Figure 7.8

```
/*
 * A program that doesn't exchange two values.
 */
#include <stdio.h>

main()
{
  int s, t;
  void swap(int x, int y);

  s = 10; t = 20;
  printf("Before swap, s=%d, t=%d\n", s, t);
  swap(s, t);
  printf("After swap, s=%d, t=%d\n", s, t);
  return 0;
}

void swap(int x, int y)    /* incorrect version */
{
  int temp;

  temp = x;
  x = y;
  y = temp;
}
```

Figure 7.8 badswap.c—An incorrect version of swapping function along with a program that uses it.

does not do what we want. It swaps the values of its parameters x and y, but does not affect the values s and t passed to it by the main program, as the program's unpleasant output shows.

```
Before swap, s=10, t=20
After swap, s=10, t=20
```

To get swap to exchange the values of variables in its calling function, we have to pass it their addresses and modify it to exchange the values indirectly through these pointers. A corrected version of swap and an example call is shown in Figure 7.9. The happy result is now

```
Before swap, s=10, t=20
After swap, s=20, t=10
```

Figure 7.10 illustrates how this new version of swap works, assuming that the addresses of s and t are 1000 and 2000, respectively, s is 5, and t is 10. When swap is called, xptr becomes 1000 and yptr becomes 2000, the addresses of s and t. The assignment temp = *xptr causes the value in location 1000 (5) to be placed in temp. Similarly, *xptr = *yptr assigns to location 1000 the value in

```
/*
 * A program that does exchange two values.
 */
#include <stdio.h>

main()
{
  int s, t;
  void swap(int *xptr, int *yptr);

  s = 10; t = 20;
  printf("Before swap, s=%d, t=%d\n", s, t);
  swap(&s, &t);
  printf("After swap, s=%d, t=%d\n", s, t);
  return 0;
}

void swap(int *xptr, int *yptr)    /* correct */
{
  int temp;

  temp = *xptr;
  *xptr = *yptr;
  *yptr = temp;
}
```

Figure 7.9 swap.c—Correct version of swapping function and a program that uses it to exchange two values.

location 2000 (10), and `*yptr = temp` completes the exchange by placing `temp`'s contents (5) in location 2000.

There are several common mistakes when dealing with pointer parameters. *Warning: Don't fail to pass a pointer to a function that expects one.* Doing so here would cause `swap` to try to exchange the values in addresses 5 and 10, which is not at all what we want. For `swap` to work correctly, it must be passed the *addresses* of the variables whose values are to be exchanged, not the values themselves. Passing the variables themselves is likely to cause an addressing exception.

Warning: Don't use the pointer as an integer in one place and as a pointer in another. Luckily, Turbo C catches such mistakes but many older compilers don't. We can avoid this problem by first writing the function without any pointer parameters. We can then transform the appropriate parameters into pointers by renaming them to reflect their new use, then replacing all their uses with the appropriate pointer name, preceded by a `*`. In fact, this is how we got the correct version of `swap` from the incorrect one. We replaced the `int` variables `x` and `y` with the pointer variables `xptr` and `yptr` and preceded all uses of these pointers with `*`. Although it is not necessary for `swap`, we may have to parenthesize references through pointer variables

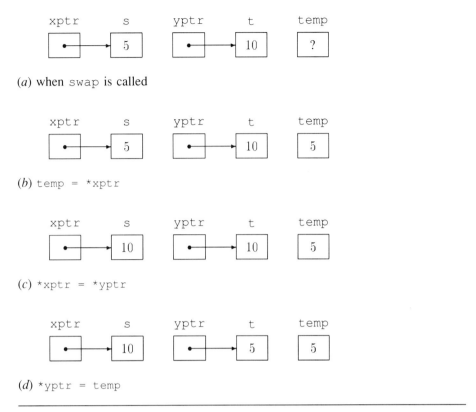

(*a*) when `swap` is called

(*b*) `temp = *xptr`

(*c*) `*xptr = *yptr`

(*d*) `*yptr = temp`

Figure 7.10   Exchanging two variables using pointers.

to guarantee the desired order of evaluation.

Warning: Don't pass a pointer's address instead of the pointer itself. An example is shown in Figure 7.11, a version of our earlier function `reverse_tab` to reverses an array in place. We have modified it to use pointers to traverse the array and to use `swap` to exchange array elements.

This version of `reverse_tab` uses `swap` to exchange the values pointed to by `ptr` and `endptr`—but does so incorrectly. We are mistakenly passing the addresses of `ptr` and `endptr` to `swap`—even though `ptr` and `endptr` already contain the addresses of the values `swap` should exchange. Since we already have the pointers we need, we do not want to take their addresses. The correct call to `swap` is

```
swap(ptr, endptr);
```

Try drawing a picture of what's happening here and trace through it by hand.

```
/*
 * A new version of "reverse_tab".  This version uses "swap",
 * but uses it incorrectly.
 */

void reverse_tab(int *ptr, int first, int last)
{
  int *endptr;
  void swap(int *xptr, int *yptr);

  endptr = ptr + last;
  for (ptr += first; ptr <= endptr; ptr++, endptr--)
    swap(&ptr, &endptr);
}

void swap(int *xptr, int *yptr)
{
  int temp;

  temp = *xptr, *xptr = *yptr, *yptr = temp;
}
```

Figure 7.11   A problematic function to reverse an array in place. It doesn't use the swap function correctly.

EXERCISES

7-13   Compile Figure 7.11 and use it in a program. What happens?

7-14   Write a function, maxmin, that returns through its parameters the largest and smallest values in an array of floating point numbers.

7-15   Write a function, stol (for string to long), that takes a string and turns it into a single long integer. The function should return an error indication. The long should be returned through a pointer parameter.

7-16   Write the function str_swap, whose arguments are pointers to strings. The values of these pointers are swapped. When is str_swap useful? (Hint: This requires pointers to pointers. Drawing a picture will help you see what's going on.)

7.5   PASSING VARIABLE NUMBERS OF ARGUMENTS

All functions we've written so far take a fixed number of arguments—but we've used functions, such as scanf and printf, that take a variable number of arguments. To see how these functions are written, we'll write a function, max, that returns the largest value in the group of values provided as its arguments. max is shown in Figure 7.12, along with an example call.

```
/*
 * A program showing how to write functions that take a
 * variable number of arguments.
 */
#include <stdio.h>
#include <stdarg.h>

main()
{
  int max(int argcnt, ...);

  printf("%d\n", max(5,1,7,3,4,2));
  return 0;
}

int max(int argcnt, ...)
{
  va_list argptr;                   /* argument pointer */
  int nextarg;
  int biggest, i;                   /* largest, index */

  biggest = -((unsigned int) ~0 >> 1);  /* very small integer */
  va_start(argptr, argcnt);
  for (i = 0; i < argcnt; i++)
    if ((nextarg = va_arg(argptr, int)) > biggest)
      biggest = nextarg;
  va_end(argptr);
  return biggest;
}
```

Figure 7.12   max.c—An example function that takes a variable number of arguments.

How can max figure out how many arguments it was actually passed? scanf and printf figure out how many arguments they have and what their types are by examining the control string. An alternative is to supply the number of arguments as a parameter, and that's what we've done with max. Its first argument is the number of additional arguments. To indicate that these other arguments are arbitrary both in number and type, we use three dots (...) as the last parameter type in both the function header and the prototype.

```
        int max(int argcnt, ...)
```

To write functions with variable numbers of arguments, we need to include the header file stdarg.h. It supplies a new data type, va_list, and a set of functions (macros, actually) that we use to access the undeclared arguments. The idea is that we use a special pointer to traverse the arguments; these functions allow us to obtain and update that pointer.

We begin by declaring the pointer to have type va_list. The pointer can have any name, but we like to use argptr, for pointer to an argument list.

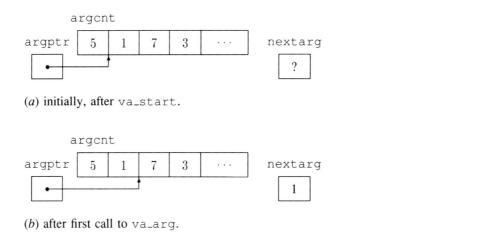

(a) initially, after va_start.

(b) after first call to va_arg.

Figure 7.13 Processing max's arguments.

```
    va_list argptr;                    /* pointer to argument list */
```

We initialize the pointer with va_start, which takes two arguments. The first is the argument pointer, the other is the name of the last parameter in the function definition, the one that appears before the three dots.

```
    va_start(argptr, argcnt);
```

This call makes argptr point just past max's first argument, argcnt.

Now we have to run through the arguments, one at a time, as illustrated in Figure 7.13. We use va_arg to do this. It also takes two arguments, the argument pointer, argptr, and the *type* of the next argument. It updates argptr to point to the next argument, and then returns the value of the thing argptr used to point to (an item of *type*). In this case, the type is always an int.

```
    nextarg = va_arg(argptr, int)
```

Functions like printf are more complicated because they must determine the type of the argument from the control string.

When we've finished processing arguments, we call va_end.

```
    va_end(argptr);
```

It turns out this call does nothing in Turbo C—so why do we need it? We don't, if our program is only compiled with Turbo C and only run on the PC. But on other machines with other compilers, va_end may reset some previously changed state information. To be portable, make sure you include the va_end when you're done processing the arguments.

Writing functions that can handle variable numbers of arguments requires extra planning and effort. But these functions are convenient—max would be much harder to use if we had to pass it an array of values. The functions in stdarg.h provide a clean interface to these arguments, allowing us to ignore the details of the underlying hardware and letting us leave them to the hardworking compiler writer who has to provide these functions.

Built-in Variable Argument Functions

Turbo C provides several library functions that can be passed an argument pointer, a variable of type va_list. Two of these are vprintf and vscanf, which are analogous to printf and scanf, respectively.

We make use of these functions in the function debug, the simple debugging aid shown in Figure 7.14. We call it with the name of the function, a formatting string, and a list of variables. It writes the word "DEBUGGING" and the function's name, and then writes the variables' values according to the formatting string.

```
DEBUGGING main: x=10, y=20
```

Using debug rather than printf when debugging helps us obtain consistent debugging output, and separates debugging statements from those that produce normal program output.

We want debug to take a variable number of arguments, just like printf does. That's because we want it to be able to write different numbers of variables in different calls. In fact, debug is very similar to printf, except that it has an additional first argument, the function name.

```
void debug(char *funcname, char *format, ...)
```

debug uses printf to write the "DEBUGGING" and the function's name. It then wants to write the variable names and values according to its format parameter—but it doesn't want to have to process the format parameter itself. That's alot of work, and we really don't want to duplicate printf, deciphering the format string and processing the various arguments. Unfortunately, however, there's no way to pass printf a pointer to the remaining arguments.

That's where vprintf comes in. vprintf takes a formatting string and a pointer to a variable argument list, and prints each of the variables in that list appropriately.

```
vprintf(char *format, va_list argptr);
```

debug works by obtaining the argument pointer with va_start and then passing it to vprintf.

```
va_start(argptr, format);   /* get argument pointer */
vprintf(format, argptr);    /* print rest */
```

```
/*
 * Another program that uses a function that takes a variable
 * number of arguments, this time to write a debugging message.
 */
#include <stdio.h>
#include <stdarg.h>

main()
{
  int x, y;
  void debug(char *funcname, char *format, ...);

  x = 10;  y = 20;
  debug("main", "x=%d, y=%d\n", x, y);
  return 0;
}

void debug(char *funcname, char *format, ...)
{
  va_list argptr;

  printf("DEBUGGING %s: ", funcname);
  va_start(argptr, format);
  vprintf(format, argptr);        /* print various arguments */
  va_end(argptr);
}
```

Figure 7.14 debug.c—A debugging aid that makes use of the built-in variable argument functions.

EXERCISES

7-17 Write min, a variable argument function that returns the value of its smallest argument.

7-18 Write search, a variable argument function that searches an array for the first occurrence of any one of a list of arguments. Its header is:

```
int *search(int table[], int argcnt, ...);
```

Have search return a pointer to the desired elements position in the table, or NULL if no such element can be found.

7.6   POINTERS TO FUNCTIONS

It would be nice to be able to pass functions as parameters. We could use this ability to write a single function that could print each element in an array in whatever format we wanted: octal, binary, every other line, indented slightly, and so on. This function, which we'll call `print_table`, would contain all of the code to traverse an array, but would print an element by calling a function we passed to it. If we had the functions `print_octal` and `print_binary` shown in Figure 7.15, we could write every element in octal by passing `print_octal` to `print_table`, or write every element in binary by passing `print_binary` to it.

Sadly, however, we can't pass functions as parameter or assign them to variables. But we can use *pointers* to functions, which can be thought of as the address of the code executed when a function is called, or as a pointer to a block of internal information about the function. Dereferencing a pointer to a function calls the function to which it points.

To declare a pointer to a function we specify the pointed-to function's return type, and its parameters. For example, the declaration

    type (`*`funcptr) (*parameter-list*) ;

declares `funcptr` as a pointer to a function that takes parameters of the types specified in *parameter-list* and returns *type*. We need the parenthesis around `*funcptr`—without them we would instead be declaring it as a function returning *type*, not a pointer to a function. (We agree this syntax is gross, but we are stuck with it. We'll explain the rationale behind C's declaration syntax in Chapter 11. For now, just memorize this form.)

We do not apply the address operator (`&`) to a function to obtain a pointer to it. Instead, we simply use the function name without following it with a parenthesized parameter list. For example, assuming the declaration

```
double (*funcptr)(int, int);
```

we can make `funcptr` point to the function `power` that we wrote earlier with the assignment

```
funcptr = power;
```

To call the function pointed to by `funcptr`, we simply dereference it as we would any other pointer, following it with a list of parameters. After the previous assignment,

```
(*funcptr)(2, 5)
```

is equivalent to

```
power(2, 5)
```

calling `power` to compute 2^5. The parenthesis surrounding `*funcptr` are necessary to guarantee the correct order of evaluation.

All we've seen so far is how pointers to functions provide us with a long-winded way of calling functions. But they are useful. Figure 7.15 uses them in `print_table`, the function we discussed earlier, and a main program that uses it to print an array of integers in octal, then in binary.

When we call `print_table`, we have to pass it an array of `int`s, an `int` that holds the number of elements in the array, and a pointer to a printing function that takes an `int` and returns `void`. Within `print_table`, we declare the parameter `funcptr` as a pointer to a function that takes an `int` and returns a `void`.

```
/*
 * Print array in octal and binary using generic function.
 */
#include <stdio.h>

#define MAX      20
#define INTBITS  16                    /* assume 16-bit ints */

main()
{
  int table[MAX], i;
  void print_table(int *ptr, int n, void (*funcptr)(int));
  void print_octal(int num);
  void print_binary(int num);

  for (i = 0; i < MAX; i++)     /* provide initial values */
    table[i] = i;
  printf("Here's the array in octal.\n");  /* print in octal */
  print_table(table, MAX, print_octal);
  printf("Here's the array in binary.\n"); /* print in binary */
  print_table(table, MAX, print_binary);
  return 0;
}

void print_table(int *ptr, int n, void (*funcptr)(int))
{
  int *endptr;

  for (endptr = ptr + n - 1; ptr <= endptr; ptr++)
  {
    (*funcptr)(*ptr);    /* print an element */
    putchar('\n');
  }
}

void print_octal(int i)
{
  printf("%06o", i);
}

void print_binary(int value)
{
  int i;

  for (i = INTBITS - 1; i >= 0; i--)
    printf("%d", (value >> i) & 01);
}
```

Figure 7.15 genprint.c—A generic array printing function and a program that uses it to print an array in octal and in binary.

```
void (*funcptr)(int);
```

Inside the loop that traverses the array, the statement

```
(*funcptr)(*ptr);                       /* print an element */
```

calls the function pointed to by `funcptr`, passing it the integer pointed to by `ptr` (the pointer used to traverse the array).

We print the array in octal with

```
print_table(table, 100, print_octal);   /* print in octal */
```

Because `print_octal` is not followed by a parameter list, we are passing a pointer to a function as `print_table`'s last parameter. Of course, had `print_octal` been followed by a parameter list, it would have been a function call whose return value was passed to `print_table`. Similarly, we print the array in binary with

```
print_table(table, 100, print_binary); /* print in binary */
```

In both cases, the compiler must know the type of the function's return value before the function name appears. We do so with the prototypes

```
void print_octal(int num);
void print_binary(int num);
```

`print_table`'s prototype seems more complicated.

```
void print_array(int *ptr, int n, void (*funcptr)(int));
```

But it really isn't—that strange looking last argument is simply a pointer to a printing function, a function that takes an integer parameter (the integer to print) and doesn't return anything.

Built-in Generic Functions

We used pointers to functions to make `print_table` general enough to print an array of integers in whatever format we want. That may be only mildly interesting, but we can use a similar technique to do something more useful—we can write functions that can search or sort any type of array. In fact, several of these functions have been written for us and placed in the standard Turbo C library. These include `lsearch` and `bsearch`, which search an array for a value, and `qsort`, which sorts a table. Appendix E describes them in detail.

To use these functions, we must provide information about the array we want to search or sort. For example, to use `qsort` to sort an array, we pass it the array, the number of elements in the array, the size of each element, and a function that can compare two array elements. So `qsort`'s header, which is found in stdlib.h, is

```
void qsort(void *table, int num, int size,
           int (*cmpfunc)(void *, void *))
```

Actually we're fudging the truth slightly: The declaration has some additional information that we're ignoring for now.

qsort's first parameter seems strange, but it is simply the address of the array's first element. Because qsort doesn't know what type of pointer it will be passed—after all, it can sort an array of integers, or an array of floats, or an array of whatever else—this address is a pointer to void, a pointer to an object of unknown type.

qsort's last parameter, a pointer to a function used to compare array elements, seems even stranger. This comparison function takes two pointers to elements in the array, and returns an int which is 0 if the items are the same, negative if the first item is less than the second, and positive if the first item is greater than the second. Its parameters are pointers to void because qsort simply passes the comparison function two pointers, without knowing their types.

Figure 7.16 shows how we can use qsort to sort an array of ints. The only tricky part is in writing the comparison function. qsort passes this function pointers to elements in the array it's sorting, and the function is responsible for dereferencing these pointers before comparing the elements. Actually, qsort passes the comparison function pointers to void, so it must first cast them into pointers of the appropriate type.

Figure 7.17 shows how we can use qsort to sort an array of floats. There is very little difference, except that now we pass it a different comparison function, cmpflt.

Coding the comparison functions and getting all of the casts right may seem somewhat difficult—but it is much, much easier than writing quicksort ourselves.

Writing a Generic Function

So just how is a generic function like qsort written? We'll illustrate by writing a simple function to sequentially search an array for a value, and using it to search an array for a value. This function, search, shown in Figure 7.18, takes the same set of arguments that qsort does, plus one additional one: a pointer to the item we're looking for. It returns a pointer to the matching item or NULL if it can't be found. Since the item can be any type, this pointer is a pointer to void.

search works by running through the array, using the comparison function to compare the current array element against the target, returning when its found the element. The trick is that it treats the array as a large sequence of bytes. To get a pointer to the start of the first element, we cast the array pointer to a pointer to a character. To get a pointer to the start of the next element, we increment this pointer by the size in bytes of an array element.

EXERCISES

7-19 Use print_table to print only nonzero array elements. How would you extend it to print values in hex and decimal? Don't change print_table.

```
/*
 * Using quicksort to sort an array of ints.
 */
#include <stdio.h>
#include <stdlib.h>

#define MAX    8       /* small table */

main()
{
    int table[MAX];
    int cmpint(void *xptr, void *yptr);

    table[0] = 17; table[1] = 10; table[2] = 89; table[3] = 26;
    table[4] = 30; table[5] = 99; table[6] = 78; table[7] = 11;

    qsort((void *) table, MAX, sizeof(int), cmpint);
    printf("%d %d %d %d %d %d %d %d\n",
           table[0], table[1], table[2], table[3],
           table[4], table[5], table[6], table[7]);
    return 0;
}

int cmpint(void *xptr, void *yptr)  /* comparison function */
{
    int x, y;

    x = * (int *) xptr;
    y = * (int *) yptr;
    return x - y;
}
```

Figure 7.16 qsort1.c—An example program using the built-in generic function qsort to sort an array of 8 ints.

7-20 Use qsort to sort a table of doubles. Then use it to sort a table of chars.

7-21 Write a version of reverse_tab that reverses an array with any type of element.

7-22 Use search to search a table of floats. Then use it to search a table of chars

7-23 Write a generic function, read_table, to fill an array with values read from its input. Use print_table as a model.

7.7   RECURSION

Many algorithms and mathematical definitions are naturally described *recursively*, that is, partially in terms of themselves. One very simple example is the mathematical

```
/*
 * Using quicksort to sort an array of floats.
 */
#include <stdio.h>
#include <stdlib.h>

#define MAX    8      /* small table */

main()
{
  float table[MAX];
  int cmpflt(void *xptr, void *yptr);

  table[0] = 17.9; table[1] = 10.8; table[2] = 89.6;
  table[3] = 26.1; table[4] = 30.5; table[5] = 99.5;
  table[6] = 78.5; table[7] = 11.9;

  qsort((void *) table, MAX, sizeof(float), cmpflt);
  printf("%f %f %f %f\n%f %f %f %f\n",
        table[0], table[1], table[2], table[3],
        table[4], table[5], table[6], table[7]);
  return 0;
}

int cmpflt(void *xptr, void *yptr)  /* comparison function */
{
  float x, y;

  x = * (float *) xptr;
  y = * (float *) yptr;
  return x - y;
}
```

Figure 7.17 qsort2.c—An example program using the built-in generic function qsort to sort an array of 8 floats.

definition of a factorial. The factorial of n (written $n!$) is the product of all integers between 1 and n (assuming n is nonnegative).

$$n! = \begin{cases} 1 & n = 0 \\ n \times (n-1)! & n > 0 \end{cases}$$

Some example factorials are $2! = 2$, $3! = 6$, $4! = 24$, and $5! = 120$.

Notice that to determine the factorial of any $n \geq 0$, we have to determine the factorial of $n - 1$. As with all recursive definitions, we have to know the function's value at one or more points. In this case, we know that $0!$ is 1.

Functions can call themselves recursively—which makes it easy to translate the mathematical definition of a factorial into the function fact that can compute a factorial. fact is shown in Figure 7.19, along with a special version of it that prints

```
/*
 * Generic table search.
 */
#include <stdio.h>
#include <stddef.h>

#define MAX 20

main()
{
  int i, table[MAX];
  int t, *tptr;                      /* target, ptr to target */
  int cmpint(void *xptr, void *yptr);
  void *search(void *table, int num, int size,
               int (*cmp)(void *, void *), void *tptr);

  for (i = 0; i < MAX; i++)
    table[i] = i;                    /* some initial values */
  while (scanf("%d", &t) == 1)
  {
    tptr = (int *) search((void *) table, MAX, sizeof(int),
                          cmpint, (void *) &t);
    (tptr == NULL) ? printf("Failed.\n")
                   : printf("Found %d at %d.\n", t, tptr - table);
  }
  return 0;
}


void *search(void *tabptr, int n, int size,
             int (*funcptr)(void *, void *), void *tarptr)
{
  char *ptr, *endptr;                    /* byte pointers */

  ptr = (char *) tabptr;
  endptr = ptr + size * n;
  for (; ptr < endptr; ptr += size)
    if ((*funcptr)((void *) ptr, tarptr) == 0)
      return (void *) ptr;            /* found it */
  return NULL;                        /* failure, return null */
}

int cmpint(void *xptr, void *yptr)  /* comparison function */
{
  int x, y;

  x = * (int *) xptr;
  y = * (int *) yptr;
  return x - y;
}
```

Figure 7.18 intgsrch.c—A program to use generic sequential search on a table of ints.

```
/*
 * Compute n! for n >= 0.
 */
#include <stdio.h>

main()
{
  long fact(int n);            /* compute factorial */
  long trace_fact(int n);      /* provides tracing info */

  printf("%ld\n", fact(4));   /* test it */
  printf("Here's a trace.\n");
  printf("%ld\n", trace_fact(4));   /* with trace */
  return 0;
}

long fact(int n)
{
  return (n <= 1) ? 1 : n * fact(n-1);
}

long trace_fact(int n)
{
  long temp;

  printf("Computing %d factorial\n", n);
  temp = (n <= 1) ? 1 : n * trace_fact(n-1);
  printf("Computed %d factorial = %ld\n", n, temp);
  return temp;
}
```

Figure 7.19 fact.c—Functions to recursively compute $n!$. One supplies tracing information, the other doesn't.

additional information allowing us to trace the recursive calls. The program's output is shown in Figure 7.20.

EXERCISES

7-24 The Fibonacci numbers are a famous mathematical sequence that can be defined recursively. For nonnegative integers

$$fib(n) = \begin{cases} 0 & n = 0 \\ 1 & n = 1 \\ fib(n-1) + fib(n-2) & n \geq 2 \end{cases}$$

```
24
Here's a trace.
Computing 4 factorial
Computing 3 factorial
Computing 2 factorial
Computing 1 factorial
Computed 1 factorial = 1
Computed 2 factorial = 2
Computed 3 factorial = 6
Computed 4 factorial = 24
24
```

Figure 7.20 The program's output when run.

The first 10 Fibonacci numbers are 0, 1, 1, 2, 3, 5, 8, 13, 21, and 34. Write recursive and iterative functions to compute the nth Fibonacci number and print the 100th number in this sequence. Which version is faster? Which would you use to print the first 100 Fibonacci numbers?

7.8 CASE STUDY—BINARY SEARCH

The simplest way to search a table is *sequential search*: We compare the value we're searching for with each table entry until we've found a match or looked through the entire table. The average successful search examines about half the table's elements—but an unsuccessful search examines them all. Although this method is reasonable for searching small unordered tables, for large *sorted* tables we can do much better. Binary search is a much faster (indeed, optimal) algorithm for searching sorted tables that happens to be easily expressed by a recursive algorithm.

In binary search, we start by comparing the target value with the table's middle element. The table is sorted, so if the target is larger, we can ignore all values smaller than the middle element and apply binary search recursively to the table's upper half. And similarly, if the target is smaller, we apply binary search recursively to the table's lower half. We stop when we've found the target (it's equal to the middle element) or there are no values left to search.

Binary search is significantly faster than sequential search. Every time we compare the target to a table element, we no longer have to consider half of the remaining values. Roughly, its time is proportional to $\log_2(n)$, where n is the number of values in the table.

We've implement binary search in a function bsearch, shown in Figure 7.21, along with a program that uses it to search a sorted table of longs. bsearch is passed the target value and pointers to the table's first and last elements. It returns a pointer to the matching table element, or the null pointer if no such element is found.

```
/*
 * Program using binary search.
 */
#include <stdio.h>
#include <stddef.h>

#define MAX     100
#define TARGET  36

main()
{
  long table[MAX], *fndptr;     /* array, pointer to an item */
  int i;
  long t;                       /* target */
  long *bsearch(long *min, long *max, long t);

  for (i = 0; i < MAX; i++)      /* initialize table with */
    table[i] = i;                /*   0,1,2,3,... */
  while (scanf("%ld", &t) == 1)
  {
    fndptr = bsearch(&table[0], &table[MAX - 1], t);
    if (fndptr != NULL)
      printf("Found %ld as element %d.\n", t, fndptr - table);
    else
      printf("Didn't find %ld.\n", t);
  }
  return 0;
}

long *bsearch(long *minptr, long *maxptr, long target)
{
  long *midptr;

  /* calculate midpoint */

  midptr = minptr + (maxptr - minptr) / 2;

  if (maxptr < minptr)          /* value in table? */
    return NULL;

  if (target == *midptr)        /* middle is target? */
    return midptr;

  return (target < *midptr)    /* search correct half */
          ? bsearch(minptr, midptr - 1, target)
          : bsearch(midptr + 1, maxptr, target);
}
```

Figure 7.21   bsearch.c—A binary search function and a program using it.

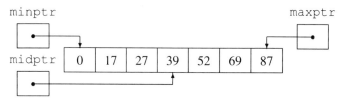

(*a*) at start: $39 < 69$, so search top half of table.

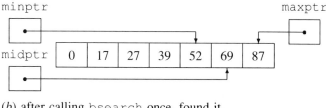

(*b*) after calling `bsearch` once, found it.

Figure 7.22   A successful binary search.

An illustration of a successful binary search on a seven-element table is shown in Figure 7.22. Figure 7.23 illustrates an unsuccessful search on the same table. With every recursive call to `bsearch`, the pointers `minptr` and `maxptr` move toward each other. The search and recursive calls terminate when the pointers cross, or the target value is found.

When `bsearch` is called, it first calculates the address of the middle element in the unsearched portion of the table (the whole table when it is first called). Because we can't add or divide pointers, we calculate the midpoint with

```
midptr = minptr + (maxptr - minptr) / 2;
```

instead of adding the two pointers together and dividing by two.

After we find the midpoint, we check whether the search has failed. The target is not present when the pointers representing the endpoints of the unsearched portion of the table cross (`maxptr < minptr`). This happens only when one element is left to search, and that element is not the target. If the search fails, we return the null pointer (automatically cast to a pointer to a `long`).

Once we know that there are unexamined table elements, we compare the target with the value pointed to by `midptr`. If the values are equal, we return `midptr`, which points to the desired table entry. Otherwise, we recursively apply `bsearch` to the appropriate section of the table.

Although we can write functions such as `fact` and `bsearch` more efficiently iteratively than recursively, we can often use recursion to make functions more com-

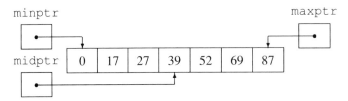

(*a*) at start: 39 > 28, so search lower half of table.

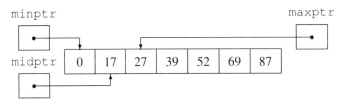

(*b*) after calling `bsearch` once, 28 > 17.

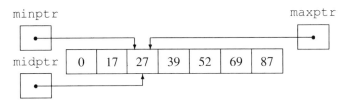

(*c*) call `bsearch` again, 28 not equal to 27. The pointers will cross on the next call.

Figure 7.23   An unsuccessful binary search.

pact or to make them reflect an algorithm or mathematical definition more closely. Recursion is a powerful technique used often in the programs in the rest of this book.

EXERCISES

7–25 Add tracing information to `bsearch` that prints messages whenever the function is entered or exited, noting the values delimiting the area to be searched.

7–26 Rewrite the binary search algorithm nonrecursively. (Watch out! It's messier than it seems.) Is this version more efficient than the recursive version? Which version is more compact?

7-27 Rewrite binary search using array subscripting rather than pointers. Which version is more compact? Which version is more readable?

7-28 Because of the overhead involved in calculating the midpoint, binary search is often slower than sequential search when searching small tables. Determine the point on your system where both functions take the same amount of time. Then write a single search function, called with the same arguments as bsearch, that does a sequential search if the table is small (less than the break-even point) and otherwise calls bsearch.

7-29 Write a generic binary search function. Use your function to search an array of ints and to search an array of chars.

7-30 Write a generic insertion sorting algorithm. Again, test your function by using it to sort an array of ints and to sort an array of chars.

7-31 Implement qsort. You can find a description of how quicksort works in almost any algorithms book.

7-32 Write a function, gentable, to generate a table of x,y points by evaluating another function over a range of x values. gentable is passed a pointer to the function to plot, the starting and ending x values, the number of points to plot, and two arrays for the x and y values. For example, we can generate 1000 values of the sin function between 0 and 1 radians with:

```
gentable(sin, 0, 1, 1000, x, y);
```

sin is a function found in the math library. To use it, you'll have to include math.h. Test your functions on various other math library functions, such as cos or tan.

7-33 Write the rest of the function plotter. It should take an array of points, scale it, and then plot the various points.

8 CONSTRUCTING LARGER PROGRAMS

Our previous programs have snuggled safely into a single source file, and our earlier functions have communicated solely through parameter passing and return values. But we aren't confined to such a simple program structure. We can construct an executable program from multiple source files, compiling each separately and then linking them together, and we can write functions that communicate through globally accessible variables. In this chapter we introduce storage classes and separate compilation, the mechanisms that support building bigger programs, and show how to use Turbo C's program builder, a useful tool for maintaining these programs. The chapter concludes by implementing sets, a useful data type that C doesn't provide.

8.1 LOCAL VARIABLES

Every identifier not only has a type, such as `int`, `double`, and so on, but also a *storage class* that provides information about its visibility, lifetime, and location. There are four storage class specifiers: `auto`, `register`, `static`, and `extern`. When we declare a variable, we can explicitly provide a storage class by preceding the variable's type with one of these specifiers. But if we don't, the compiler provides a default storage class for us.

The Storage Class Auto

The local variables we declare inside our functions are given the storage class `auto` by default. We can use the keyword `auto` to make the storage class explicit—but no one does, since a declaration such as

```
{
    auto int x, y;
     . . .
}
```

is exactly equivalent to

```
{
    int x, y;
      . . .
}
```

Although we haven't yet done so, we can also declare local variables at the beginning of any statement group or *block*, a convenience that aids modularity. We take advantage of this feature in the function searchstr, shown in Figure 8.1. This function takes two strings, s and t, searches s for the first occurrence of t, and returns its location. The statement

```
printf("%d\n", searchstr("Alex was here", "was"));
```

prints a five.

searchstr uses two nested loops. The outer loop walks a pointer, p, through the string s. The inner loop compares the target string t, with the group of characters in s to which p points. To do this comparison, we walk two other pointers, x and y, through these strings, as shown in Figure 8.2. We declare these pointers within the block containing the inner loop to clarify that this is the only place we use them.

An auto variable is visible only from the point of its declaration until the end of the block in which it is declared. That means we can't access it directly from a block outside the one in which it is declared; in fact, trying to do so causes a compile-time error. In Figure 8.1, placing

```
printf("Exit with *x is %c, *y is %c", *x, *y);
```

outside the inner block but before the function's end results in an "undefined variable" message.

auto variables have a short lifetime: from block entry to block exit. When we enter a block, space is reserved for its local variables; when we exit the block, this space is freed. (The name auto derives from this *automatic* creation and removal on block entry and exit.) As a result, the next time we enter a block, its auto variables may not even use the same physical memory locations—so we can't count on them still having the values they had before.

Initializing Local Variables

Despite their name, automatic variables are not automatically initialized to zero. Instead, they simply start with whatever was previously in the memory location allocated for them—usually garbage. *Warning: To prevent hard-to-find problems, initialize all* auto *variables before using them.* Conveniently, we can initialize a variable when we declare it simply by following its name with an equals sign and an arbitrary expression. This expression is evaluated whenever the function is called and the result assigned to the declared variable. For example,

```
int i = 0;
```

declares i as an integer and then initializes it to zero. The initializing expression can be any legal C expression, which means that it can include function calls, already declared local variables, and parameters.

```
/*
 * Search one string for another.
 */
#include <stdio.h>

main()
{
  int searchstr(char *string, char *target);

  printf("%d\n", searchstr("Alex was here", "was"));
  return 0;
}

/*
 * Return position of t in s.
 */
int searchstr(char *s, char *t)
{
  char *p;

  for (p = s; *p != '\0'; p++)            /* run p through s */
  {
    char *x, *y;      /* ptr to next part of s, start of t */

    x = p;   y = t;
    for (; *x != '\0' && *y != '\0' && *x == *y; x++, y++)
      ;
    if (*y == '\0')
      return p - s;                       /* where t is in s */
  }
  return -1;                              /* failure */
}
```

Figure 8.1   strsrch.c—A function to search one string for another string and a program that uses it.

We can also initialize automatic arrays, simply by supplying a brace-enclosed, comma-separated list of expressions. The values in this list become the initial values of the corresponding array elements. There's one restriction: The initial values for the array elements must be computable at compile-time.

Figure 8.3 contains a little function, daycalc, that given a date (month, day, and year), returns the day of the year. So

```
printf("%d\n", daycalc(6,24,1988));
```

prints 176. daycalc uses a table, days, that contains the number of days in each month. We initialize it with

```
int days[] =
    {31, 28, 31, 30, 31, 30, 31, 31, 30, 31, 30, 31};
```

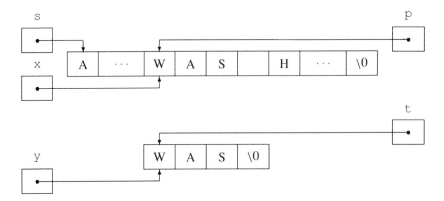

(*a*) At beginning of `was` (p has already moved through the first few characters).

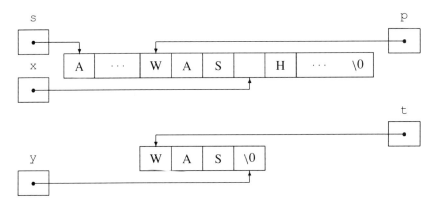

(*b*) At the end of `was`. We've found the matching substring.

Figure 8.2 How `searchstr` works.

Because we don't provide a subscript, the compiler allocates just enough space for all initialized elements, 12 in this case. We can supply an array size, but it must be large enough to hold the given elements. If it's larger, the extra elements are initialized to zero. Unfortunately, there's no convenient way to initialize only selected elements.

Letting the compiler calculate the array's size is especially useful when we initialize character strings, since it saves us the trouble of computing their length. The following,

```
char message[] =
    {'t', 'h', 'a', 'n', 'k', 's', '!', '\0'};
```

declares `message` to be an array of eight characters, initialized with the string "thanks!". Since we specified each of the characters in the string, we were stuck with providing the terminating null character ourselves. But there's a convenient shorthand

```
/*
 * Given month, day, year, return day of year.
 */
#include <stdio.h>

main()
{
  int daycalc(int month, int day, int year);

  printf("%d\n", daycalc(6,24,1988));
  return 0;
}

int daycalc(int month, int day, int year)
{
  int days[] =
      {31, 28, 31, 30, 31, 30, 31, 31, 30, 31, 30, 31};
  int i = 0;
  int total = day;

  for (; i < month - 1; i++)
    total += days[i];    /* sum days in preceding months */
  if (month > 2 && year % 4 == 0
          && year % 100 != 0 || year % 400 == 0)
    total++;              /* add leap year */

  return total;
}
```

Figure 8.3   daycalc.c—A function to determine which day of the year it is.

```
        char *message = "thanks!";
```

that automatically places the null at the string's end.

The Storage Class Register

Automatic variables are stored in memory. But accessing a memory location takes time, much more time than accessing one of the machine's registers. In fact, if it were possible we'd like to have all of our variables stored in registers rather than memory. We tell the compiler to store a variable or function parameter in a machine register by giving it the storage class `register`. The declaration

```
        register char *ptr;
```

declares `ptr` as a `register` variable. Making frequently accessed variables `register` leads to faster and slightly smaller programs.

Unfortunately, there are some restrictions on `register` variables. Since a machine register is usually a single word, many compilers only allow those variables that

```
/*
 * Main program to test our string reversing function.
 */
#include <stdio.h>
#include <string.h>

main()
{
  char s[] =
       {'s', 'd', 'r', 'a', 'w', 'k', 'c', 'a', 'b', '\0'};
  char *strrev(char *string);
  printf("%s\n", strrev(s));
}

/*
 * Reverse a string in place, returning pointer to
 * beginning of the string.
 */
char *strrev(char *ptr)
{
  register char *fptr = ptr;
  register char *rptr = fptr + strlen(fptr) - 1;
  register char tmp;

  for (; fptr < rptr; fptr++, rptr--)
    tmp = *fptr, *fptr= *rptr, *rptr = tmp;
  return ptr;
}
```

Figure 8.4 A new version of strrev that uses pointers placed in registers.

fit into a word to be placed in registers. This means that we can normally only place int, char, or pointer variables in registers. In addition, most machines also have only a few registers available to user programs, usually two or three. The compiler simply ignores our register declaration and places the variable in memory if it isn't of the right type or if there aren't enough registers. Lastly, and perhaps obviously, since a register variable is not kept in memory, we can't take its address with &.

Figure 8.4 is a program that reverses a string using a version of strrev that places the pointers it uses into registers. This function is about 20-25 percent faster and contains about 7-10 percent fewer machine language instructions than its registerless counterpart.

Since there are usually few available registers, carefully select the variables you place in them. (Otherwise, the compiler will select them for you.) Don't bother to declare variables as register until you've written the program and found it too slow. Then place into registers the most often used variables in the functions that take the most time.

```
/*
 * Keep a count of times function is called (buggy version).
 */
#include <stdio.h>

main()
{
  void testfunc(void);

  testfunc(); testfunc(); testfunc();
  return 0;
}

void testfunc(void)
{
  int cnt = 0;

  printf("testfunc call #%d\n", ++cnt);  /* increment once/call */
}
```

Figure 8.5 tstfnc1.c—An incorrect try at counting function calls. No matter how many times we call it, it always writes a one.

The Storage Class Static

We saw that a local variable lives only as long as the block in which it resides. But what do we do when we want a local variable to retain its value across function calls? Suppose, for example, that we want to modify a function to print a message that includes the number of times it is called. This might be useful when debugging: any output the function produced would be identified by the time the function was called. To do so, the function must somehow maintain a count that it updates each time it is called.

Our first thought might be that we could write the function as shown in Figure 8.5. This doesn't work, however, because cnt is initialized to zero every time we call testfunc. No matter how many times we call it, it still writes a one. To fix it we give cnt the storage class static, as we've done in Figure 8.6.

A static local variable lives as long as the program containing it does. Space for it is allocated and initialized once, at compile time. statics are initialized to zero by default, but as with any other local variable, we can provide an initializing expression. The one restriction is that the expression must be computable at compile time.

In the new version of testfunc, cnt is assigned a zero when the program starts. Each time testfunc is called, it increments cnt and prints it. Since cnt is static its value is preserved across calls. So the first time we call testfunc it writes a one, the next time, a two, and so on.

```
/*
 * Keep a count of times function is called (working version).
 */
#include <stdio.h>

main()
{
  void testfunc(void);

  testfunc(); testfunc(); testfunc();
  return 0;
}

void testfunc(void)
{
  static int cnt = 0;

  printf("testfunc call #%d\n", ++cnt);
}
```

Figure 8.6   tstfnc2.c—A correct version of a function that counts and prints the number of times it's called.

Figure 8.7 provides a more realistic use of static variables. It's a little program that line numbers its input and writes a page number on the top of every page. This program is broken into several pieces: getline to read a line of input, numline to write a line of output, and the main program. We've been using getline for quite some time: it simply reads a line of input into an array. numline writes a line of output, keeping track of the number of lines and pages written, and writing a page number at the top of every new page. The idea behind numline is to encapsulate all line numbering and page handling in a single function, so that the main program worries only about reading and writing lines. numline keeps the page number and line numbers in static variables so that their values remain between successive calls to it. Their initialization occurs once, when numline is first called.

EXERCISES

8-1 Rewrite strsearch more compactly, and then add appropriate register declarations. How much more efficient is this version?

8-2 Modify getline to use register declarations.

8-3 Modify page (Chapter 3) to line number its output lines.

8-4 Write the opposite of daycalc, a function that, given an integer day and a year, returns the corresponding month and day of the month. Given 40 and 1987, it should

```c
/*
 *  Print lines with automatic page and line numbering
 */
#include <stdio.h>

#define MAXLEN   80        /* longest line */
#define PAGELEN  60        /* page length */

main()
{
  char input[MAXLEN + 1];    /* input line */
  void numline(char *line);
  int getline(char *line, int max);

  while(getline(input, MAXLEN) != -1)
    numline(input);
  return 0;
}

void numline(char *line)
{
  static int pageno = 0;             /* current page number */
  static unsigned long lineno = 0L;  /* current line number */
  static int pageline = PAGELEN;     /* lines used on page  */

  if (pageline == PAGELEN)           /* new page, write pageno */


  {
    printf("\fPage Number: %d\n\n", ++pageno);
    pageline = 0;
  }
  printf("%6lu %s\n", ++lineno, line);
  pageline++;
}

int getline(char *ptr, int max)
{
  int c;
  char *startptr = ptr;
  char *endptr = startptr + max;

  while ((c = getchar()) != '\n' && c != EOF)
    if (ptr < endptr)
      *ptr++ = c;
  *ptr = '\0';
  return (c == EOF) ? -1 : ptr - startptr;
}
```

Figure 8.7 pagenum.c—Using `statics` in a program to page number its input.

return 2 for the month and 9 for the day.

8–5 Write a function that converts a string to an integer. The function should return a pointer to a `static` variable containing the integer's value. The function should return `NULL` if there's an error.

8.2   GLOBAL VARIABLES

So far we have declared variables only at the beginning of blocks. It turns out, however, that we can declare variables outside any function, anywhere in the file. Functions can access these variables—which resemble the global variables of Pascal and the common variables of FORTRAN—simply by referring to them by name; we don't have to pass them as parameters. Global variables have the same lifetime and initialization rules as `static`s.

We illustrate one common use of global variables in Figure 8.8, a new version of octdmp, the octal dump program we wrote in Chapter 5. That program saved input characters in an array until it had accumulated enough to fill an entire output line. Now we've made this array (`chars`) global, along with the number of items in it (`ingroup`) and the count of input characters read (`cnt`). Both `main` and `print_group` (the function used to output the characters) access this array by referring to it by name.

We don't have to explicitly initialize global counters, such as `cnt` or `ingroup`, to zero, since they start out as zero by default. This implicit initialization is convenient and is taken advantage of by countless programs, but explicitly initializing global variables makes our programs more readable.

Using these globals makes it is easier to call `print_group`, since we no longer have to provide parameters. But it also makes our program less general, since `print_group` now only works with a particular global array named `chars`. When using global variables, consider carefully the tradeoff between readability and convenience. A little extra effort to avoid globals and having all functions communicate through parameters increases modularity and aids readability. *Warning: In longer programs, external variables obscure the connections between functions, decreasing readability and modular independence.* Any of a program's functions can easily change a global variable, leading to subtle errors when the change is accidental. We try to use globals only for tables or for variables shared between routines when it is inconvenient to pass them as parameters.

EXERCISES

8–6 Write a program to count the number of occurrences of each unique input character (except for control characters). That is, the program prints how many a's it read, how many b's, how many spaces, and so on. To do this, the program needs to use a table of counters: one to count a's, one to count b's, and so on. Break the program into two pieces: the main program, which reads in a character and updates the table, and

```
/*
 * Octal dump (using globals).
 */
#include <stdio.h>
#include <ctype.h>

#define MAXCHARS  8       /* Number of chars on an output line */

int   chars[MAXCHARS];    /* chars for current output line */
int   ingroup;            /* chars in group */
long cnt;                 /* chars in input */

main()
{
  void print_group(void);   /* no parameters now */

  for (; (chars[ingroup] = getchar()) != EOF; cnt++)
    if (++ingroup == MAXCHARS)
    {
      print_group();
      ingroup = 0;
    }
  if (ingroup)
    print_group();
  return 0;
}

void print_group(void)
{
  int i;
  void print_space(int c);

  printf("%06ld  ", cnt - ingroup + 1);
  for (i = 0; i < ingroup; i++)    /* print octal codes */
    printf(" %03o", chars[i]);
  printf("\n        ");
  for (i = 0; i < ingroup; i++)
  {
    putchar(' ');                  /* space */
    if (isspace(chars[i]))
      print_space(chars[i]);       /* whitespace */
    else if (isprint(chars[i]))
      printf("  %c", chars[i]);     /* printable */
    else
      printf("   ");                /* other chars */
  }
  putchar('\n');
}
```

```
/*
 * print_space (doesn't use globals).
 */
void print_space(int c)
{
  int label;

  if (c == ' ')
    printf("    ");
  else
  {
    switch(c)
    {
      case '\b' :  label = 'b';  break;
      case '\f' :  label = 'f';  break;
      case '\n' :  label = 'n';  break;
      case '\r' :  label = 'r';  break;
      case '\t' :  label = 't';  break;
      case '\v' :  label = 'v';  break;
      default   :  label = '?';  break;
    }
    printf(" \\%c", label);
  }
}
```

Figure 8.8 octdmp.c—A new version of our octal dump program that uses global variables.

a function `print_table` that writes the characters and their counts. Use a global variable to hold the table.

8–7 Modify the character-counting program so that it behaves sensibly when it encounters control characters. It should print counts for these characters, but it shouldn't print the characters themselves.

8–8 Rewrite the program in the previous exercise so that the table is local to `main`.

8–9 Modify both versions to limit the scope of any index variables used. Does this make them more readable? Does this make them more compact?

8.3   EXTERNAL DECLARATIONS

In Figure 8.8 we conveniently define three global variables before any of the functions that use them.

```
int chars[MAXCHARS];
int ingroup
long cnt;
```

These definitions do two things. They allocate storage for the variables, and they provide the type information necessary to access these variables simply by referring to them by name.

But what about a function that needs to access a global variable defined after it or in another source file? Suppose, for example, that for some strange reason we wanted to organize our octal dump program with the variable definitions at the bottom of the file rather than at the top, as shown in Figure 8.9 (we're much more likely to place the variables in a separate file, but the same idea applies to both cases). Since these variable definitions now follow the functions that use them, we need some mechanism to provide the necessary type information. We do so by declaring the global variables within each function, preceded by the storage class specifier `extern`.

```
extern int chars[], ingroup;
extern long cnt;
```

These declarations are called *external declarations*. They tell the compiler what the types of these variables are, and that space for them is allocated elsewhere. But no space is allocated for a variable preceded with `extern`. Because external declarations don't allocate space, we need not provide bounds for any arrays.

An `extern` within a function provides the type information to just that one function. We can provide the type information to all functions within a file by placing external declarations before any of them, as we've done in Figure 8.10.

Because a global variable definition also declares the variable's type, we don't need external declarations if the global variable is defined before the functions that use it. Because a global variable definition allocates storage for the variable, a global variable should be *defined* only once, but should be *declared* by all functions that need to reference it.

The distinction between definition and declaration also applies to functions. We define a function when we specify its parameters and function body. This causes the compiler to allocate space for the function's code and provides type information for its parameters. We declare a function when we provide its prototype—but since functions are external by default, we can leave `extern` off from their declarations. So

```
void print_group(void);
```

is really a shorthand form for

```
extern void print_group(void);
```

Function declarations outside of any function work the same way as variable declarations outside of any function—they provide the necessary type information to all functions in the source file. This means that if we supply prototypes once, at the top of the source file, we don't have to supply them within each of the functions. We did so in Figure 8.10.

If we don't provide a prototype, the compiler assumes that the function returns an `int`. But we shouldn't take advantage of this—our programs are more readable if we provide prototypes for all functions, even those that return `int`.

```
/*
 * Octal dump program (time time organized differently)
 */
#include <stdio.h>
#include <ctype.h>

main()
{
  extern int chars[];
  extern int ingroup;
  extern long cnt;
  void print_group(void)


    . . .
}

void print_group(void)
{
  extern int chars[], ingroup;
  extern long cnt;            `
  void print_space(int c)


    . . .
}

void print_space(int c)
{
    . . .
}

int chars[MAXCHARS];       /* chars for current output line */
int ingroup;               /* chars in group */
long cnt;                  /* chars in input */
```

Figure 8.9 One way to use the storage class specifier `extern`. Each function has an external declaration for each of the global variables to which it refers.

EXERCISES

8-10 Remove `chars`'s external *declarations* from Figure 8.8. What happens when you try to compile it? Remove `chars`'s external *definition* from Figure 8.8. What happens when you try to compile it? Are the error messages from the compiler or the linker?

```
/*
 * Octal dump w/variables declared at the bottom
 */
#include <stdio.h>
#include <ctype.h>

extern int chars[], ingroup;
extern long cnt;
extern void print_group(void);
extern void print_space(int c);

main()
{
  . . .
}

void print_group(void)
{
  . . .
}

void print_space(int c)
{
  . . .
}

int chars[MAXCHARS];    /* chars for current output line */
int ingroup;            /* chars in group */
long cnt;               /* chars in input */
```

Figure 8.10 Another way to use the storage class specifier `extern`. We place global external declarations before any of the function's that use them.

8.4   SEPARATE COMPILATION

Our programs have so far resided in individual files. The major problem with this is that we've had to copy the source of useful functions like `getline` into all of the programs that use them. Fortunately, however, we can spread the source of a C program over many files, which we compile separately and then link together. Figure 8.11 shows what happens when we compile a program composed of several source files. Each source file compiles into an *object module* containing its machine language code, a list of the names and addresses of all external functions and variables defined in it, and a list of all of its external references to functions and variables defined in other source files. (In fact, any global definition or external declaration causes the external's name to be given to the linker.) The *linker* then creates an executable file from the various object modules by turning all external references into the variable's or function's address.

While resolving external references, the linker adds any referenced library func-

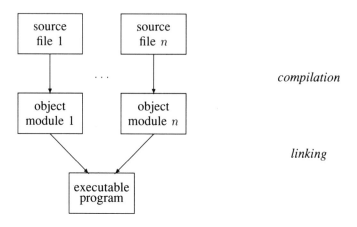

Figure 8.11 The process of compilation and linking.

tions. A library is a group of object modules that have been compiled in advance and stored in a special format. Turbo C only links those library functions or variables we actually require; other linkers automatically include the entire library. Although we don't have to do anything special to use the standard I/O library, to use other libraries we have to provide their names to the linker.

To illustrate how to compile and link multiple source files using Turbo C, we'll break our page-numbering program (Figure 8.7) into several source files. The first is pageno.c, which contains `main` and `numline`. The second is inout.c, which holds our old friend `getline` and its sibling, `putline`, which writes a string to the standard output, followed by a new line. And the last is inout.h, which is a header file containing the function prototypes for `getline` and `putline`. pageno.c is shown in Figure 8.12, inout.h in Figure 8.13, and inout.c in Figure 8.14.

Why did we choose this organization? The main reason for placing `getline` and `putline` in a source file of their own is that they are generally useful functions. This way we can compile the file once and then link it with many different programs. We provide the header file so that the individual functions using `getline` and `putline` don't need to provide their prototypes. When a source file includes this header file, it's as though we put prototypes before any of its functions. In the `#include`, we surround inout.h by quotation marks instead of angle brackets to indicate that it is our own include file, and not one that is system-supplied. Consequently, the preprocessor won't search the standard system locations for it.

We've studied how to compile and link a program spread out over several files, but we've ignored specifics. Now we'll look first at the command-line environment,

```
/*
 * Print lines with automatic page and line numbering.
 */
#include <stdio.h>
#include "inout.h"

#define MAXLEN   80          /* longest line */
#define PAGELEN  60          /* page length */

main()
{
  char input[MAXLEN + 1];    /* input line */
  void numline(char *line);

  while(getline(input, MAXLEN) != -1)
    numline(input);
  return 0;
}

void numline(char *line)
{
  static int pageno = 0;             /* current page number */
  static long lineno = 0;            /* current line number */
  static int pageline = PAGELEN;     /* lines used on page  */

  if (pageline == PAGELEN)           /* new page, write pageno */
  {
    printf("\fPage Number: %d\n\n", ++pageno);
    pageline = 0;
  }
  printf("%6ld %s\n", ++lineno, line);
  pageline++;
}
```

Figure 8.12 pageno.c—The main program and the function numline of our line numbering program.

```
/*
 * inout.h -- Prototypes for inout.c:
 *    getline - read an input line into a string (Chapter 6).
 *    putline - new function to write a string.
 */

int getline(char *line, int max);
void putline(char *line);
```

Figure 8.13 inout.h—The header file for inout.c.

```
/*
 * inout.c -- Two useful I/O functions:
 *      getline - read an input line into a string.
 *      putline - write a string as output line.
 */
#include <stdio.h>
#include "inout.h"

int getline(char *startptr, int max)
{
  register int c;
  register char *ptr = startptr;
  register char *endptr = startptr + max - 1;

  while ((c = getchar()) != '\n' && c != EOF)
    if (ptr < endptr)
      *ptr++ = c;
  *ptr = '\0';
  return (c == EOF) ? -1 : ptr - startptr;
}

void putline(char *startptr)
{
  register char *ptr = startptr;

  for (; *ptr != '\0'; ptr++)
    putchar(*ptr);
  putchar('\n');
}
```

Figure 8.14 inout.c—Two useful input/output functions, getline and putline.

then at the interactive environment.

Separate Compilation with tcc

Normally, tcc tries to compile and link whatever source files we give it. So we can compile a group of files simply by listing their names.

    tcc pageno.c inout.c

This compiles these files, and links the resulting object modules together to form an executable program named after tcc's first argument; pageno.exe, in this case. We can use the -e option to provide a different name, as in

    tcc -epgno pageno.c inout.c

which creates an executable program named pgno.exe. There can be no spaces between the -e and the file name that follows it.

As an alternative, we can compile the files individually, at different times, and then link everything together once we have the necessary object modules. The -c option tells tcc to "compile only", *without linking*. The command

    tcc -c inout.c

compiles inout.c into the object module inout.obj. Similarly,

    tcc -c pageno.c

compiles pageno.c into the object module pageno.obj. To link these object modules together, we again use tcc.

    tcc pageno.obj inout.obj

By default, tcc not only compiles any named .c files, but also links the resulting object files with any named .obj files. In this case, there are no .c files, so it simply links the object modules together. Had we already compiled inout.c successfully, we could use the single command

    tcc pageno.c input.obj

to compile pageno.c into an object module, to link it with inout.obj and the standard libraries, and to create the executable program pageno.exe.

(We have assumed that the library and include file options were placed in a configuration file, as discussed in Appendix A. If not, you'll have to specify the include directory when compiling and the library directory when linking.)

Separate Compilation with tc

To conveniently compile and link multiple files in the interactive environment we need to build a *project file*. In the simplest case, a project file simply lists the names of the relevant source files. For our example, its contents are simple.

    pageno.c
    inout.c

We don't need the .c suffix, but we prefer to provide it. The project file's name should end in .prj, such as pageno.prj. The project file's name determines the name of the executable program. In this case, as before, our executable is named pageno.exe.

After we've created the project file, we need to tell Turbo C its name. To do so, we hit *ALT-P* to get to the PROJECT menu, select the "project name" entry, and enter the project file name. Once we've done this, hitting *F9* compiles and links our files, and creates the appropriate executable program. Hitting *ALT-R* is just like *F9*, but it also runs the newly created program.

There are times when we want to compile a single file into an object module without linking. Why? Because we may want to link the same code into many files, without having to recompile the same source file many times. To compile a source file without linking, use the COMPILE-TO-OBJECT entry of the compiler menu. To compile a group of files that includes already compiled objects, include the object names in the project file.

    pageno.c
    inout.obj

```
/*
 * queues.h -- Prototypes for queue functions.
 */

void enqueue(int);        /* add item to queue */
int dequeue(void);        /* take item away from queue */
int emptyqueue(void);     /* is queue empty? */
```

Figure 8.15 queues.h—The header file for the queues package.

A Bigger Project—Queues

To further illustrate separate compilation, we implement a program that computes the average waiting times of riders waiting for a bus. Its input describes the time that either a person or bus arrived at the bus stop. The input consists of triplets of integers, one per line. The first integer is a code (0 indicates a person, 1 a bus), the second is the arrival time, and the third indicates how many people arrived or how many seats are available on the bus. The program's output identifies the arrivals and prints the total and average waiting time. The input

```
0 2 2
0 6 1
1 7 5
0 8 2
1 10 7
```

produces the output

```
2 people arrived at time 2
1 people arrived at time 6
Bus arrived at time 7 (5 seats)
2 people arrived at time 8
Bus arrived at time 10 (7 seats)
5 people waited 15, average wait 3.00
```

The program simulates the lines of people waiting for the bus. Whenever a person arrives, it saves their arrival time. When a bus arrives, the program lets those who have waited the longest onto the bus first, updating a count of the total waiting time. We use a queue to store these arrival times. A queue is a "first-in, first-out" data structure that behaves like a line for a movie: the people who arrive first are at the front, those who arrive last are at the back. We implement three queue operations: enqueue, which adds an item to the rear of the queue; dequeue, which takes an item away from the front of the queue; and emptyqueue, which returns nonzero if the queue is empty. Since queues are generally useful, we place these functions in a separate file, queues.c. We also provide a header file, queues.h, that contains their prototypes. These files are shown in Figure 8.15 and Figure 8.16.

The simplest way to implement a queue is as an array and a count. Adding an item is easy: we increment the count and count and add the item to the array's end. But

```
/*
 * queues.c -- Simple queue manager, no error checking.
 */
#include "queues.h"                    /* include prototypes */

#define MAXQUEUE 100                   /* number of queue items */

int queue[MAXQUEUE];                   /* holds the queue */
int *fptr = queue, *rptr = queue;  /* ptrs to its front/rear */

int *next(int *ptr)        /* update pointer to next item */
{
  return (ptr == queue + MAXQUEUE - 1) ? queue : ptr + 1;
}

void enqueue(int item)     /* add item to queue */
{
  *rptr = item;
  rptr = next(rptr);
}

int dequeue(void)          /* take top item off queue */
{
  int temp = *fptr;

  fptr = next(fptr);
  return temp;
}

int emptyqueue(void)       /* does queue have items left? */
{
  return fptr == rptr;
}
```

Figure 8.16 queues.c—The source file for managing queues.

deleting an item is difficult: not only do we have to decrement the count, but we also have to shift all array elements over one place. As an alternative, we can maintain two pointers into the array: fptr points to the queue's first item, rptr points to its last, as shown in Figure 8.17. Adding an element is still easy: we increment rptr and place a value at the location to which it points. But now deleting an item is also easy: we simply increment fptr and return the item to which it pointed. Since all of the queue operations work with the queue array and these pointers, we make them global.

```
    int queue[MAXQUEUE];                  /* holds the queue */
    int *fptr = queue, *rptr = queue;  /* ptrs to front/rear */
```

The functions implementing the queue can access them by referring to them by name.

(*a*) The empty queue.

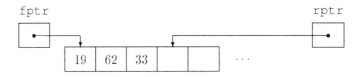

(*b*) The queue after adding two elements.

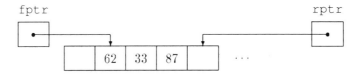

(*c*) The queue after deleting the first element and adding a new element.

Figure 8.17   Adding and deleting queue items.

The queue operations are straightforward, although we've ignored something: The way we use pointers allows the queue to move around the array. After enqueueing three items and dequeueing two of them, the first item in the queue is actually the third item in the array. This queue movement means that whenever `fptr` or `rptr` points to the array's last element, updating it should cause it to point to the array's first element. To handle this case, `enqueue` and `dequeue` both use a function `next` to return the appropriate pointer value.

In addition to the file containing queue-handling functions, this program is composed of several other source files. The first, wait.c, is shown in Figure 8.18. It contains the main function to handle reading input lines, to decide whether the next arrival is a person or bus, and to print the final statistics.

The second file, handle.c, contains the functions `person` and `bus` which handle the arrival of new riders or busses, using `enqueue` and `dequeue` to add or delete arrival times from the queue. They also update the counts of riders, busses, and the total amount of waiting time. We define these counters in wait.c

```
      long people,                             /* total people */
           busses,                             /* total busses */
/*
 * wait.c -- Compute average waiting time.
 */
#include <stdio.h>
#include "inout.h"
#include "handle.h"

#define MAXLEN 80

long people,                         /* total people */
    busses,                          /* total busses */
    waiting;                         /* total waiting time */

main()
{
  char buffer[MAXLEN + 1];           /* hold input line */
  int  code, time, count;            /* input numbers */

  while (getline(buffer, MAXLEN) != -1)
    if (sscanf(buffer,"%d %d %d", &code, &time, &count) != 3)
      putline("Bad input line -- ignored");
    else
      switch(code)
        {
          case 0:  person(time, count);
                   break;
          case 1:  bus(time, count);
                   break;
          default: printf("Invalid code of %d\n", code);
                   break;
        }
  if (people == 0)
    putline("No people?");
  else
    printf("%ld people waited %ld, average wait %.2f\n",
           people, waiting, (double) waiting/people);
  return 0;
}
```

Figure 8.18   wait.c—The main program for bus simulator.

```
      waiting;                             /* total waiting time */
```

And we place external declarations for them in handle.c.

```
    extern long people;
    extern long busses, waiting;
```

As we did with inout.c, we provide a header file that contains prototypes for the functions in handle.c. This file, handle.h, is shown in Figure 8.19. handle.c itself is shown in Figure 8.20.

```
/*
 * handle.h -- Prototypes for functions in handle.c.
 */
void person(int time, int persons);
void bus(int time, int capacity);
```

Figure 8.19 handle.h—The header file for handle.c.

We've already seen the final pieces of the program, the functions `getline` and `putline`, which we assume are once again in the file inout.c.

Figure 8.21 shows the components of the package and how they fit together. We can build the program with `tcc` using one simple command.

    tcc queues.c wait.c handle.c inout.c

With `tc`, we can use a simple project file.

    queues.c
    handle.c
    wait.c
    inout.c

If we assume that inout.c was previously compiled (when we were developing pageno), we can avoid compiling it again by using a slightly different command.

    tcc queues.c wait.c handle.c inout.obj

Or by using a slightly different project file.

    queues.c
    handle.c
    wait.c
    inout.obj

Actually, we probably want a more sophisticated project file, which we'll see how to create in the next section.

More Advanced Project Files

Separate compilation and linking lets us break large programs into smaller, more manageable pieces that we can develop separately and later link together. When we make a change, we need only recompile the files affected by it, not the entire program. Unfortunately, keeping track of which files need to be recompiled is often difficult, especially as our programs grow larger and more complex. What we really want is a way to automatically recompile only the files affected by our latest change. It turns out that tc's project files allow us to do just that. When we supply a project file, tc doesn't necessarily recompile all the files listed within it, only those it has to.

```
/*
 * handle.c -- Update the counts.
 */
#include <stdio.h>
#include "queues.h"
#include "handle.h"

void person(int time, int persons)
{
  extern long people;

  people += persons;
  printf("%d people arrived at time %d\n", persons, time);
  while (persons--)
    enqueue(time);
}

void bus(int time, int capacity)
{
  extern long busses, waiting;

  printf("Bus arrived at time %d (%d seats)\n", time, capacity);
  busses++;
  while (capacity-- && !emptyqueue())
    waiting += time - dequeue();
}
```

Figure 8.20   handle.c—The functions to handle updating counters.

There are two reasons why we have to recompile a source file. One is simply that we changed it. In this case, we need to compile it to create a new object module. The other is that the file uses functions or global variables in some other source file that we've changed. In this case, not only do we have to compile the file we changed, but all of those other files that use it.

tc takes care of the first case by default. When we try to create an executable program, tc automatically recompiles any source files we changed, and then relinks the resulting object modules with the rest of the project's object modules. The second case is more difficult. We need to tell tc explicitly about the source files that are somehow related. We do so by following the source file's name with a parenthesized list of files. Changing any of these files causes the source file to be recompiled.

For our program, the project file is:

```
wait.c      (handle.h)
handle.c    (handle.h queues.h)
queues.c    (queues.h)
inout.obj
```

What does this file mean? The first line means that wait.c should be recompiled

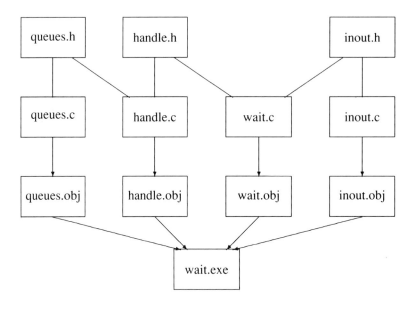

Figure 8.21 The process of compilation and linking our bus simulator.

not only if we change it but also if we change handle.h. The second line means that handle.c should be recompiled if it changes, or if we change handle.h or queues.h. The third line means that queues.c must be recompiled if it or queues.h changes. And the fourth line means that inout.obj should always be linked with the other object modules.

Why do we want this behavior? Because main, in wait.c, calls person and bus, two functions in handle.c. If these functions change internally, we need only recompile handle.c. But, if their prototypes change, we need to recompile wait.c as well. Similarly, if we change the queues, perhaps to use a different implementation, we need to recompile queues.c and handle.c, the file that uses these routines.

This project file is assuming that inout.c has already been compiled as part of some other program. By placing inout.obj in the project file, we imply that it's not expected to change as part of this project.

EXERCISES

8-11 Add `register` declarations to queues.c. Does the program's performance increase noticeably?

8-12 What happens when we add items to an already full queue? Modify the queue-handling functions to return values on errors.

8-13 Write a project file that assumes that both the input/output functions and the queue-handling functions have been written and compiled by someone else.

8.5 PRIVATE GLOBAL VARIABLES AND FUNCTIONS

By default, function names and global variables are made available to any file that declares them with `extern`. So wait.c can directly access the queue and its pointers by including the external declarations

```
extern int queue[];
extern int *fptr, *rptr;
```

The problem is that we really want to limit the access to these variables to the functions within queues.c—we don't want other modules to be messing around with the internal implementation of queues.

To prevent unwanted access to these variables, we have to declare them as `static`.

```
static int queue[MAXQUEUE];   /* array holding queue */
static int *fptr = queue,     /* ptrs to queue front/rear */
           *rptr = queue;     /*   and rear of queue */
```

`static` variables and functions are not made available to the linker and therefore cannot be accessed by other files. In fact, a `static` external variable or function is visible only to the part of the source file following its declaration. That means only the queue-handling functions can access `queue`, `fptr`, and `rptr`.

Preceding a function name with `static` prevents the direct use of these functions from other files. queues.c makes use of a function `next` to determine the next value for the queue pointers. Since we don't want functions outside of queues.c to use this function, we declare it with `static`.

```
static int *next(int *ptr)   /* update ptr to next item */
{
    return (ptr == queue + MAXQUEUE - 1) ? queue : ptr + 1;
}
```

EXERCISES

8-14 A stack is the reverse of a queue: The first thing placed on it is the last thing taken off, just like a stack of cafeteria trays. Stacks generally have a small set of operations including `push`, which adds an item to a stack, `pop`, which takes an item off, and `isempty`, which returns nonzero if the stack is empty. Write these operations.

8-15 Use the stack operations created in the previous exercise to write a program to reverse its input.

8.6   **TYPE MODIFIERS**

Storage classes provide information about a variable's lifetime and visibility. *Type modifiers* provide some additional information about how the variable is going to be used. Turbo C provides two *type modifiers*: `const` and `volatile`.

`const` informs the compiler that a particular object is not supposed to change. For example,

```
const int PAGELEN = 60;
```

declares `PAGELEN` as an `int` and tells the compiler that its value should remain constant throughout its lifetime. This causes the compiler to forbid any assignments to `PAGELEN` (including trying to increment or decrement it). Up to now we've been using `#define`, but we prefer `const`, since it allows us to easily limit the constant's scope. `const` also allows the compiler to flag as an erorr any attempt to assign a value to that variable. But `const` doesn't completely eliminate the need for `#define`. We can't use `const int` in any expression that must be evaluated at compile time, such as the subscript in an array declaration.

We can use `const` to modify any object, even those indirectly accessed through a pointer. The following declares `ptr` as a pointer to a constant `int`.

```
const int *ptr;              /* pointer to constant int */
```

What this means is that any attempt to change a value indirectly through `ptr`, as in `(*ptr)++`, is in error. But we can still change `ptr`. To declare a constant pointer, we declare the pointer in a slightly different way.

```
int a[100];

int *const aptr = a;       /* constant pointer to an int */
```

makes it a mistake to try to modify `ptr`. This says that `aptr` is a constant and can't be changed, even though we can modify whatever it points to.

The other type modifier, `volatile`, is the complete opposite of `const`. It means that the value could change at any time, and that the compiler should be aware of this when doing optimizations. We use this modifier only when we have a variable that's being updated by external sources, such as interrupt routines.

EXERCISES

8-16 Modify pageno and daycalc to use `const`s where appropriate.

8-17 We lied earlier about qsort's header; it's really

```
void qsort (void *base, int nelem, int width,
            int  (*cmp)(const void *, const void *));
```

Modify the comparison functions that we wrote in Chapter 7, `intcmp` and `fltcmp`, to work appropriately with this declaration.

8.7   CASE STUDY—ABSTRACT DATA TYPES

When Pascal and C are compared, C is frequently criticized for its lack of a "set" data type. A set is simply an unordered collection of values with certain operations defined on it. Some of the more common operations are adding and deleting values, and testing to determine if a value is in a set. In this section, we implement these set operations and a program to use them.

We implement sets as an *abstract data type* by creating a SET data type and functions for the various set operations. Programs using sets know only the names of these operations, restrictions on their use, and the order and expected type of parameters. To keep the details of their implementation hidden from their users, we package the set operations in a single module we compile separately. This allows us to change the implementation or add operations without having to rewrite the programs using them.

The concept of an abstract data type shouldn't seem strange. We have been using `floats` and `doubles` without knowing either their internal representation or the implementation details of operators such as + or /.

Implementing Sets

We implement sets as bit arrays, one bit per set element. C doesn't provide bit arrays, but we can simulate them using an array of `unsigned ints`. To access the bit corresponding to a given set element, we have to determine its location: the array element that contains the bit, and where that bit is located within that array element. We do so by dividing the set element by the number of bits in an `int`; the remainder is the bit's position within the array element. Figure 8.22 shows a sample computation. With this representation, the set operations are simple. We add an element to a set by turning on the bit it indexes, and delete it by turning that bit off. And we check membership by examining the bit's value.

Defining the SET Type

Programs using sets don't have to know that they are implemented as a bit array. In fact, we want programs to be able to declare a SET type as if the language provided one. To do so, we need a new C facility, `typedef`, which allows us to define synonyms for existing types. A `typedef` looks like a variable declaration with the name of the new type found where the variable usually occurs. These `typedefs`

```
typedef void *SET;
typedef int  ELEMENT;
```

make SET a synonym for `void *` and ELEMENT a synonym for `int`. We can use these types as if they were basic types. For instance, the declaration

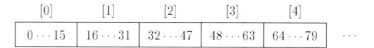

(*a*) Element 69 is in word 4 (69 / 16).

$$4$$

| 0111101010001111 |

(*b*) Element 69 is bit 5 in word 4 (69 % 16). This bit is 0, so 69 isn't in the set.

Figure 8.22 Locating the bit representing a set element; here, 69. First we select the array element, then the bit within it.

```
ELEMENT x;
SET s;
```

declares x as an int and s as a pointer to void. Types created with typedef are in effect from the typedef until the end of the file.

The SET and ELEMENT types are defined in the header file sets.h, shown in Figure 8.23. In addition, it includes prototypes for the various set operations. As expected, we have to include sets.h in all files containing functions that manipulate sets.

The SET Operations

sets.c, shown in Figure 8.24, contains the set operations we discussed earlier, along with two new ones. set_create uses malloc to allocate an array of unsigned integers large enough to hold the desired number of set elements. set_destroy uses free to return this storage. Despite our implementing SETs as arrays of integers, we make the SET type a typedef to a pointer to void to hide the internal details of their implementation. The functions dealing with the internals of a SET cast it into a pointer to an unsigned int before using it.

We build the basic set operations on top of three bit-manipulating functions. get_bit and set_bit set or return the bit representing a set element. Both use get_bit_pos to compute the location of the desired bit. Because these functions are internal to the SET type's implementation, we keep them hidden by declaring them as static.

```
/*
 * sets.h -- Definitions to use "sets" of integers.
 *              (1) Type definitions for set data type.
 *              (2) Prototypes for set functions.
 */
typedef void *SET;
typedef int ELEMENT;

extern SET set_create(int n);
extern void set_destroy(SET a);
extern void set_add(SET s, ELEMENT e);
extern void set_delete(SET s, ELEMENT e);
extern int set_member(SET s, ELEMENT e);
```

Figure 8.23   sets.h—The header file for sets.

Using Sets

Figure 8.25 uses sets in a program that partitions its input into values that appear once and those that appear many times. We could use this program to verify that no identification number appears more than once.

The program uses two sets. unique contains the values appearing once, dup contains the duplicates. When the program starts, we create these sets with set_create. We read values with getline and turn them into integers with sscanf. After we read a value, we check whether it is a member of unique. If it is, we remove it from unique and add it to dup. Otherwise, we simply add it to unique. Once we're done, we print the members of these two sets. To print a set, we run through all possible set values, printing those values that are set members.

To create an executable program from Figure 8.25, we need to link in the object module containing the implementation of the data type (compiled from sets.c). In addition, since we are using getline, we need to include its object module. Luckily, a simple project file does the job.

```
dups.c (sets.h)
sets.c (sets.h)
inout.obj
```

The compilation process for our sample program is shown in Figure 8.26.

Some Notes On Abstract Data Types

This example illustrates two important points. The first is that we should separate the details of a function or data type's implementation from those of its use. The program in Figure 8.25 would be considerably more complex and consequently harder to understand if it also contained the definitions of getline and of the set operations.

```c
/*
 * sets.c -- The routines to handle sets.
 *    Local functions:
 *      get_bit_pos - locate bit representing element.
 *      set_bit - turn on/off bit representing element.
 *      get_bit - get value of bit representing element.
 *    Interface functions:
 *      set_create - create a set of "n" elements.
 *      set_destroy - get rid of a set.
 *      set_add - add an element to a set.
 *      set_delete - take an element from a set.
 *      set_member - is an element a member of a set?
 */
#include <stddef.h>
#include <alloc.h>
#include "sets.h"

static const int wordsize = 16;     /* 16 bit ints */

static void get_bit_pos(int *word_ptr, int *bit_ptr, ELEMENT elem)
{
  *word_ptr = elem / wordsize;
  *bit_ptr = elem % wordsize;
}


static void set_bit(SET s, ELEMENT elem, int inset)
{
  int word, bit;                  /* element's position */
  unsigned int *p = (unsigned int *) s;   /* set pointer */


  get_bit_pos(&word, &bit, elem);
  inset ? (p[word] |= (01 << bit)) : (p[word] &= ~(01 << bit));
}

static int get_bit(SET s, ELEMENT elem)
{
  int word, bit;                  /* element's position */
  unsigned int *p = (unsigned int *) s;   /* set pointer */


  get_bit_pos(&word, &bit, elem);
  return (p[word] >> bit) & 01;
}

SET set_create(int n)
{
  int words = (n / wordsize) + ((n % wordsize) != 0);
  unsigned int *p = (unsigned int *) malloc(words * sizeof(int));
  int i;


  if (p != NULL)
    for (i = 0; i < words; p[i++] = 0)
      ;
  return (SET) p;
}
```

```
void set_destroy(SET s)
{
   free((void *) s);
}

void set_add(SET s, ELEMENT elem)
{
   set_bit(s, elem, 1);
}

void set_delete(SET s, ELEMENT elem)
{
   set_bit(s, elem, 0);
}

int set_member(SET s, ELEMENT elem)
{
   return get_bit(s, elem);
}
```

Figure 8.24   sets.c—An implementation of a simple sets package.

We can understand how it works without knowing that sets are implemented as bit arrays or that getline reads characters one at a time.

The other point is that wherever possible, we should build our programs on top of functions we have already written. We should create modules, like our sets, that can easily be used by new programs. Doing so effectively adds features to the language, allowing us to build programs much more quickly than we could if we had to start from scratch each time.

EXERCISES

8-18 Other common set operations include set_union and set_inter. set_union takes two sets and returns a set containing all the items in either of those two sets. set_inter is similar, but returns a set containing the items that are in both of those sets.

8-19 The difference of two sets is the elements in the first set that are not also present in the second set. Write a function, set_diff, that places the difference of two sets into a third set.

8-20 Write a function, print_set, that prints out the elements of a set in traditional set notation. For example, a set containing the elements 3, 7, and 14, should print as 3, 7, 14. Can this be implemented without adding set operations?

8-21 Our implementation of sets isn't particularly space-efficient for sets containing only

```c
/*
 * Identify duplicates in the input.
 */
#include <stdio.h>
#include <stddef.h>
#include "sets.h"
#include "inout.h"

#define ITEMS   1000        /* hold 0 through 999 */
#define MAXLEN    80        /* longest line */

main()
{
  SET unique, dup;          /* unique and duplicate elements */
  ELEMENT value;            /* value read */
  char buffer[MAXLEN + 1];  /* line containing value */
  void set_print(SET s, char *name);

  if ((unique = set_create(ITEMS)) == NULL ||
      (dup = set_create(ITEMS)) == NULL)
    putline("Couldn't create sets...terminating");
  else
  {
    while (getline(buffer, MAXLEN) != -1)
      if (sscanf(buffer, "%d", &value) != 1)
        putline("Bad input...skipping");
      else if (value < 0 || value >= ITEMS)
        printf("Out of range: %d\n", value);
      else if (set_member(unique, value))
        set_delete(unique, value), set_add(dup, value);
      else if (!set_member(dup, value))
        set_add(unique, value);
    set_print(unique, "Unique Values");
    set_print(dup, "Duplicate Values");
  }
  return 0;
}

void set_print(SET set, char *name)
{
  ELEMENT i;      /* next potential element */

  putline(name);
  for (i = 0; i < ITEMS; i++)
    if (set_member(set, i))
      printf("%d\n", i);
}
```

Figure 8.25 dups.c—A program to check for duplicate input values.

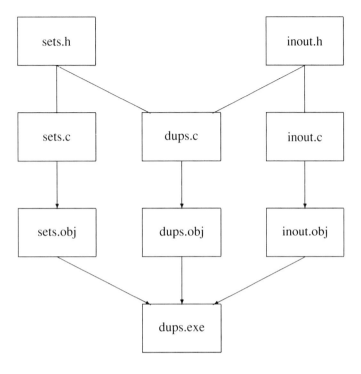

Figure 8.26   The process of compiling and linking the sets package.

a few elements. An alternative is to use sorted arrays of `ints` rather than bit arrays. Now when we add an element to the set, we place it in its correct place in the array. We check for membership by searching the array. And we delete an element by shifting array items. Implement sets using sorted arrays.

8–22 Extend the previous exercise to implement set union and set intersection.

9   THE
PREPROCESSOR

Many useful features of C aren't implemented by the compiler, but instead by a program that processes C source files before the compiler ever sees them. This chapter is a detailed discussion of that program, the C preprocessor. We introduce macros and show how they can make our programs more efficient and more readable. We examine header files in more detail and show how we can use them to effectively extend the language. And we study conditional compilation and show how it aids debugging and portability. This chapter concludes by using the preprocessor to improve an inconvenient function interface.

9.1   PREPROCESSOR DIRECTIVES

The preprocessor reads a source file, performs various actions on it, and passes the resulting output to the C compiler. We tell it what to do by placing special *preprocessor command lines* in the source file. These lines begin with a *preprocessor directive* in column one. Turbo C's preprocessor directives are shown in Table 9.1. Some of them should be familiar; we have already used #include and #define in many of our programs.

In Turbo C, the preprocessor is part of the compiler, and we have to run a separate program, cpp, to actually see the result of its processing. We use cpp the same way we use tcc—but instead of producing an executable program, cpp creates a text file that contains the result of its processing. This file's name ends with .i instead of .c. Figure 9.1 shows a file testcpp.c, and Figure 9.2 shows the output file testcpp.i that results from

    cpp testcpp.c

The preprocessor's output doesn't include lines that are part of comments or directives. Unlike the actual preprocessor, each line in cpp's output begins with the input file name and line number—which means that we can't then compile the resulting file. Luckily, we can use the -P- option to cpp to suppress this extra information.

DIRECTIVE	USE
#include	Include text from a file
#define	Define a macro
#undef	Undefine a macro
#if	Test if a compile-time condition holds
#ifdef	Test if a symbol is defined
#ifndef	Test if a symbol is not defined
#else	Indicate alternatives if a test fails
#elif	Combination of #if and #else
#endif	End a preprocessor conditional
#line	Give a line number for compiler messages
#error	Terminate processing early
#pragma	Implementation dependent directive

Table 9.1 C preprocessor directives and their uses.

9.2   SIMPLE MACRO SUBSTITUTION

We have used #define to define various symbolic constants, such as the number of elements in an array and the number of bits in a word. Doing so makes our programs easier to read and easier to change. It can be difficult to decipher what a numeric value does, since the same value can mean different things in different places. The value 10 may be an interest rate, the size of an array, or a base for number conversion. By providing a descriptive name for each unique use of a constant, we clarify its purpose, and allow us to change its value throughout the program simply by changing the line defining its name.

We have not yet done so, but we can use #define to give symbolic names to any arbitrary piece of text, not just numeric constants. We can do this because #define is more powerful than we have let on; it is actually a general mechanism for text replacement. The preprocessor command line

        #define *NAME TEXT*

instructs the preprocessor to replace all subsequent *unquoted* occurrences of *NAME* with *TEXT*. There are no restrictions on *TEXT*, but *NAME* must be an identifier and is usually written in all uppercase letters to distinguish defined names from the variable and function names handled by the compiler. A defined name is often called a *macro*, and the process of substituting its replacement text is called *macro substitution*.

One common use for #define is to give symbolic names to string constants. After encountering

        #define DIGITS "0123456789"

```
/*
 * A sample source file to be run through cpp.
 */
#define MAX 100

main()
{
  int a[MAX], i;

  for (i = 0; i < MAX; i++)
    a[i] = 0;
}
```

Figure 9.1   testcpp.c—A sample source file.

```
testcpp.c 1:
testcpp.c 4:
testcpp.c 6: main()
testcpp.c 7: {
testcpp.c 8:   int a[100], i;
testcpp.c 9:
testcpp.c 10:   for (i = 0; i < 100; i++)
testcpp.c 11:     a[i] = 0;
testcpp.c 12: }
testcpp.c 13:
```

Figure 9.2   The output file testcpp.i that results when we run it through cpp.

the preprocessor replaces each occurrence of DIGITS with the string constant "0123456789".
Another common use is to give symbolic names to arbitrary expressions.

```
#define TWOPI    (3.1415926 * 2.0)
```

The preprocessor simply substitutes the expression for its defined name, *without evaluating it*. It replaces

```
circumf = radius * TWOPI;
```

with

```
circumf = radius * (3.1415926 * 2.0);
```

We are allowed to define names in terms of other names, and to define them in
any order, as long as all definitions precede any use.

```
#define MIN     1               /* first array element */
#define MAX     99              /* last array element */
#define COUNT   (MAX - MIN + 1) /* total number of items */
```

When we define a name, the preprocessor simply remembers the replacement text, but does not substitute for any defined names it contains. Later, when we use the name, the preprocessor substitutes the replacement text and then performs macro substitution on any defined names it contains. So if the preprocessor finds this expression to compute a midpoint

```
mid = COUNT / 2;
```

it first substitutes for COUNT

```
mid = (MAX - MIN + 1) / 2;
```

and then for MAX and MIN.

```
mid = (99 - 1 + 1) / 2;
```

Even though the preprocessor doesn't evaluate expressions, using names that expand into expressions doesn't make our programs run slower. Turbo C computes the value of expressions involving only constants at compile time.

Warning: Failing to parenthesize expressions in the replacement text can cause unexpected order of evaluation problems. Not parenthesizing COUNT's definition

```
#define COUNT    MAX - MIN + 1    /* asking for trouble! */
```

results in an incorrect expression to compute the midpoint.

```
mid = 99 - 1 + 1 / 2;
```

Syntactic Replacement

We can use #define to hide confusing or error-prone parts of C's syntax. The definitions

```
#define FOREVER  for(;;)       /* infinite loop */
#define IS       ==            /* equality test */
```

help make infinite loops more explicit

```
FOREVER
  printf("Reflex test - hit the interrupt key\n");
```

and prevent the common mistake of using = instead of == for equality tests.

```
if (ptr IS NULL)
  printf("Malloc failed.\n");
```

In fact, we can actually hide enough of C's syntax to make it resemble another language, such as Pascal. We can use the definitions in Figure 9.3 to write C programs in a Pascal-like syntax, letting the preprocessor translate them into the form the compiler expects. Figure 9.4 shows a new version of our earlier program to compute powers, rewritten to use these definitions.

Major syntactic replacement also has its drawbacks. First, defined names must be identifiers, so we can't redefine operators and other nonalphabetic tokens such as comment delimiters, which limits how much C syntax we can hide. Second, the

```
/*
 * pascal.h -- Definitions for Pascal-like syntax.
 */
#define    INTEGER      int
#define    REAL         double
#define    IF           if (
#define    THEN         )
#define    ELSE         else
#define    WHILE        while (
#define    DO           )
#define    BEGIN        {
#define    END          }
#define    PROCEDURE    void
#define    FUNCTION
#define    AND          &&
#define    OR           ||
#define    MOD          %
#define    RETURN       return
#define    WRITE        printf
#define    READ         scanf
```

Figure 9.3 pascal.h—Definitions used to create a Pascal-like syntax.

compiler doesn't know about our extended syntax, so any error messages resulting from using our definitions incorrectly will correspond to C's syntax, making it hard to find these mistakes. And third, most people don't use an extended syntax, so it is hard for them to maintain programs written in one. Despite these limitations, some large programs, including a command interpreter and an object code debugger, have been written in an ALGOL-like syntax defined using the preprocessor.

Because the replacement text is arbitrary, the preprocessor doesn't do any syntax checking, leaving this task to the compiler. *Warning: Syntax errors within a definition are detected when we use the name, not when we define it.* The incorrect definition

```
#define PI = 3.1415926;   /* wrong: don't want "=" or ";" */
```

contains two common syntax errors: following a name with an assignment operator and terminating a definition with a semicolon. If we follow this definition with

```
circumf = 2 * PI * radius;
```

Turbo C reports errors for the incorrect statements

```
circumf = 2 * = 3.1415926; * radius;
```

that result from the preprocessor's substitutions. Remember that the preprocessor doesn't know C—it blindly replaces names with replacement text.

```
/*
 * Power rewritten using our Pascal-like syntax.
 */
#include <stdio.h>
#include "pascal.h"

main()
{
  INTEGER x, y;                        /* user inputs */
  REAL power(INTEGER x, INTEGER y); /* computes x to the y */

  WHILE WRITE("Enter x,y: "), READ("%d,%d", &x, &y) == 2 DO
    WRITE("%d to the %d is %f\n", x, y, power(x,y));
  RETURN 0;
}

REAL FUNCTION power(INTEGER x, INTEGER y)
{
  REAL p = 1.0;        /* start with x to the 0 */

  IF y >= 0 THEN
    WHILE y-- DO       /* positive powers */
      p *= x;
  ELSE
    WHILE y++ DO       /* negative powers */
      p /= x;
  RETURN p;
}
```

Figure 9.4 paspow.c—Our old `power` function, rewritten using Pascal-like syntax.

EXERCISES

9–1 Write constant definitions for the maximum and minimum values of the types `short`, `int`, and `long` on the PC. Write similar constant definitions for their unsigned counterparts.

9.3   **MACRO SUBSTITUTION WITH PARAMETERS**

So far we've defined names so that they are always replaced by the same text. We can vary the replacement text by defining a macro with parameters.

> `#define` *macro-name* (*name-1*, ..., *name-n*) *replacement-text*

Subsequent occurrences of the macro name are known as *macro calls*.

> *macro-name* (*text-1*, ..., *text-n*)

Macro calls look like function calls but behave differently. When we call a macro, we supply its arguments, and the preprocessor performs *macro expansion*, replacing the call with macro's replacement text and then replacing the macro's parameters with its arguments. In effect, the replacement text is a template, filled in when the macro is called.

GETBIT is a simple macro to return the value of an `int`'s nth bit.

```
#define GETBIT(w, n) (((unsigned int) (w) >> (n)) & 01)
```

To prevent order-of-evaluation problems when GETBIT is expanded, we parenthesized all occurrences of its parameters in its replacement text, as well as the replacement text itself. Following this definition, an expression like

```
GETBIT(value, i)
```

is a macro call. The preprocessor substitutes `value` for w and `i` for n in GETBIT's replacement text.

Figure 9.5 is a version of `print_binary` from Chapter 7 rewritten to use GET-BIT. Although we could have written GETBIT as a function, as we did in Chapter 4, we didn't simply because it is much less work to write it as a macro. Of course, we didn't have to write either a macro or a function to get the desired bit; the original version of the program accessed the bit directly. But using the macro aids readability without affecting efficiency.

Some Useful Macros

Macros can do things that functions can't. Consider the macro INRANGE, which returns a nonzero value only if its third parameter falls between its other two parameters.

```
#define INRANGE(x,y,v) ((v) >= (x) && (v) <= (y))
```

If the macro call

```
INRANGE(1, 100, inp)
```

appears after this definition, it is replaced with

```
((inp) >= (1) && (inp) <= (100))
```

`inp` replaces v, 1 replaces x, and 100 replaces y.

Because INRANGE is a macro and not a function, it can find the minimum of any pair of values with the same data type, `ints`, `floats`, `doubles`, whatever. If we wrote INRANGE as a function, we would have to type cast its arguments if their type differed from that of its parameters, or we would have to have different versions of INRANGE for each data type. We also gain efficiency by writing INRANGE as a macro, since macro calls are done during preprocessing instead of at run time, eliminating the overhead of a function call (argument passing, variable allocation, calling and returning from the function).

We can use macros to save ourselves typing and lessen the chance of error. The macro ALLOC

```
/*
 * Print an integer in binary.
 */
#include <stdio.h>

#define GETBIT(w, n)        (((unsigned int) (w) >> (n)) & 01)

const int INTBITS = 16;    /* assume 16-bit ints */

main()
{
  void print_binary(int value);

  print_binary(1961);
  return 0;
}

void print_binary(int value)
{
  int i = INTBITS;

  while (--i >= 0)
    printf("%d", GETBIT(value,i));
  putchar('\n');
}
```

Figure 9.5 pbinary.c—A program accessing bits using a macro rather than a function.

```
#define ALLOC(type) ((type *) malloc(sizeof(type)))
```

allocates one item of `type`, automatically computing its size and taking care to cast `malloc`'s return value into a pointer to the correct type. After this definition, the statement

```
ptr = ALLOC(int);
```

expands into

```
ptr = ((int *) malloc(sizeof(int)));
```

ALLOC can't be a function, since functions can't take types as arguments. A useful variant is SALLOC, which automatically computes a string's length and allocates sufficient space for the string.

```
#define SALLOC(s) ((char *) malloc((unsigned) strlen(s) + 1))
```

We could write SALLOC as a function, but as a macro it is much more efficient.

We can also write macros that hide certain language idioms—once again making our programs more readable without losing efficiency. The macros STREQ, STRLT, and STRGT hide the hideousness of strcmp's return value.

```
/*
 * Macros to get/set bits:
 *     onbit - return a word with only bit n ON.
 *     offbit - return a word with only bit n OFF.
 *     setbiton - return word with bit N ON.
 *     setbitoff - return word with bit N OFF.
 *     getbit - return value of bit N in word.
 *     setbit - set bit N to VALUE.  \
 *     getbits - return value of bits N thru N+K.
 *     setbits - set bits N thru N+K to value.
 */
#define ONBIT(n)          (01 << (n))
#define OFFBIT(n)         ~(01 << (n))

#define SETBITON(w,n)     ((unsigned int) (w) | ONBIT(n))
#define SETBITOFF(w,n)    ((unsigned int) (w) & OFFBIT(n))

#define GETBIT(w,n)       ((((unsigned int) (w)) >> (n)) & 01)
#define SETBIT(w,n,v)     ((v == 0) ? SETBITOFF(w,n) \
                                    : SETBITON(w,n))

#define GETBITS(w,n,k)    (( ((unsigned int) (w)) & \
                            (~(~0 << k) << n)) >> n)
#define SETBITS(w,n,k,v)  (((unsigned int) w & \
                            ~(~(~0 << k) << n)) | (v << n))
```

Figure 9.6   bits.h—Macros to get and set bits within a word.

```
#define STREQ(x,y) (strcmp((x),(y)) == 0) /* equal? */
#define STRLT(x,y) (strcmp((x),(y)) < 0)  /* x < y? */
#define STRGT(x,y) (strcmp((x),(y)) > 0)  /* x > y? */
```

They test whether one string is lexicographically equal to, less than, or greater than another string. Without these macros, the program's reader must remember the meaning of the various return values of strcmp to understand the string comparison being performed.

Using Macros in Macro Definitions

We are allowed to use macros with parameters in defining other macros, as we've done in Figure 9.6, which contains a full set of bit-shifting macros. To keep these macros simple, we have written them in terms of several mask-creating macros. Even so, some of them are too long to fit on a line. We indicate that a macro is continuing onto another line by placing a backslash at the end of the line. Figure 9.7 is a new version of our Chapter 4 word-packing program that uses these macros instead of the functions it used before.

Assuming these definitions, the preprocessor replaces a macro call such as

```c
/*
 * New version of Chapter 4 program to pack employee information.
 * This version uses macros rather than functions.
 */
#include <stdio.h>
#include "bits.h"


#define SINGLE    0     /* indicate marital status */
#define MARRIED   1
#define SEPARATED 2
#define DIVORCED  3
#define MALE      1     /* indicate sex */
#define FEMALE    0
#define MSBIT     0     /* marital status: bits 0-1 */
#define MSBITS    2
#define AGEBIT    2     /* age: bits 2-8 */
#define AGEBITS   7
#define SEXBIT    9     /* sex: bit 9 */
#define YRSBIT    10    /* year: bits 10-15 */
#define YRSBITS   6

main()
{
  unsigned int mstat, sex, age, years;
  unsigned int info = 0;   /* holds the info */

  printf("male=%d, female=%d? ", MALE, FEMALE);
  scanf("%d", &sex);
  printf("age? ");
  scanf("%d", &age);
  printf("single=%d, married=%d, separated=%d, divorced=%d? ",
         SINGLE, MARRIED, SEPARATED, DIVORCED);
  scanf("%d", &mstat);
  printf("years employed? ");
  scanf("%d", &years);

  info = SETBIT(info, SEXBIT, sex);
  info = SETBITS(info, AGEBIT, AGEBITS, age);
  info = SETBITS(info, MSBIT, MSBITS, mstat);
  info = SETBITS(info, YRSBIT, YRSBITS, years);
  printf("Here's the info: 0x%04x\n", info);
  printf("Sex: %d\n", GETBIT(info, SEXBIT));
  printf("Age: %d\n", GETBITS(info, AGEBIT, AGEBITS));
  printf("Marital status: %d\n", GETBITS(info, MSBIT, MSBITS));
  printf("Years employed: %d\n", GETBITS(info, YRSBIT, YRSBITS));
  return 0;
}
```

Figure 9.7 newbits.c—A new version of our earlier program to pack employee information into a single word.

```
word = SETBIT(word,2,1);      /* turn on bit 2 in word */
```

with

```
word = ((1 == 0) ? SETBITOFF(word,2) : SETBITON(word,2));
```

Then it expands the macros SETBITOFF and SETBITON.

```
word = ((1 == 0) ? ((unsigned int) word & OFFBIT(2))
                 : ((unsigned int) word | ONBIT(2)));
```

And finally it expands OFFBIT and ONBIT, resulting in the expression we want.

```
word = ((1 == 0) ? ((unsigned int) word & ~(01 << (2)))
                 : ((unsigned int) word | (01 << (2))));
```

We can also use macros as the arguments of macro calls. We can use the macro SQUARE

```
#define SQUARE(x)  ((x)*(x))
```

to compute n^4.

```
SQUARE(SQUARE(n))      /* quadruple a value */
```

The preprocessor expands this expression into

```
((SQUARE(n))  *  (SQUARE(n)))
```

replacing SQUARE's parameter x with SQUARE(n). Since there are still defined names in this expression, the preprocessor applies macro substitution to them, eventually generating the expression

```
((((n)  *  (n)))  *  (((n)  *  (n))))
```

Despite all the parentheses, this correctly computes n^4.

Potential Problems

Macros are useful—but they also have several potential pitfalls. One drawback is that a macro's code appears everywhere the macro is called, while a function's code appears only once, regardless of how many times the function is called. When minimal program size is important, write large, often-used macros as functions.

Warning: A macro argument, unlike a function argument, may be evaluated more than once. The call

```
SQUARE(i + j)
```

expands into

```
((i + j)  *  (i + j))
```

causing two evaluations of i + j. This may not seem particularly troublesome, but it is, especially when the arguments have side effects. Suppose we want to compute a^2 and then increment a. Unfortunately,

```
SQUARE(a++)
```

isn't correct, as it expands into

```
((a++) * (a++))
```

which does something very different. Use expressions as macro arguments sparingly, and avoid them entirely when they contain side effects.

Warning: Forgetting to put parentheses around a macro's parameters within its replacement text can result in incorrect orders of evaluation. Leaving them off the definition of SQUARE

```
#define SQUARE(x) (x * x) /* SLOPPY: underparenthesized */
```

causes

```
SQUARE(i + j)
```

to expand into

```
i + j * i + j
```

which does not return the $(i + j)^2$. Careful parenthesizing eliminates potentially incorrect orders of evaluation.

Most of these pitfalls can be avoided by can be avoided by remembering that macros are not functions.

Macro Operators

Turbo C provides two special operators, # and ##, that can appear in macro definitions. The first, #, precedes a parameter name. It means place double quotes around the argument that is substituted for the parameter. We use it in the macro DUMP, which writes a variable's name and value. dump is useful when debugging.

```
#define DUMP(name, format) \
        printf(#name "=" format "\n", name)
```

The call

```
DUMP(x,"%d");   /* dump x's value as integer */
```

expands into

```
printf("x" "=" "%d" "\n", x);
```

The preprocessor places double quotes around the x passed as the macro's first argument. The compiler then concatenates the resulting strings into a single string.

```
printf("x=%d\n", x);
```

The other operator, ##, turns two tokens into a single token. We use it in the macro TWOPOW.

```
#define TWOPOW(power)  two ## power   /* twoX */
```

When the preprocessor sees

```
TWOPOW(4)
```

it first substitutes 4 for `power`

```
two ## 4
```

and then joins these together to form a single identifier, `two4`.

Why would we ever want to do this? Possibly for flexibility. The current version of `TWOPOW` assumes that we have defined a set of constants

```
#define two1   2    /* 2 to the 1st */
#define two2   4    /* 2 to the 2nd */
#define two4   16   /* 2 to the 4th */
      . . .
```

and creates the reference to the appropriate constant. But if we decide we don't want numerous constants and that we would rather compute the power of two, a simple change to `TWOPOW`'s definition is sufficient.

```
#define TWOPOW(power) (1 << (power))
```

If we don't use the macro to construct the identifiers, we end up searching our entire program to find all their uses.

Undefining Names

Once we have defined a name, *all* subsequent occurrences are replaced with its replacement text. It is sometimes desirable to limit the scope of a name definition, either to highlight that the name is used only in a small section of the program, or to allow the name to be redefined. We use the directive

```
#undef NAME
```

to undefine a defined name, stopping macro substitution for it. We can then use `#define` to redefine the name. We'll get a warning if we try to redefine a name without first undefining it.

One use for `#undef` is to let us select between a macro and a function to accomplish a particular task. We need this ability because in some applications we're more concerned with speed; in others size. Macros give us speed; functions save space.

When we include `ctype.h`, we define a number of character-testing macros. Suppose that we decide that we want to use these macros except that we want `isalpha` to be a function, rather than a macro. (Why? Perhaps because we have side effects in its arguments, or perhaps because we want to add debugging information to it.) All we have to do is undefine `isalpha` after we include `ctype.h`, and then provide our own function named `isalpha`. We've done just that in Figure 9.8.

EXERCISES

9–2 Write a macro, `PRINTINT`, that takes an integer parameter and writes it to the standard output using `printf`. Can you write a macro to print a value of an arbitrary type appropriately?

```
/*
 * countem2.c -- New version of countem program from Chapter 5.
 */
#include <stdio.h>
#include <ctype.h>                /* defines ctype macros */

#define PRINT_TOTALS(x,total) \
        printf(#x "\t%7ld %4.1f%%\n", x, ((x) * 100.0 / (total)))

#undef isalpha                    /* want our own definition */

int isalpha(int c)
{
  return (c >= 'a' && c <= 'z') || (c >= 'A' && c <= 'Z');
}

main()
{
  int c;
  long spaces, letters, digits, puncts, others, tot;

  spaces = letters = digits = puncts = others = 0L;
  while ((c = getchar()) != EOF)
    if (isspace(c))
      spaces++;                   /* whitespace */
    else if (isalpha(c))
      letters++;                  /* upper- or lowercase letter */
    else if (isdigit(c))
      digits++;                   /* digit */
    else if (ispunct(c))
      puncts++;                   /* punctuation */
    else
      others++;
  tot = spaces + letters + digits + puncts + others;
  printf("Total    %7ld\n\n", tot);
  if (tot != 0)
  {
    PRINT_TOTALS(spaces,tot);
    PRINT_TOTALS(letters,tot);
    PRINT_TOTALS(digits,tot);
    PRINT_TOTALS(puncts,tot);
    PRINT_TOTALS(others,tot);
  }
  return 0;
}
```

Figure 9.8 countem2.c—A new version of our program to print a breakdown of the different types of characters in its input.

9-3 Write a macro, `INDEX`, that expands into a `for` loop that indexes a variable from a minimum to a maximum.

```
INDEX(i, 1, 100) printf("This is %d\n", i);
```

expands into

```
for (i = 1; i <= 100; i++) printf("This is %d\n", i);
```

`INDEX` should work even if the loop bounds are expressions.

9-4 Write the macros `DIV` and `DIVMOD`. `DIV(x,y)` returns the value of x/y for nonzero values of y, otherwise it returns zero. `DIVMOD(d,r,x,y)` divides x by y, storing the result in d and the remainder in r.

9-5 Write a macro, `MSG(flag,msg)`, that writes the string `msg` only if `flag` is not zero.

9-6 Write a macro, `NULLPTR(type)`, that returns a null pointer correctly cast to the passed type. When is this macro useful?

9-7 Write a macro, `DEREF(ptr, type)`, that dereferences `ptr` only if it is not null. If `ptr` is null, the macro prints an error message and returns zero, cast to the appropriate type.

9-8 Examine some of the C programs you have written. Are there complicated expressions that could be greatly simplified by using macros? Write these macros.

9.4   FILE INCLUSION

We have been using file inclusion right from the start. The directive `#include` instructs the preprocessor to replace the current line with the entire contents of the specified file. If we don't provide a full path name, the preprocessor searches for the file in various locations determined by the `#include` form used. The form

```
#include <filename>
```

has the preprocessor look in only those locations specified by the -i option or the OPTIONS/ENVIRONMENT/INCLUDE menu entry. It is used to access system-supplied include files.

The alternative form

```
#include "filename"
```

is used for include files that we create. It looks in a default directory first, and searches the other locations only if the file is not found locally. This form is used only with local include files. Preprocessing stops if an include file cannot be found. Included files can include other files; most preprocessors allow at least five levels of nesting. Of course, an included file shouldn't include itself or any file that includes it.

File inclusion allows us to create a file of useful definitions that we can include in all our programs. Definitions like those shown in Figure 9.9 can extend C in a useful way while requiring little effort on our part. Most of these definitions and

```
/*
 * defs.h -- Our default definitions.
 */
#include <stdio.h>                 /* we always need these */
#include <stddef.h>
#include <string.h>
#include <ctype.h>

#define TAB      '\t'
#define PAGE     '\f'
#define BELL     '\a'
#define CR       '\n'

#define FOREVER for(;;)
#define IS       ==
#define ISNOT    !=

#define MIN(x,y)       ((x) < (y) ? (x) : (y))   /* smaller */
#define MAX(x,y)       ((x) < (y) ? (y) : (x))   /* larger */
#define INRANGE(x,y,v) ((v) >= (x) && (v) <= (y))

#define SWAP(tmp,x,y) (tmp = x, x = y, y = tmp)


#define STREQ(x,y) (strcmp(x,y) == 0)
#define STRLT(x,y) (strcmp(x,y) < 0)
#define STRGT(x,y) (strcmp(x,y) > 0))


#define ALLOC(x) ((x *) malloc((unsigned) sizeof(x)))
#define SALLOC(s) ((char *) malloc((unsigned) strlen(s) + 1))
```

Figure 9.9 defs.h—A header file containing generally useful definitions used by many programs.

macros were explained in earlier sections. We have, however, added a macro SWAP that exchanges two variables, and the macros MAX and MIN that return the maximum and minimum value of their arguments, respectively.

File inclusion allows us to define a set of useful operations entirely within an include file. In fact, we've already done so with the bit-accessing macros we wrote earlier. We put them into the header file bits.h, and then include it in whatever programs need these macros. Should we find that these macros are generally useful, we can include bits.h from defs.h. Doing so effectively extends the language to provide additional functions we find useful, while preserving the efficiency of programs that use them.

```
/*
 * bool.h -- Header file defining BOOLEAN data type.
 */
#define BOOLEAN     short

#define TRUE        1
#define FALSE       0

#define NOT         !
#define AND         &&
#define OR          ||

#define BOOLVAL(x)  (x) ? "TRUE" : "FALSE"
```

Figure 9.10 bool.h—A header file defining a BOOLEAN data type.

Including Data Type Definitions

We can define a seemingly new data type completely within a header file. As an example, Figure 9.10 shows the include file bool.h, which contains definitions that make it appear as though C has a Boolean data type. These definitions help us write more readable code, and make it easier to translate programs written in a language that has a Boolean type.

We use short to hold BOOLEANs, since we need only store the two values zero FALSE and one TRUE. For consistency with other languages, we define the constants NOT, AND, and OR as alternatives to C's equivalent logical operators. BOOLVAL returns a string representing the BOOLEAN's value, which comes in handy when debugging.

Any program can pretend that C has BOOLEANs by including bool.h and using these definitions. We use them in Figure 9.11, a new version of uniq, the Chapter 6 program to filter duplicate lines. We'd already made use of constants for TRUE and FALSE; this version differs in that the constants are in a header file and do not have to be defined, and that first is now a BOOLEAN rather than int. Notice that since we've defined bool.h ourselves, we surround the #include with quotes rather than angle brackets.

EXERCISES

9–9 Define a header file that provides a group of functions for manipulating sets of small integers (from 0 to 31). Write macros for adding an item to the set, deleting an item, testing whether an item is in the set, and taking the union and intersection of two sets.

9–10 Define a header file that provides a set of macros for traversing arrays. These include

```
INIT(array, elements, ptr, value)
```

```
/*
 * A new version of our program to strip duplicate lines.
 */
#include "defs.h"              /* our definitions */
#include "bool.h"              /* our Boolean type */
#include "inout.h"             /* getline/putline */

#define MAXLEN 80              /* longest line length */

main()
{
  char curr[MAXLEN + 1],       /* current line */
       prev[MAXLEN + 1];       /* previous line */
  BOOLEAN first = TRUE;        /* first time through? */

  while(getline(curr, MAXLEN) != -1)
  {
    if (first || !STREQ(prev, curr))
    {
      putline(curr);
      first = FALSE;
    }
    strcpy(prev, curr);
  }
  return 0;
}
```

Figure 9.11   newuniq.c—Using the BOOLEAN definitions in a new version of uniq.

that expands into a loop initializing each array element to a particular value,

        FWALK(array, elements, ptr, func)

that expands into a loop executing a function on each array element (going from beginning to end), and

        RWALK(array, elements, ptr, func)

that does the same thing but in the opposite direction.

9.5   CONDITIONAL COMPILATION

We can use the preprocessor to select which lines of the source file are actually compiled, a process known as *conditional compilation*. Conditional compilation lets us compile a program's source into different versions, depending on our needs. There are two types of compile-time tests: We can check whether a name is defined, and we can check whether an expression has a particular value.

Testing Name Definition

We use #ifdef and #ifndef to test whether a name is defined. #ifdef is the compile-time equivalent of an if whose expression is restricted to a single name.

```
#ifdef name
  first-group-of-lines
#else
  second-group-of-lines
#endif
```

The processor and compiler process *first-group-of-lines* when *name* is defined, and *second-group-of-lines* if it is not. The #else is optional. If we omit it and the test fails, the preprocessor simply ignores the lines preceding the matching #endif. Every #ifdef or #ifndef must have an #endif.

Figure 9.12 uses #ifdef in a new version of the insertion sort program from Chapter 2. This version conditionally includes statements that provide debugging output. These statements are included only if the name DEBUG is defined when the function is compiled.

If DEBUG is defined when the preprocessor evaluates the first #ifdef, the compiler receives

```
{
  printf("Moving %d from %d to %d\n", a[num], num - 1, num);
  a[num] = a[num - 1];
}
```

but doesn't see the statement between the #else and the #endif. It only sees that statement if DEBUG is not defined.

What are the alternatives to having the preprocessor decide whether debugging output should be produced? We could add output statements whenever debugging output is desired, and then remove them once the program has been debugged. But then our programs aren't as maintainable, since the debugging statements aren't available when we want to update the program. We could use run-time tests, but then our programs are larger, because the debugging statements appear in the program's object module even when debugging output is not desired, and slower, because the tests are not done at run time rather than compile time. The preprocessor approach does have one disadvantage: The many preprocessor tests make the source less readable.

The other test, #ifndef, tests whether a name has not been defined. It appears most often in include files to ensure that even if the file is included more than once, any definitions it contains won't be.

We use #ifndef in Figure 9.13, a modified version of bool.h, called boolean.h, that defines BOOLEAN only if it hasn't already been defined. The file's first line

```
#ifndef BOOLEAN
```

causes the various names contained in the file to be defined only if BOOLEAN is undefined. If BOOLEAN is already defined, we assume that the file has already been included and that we can ignore its definitions. Remember that both #ifdef and #ifndef test only whether the name is defined in the preprocessor; they do not test whether the name of an identifier, function, or type has been declared.

```c
/*
 * A new version of Chapter 2's insertion sort program
 * (modified to include debugging statements).  To get
 * the debugging statements, define DEBUG.
 */
#include <stdio.h>
#include "inout.h"

#define MAX      100  /* maximum number of values to sort */
#define MAXLEN    80  /* longest line */

main()
{
  int n = 0;                 /* number of values in table */
  int table[MAX];            /* table of values */
  int next;                  /* current value */
  char line[MAXLEN + 1]; /* input line */
  void insert(int a[], int val, int num);
  void print_table(int a[], int num);

  while (n < MAX && getline(line, MAXLEN) != -1)
    if (sscanf(line, "%d", &next) != 1)
      putline("Bad input...skipping");
    else
      insert(table, next, n++);
  print_table(table, n);
  return 0;
}

/*
 * Place value in correct place in array.
 */
void insert(int a[], int val, int num)
{
  for (; num > 0 && val < a[num - 1]; num--)
#ifdef DEBUG
  {
    printf("Moving %d from %d to %d\n", a[num], num - 1, num);
    a[num] = a[num - 1];
  }
#else
    a[num] = a[num - 1];
#endif
#ifdef DEBUG
  printf("Inserting %d at position %d\n", val, num);
#endif
  a[num] = val;
}
```

```
/*
 * Print array in sorted order.
 */
void print_table(int a[], int num)
{
  int i;

  for (i = 0; i < num; i++)
#ifdef DEBUG
    printf("a[%d] = %d\n", i, a[i]);
#else
    printf("%d\n", a[i]);
#endif
}
```

Figure 9.12   newisort.c—Insertion sort program with debugging statements.

```
/*
 * Header file defining BOOLEAN data type.
 */
#ifndef BOOLEAN

#define BOOLEAN     short
#define TRUE        1
#define FALSE       0

#define NOT         !
#define AND         &&
#define OR          ||

#define BOOLVAL(x)  (x) ? "TRUE" : "FALSE"

#endif
```

Figure 9.13   boolean.h—A new version of the include file that defines BOOLEAN.

Defining Names

So where do these names we're testing come from? We test whether DEBUG is defined to decide whether to include the debugging statements. But how do we make sure DEBUG is defined? One way is to simply add the line

```
#define DEBUG
```

at the top of our source file when we want debugging statements. We then remove it when they are no longer necessary. But this forces us to edit the source file. The

-D compiler option provides an alternative: -D*Name* defines a name, just as if we had typed

        #define *NAME*

at the beginning of each of the source file we're compiling. Assuming our program is named newisort.c, we would compile it with

>   tcc -c -DDEBUG newisort.c

to obtain debugging output. In tc, we select the COMPILE/DEFINES menu entry and enter the names we want defined.

There are two other forms of the -D option. We can give a *NAME* a value, as opposed to simply defining it, using

>   tcc -D*NAME*=*VALUE* *filenames*

There can be no blanks surrounding the =. So

>   tcc -DMAXLEN=256

gives MAXLEN an initial value of 256.

Predefined Names

In addition to names we define ourselves, most preprocessors also predefine some names for us. These include the machine the program is running on, its host operating system, and the name of the compiler being used. Table 9.2 contains the names defined by the Turbo C compiler.

A program can test these predefined names to determine what type of environment it's running in, and adjust environment dependencies accordingly. The Turbo C compiler, for example, defines the name __TURBOC__ (a name containing two leading and two trailing underscores). Our programs can make use of this to compile differently under Turbo C than they would under other compilers. This allows them to take advantage of special Turbo C features, such as function prototypes, without losing portability.

Figure 9.14 is an example. It's a new version of the header file, inout.h, that supplies prototypes for getline and putline. If __TURBOC__ is defined, as it is when we're compiling with Turbo C, these prototypes are processed. Otherwise, we're using some other compiler and the old-style declarations are used. As long as the program doesn't rely on the automatic parameters made possible by prototypes, it should run well under either style compiler. Actually, we also have to make a similar change in inout.c, a topic discussed in more detail in Chapter 16.

Most processors also define a set of variables with useful *values*. Almost all preprocessors, including Turbo C, predefine the names __LINE__ and __FILE__ as the current line number and current source file name. We illustrate one use of these definitions in the definition of the macro ASSERT, shown in Figure 9.15.

ASSERT's argument is an expression representing a programmer assumption. If the assumption doesn't hold, it writes a message that includes the line number and source file where the assertion was made. We can insert a call to ASSERT wherever

NAME	VALUE OR TEST
__LINE__	Current line number (an integer)
__FILE__	Current file name (a string constant)
__DATE__	Current date (a string: MMMDDYYYY)
__TIME__	Current time (a string: HHMMSS)
__STDC__	ANSI compatibility?
__TURBOC__	Current Turbo C version number (in hex)
__MSDOS__	Compiling under DOS
__PASCAL__	Pascal calling conventions (-p)?
__CDECL__	C calling conventions (no -p)?
__TINY__	Using tiny memory model?
__SMALL__	Using small memory model?
__MEDIUM__	Using medium memory model?
__COMPACT__	Using compact memory model?
__LARGE__	Using large memory model?
__HUGE__	Using huge memory model?

Table 9.2   Various Turbo C predefined preprocessor names.

```
/*
 * inout.h -- prototypes for inout.c (new version)
 *    getline - read an input line into a string (Chapter 3)
 *    putline - write a string
 */

#ifdef __TURBOC__
  extern int getline(char *line, int max);
  extern void putline(char *line);
#else
  extern int getline();
  extern void putline();
#endif
```

Figure 9.14   inout.h—New version of the header file that provides the prototypes for `getline` and `putline`.

```
/*
 * assert.h -- Our version of the ASSERT macro.
 */

#define ASSERT(cond) \
   ( (cond) ? 1 \
            : (printf("Assertion (" #cond ") failed (%s,%d)\n", \
               __FILE__, __LINE__), 0))
```

Figure 9.15 assert.h—The definition of our ASSERT macro.

function makes a critical assumption, documenting the assumption and indicating it when it fails. Invariably, a false assumption will cause our program to fail; ASSERT helps us find such assumptions.

When ASSERT is called, the preprocessor replaces __LINE__ and __FILE__ with the line number and file name of the call. This way the error message indicates where the failed assumption occurred in the source file. We wrote ASSERT as a conditional expression to allow functions to test assertions and exit when they fail.

Figure 9.16 contains a new version of reverse_tab that uses ASSERT to make explicit its assumption that it is passed a non-null pointer, and that its first array bound is less than the second. If we accidentally pass reverse_tab a null pointer, we get a useful error message.

```
Assertion (first <= last) failed (ASSERT.C,26)
```

This message was generated because the call to ASSERT

```
ASSERT(first <= last);
```

expands into

```
((first <= last)
   ? 1
   : (printf("Assertion (" "first < last" ") failed (%s,%d)\n",
            test.c, 31), 0));
```

which causes the error message to print when the program runs. The ASSERT provides some indication of where the problem lies. An error message from a failed assertion provides à better starting point for locating bugs than missing output or a potentially cryptic system message.

More General Compile-Time Tests

#ifdef and #ifndef are special cases of a more general compile-time test. The directive

```
#if constant-expression
   first-group-of-lines
#else
   second-group-of-lines
#endif
```

```
/*
 * Bad call to function to reverse an array in place.
 */
#include "defs.h"
#include "assert.h"

#define MAXLEN 10

main()
{
  int i, table[MAXLEN];
  void reverse_tab(int *ptr, int first, int last);

  for (i = 0; i < MAXLEN; i++)
    table[i] = i;         /* provide initial values */
  reverse_tab(table, MAXLEN - 1, 0);   /* bad call! */
  return 0;
}

void reverse_tab(int *ptr, int first, int last)
{
  int *endptr = ptr + last;
  int temp;

  ASSERT(ptr != NULL);
  ASSERT(first <= last);

  for (ptr += first; ptr <= endptr; ptr++, endptr--)
    SWAP(temp, *ptr, *endptr);
}
```

Figure 9.16 assert.c—Making an assumption explicit with the ASSERT macro.

evaluates *constant-expression* and compares its value with zero to determine the group of lines to process. As before, the #else is optional.

We can use a simple form of #if to "comment out" sections of code that contain comments when we are using a C compiler that does not allow nested comments.

```
    #if 0              /* begin ignored section */
      lines-to-be-commented out
    #endif             /* end ignored section */
```

Since the #if's expression is always zero, the *lines-to-be-commented-out* are always ignored.

We could also use #if to have our program compile differently, depending on which version of Turbo C it is running under. We might want to do so because we want to use the graphics library functions provided with Turbo C 1.5, and our own routines otherwise.

```
#if __TURBOC__ < 0x0150
    Code for Turbo C, version 1.0-1.4
#else
    Code for version 1.5 or later
#endif
```

This works because __TURBOC__ is defined as a hexadecimal constant representing the version of the Turbo C compiler you are using. The high byte is the version number, the low byte the release: version 1 is 0x0100, version 1.2 is 0x0120, and so on.

We can combine #if with a special preprocessor operator, defined, to test for name definition. defined takes a *NAME* (which must be surrounded by parentheses) and returns a nonzero value only if the *NAME* is defined. We can rewrite our earlier

```
#ifdef __TURBOC__
```

as

```
#if defined(__TURBOC__)
```

Similarly, we could test whether BOOLEAN was not defined with

```
#if !defined(BOOLEAN)
```

Because defined is a new addition to the language, many compilers don't yet provide it. This means that you need to use the old form if you are planning to port your programs to an older C compiler.

Turbo C provides one other recent addition to C, #elif. We can use it to write #ifs of the form

```
#if test-1
 . . .
#else
#if test-2
 . . .
#endif
#endif
```

more compactly

```
#if test-1
 . . .
#elif test-2
 . . .
#endif
```

We replace any #else immediately followed by an #if with #elif and then remove its #endif.

___

EXERCISES

9-11 Modify bits.h to define the various macros only if they have not already been defined.

9-12 Write a program that prints the version of Turbo C used to compile it.

9-13 Write a program that prints (in a nice way) the memory model used to compile it.

9.6   OTHER PREPROCESSOR DIRECTIVES

There are three other preprocessor directives. The first, `#line`, tells the preprocessor from which input file and line a line in its input was derived.

> `#line` *line-number* *"filename"*

`#line` appears most frequently in C programs that have been generated or modified by other programs (*pre-preprocessors*) before they are seen by the preprocessor or compiler. Because line numbers referred to in a preprocessor or compiler error message may not correspond exactly to the line where the error occurred in the source file used to generate these programs, the pre-preprocessors use `#line` to make error messages refer to the correct lines in the original source file.

We use `#error` most frequently inside preprocessor conditionals. When the preprocessor encounters a `#error`,

> `#error` *error-message*

it writes an error message and terminates preprocessing early.

> `Fatal:` *filename line* `Error directive:` *error-message*

A program could use

```
#if TURBOC < 0x0150
#error No graphics library (not version 1.5 or later)
#else
    normal code
#endif
```

to terminate preprocessing unless it was running version 1.5 Turbo C or later, perhaps because it needs the graphics functions available only with those versions.

The final directive is `#pragma`, whose behavior differs between compilers. In Turbo C, we can use it to turn various warnings on and off.

```
#pragma -wrch    /* no warnings about unreachable code */
#pragma +wcln    /* warn about long constants */
#pragma .wsus    /* default suspicious pointer warning */
```

Preceding the warning with a − turns it off, a + turns it on, and a . restores the default. Appendix D lists all of the warnings and their abbreviations.

EXERCISES

9-14 Write a program that removes all lines beginning with an at-sign (@) from C source files. This allows us to have convenient single-line comments. The program should provide `#line`s to ensure error messages refer to the line in the original source file.

9-15 Modify boolean.h to terminate processing if it is included when a BOOLEAN type has already been defined.

```
/*
 * Header file for search function.
 */

#define SEARCH(type, a, n, tptr, cfp) \
        (type *) search((void *) a, n, sizeof(type), cfp, tptr)

extern void *search(void *tabptr, int n, int size,
                    int (*funcptr)(void *, void *), void *tarptr);
```

Figure 9.17 search.h—Header file for generic search routine.

9.7   CASE STUDY—IMPROVING FUNCTION INTERFACES

In Chapter 7 we presented a function that could search any type of array for a particular value. While it's a powerful function, it's painful to use. Searching an array of ints required a complicated function call with lots of casting, something like:

```
iptr =
    (int *) search((void *)table, MAXLEN, sizeof(int),
                   cmpint, &i);
```

We can take advantage of header files and macros to make search easier to use. First, we create a header file, search.h, that provides the necessary prototypes and defines a macro, SEARCH, to hide the underlying type casting. This file is shown in Figure 9.17. The search function itself is placed in search.c, which is shown in Figure 9.18.

Then, we place any necessary comparison functions in a file of their own and create a header file, cmpfunc.h, that provides prototypes for these functions and defines macros for searching tables of a particular type. In this case, we have one comparison function, cmpint, so we define one macro, INTSEARCH, for searching a table of ints. The header file is shown in Figure 9.19. The file containing cmpint is shown in Figure 9.20.

And finally, we make the file containing the call to search include cmpfunc.h. Now using search is a breeze. We can search a table of ints with

```
tptr = INTSEARCH(table, MAXLEN, &t);
```

The revised program containing this search is shown in Figure 9.21.

This much work probably isn't warranted to avoid writing a set of functions to do linear searches of different data types. But fast searches and sorts involve complicated algorithms that we don't want to have to reimplement for every data type. For these, the method outlined in this section provides a useable interface with a minimum of effort.

```
/*
 * The search function.
 */
#include <stddef.h>
#include "search.h"

void *search(void *tabptr, int n, int size,
             int (*funcptr)(void *, void *), void *tarptr)
{
  char *ptr, *endptr;                    /* byte pointers */

  ptr = (char *) tabptr;
  endptr = ptr + size * (n - 1);
  for (; ptr <= endptr; ptr += size)
    if ((*funcptr)((void *)ptr, tarptr) == 0)
      return (void *) ptr;               /* found it */
  return NULL;                           /* failure, return null */
}
```

Figure 9.18   gsearch.c—The generic search function.

```
/*
 * Header for file containing comparison functions.
 */
#include "search.h"

#define INTSEARCH(table,items,tptr) \
        SEARCH(int, table, items, tptr, cmpint)

extern int cmpint(void *xptr, void *yptr);
```

Figure 9.19   cmpfunc.h—Header file to make it easier to use the generic search function.

EXERCISES

9–16 Provide a nice interface for searching arrays of `chars` and arrays of `doubles`.

9–17 Provide a nice interface for using the `qsort` library function with arrays of `ints`, arrays of `chars`, and arrays of `doubles`.

9–18 Provide a set of function for manipulating arrays. This set should include `walk_array`, which applies a function to every array element, and `map_array`, which is just like `walk_array`, but it quits if the function it applies returns zero. Provide a nice interface for using them with arrays of `ints` and arrays of `doubles`.

```
/*
 * Comparison function for integers.
 */
#include "cmpfunc.h"

int cmpint(void *xptr, void *yptr)
{
  int x, y;

  x = * (int *) xptr;
  y = * (int *) yptr;
  return x - y;
}
```

Figure 9.20 cmpfunc.c—The comparison function.

```
/*
 * Generic table search using our nice interface to the
 * search function.
 */
#include <stdio.h>
#include <stddef.h>
#include "cmpfunc.h"

#define MAXLEN 20

main()
{
  int i, table[MAXLEN];
  int t;                   /* target */
  int *tptr;               /* ptr to target's position in table */


  for (i = 0; i < MAXLEN; i++)
    table[i] = i;                    /* some initial values */
  while (scanf("%d", &t) == 1)
    if ((tptr = INTSEARCH(table, MAXLEN, &t)), tptr == NULL)
      printf("Search failed.\n");
    else
      printf("Search found %d at position %d\n", t, tptr - table);
  return 0;
}
```

Figure 9.21 testsrch.c—The main program using the generic search function.

10 MULTIDIMENSIONAL ARRAYS

So far our programs have needed only simple, one-dimensional arrays. In this chapter we introduce two-dimensional arrays, concentrating on how we can use pointers to gain performance improvements. We present several programs that manipulate two-dimensional arrays using traditional array subscripting, and then rewrite them more efficiently using pointers. We also briefly cover three- and higher-dimensioned arrays. The chapter concludes by implementing the Game of Life, once with array subscripting and once using pointers. This chapter contains much detail, but studying it carefully will result in faster programs and a thorough understanding of important fine points of the language.

10.1 TWO-DIMENSIONAL ARRAYS

We declare two-dimensional arrays by enclosing the bounds of each dimension separately in brackets. The declaration

```
#define  MAX_STUDENTS   10
#define  MAX_TESTS       3
    . . .
int   scores[MAX_STUDENTS][MAX_TESTS];
```

defines `scores` to be a two-dimensional array of `int`s containing a total of 30 elements. We usually think of the first dimension as representing the rows of a matrix and the second as the columns, so we have declared `scores` to have 10 rows of 3 columns each. One use of `scores` would be to hold the test scores for students in a class. Each row corresponds to the test scores for a particular student, each column corresponds to the scores for a particular test.

As you might have guessed, we access the elements of two-dimensional arrays using double sets of brackets. The first index selects the row, the second selects the column within that row. Each dimension of the array can be indexed from zero to its maximum size minus one, so the legal indexes for `scores` range from `scores[0][0]` to `scores[9][2]`.

We illustrate two-dimensional arrays with a simple program, shown in Figure 10.1, that reads items into a two-dimensional array and then prints them. Two functions do most of the work. `read_scores` reads the items into the array, and `print_scores`

```
/*
 * Read and print student scores, one student per line.
 */
#include <stdio.h>
#include "ioscores.h"

#define MAX_STUDENTS 10

main()
{
  int scores[MAX_STUDENTS][MAX_TESTS];

  if (read_scores(scores, MAX_STUDENTS) == MAX_STUDENTS)
    print_scores(scores, MAX_STUDENTS);
  else
    printf("Couldn't read all students successfully\n");
  return 0;
}
```

Figure 10.1 tstscrs.c—A main program that uses read_scores and print_scores.

```
/*
 * ioscores.h -- Prototypes for score manipulating functions.
 */
#define MAX_TESTS 3

extern int read_scores(int s[][MAX_TESTS], int maxrow);
extern void print_scores(int s[][MAX_TESTS], int maxrow);
```

Figure 10.2 ioscores.h—Header file containing the prototypes for our input and output functions.

prints them, one row per line. Each input line contains a single score, with all of the scores for a given student preceding those of the next. Each output line contains the test scores for a particular student. Both functions use two variables, student and test, to index the array; student selects the row and test selects the element within that row. We place the prototypes for these functions in ioscores.h, shown in Figure 10.2. The functions themselves are in the file ioscores.c, shown in Figure 10.3.

read_scores and print_scores are straightforward—except for their first parameter declaration.

```
    int s[][MAX_TESTS]
```

```
/*
 * ioscores.c -- Functions to read and print a 2-d array.
 */
#include <stdio.h>
#include "ioscores.h"
#include "inout.h"                      /* from chapters 8 and 9 */

#define  MAXLEN    80

int read_scores(int s[][MAX_TESTS], int maxrow)
{
  int student, test;
  char line[MAXLEN + 1];

  for (student = 0; student < maxrow; student++)
    for (test = 0; test < MAX_TESTS; test++)
      if (getline(line, MAXLEN) == -1 ||
            sscanf(line, "%d", &s[student][test]) != 1)
        return -student;   /* negative return is problem */
  return maxrow;   /* read all scores we're supposed to */
}

void print_scores(int s[][MAX_TESTS], int maxrow)
{
  int student, test;          /* our indices */

  for (student = 0; student < maxrow ; student++)
    for (test = 0; test < MAX_TESTS; test++)
      printf("%d%c", s[student][test],
                (test != MAX_TESTS - 1) ? ' ' : '\n');
}
```

Figure 10.3   ioscores.c—Reading and printing test scores using conventional array subscripting.

To be able to subscript a two-dimensional array correctly, the compiler needs to know the number of columns in each row, and we must provide it in the array's parameter declaration. But as with one-dimensional arrays, when we pass a two-dimensional array as a parameter, we are really only passing a pointer—a pointer to its first *row*—and the compiler need not know how many rows the array has.

Internal Representation of Two-Dimensional Arrays

Two-dimensional (2D) arrays are stored in "row major" order, as illustrated in Figure 10.4. That is, the elements of the first row are stored consecutively in memory, then the elements of the second row, and so on. When we refer to an array element, as with `scores[7][2]`, the compiler finds the element's location from the two subscripts and its knowledge of the number of columns in each row. Using our earlier

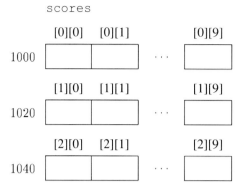

Figure 10.4 Internal representation of two-dimensional array; here, `scores`.

declaration of `scores`, and assuming that `scores` starts at location 1000, we find `scores[7][2]` at

> &`scores[0][0]` + *words for 3 × 7 elements in rows 0 through 6*
>   + *words for the 2 elements preceding it in row 7*

or

$$1000 + 21 \times sizeof(int) + 2 \times sizeof(int)$$

which is 1046. In general, we find `scores[i][j]` at

> &scores[0][0] + i × MAX_TESTS × sizeof(int) + j × sizeof(int)

Why do we care about the internal layout of two-dimensional arrays? Because it allows us to traverse them with pointers as though they were giant one-dimensional arrays, which leads to more efficient programs. Figure 10.5 contains a small program that uses a function `init_2d` to initialize to zero all of the elements in a large two-dimensional array. The constants defining the size of the array are in the header file shown in Figure 10.6, along with a function prototype for `init_2d`.

We've provided two versions of this function. The first, shown in Figure 10.7, uses two indices, `x` and `y`, and traditional two-dimensional array subscripting. The second, shown in Figure 10.8, uses a single pointer, `ptr`. We initialize it to the address of the array's first element with

> ptr = &table[0][0];

We then repeatedly increment the pointer, placing a zero in the item it points to, until it is equal to the address of the array's last element,

> &table[MAXROWS - 1][MAXCOLS - 1]

This pointer version takes approximately one-third the time of the first version, a significant savings.

```
/*
 * Initialize two-d array to zero.
 */
#include <stdio.h>
#include "init.h"

main()
{
  int table[MAXROWS][MAXCOLS];

  printf("initializing...\n");
  init_2d(table, 0);
  printf("...done\n");
  return 0;
}
```

Figure 10.5 init.c—A program that uses the function init_2d to initialize a two-dimensional array's elements to zero.

```
/*
 * init.h -- Header file for program to initialize two-d array
 */

#define MAXROWS 150
#define MAXCOLS 200

extern void init_2d(int table[][MAXCOLS], int value);
```

Figure 10.6 init.h—The header file used by init_2d.

Initializing Two-Dimensional Arrays

We can initialize two-dimensional arrays in the same way we initialize their one-dimensional counterparts: by following their declaration with a list of values enclosed in braces. For example,

```
int square[3][3] = {1, 1, 1, 2, 2, 2, 3, 3, 3};
```

initializes the elements in square's first row to one, those in its second row to two, and those in its third row to three. The problem with using this form is that it is not immediately apparent which values go with which elements. We can initialize two-dimensional arrays row by row, by surrounding the elements in each row with braces. The declaration

```
int square[3][3] = {{1,1,1}, {2,2,2}, {3,3,3}};
```

is a more readable equivalent to the previous one.

```
/*
 * Array-subscripting version.
 */
#include "init.h"

void init_2d(int table[][MAXCOLS], int value)
{
  int x, y;

  for (x = 0; x < MAXROWS; x++)
    for (y = 0; y < MAXCOLS; y++)
      table[x][y] = value;
}
```

Figure 10.7 init1.c—Array-subscripting version of init_2d.

```
/*
 * Pointer-indexing version.
 */
#include "init.h"

void init_2d(int table[][MAXCOLS], int value)
{
  int *ptr = &table[0][0];
  int *endptr = &table[MAXROWS - 1][MAXCOLS - 1];

  for (; ptr <= endptr; *ptr++ = value)
    ;
}
```

Figure 10.8 init2.c—Pointer-indexing version of init_2d.

Since the compiler can determine the size and structure of an array from the values we provide, we don't have to specify its first dimension (the number of rows). We can rewrite the above declaration of square as

```
int square[][3] = {{1,1,1}, {2,2,2}, {3,3,3}};
```

Missing values are set to zero by default, so there is no need to supply values for all array elements. The declaration

```
int square[3][3] = {{1,1}, {1}};
```

initializes the first two elements of the first row and the first element in the second row to one, and all other elements to zero. Unfortunately, there is no way to initialize only selected rows. The simplest way to initialize rows that do not require initialization themselves, but precede rows that do, is to initialize their first element to zero.

EXERCISES

10–1 Write a function, `read_student`, that reads in a student identification number, followed by the student's test scores. The student number should be used to select the row in the array. Implement an appropriate error-testing and flagging mechanism.

10–2 Write a function, `print_tests`, that prints the elements of `scores`, one column per line. Each line of output contains all of the scores for a particular test.

10–3 Write a function to determine whether a particular square two-dimensional array is a magic square (all rows, columns, and diagonals add to the same value).

10–4 Write a function to determine whether a particular square two-dimensional array is an identity matrix (ones on the diagonal; zeros everywhere else). Can you write this function, treating the array as though it were one-dimensional?

10.2   POINTERS AND TWO-DIMENSIONAL ARRAYS

The name of a two-dimensional array, like the name of a one-dimensional array, is the address of the array's first element or, more precisely, a pointer to its first *row*. As we discovered in Chapter 6, any array access is automatically converted to an equivalent pointer expression. Whenever we reference an element in a two-dimensional array using two subscripts, C converts the array access into an equivalent pointer expression. `scores[i][j]`, for example, is converted into the equivalent pointer expression

```
*(*(scores + i) + j)
```

Figure 10.9 shows how this bizarre-looking expression obtains the value of scores(i)(j). The rest of this section clarifies why this expression works, and how we can use pointers to efficiently traverse two-dimensional arrays.

Traversing Columns

We will illustrate the relationship between pointers and two-dimensional arrays with a simple function, `test_avg`, that computes the average of the values in a given column of an array. The call

```
test_avg(scores, MAX_STUDENTS, i)
```

returns the average of the `i`th column in the first `MAX_STUDENTS` rows, which is the average score on a particular test. `test_avg` works correctly only if `i` is less than `MAX_TESTS`, but to simplify things we don't bother with error checking.

Figure 10.10 contains a main program that uses `test_avg` to compute the average of each of the columns in the array. We've written two versions of `test_avg` itself. Once again, the first version, shown in Figure 10.11, uses array subscripting, and the second, shown in Figure 10.12, uses pointers.

When we declare a two-dimensional array, the array name is declared as a constant pointer to the array's first row. *Warning: The name of a two-dimensional array is not a pointer to the first item in it.* As an example,

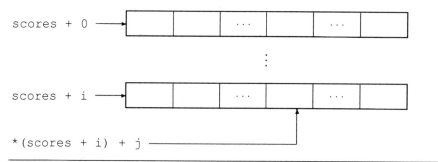

Figure 10.9 Using `*(*(scores + i) + j)` to access `scores[i][j]`.

```
/*
 * Read scores and print average on each test.
 */
#include <stdio.h>
#include "ioscores.h"

#define MAX_STUDENTS   10

main()
{
  int scores[MAX_STUDENTS][MAX_TESTS];
  int i;
  double test_avg(int s[][MAX_TESTS], int rows, int n);

  if (read_scores(scores, MAX_STUDENTS) == MAX_STUDENTS)
    for (i = 0; i < MAX_TESTS; i++)
      printf("Average on test %d is %.2lf\n",
             i, test_avg(scores, MAX_STUDENTS, i));
  else
    printf("Couldn't read all students successfully\n");
  return 0;
}
```

Figure 10.10 testavg.c—A main program to use `test_avg` to compute the average of each of the columns.

```
/*
 * Array-subscripting version of our function to compute
 * the average of a column in a 2d array.
 */
#include "ioscores.h"

double test_avg(int s[][MAX_TESTS], int rows, int n)
{
  double sum = 0.0;               /* column total */
  int    i;                       /* row index */

  for (i = 0; i < rows; i++)
    sum += s[i][n];
  return sum / rows;
}
```

Figure 10.11 tstavg1.c—An array-subscripting version of test_avg.

```
    int scores[MAX_STUDENTS][MAX_TESTS];
```

allocates space for a two-dimensional array, and defines scores as a pointer to the array's first row. When we pass scores as a parameter, we are passing a pointer to its first row. In test_avg we declare this parameter as

```
    int (*rowptr)[MAX_TESTS]
```

That is, as a pointer to an array of MAX_TESTS ints. We need the parentheses around *rowptr because * has lower precedence than []. Without them, as in

```
    int *rowptr[MAX_TESTS];
```

rowptr would be declared as an array of MAX_TESTS elements, each a pointer to an int.

Because pointer arithmetic is done in units of the pointed-to thing, incrementing a pointer to a row makes it point to the next row. This allows us to traverse a two-dimensional array by initializing a pointer (rowptr) to the first row of the array and incrementing the pointer (rowptr++) each time we need to get to the next row. But once we have a pointer to a row, we still need a way to access its elements. Fortunately, dereferencing a pointer to an array gives the array, or more accurately, a pointer to the array's first element. This means that since rowptr points to a particular row, *rowptr is a pointer to that row's first element. We use *rowptr as though it were the name of an array (the array containing the MAX_TESTS elements in that row), so (*rowptr)[n] accesses the nth element in the row, as shown in Figure 10.13.

We compiled and ran both versions on several different computers. On the average, the pointer version took less than two-thirds the time of the straightforward array-subscripting version. Why is there so much improvement? Normally when we do a two-dimensional array access, such as scores[i][j], to locate the desired

```
/*
 * Pointer-indexing version of our function to compute the
 * average of a column in a 2d array.
 */
#include "ioscores.h"

double test_avg(int (*rowptr)[MAX_TESTS], int rows, int n)
{
    double sum = 0.0;              /* column total */
    int (*endptr)[MAX_TESTS];      /* will point to last row */

    for (endptr = rowptr + rows; rowptr < endptr; rowptr++)
        sum += (*rowptr)[n];
    return sum / rows;
}
```

Figure 10.12   tstavg2.c—A pointer-indexing version of test_avg.

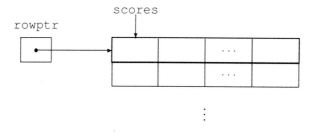

(*a*) rowptr starts off pointing to the first *row* in scores.

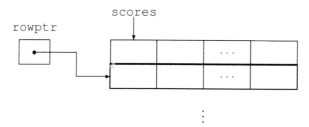

(*b*) Incrementing rowptr causes it to point to the next row of scores.

Figure 10.13   What happens when we increment a pointer to a row.

```
/*
 * Read scores and print average for each student.
 */
#include <stdio.h>
#include "ioscores.h"

#define MAX_STUDENTS 10

main()
{
  int i, n;
  int scores[MAX_STUDENTS][MAX_TESTS];
  double student_avg(int s[][MAX_TESTS], int n);

  if ((n = read_scores(scores, MAX_STUDENTS)) == MAX_STUDENTS)
    for (i = 0; i < MAX_STUDENTS; i++)
      printf("Average for student %d is %.2lf\n",
             i, student_avg(scores, i));
  else
    printf("Only %d students read successfully\n", -n);
  return 0;
}
```

Figure 10.14 rowavg.c—A program that prints the average of each of the rows in a two-dimensional array.

element, the compiler must do the complicated address calculation we saw earlier. This calculation first figures out which row the element is in, then where it is in that row. But when we use the row pointer, (*rowptr)[n], the compiler already knows which row the element is in, eliminating a major portion of the address calculation. Later exercises show how we can improve this function even further.

Traversing Rows

We can use pointers to process rows as well as columns. Figure 10.14 is a program that uses a new function, student_avg, to compute the average of a row. Figure 10.15 and Figure 10.16 contain array-subscripting and pointer-indexing versions of student_avg, respectively.

When we use pointers, we traverse a row of a two-dimensional array just as we traverse a one-dimensional array: We initialize a pointer to the row's first element and increment it until it points to the row's last element.

Again we find a large performance improvement. The pointer version takes less than one-third the time of the array-subscripting version. Why? Because we now access the various elements within a row simply by incrementing a pointer—completely eliminating any address calculations.

```
/*
 * Compute row average using array subscripting.
 */
#include "ioscores.h"

double student_avg(int s[][MAX_TESTS], int n)
{
  int i = 0;                      /* index to next row */
  long sum = 0;                   /* total so far */

  for (; i < MAX_TESTS; sum += s[n][i++])
    ;
  return (double) sum / MAX_TESTS;
}
```

Figure 10.15 rowavg1.c—An array-subscripting version of student_avg.

```
/*
 * Compute row average using pointer indexing.
 */
#include "ioscores.h"

double student_avg(int s[][MAX_TESTS], int n)
{
  int  *colptr = &s[n][0];             /* ptr to first element */
  int  *endptr = colptr + MAX_TESTS;   /* ptr to last element */
  long sum = 0;                        /* total so far */

  for (; colptr < endptr; sum += *colptr++)
    ;
  return (double) sum / MAX_TESTS;
}
```

Figure 10.16 rowavg2.c—A pointer-indexing version of student_avg.

Accessing Rows

We just wrote a specialized function to compute the average of a row within a two-dimensional array. But suppose that we already have a function, avg_table, that can compute the average of a one-dimensional array. How can we use it and save ourselves the trouble of writing our earlier function? Easily—we just pass the function the address of the first element in the desired row, along with the number of elements in that row. To sum up the values in row five, for example, we use

```
avg_table(&scores[5][0], MAX_TESTS)
```

It turns out there is an even more concise way to provide the address of the first element in a row. We simply follow the array name with a single subscript: the row number. So we can rewrite the call above as

```
avg_table(scores[5], MAX_TESTS)
```

This works because `scores[5]` is exactly equivalent to `&scores[5][0]`. In general, `scores[i]` is equivalent to `&scores[i][0]`. To see why, remember that C turns any array access into a pointer expression. So `scores[i]` is turned into `*(scores + i)`. Adding `i` to `scores` gives us a pointer to the `i`th row. And dereferencing it gives us a pointer to the first element in the `i`th row. Use whichever form you find most understandable.

Figure 10.17 contains a new version of our earlier program to compute the average student score. This version uses `avg_table`.

EXERCISES

10-5 Rewrite `read_scores` and `print_scores` to use pointers.

10-6 Write a function, `print_2d_rev`, that prints the values in a two-dimensional array in reverse order, last row first and first row last. First, write it using the usual array subscripting; then rewrite it so that the rows are indexed with a pointer. Finally, rewrite it so that all elements are indexed with pointers. Which of the three versions is the fastest?

10-7 Write a function, `sort_scores`, that takes two arguments: `scores`, a two-dimensional array of `int`s, and `n`, the column to sort on. The array should be sorted so that the nth column is sorted from low to high.

10-8 We can improve `test_avg` by treating it as a one-dimensional array and traversing it with a pointer. We initialize a pointer to the nth column, and increment by `MAX_TESTS` to access the nth column of subsequent rows. Make this improvement.

10-9 Write a fast function to initialize an identity matrix. An identity matrix has ones on the diagonal and zeros everywhere else.

10-10 Write a fast function to compare two two-dimensional arrays. The function should return the subscript of the first place where the arrays differ.

10-11 Write a generic function for traversing a two-dimensional array. This function is passed pointers to the first and last elements in the array, the number of rows and columns in it, and a function to execute once for each array element.

10-12 In general, at compile time we don't know how many columns we'll have in a two-dimensional array. We can get around this problem by using a one-dimensional array that contains the same number of elements required by our two-dimensional array. Write macros that let us do this conveniently. We need macros to declare the array, and to access an element in it.

10-13 Write a function that dynamically allocates a two-dimensional with the appropriate number of rows and columns. Any program that uses this function will have to declare the array it returns as a single pointer, and not as a two-dimensional array.

```
/*
 * Read scores and print average for each student.
 */
#include <stdio.h>
#include "ioscores.h"

#define MAX_STUDENTS 10

main()
{
  int i;
  int scores[MAX_STUDENTS][MAX_TESTS];
  double avg_table(int *ptr, int n);

  if (read_scores(scores, MAX_STUDENTS) == MAX_STUDENTS)
    for (i = 0; i < MAX_STUDENTS; i++)
      printf("Average for student %d is %.2lf\n",
             i, avg_table(scores[i], MAX_TESTS));
  else
    printf("Couldn't read students successfully\n");
  return 0;
}

/*
 * Compute the average of an array with "n" elements
 */
double avg_table(int *ptr, int n)
{
  long sum = 0;                  /* holds total */
  int *endptr = ptr + n - 1; /* pointer to last element */

  for (; ptr <= endptr; sum += *ptr++)
    ;
  return (double) sum / n;
}
```

Figure 10.17 avgtab.c—A second version of our program to print average student scores.

10.3   THREE-DIMENSIONAL ARRAYS

It turns out that C also allows three and higher-dimensioned arrays. We declare, initialize, and subscript these as we do for two-dimensional arrays. For example,

```
#define MAX_CLASSES   2
#define MAX_STUDENTS 10
#define MAX_TESTS     3
     . . .
  int classes[MAX_CLASSES][MAX_STUDENTS][MAX_TESTS];
```

```
/*
 * Read and print student scores, one student per line.
 */
#include <stdio.h>
#include "ioclass.h"       /* for read_scores/write_scores */

#define MAX_CLASSES   2

main()
{
  int classes[MAX_CLASSES][MAX_STUDENTS][MAX_TESTS];

  if (read_classes(classes, MAX_CLASSES) == MAX_CLASSES)
    print_classes(classes, MAX_CLASSES);
  else
    printf("Couldn't read all classes successfully\n");
  return 0;
}
```

Figure 10.18 classes.c—A program to read and print three-dimensional arrays.

declares a three-dimensional array holding 60 elements organized into 2 two-dimensional arrays of 10 rows and 3 columns each. We could use it to store the test scores for students in two different classes, with each of the two-dimensional arrays holding the scores for the students in one class. As you may have guessed, the name of a three-dimensional array is defined as a pointer to the first two-dimensional array inside it.

We access three-dimensional arrays using three subscripts; classes[0][1][2] refers to the third column of the second row of the first two-dimensional array. Or, in plain English, the third test score of the second student in the first class.

N-Dimensional Arrays and Parameters

When we declare an N-dimensional array parameter, we must supply all dimensions except the first, regardless of what N actually is. This is because when we pass an N-dimensional array as a parameter, we really pass a pointer to the first $N - 1$ dimensional array it contains.

Figure 10.18 provides an example. It contains a program that reads values into classes and then prints them. To do so, it makes use of the two functions, read_classes and print_classes. Both functions are passed two parameters: a three-dimensional array and the number of two-dimensional arrays it contains.

We've placed their prototypes in the file ioclass.h and the functions in io-class1.c. These files are in Figure 10.19 and Figure 10.20, respectively. The functions expect to be passed classes, but since we're really only passing a pointer,

```
/*
 * ioclass.h -- Prototypes for functions to read and print
 *              lass scores.
 */
#include "ioscores.h"

#define MAX_STUDENTS 10

int read_classes(int c[][MAX_STUDENTS][MAX_TESTS], int n);

void print_classes(int c[][MAX_STUDENTS][MAX_TESTS], int n);
```

Figure 10.19   ioclass.h—Header file defining prototypes for our input/output functions.

we can declare the prototypes using either array indexing notation

```
    void print_classes(int c[][MAX_STUDENTS][MAX_TESTS], int n)
```

or pointer notation.

```
    void print_classes(int (*ptr)[MAX_STUDENTS][MAX_TESTS],
                        int n)
```

The latter form declares `ptr` as a pointer to a two-dimensional array. But because `read_classes` and `print_classes` use array-indexing to process `classes`, we've used the first form.

N-Dimensional Arrays and Pointers

`read_classes` uses `read_scores` to read the scores into the individual two-dimensional arrays in `classes`. It first reads in the scores for the first class, then the scores for the second class, and so on. And `print_classes` does something similar, except that it uses `print_scores` to print these arrays. But both `read_scores` and `print_scores` expect a pointer to the first row in a two-dimensional array. How can we provide them with one, when we're working our way through a three-dimensional array?

In C, any N-dimensional array is treated as though it were an array of $N - 1$-dimensional arrays. A two-dimensional array, for example, is treated as an array of one-dimensional arrays, a three- or higher dimensional array is treated as an array of two-dimensional arrays, and so on. By treated, we mean several things. First, regardless of the number of dimensions in it, any array is stored as a single one-dimensional array, as shown in Figure 10.21. Second, any array name is defined as a constant pointer to the first N-1-dimensional array within it. `classes`, for example, is defined as a pointer to its first two-dimensional array. Third, any N-dimensional array access is translated into a sequence of pointer additions and dereferences, with one addition and dereference for each dimension of the array. And finally, pointer

```
/*
 * Functions to read/print a 3d array.
 */
#include <stdio.h>
#include "ioclass.h"

int read_classes(int c[][MAX_STUDENTS][MAX_TESTS], int n)
{
  int class;

  for (class = 0; class < n; class++)
    if (read_scores(c[class], MAX_STUDENTS) != MAX_STUDENTS)
      return -class;
  return class;
}

void print_classes(int classes[][MAX_STUDENTS][MAX_TESTS], int n)
{
  int class;

  for (class = 0; class < n; class++)
  {
    print_scores(classes[class], MAX_STUDENTS);
    putchar('\n');
  }
}
```

Figure 10.20   ioclass1.c—Array-subscripting versions of our functions to read and print a three-dimensional array.

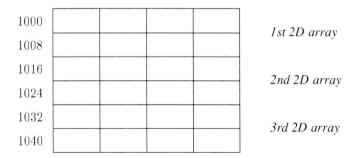

Figure 10.21   Storage layout for a 3 × 2 × 4 three-dimensional array of ints.

```
/*
 * Pointer version of our 3D array reading and printing
 * functions.
 */
#include <stdio.h>
#include "ioclass.h"

int read_classes(int (*ptr)[MAX_STUDENTS][MAX_TESTS], int n)
{
  int (*saveptr)[MAX_STUDENTS][MAX_TESTS] = ptr;
  int (*endptr)[MAX_STUDENTS][MAX_TESTS];

  for (endptr = ptr + n - 1; ptr <= endptr; ptr++)
    if (read_scores(*ptr, MAX_STUDENTS) != MAX_STUDENTS)
      return saveptr - ptr;   /* negative value on error */
  return ptr - saveptr;
}

void print_classes(int (*ptr)[MAX_STUDENTS][MAX_TESTS], int n)
{
  int (*endptr)[MAX_STUDENTS][MAX_TESTS];

  for (endptr = ptr + n - 1; ptr <= endptr; ptr++)
  {
    print_scores(*ptr, MAX_STUDENTS);
    putchar('\n');
  }
}
```

Figure 10.22 ioclass2.c—Pointer-indexing versions of our input and output functions.

arithmetic with any N is calculated based on the size of the $N - 1$-dimensional arrays it contains.

One result of all these features is that classes[i] is automatically translated into *(classes + i), which is a pointer to the first row in ith two-dimensional array within classes. And that's exactly what we want to pass to read_scores and print_scores.

```
    print_scores(classes[i], MAX_STUDENTS);
```

Another result is that we can use pointers to traverse any *N*-dimensional array— although the code can be confusing and hard to read when we traverse higher-dimensioned arrays. If we have a pointer ptr that points to some two-dimensional array within classes, incrementing it with ptr++ causes it to point to the next two-dimensional array. And because dereferencing a pointer gives a pointer to the array's first element, *twodptr is a pointer to the first row of a two-dimensional array and **twodptr is a pointer to its first element. As an example, Figure 10.22 contains pointer versions of read_scores and print_scores.

Initializing Two-Dimensional Arrays

We can initialize any array, regardless of its dimension, by providing a brace-enclosed list of elements. If any of these elements are arrays, we can also enclose their values in braces. For example

```
int x[2][3][4] =
   {{{ 0,  1,  2,  3}, { 4   5,  6,  7}, { 8,  9, 10, 11}},
    {{ 2, 13, 14, 15}, {16, 17, 18, 19}, {20, 21, 22, 23}}};
```

As with any array, we could just list the array's elements.

```
int x[2][3][4] =
   { 0,  1,  2,  3,  4,  5,  6,  7,  8,  9, 10, 11,
    12, 13, 14, 15, 16, 17, 18, 19, 20, 21, 22, 23};
```

EXERCISES

10-14 Write a function, read_classes, that reads in the test scores for each class. Assume that the number of students in the class precedes the scores for that class.

10-15 Write a function that sums the elements in a three-dimensional array using a single pointer to traverse the array. How much faster is this than using three-dimensional subscripting?

10-16 Repeat the previous exercise for some higher-dimensioned array. Can you generalize your function to work on any *N*-dimensional array? Explain why the function is substantially faster when pointers are used.

10-17 Write a function to print the total values of each of the two-dimensional arrays contained in classes. There should be one value output for each two-dimensional array in classes.

10-18 Repeat the previous exercise using pointer subscripting. Is this version significantly faster? Why or why not?

10-19 Write a function to calculate and print the average of each test by class. The order of output should be all the scores for the first test in the first class, then all the scores for the first test in the second class, and so on.

10.4   CASE STUDY—THE GAME OF LIFE

To illustrate the power of pointers, we conclude this chapter by implementing the Game of Life, a simulation of population growth dynamics developed by British mathematician John Horton Conway. In Life, a board represents the world, and each cell represents a single location. A cell is either empty or contains a single inhabitant. The game uses three simple rules to model population changes:

Survival An inhabited cell remains inhabited if exactly two or three of its neighboring cells are inhabited. (A cell has eight neighbors, four adjacent orthogonally and four adjacent diagonally.)

Death An inhabited cell becomes uninhabited if fewer than two or more than three of its neighbors are inhabited.

Birth An uninhabited cell becomes inhabited if exactly three of its neighbors are inhabited.

All births and deaths occur simultaneously, together causing the creation of a new generation.

Figure 10.23 shows some sample configurations and their first few generations. Sadly, most worlds eventually become uninhabited. But not to worry—some worlds do develop a stable, inhabited population, while others reach a dynamically stable population that oscillates between states. We usually let the game run until a stable population is reached.

An Array-Subscripting Version

life divides nicely into three separate tasks: reading an initial description of a world, computing the next generation, and displaying the next generation. Each of these corresponds to a single function, placed into its own source file. getworld reads a description of a world and records its initial inhabitants. nxtworld examines the current generation to determine the contents of the next generation. And putworld displays the current generation.

The world itself is a two-dimensional array of BOOLEANs; TRUE indicates an inhabited cell, FALSE an uninhabited cell. For convenience and readability, we've used typedef to define a type WORLD as a two-dimensional array of BOOLEANs. This typedef appears in life.h, shown in Figure 10.24, along with definitions of various useful constants for the size of the world and the characters used to display cells. To simplify counting a cell's neighbors, a WORLD actually includes room for an extra uninhabited border of cells. The displayable world is 20 by 78, the space available on the average display after writing a border around the world and a line identifying the current generation.

The main program is shown in Figure 10.25. After using getworld to read the initial world, it computes the requested number of generations, using putworld to display the current world, and nxtworld to calculate the contents of the next world. It stops when it has displayed the requested number of generations or the world has reached a stable state.

getworld, shown in Figure 10.26, is straightforward but lengthy. It reads the desired number of rows and columns for the world, the number of generations to compute and display, and the positions of each of the world's inhabitants. Its size stems from its extensive error checking. getworld prompts for each expected input, reading input lines with our old friend getline, and using sscanf to grab the various values. It verifies that each value is in range and writes an appropriate error

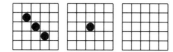

(*a*) A game that dies out quickly.

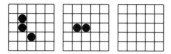

(*b*) A game that dies a little more slowly.

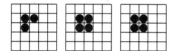

(*c*) A game that rapidly reaches a stable state.

(*d*) A game that reaches an oscillating state.

Figure 10.23   Various worlds for the game of Life and their population changes.

message when one isn't. The input reading stops when the user enters the end-of-file character (a control-*Z*).

nxtworld, shown in Figure 10.27, computes the next generation by examining each cell of the current generation, counting how many inhabited neighbors it has, and applying the rules to see whether it is inhabited in the next generation. All changes must be made at the same time, so nxtworld is passed a pointer to another world where it can record the next generation. When nxtworld returns, the main program makes the next world the current world. nxtworld updates a counter of inhabitants and returns a count of changes so the main program can easily determine if a generation has been annihilated or has reached a stable state.

The last piece of the program, putworld, shown in Figure 10.28, displays the

```
/*
 * life.h -- Header file for life game.
 */
#include "defs.h"                    /* from chapter 9 */
#include "boolean.h"                 /* from chapter 9 */

#define   BORDER    'X'              /* border around world */
#define   MARKER    '#'              /* occupied cell marker */
#define   MAXROW    20               /* legal rows: 1..20 */
#define   MAXCOL    78               /* legal columns: 1..78 */
#define   NUMROWS   (MAXROW + 2)     /* extra cells surrounding */
#define   NUMCOLS   (MAXCOL + 2)     /* (simplify neighbors) */
#define   MAXLEN    80               /* longest input line */

typedef BOOLEAN WORLD[NUMROWS][NUMCOLS];
typedef BOOLEAN (*ROWPTR)[NUMCOLS];
```

Figure 10.24   life.h—Header file for the life program.

current generation. It indicates the world's border with X's, inhabited cells with a #, and uninhabited cells with a blank.

To put all these different pieces together to form the Game of Life, we supply a simple project file.

    life.c (life.h)
    getworld.c (life.h)
    nxtworld.c (life.h)
    outworld.c (life.h)
    inout.obj

A New Version Using Pointers

All of the functions in the current version of life use traditional two-dimensional array subscripting. That makes it easy to write and easy to understand—and unbearably slow. When simulating large worlds, there is an annoying pause between successive generations. So we need to speed up the program. But how?

It turns out that the program spends most of its time in nxtworld, calculating the next generation. nxtworld is devoted almost entirely to traversing a two-dimensional array. Since it accesses rows sequentially within the array, and array elements sequentially within rows, we should find a performance improvement if we use pointers to traverse the array.

The pointers we need are diagrammed in Figure 10.29. The basic idea is straightforward. We traverse the current world one row at a time, using a single row pointer, cwrptr (which stands for current world row pointer). We use another pointer, colptr, to process each row. The tricky part comes when we count the neighbors—we need to access elements in the rows preceding and following the one pointed to

```
/*
 * life.c -- Main program for the Game of Life.
 */
#include "life.h"
#include "inout.h"  /* from Chapters 8/9 */

int rows;           /* # of rows actually used */
int cols;           /* # of columns actually used */
int inhabs;         /* # of inhabitants */
int gen;            /* current generation */
int endgen;         /* last generation */

main()
{
  static WORLD world1, world2; /* need two worlds */
  ROWPTR currptr = world1,  /* pointers to current */
         nextptr = world2,  /*   and future worlds */
         temp;              /* used to exchange worlds */
  int getworld(WORLD x);
  BOOLEAN nxtworld(WORLD x, WORLD y);
  void putworld(WORLD x);

  if (!getworld(currptr))          /* bad input */
  {
    putline("Quitting early.  Couldn't read input world\n");
    return 1;                      /* error exit */
  }
  for (gen = 1; gen <= endgen; gen++)
  {
    putworld(currptr);
    if (!inhabs || !nxtworld(currptr, nextptr))
      break;     /* no inhabitants or stable world */
    SWAP(temp, currptr, nextptr);
  }
  putline(!inhabs ? "All inhabitants are dead"
                  : ((gen <= endgen) ? "Stable" : "Finished"));
  return 0;
}
```

Figure 10.25   life.c—The main program for the Game of Life.

by cwrptr. To do this efficiently, we need two additional pointers, pcolptr and ncolptr, that point to the same column as colptr, but in the rows before and after it. As we traverse the current row, we increment these pointers as well. The pointer version of nxtworld is shown in Figure 10.30.

A small change in our earlier project file is sufficient to compile the new version.

life.c (life.h)
getworld.c (life.h)
nxtwrld2.c (life.h)

```c
/*
 * getworld.c -- Handle life game input.
 */
#include "life.h"
#include "inout.h"

int getworld(WORLD world)
{
  char buffer[MAXLEN + 1]; /* input line */
  int c, r;                /* next position */
  extern int rows, cols, endgen, inhabs;

  FOREVER                    /* for (;;) */
  {
    printf("Enter ROWS COLS GENERATIONS: ");
    if (getline(buffer, MAXLEN) == -1)
      return 0;              /* no inhabitants */
    if (sscanf(buffer, "%d %d %d", &rows, &cols, &endgen) != 3)
      putline("Didn't enter three numeric values.");
    else if (!INRANGE(1, MAXROW, rows))
      printf("Row %d isn't between 1 and %d\n", rows, MAXROW);
    else if (!INRANGE(1, MAXCOL, cols))
      printf("Column %d isn't between 1 and %d\n", cols, MAXCOL);
    else
      break;                 /* got valid values */
  }
  FOREVER                    /* for (;;) */
  {
    printf("Enter position of next cell: ");
    if (getline(buffer, MAXLEN) == -1)
      break;                   /* end of input */
    if (sscanf(buffer, "%d %d", &r, &c) != 2)
      printf("Didn't enter two numeric values\n");
    else if (!INRANGE(1, rows, r) || !INRANGE(1, cols, c))
      printf("%d, %d is out of range\n", r,c);
    else if (world[r][c])
      printf("%d, %d is already inhabited\n", r, c);
    else
    {
      world[r][c] = TRUE;
      inhabs++;
    }
  }
  return inhabs;
}
```

Figure 10.26 getworld.c—A function to read the description of the world.

```
/*
 * nxtworld.c -- Handle computing the next generation.
 */
#include "life.h"

BOOLEAN nxtworld(WORLD curr, WORLD next)
{
  int changed = 0;          /* cells that changed */
  int r, c;                 /* row, column index */
  int neighbors;            /* count neighbors */
  extern int inhabs, rows, cols;

  for (inhabs = 0, r = 1; r <= rows; r++)
   for (c = 1; c <= cols; c++)
   {
     neighbors =  curr[r - 1][c - 1] + curr[r - 1][c] +
                  curr[r - 1][c + 1] + curr[r + 1][c - 1] +
                  curr[r + 1][c]     + curr[r + 1][c + 1] +
                  curr[r][c - 1]     + curr[r][c + 1];

     if ((neighbors == 3) || (neighbors == 2 && curr[r][c]))
     {
       next[r][c] = TRUE;
       inhabs++;
     }
     else
       next[r][c] = FALSE;
     changed += next[r][c] != curr[r][c];
   }
  return changed;
}
```

Figure 10.27 nxtworld.c—Compute the next generation.

outworld.c (life.h)
inout.obj

This new version takes less than one-fifth the time of the original, an impressive savings. We leave making similar changes to putworld as an exercise for the reader.

EXERCISES

10–20 Rewrite putworld to traverse its array using pointers. How much more efficient is it?

10–21 Modify life so that it dynamically allocates space for the world. Can you make this version run even faster than ours?

```
/*
 * outworld.c -- Handle printing the generation.
 */
#include "life.h"

#define PUTBORDER()  for (c = 0; c <= cols + 1; c++) \
                         putchar(BORDER)

void putworld(WORLD world)
{
  int c, r;
  extern int rows, cols, gen, endgen;

  printf("Generation %d out of %d\n", gen, endgen);
  PUTBORDER();
  putchar('\n');
  for (r = 1; r <= rows; r++)
  {
    putchar(BORDER);
    for (c = 1; c <= cols; c++)
      putchar(world[r][c] ? MARKER : ' ');
    putchar(BORDER);
    putchar('\n');
  }
  PUTBORDER();
  putchar('\n');
  putchar('\n');
}
```

Figure 10.28 outworld.c—Display the contents of a generation.

10-22 Modify life to check for an oscillating stable state in any of the last 10 generations. Use a three-dimensional array to hold the necessary generations.

10-23 Write a program to produce a histogram of its input.

10-24 Modify your solution to the previous exercise to produce a vertical histogram.

10-25 Write a library package that allows us to write to a two-dimensional array rather than the screen. The idea is that we perform numerous updates on this array (such as adding and deleting characters) and then do a library call to replace the screen with the contents of the array. Modify life so that it uses this package.

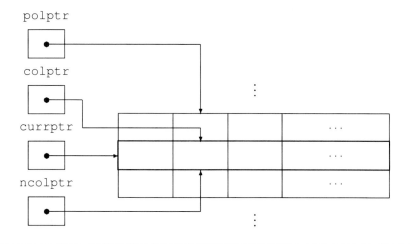

Figure 10.29   The pointers used to traverse a Life world.

```c
/*
 * nxtwrld2.c -- Compute next generation.
 */
#include "life.h"

BOOLEAN nxtworld(ROWPTR curr, ROWPTR next)
{
  extern int rows, cols, inhabs;
  ROWPTR cwrptr = curr + 1;         /* first row current world */
  ROWPTR nwrptr = next + 1;         /* first row next world */
  ROWPTR endcwrptr = cwrptr + rows; /* last row current world */
  int changed = 0;                  /* changes to world */
  int neighbors;                    /* # of cell neighbors */


  for (inhabs = 0; cwrptr <= endcwrptr; cwrptr++, nwrptr++)
  {
    BOOLEAN *colptr   = *(cwrptr) + 1;       /* current col */
    BOOLEAN *pcolptr  = *(cwrptr - 1) + 1; /* previous row */
    BOOLEAN *ncolptr  = *(cwrptr + 1) + 1; /* next row */
    BOOLEAN *endcolptr = colptr + cols;      /* last col */
    BOOLEAN *nxtptr   = *(nwrptr) + 1;       /* next world col */

    while (colptr < endcolptr)
    {
      neighbors =  pcolptr[-1] + pcolptr[0] + pcolptr[1] +
                   ncolptr[-1] + ncolptr[0] + ncolptr[1] +
                   colptr[-1] + colptr[1];
      if ((neighbors == 3) || (neighbors == 2 && *colptr))
      {
        *nxtptr = TRUE;
        inhabs++;
      }
      else
        *nxtptr = FALSE;
      changed += *nxtptr != *colptr;
      colptr++, nxtptr++, pcolptr++, ncolptr++;
    }
  }
  return changed;       /* nonzero if not stable */
}
```

Figure 10.30   nxtwrld2.c—A new version of `nxtworld` that uses pointers to traverse the array.

11 ARRAYS

OF

POINTERS

Our earlier programs have made ample use of arrays, but only arrays of integers, characters, and reals. This chapter examines another kind of array, arrays of pointers, by examining arrays of strings and arrays of pointers to functions. We show how to initialize these arrays at compile time, how to construct them dynamically at run time, and how to use pointers to efficiently traverse them. Because some of these arrays require complex type declarations, we also digress into a detailed description of C's declaration syntax. The chapter concludes with an implementation of a fast string sorting program.

11.1   ARRAYS OF POINTERS—RAGGED ARRAYS

Two-dimensional arrays contain the same number of elements in each row. But this can be inefficient. Suppose we define a table that holds character strings for each of the days of the week.

```
char day_table[][10] =
  {
    {'m', 'o', 'n', 'd', 'a', 'y', '\0'},
    {'t', 'u', 'e', 's', 'd', 'a', 'y', '\0'},
    {'w', 'e', 'd', 'n', 'e', 's', 'd', 'a', 'y', '\0'},
    {'t', 'h', 'u', 'r', 's', 'd', 'a', 'y', '\0'},
    {'f', 'r', 'i', 'd', 'a', 'y', '\0'},
    {'s', 'a', 't', 'u', 'r', 'd', 'a', 'y', '\0'},
    {'s', 'u', 'n', 'd', 'a', 'y', '\0'}
  };
```

We have to declare each row to hold enough characters in the longest string. The result is that we waste space in the rows containing shorter strings, as shown in Figure 11.1*a*.

What we really want is an array whose rows can vary in length, called a *ragged array*. We can build a ragged array out of an array of pointers. Each entry in the array is a pointer to a string. We initialize the array by supplying a list of character strings.

m o n d a y \0
t u e s d a y \0
w e d n e s d a y \0
t h u r s d a y \0
f r i d a y \0
s a t u r d a y \0
s u n d a y \0

(*a*) Using a 2D array of characters. Space is wasted at the end of each row.

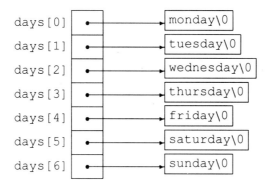

(*b*) An array of pointers to strings. No space is wasted for each string, but we use additional space to store the pointers.

Figure 11.1 Two different ways to have a table of character strings.

```
char *days[] =
{
    "monday",  "tuesday", "wednesday", "thursday",
    "friday", "saturday", "sunday"
};
```

This declares days to be an array of pointers to characters. Since we omitted the subscript from days, the compiler makes the array just large enough to hold the elements we supply. In this case, the compiler allocates space for an array containing

```
/*
 * Main program that prints a table of days.
 */
#include <stdio.h>

char *days[] =
{
  "monday",  "tuesday", "wednesday", "thursday",
  "friday", "saturday", "sunday"
};

main()
{
  void print_strings(char *table[], int n);

  print_strings(days, sizeof(days)/sizeof(char *));
  return 0;
}
```

Figure 11.2   prdays.c—A program to print a table of days of the week, one per line.

seven pointers, and assigns each element a pointer to the corresponding string, as shown in Figure 11.1*b*.

We access the elements of an array of pointers in the same way we access the elements of an array of any other type. Figure 11.2 contains a program that prints a table of strings, one per line. To do so, it makes use of a function, print_strings, shown in Figure 11.3, that is passed a table of character strings, along with the number of entries in the table, and prints the pointed-to strings, one per line. We print days with

```
    print_strings(days, 7);          /* print days */
```

Or, as an alternative, we can let the compiler calculate the number of items in days for us.

```
    print_strings(days, sizeof(days)/sizeof(char *));
```

We do the actual printing with printf, using the %s formatting code. The %s format expects a pointer to the first character of a string, which is exactly what each of the entries in days is.

Accessing Individual Items

We haven't yet worried about accessing the individual items within a ragged array. In print_strings, for example, we simply pass a pointer to the beginning of the row (or string) we want to print. But imagine for the moment that we didn't have printf, and instead had to use putchar to write the characters. Then we would need to access each of the items in the string, as we've done in Figure 11.4.

```
/*
 * Print a table of strings, one per line.
 */
#include <stdio.h>

void print_strings(char *table[], int n)
{
  int i;

  for (i = 0; i < n; i++)
    printf("%s\n", table[i]);
}
```

Figure 11.3 prstr1.c—A function to print a table of character strings, one per line. This version uses printf to write the strings.

```
/*
 *  Print a table of character strings, one per line.
 */
#include <stdio.h>

void print_strings(char *table[], int n)
{
  int i, j;

  for (i = 0; i < n; i++)
  {
    for (j = 0; table[i][j] != '\0'; j++)
      putchar(table[i][j]);
    putchar('\n');
  }
}
```

Figure 11.4 prstr2.c—Another version of our array printing function; this one uses putchar.

It turns out that we can use two-dimensional subscripting to access individual characters in the array. If table is an array of pointers to characters, table[i][j] refers to the jth character in its ith row. This seems strange—especially since table is only a one-dimensional array. Why does it work? table[i] is a pointer to the first character in a string, so adding j to it gives a pointer to the jth character in the string. So we can access the jth character with

        *(table[i] + j)

which is equivalent to table[i][j], as shown in Figure 11.5. More concretely,

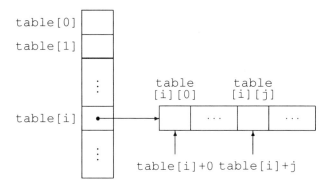

Figure 11.5 Accessing an individual character within an array of pointers to character strings.

since `table[0]` is a pointer to the string `monday`, we can access the `'n'` with `table[0][2]`.

Although we can use two-dimensional accessing, we saw in the previous chapter it is better to avoid it wherever possible and use pointers instead. Figure 11.6 does just that in a new version of `print_strings`. This version uses a single pointer to a character, `ptr`, to traverse the individual strings it prints. We initialize `ptr` to point to the string's first character with

    ptr = table[i]

This initialization works because each entry in `table` is a pointer to the first character in a string. Once we've assigned that pointer to `ptr`, we can traverse the string as we would traverse any other string. We dereference the pointer to access the individual characters and increment it to go onto the next one. This version takes about one-fourth the time of the previous version, making it worthwhile to try to eliminate two-dimensional array accessing wherever possible.

Dynamic String Allocation

Up to now, we have initialized our arrays of pointers at compile-time, leaving the task of allocating space for the pointed-to strings to the compiler. We did this because we knew the contents of the table at compile-time. But what about when the table's entries aren't known at compile time? We might, for example, want to write a program that sorts its input lines. The program must read its input into some kind of table in order to sort it. But what kind? Since some input lines are likely to be much longer than others, we don't want to use a two-dimensional array—it would waste too much

```
/*
 * Print an array of character strings, this time using
 * pointers.
 */
#include <stdio.h>

void print_strings(char *table[], int n)
{
  int i;
  char *ptr;

  for (i = 0; i < n; i++)
  {
    for (ptr = table[i]; *ptr != '\0'; ptr++)
      putchar(*ptr);
    putchar('\n');
  }
}
```

Figure 11.6 prstr3.c—Our third version of print_strings. This one uses a pointer to traverse each of the strings.

space. Instead, we need to read the input into an array of strings, and allocate the space for each entry ourselves.

We write this sorting program at the end of the chapter. For now we illustrate run-time string allocation with a simple program, shown in Figure 11.7, to reverse its input. This program uses two functions: read_strings, which reads its input into a table of strings, one line per string; and print_rev_strings, which prints the table of strings in reverse order. Their prototypes are shown in Figure 11.8; the functions themselves are shown in Figure 11.9.

read_strings takes three parameters: an empty table of pointers, a pointer to a counter, and a maximum array size. It fills in the table with pointers to dynamically allocated strings containing the input lines, and the pointed-to counter with the number of lines read. read_strings uses getline to read each input line into an array line, and the Turbo C string library function strdup to make a dynamically allocated copy of line. strdup takes a pointer to a string, calls malloc to allocate enough storage for a copy of the string, and then uses strcpy to copy the string into the newly allocated storage. When it is all through, it returns a pointer to this newly created copy. read_strings takes this pointer and places it in the table. The result is that each table entry becomes a pointer to a block of storage allocated by malloc and containing a single input line, as shown in Figure 11.10. print_rev_strings is similar to print_strings, except that it prints the last element first and the first element last.

This program relies heavily on dynamic allocation, and on a small microcomputer might easily run out of storage. What should we do when strdup (really malloc)

```
/*
 * Reverse input, one line at a time.
 */
#include <stdio.h>
#include <stddef.h>
#include "strtab.h"

#define   MAXLINES      100      /* lines to store */

main()
{
  int lines;                      /* input lines read */
  char *strings[MAXLINES];       /* array of pointers to strings */
  if (!read_strings(strings, &lines, MAXLINES))
  {
    printf("Ran out of memory after reading %d lines\n\n", lines);
    return 1;       /* out of memory error */
  }
  if (lines == MAXLINES)
    printf("More than %d lines of input\n\n", lines);
  print_rev_strings(strings, lines);
  return 0;
}
```

Figure 11.7   revinp.c—A program to reverse its input, one line at a time. It reads the input into a table of character strings and then prints that table in reverse order.

```
/*
 * strtab.h -- Prototypes for the functions that manipulate the
 *             string table.
 */

void print_rev_strings(char *table[], int n);
int read_strings(char *table[], int *ptr, int max);
```

Figure 11.8   strtab.h—Header file containing prototypes for our functions to read and print tables of strings.

```
/*
 * strtab.c -- Functions to read and print string table.  These
 *             use getline/putline (Chapter 8).
 */
#include <string.h>
#include <stddef.h>        /* for NULL */
#include "inout.h"         /* prototypes for getline/putline */

#define  MAXLEN   80       /* chars per line */

int read_strings(char *table[], int *cntptr, int max)
{
  char *sptr;                /* ptr to space allocated by malloc */
  char line[MAXLEN + 1]; /* current input line */

  *cntptr = 0;
  while ((getline(line, MAXLEN)) != -1 && *cntptr < max)
    if ((sptr = strdup(line)) != NULL)
      table[(*cntptr)++] = sptr;
    else
      return 0;            /* error, couldn't allocate */
  return 1;                /* alright */
}

void print_rev_strings(char *table[], int n)
{
  while (--n >= 0)
    putline(table[n]);
}
```

Figure 11.9 strtab.c—Contains our functions to read and print tables of strings.

fails? Unfortunately, there is no general solution, so we have to decide what to do on a case-by-case basis. In this program, when strdup fails, we stop reading input, print a warning, and then print what we've read.

EXERCISES

11-1 Write a function, print_tab_len, that prints the length of each character string in a table of character strings.

11-2 Write a function, reverse_tab, that reverses each of the strings in a table of character strings. (Hint: Use strrev from Chapter 8 to reverse the individual strings.)

11-3 Using normal array subscripting, write a function search_tab that takes two arguments—a table of character strings, table, and a character string, target. The function

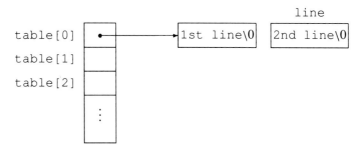

(*a*) After placing the first input line in the table and then reading the second input line.

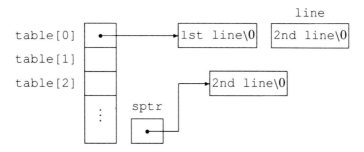

(*b*) After allocating space for the second input line, and copying the line into that space.

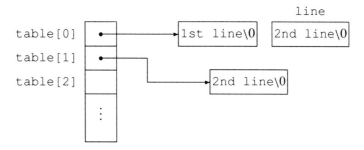

(*c*) After copying the line into that space, and hooking the line into the table.

Figure 11.10 How we can build a table of strings dynamically at run time.

```
/*
 * Print a table of character strings, one per line.
 */
#include <stdio.h>

void print_strings(char **ptr, int n)
{
  char **endptr = ptr + n - 1;  /* pointer to last element */

  for (; ptr <= endptr; ptr++)
    printf("%s\n", *ptr);
}
```

Figure 11.11 prstr4.c—Yet another version of print_strings. This one uses a pointer to traverse the table of strings.

searches char_tab for target and returns a pointer to the matching string in the table. If target is not in the table, NULL is returned.

11-4 Write a function, month_name, that takes a single-integer argument and returns a pointer to the associated month name. The month names should be kept in a static table of character strings local to the function.

11-5 Write a program, tail, that prints the last *n* lines of its input (*n* is a program constant). Use the program in Figure 11.7 as a model. Make reasonable assumptions about the maximum line length and the maximum number of lines in the input (using the constants MAXLEN and MAXLINES, respectively). Be sure to test the return from malloc and do something reasonable if it fails.

11.2   POINTERS AND ARRAYS OF POINTERS

In the previous section, we used normal array subscripting to traverse our arrays of pointers. We can, however, use pointers to traverse these arrays, just as we can with any other array. We do so in Figure 11.11, a new version of print_strings, our function to print a table of strings, one per line.

Like before, we call print_strings by passing it an array of pointers to strings and the number of items in the array. But now the array parameter is declared differently.

```
print_strings(char **ptr, int n)
```

We've seen that when we pass an array, we are really passing a pointer to its first element. So when we pass an array of ints, we pass a pointer to an int. When we pass an array of chars, we pass a pointer to a char. And when we pass an array of pointers to character, we pass a pointer to a pointer to a char, ptr's type.

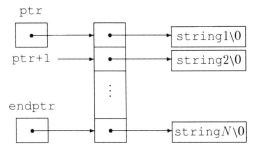

Figure 11.12   Using pointers to traverse an array of strings.

`print_strings` uses our standard method for traversing an array: We set a pointer, `ptr`, to the array's first element, and keep incrementing it until it points past the array's last element, as shown in Figure 11.12. Each time through the loop we want to pass `printf` a pointer to the first character in the next string in the table. Since `ptr` points to the string, we have to dereference it when we pass it to `printf`.

```
printf("%s\n", *ptr);
```

`search_strings`, a function to search a string for any one of a group of strings, provides a second example. The function takes three arguments: a string, and pointers to the beginning and end of an array of pointers to strings. `search_strings` returns nonzero if any of the strings in the array occur in the first string. To search for any one of the `days` in an input line we could use

```
search_strings(line, days, days + 6)
```

Just like `print_strings`, it runs a pointer through a table of strings. The only difference is that now, instead of calling `printf`, it calls `search_str`, the function we wrote earlier to search one string for another string. Figure 11.13 contains the prototypes for `search_strings` and `search_str`, Figure 11.14 contains the functions, and Figure 11.15 contains a main program that shows how these functions are used.

Both `print_strings` and `search_strings` simply pass a pointer to the next string to a function that processes it—they don't access the individual characters in the strings directly. But we can't always avoid doing that. Imagine once again that we don't have `printf`. Figure 11.16 is yet another version of `print_strings` that uses `putchar` to print the individual characters in the strings, this time using a pointer to traverse the array.

```
/*
 * srchstr.h -- Prototypes for search_strings/search_str
 */

char *search_strings(char *string, char **ptr, char **endptr);
int search_str(char *s, char *t);
```

Figure 11.13 srchstr.h—A header file defining prototypes for our string searching functions.

```
/*
 * srchstr.c -- Given a string, and an array of patterns,
 *       `         see if the string contains any of the patterns
 */
#include <stdio.h>
#include <stddef.h>
#include "srchstr.h"

char *search_strings(char *string, char **ptr, char **endptr)
{
  for (; ptr <= endptr; ptr++)
    if (search_str(string, *ptr) != -1)
      return *ptr;          /* return pointer to match */
  return NULL;              /* no match */
}

int search_str(char *s, char *t)        /* find t in s */
{
  char *p = s;

  for (; *p != '\0'; p++)               /* run p through s */
  {
    char *x = p, *y = t;  /* ptr to next part of s, start of t */

    for (; *x != '\0' && *y != '\0' && *x == *y; x++, y++)
      ;
    if (*y == '\0')
      return p - s;                     /* where t is in s */
  }
  return -1;                            /* failure */
}
```

Figure 11.14 srchstr.c—The function `searchstr` for searching a table of strings. It uses a pointer to traverse the table.

```
/*
 * Main program to test search_strings
 */
#include <stdio.h>
#include "srchstr.h"
#include "inout.h"          /* prototypes for getline/putline */

#define MAXLEN 80

char *days[] = {"Monday", "Tuesday", "Wednesday", "Thursday",
                "Friday", "Saturday", "Sunday"};

const int numdays  = sizeof(days)/sizeof(days[0]);

main()
{
  char line[MAXLEN + 1];
  char *match;

  while (printf("Enter line: "), getline(line, MAXLEN) != -1)
    if ((match = search_strings(line, days, days + numdays - 1))
          != NULL)
      printf("Line contains: %s\n", match);
    else
      putline("Line didn't contain any days.");
  return 0;
}
```

Figure 11.15 testsrch.c—A main program using our string-searching functions.

We access the individual characters in the string the same way we accessed individual elements when we had a row pointer. If pointer is used to traverse the array of strings,

```
(*ptr)[j]
```

refers to the jth character in whatever string `ptr` points to. Why? Because `ptr` points to an item in the table of pointers, `*ptr` is the value of that pointer, which means that `*ptr` is the address of the first character in the string. Adding j to `*ptr` gives us the address of the jth character, and dereferencing that with

```
*(*ptr + j)
```

gives us the character. This expression is equivalent to the previous one. Figure 11.17 shows what's going on here in more detail.

EXERCISES

```
/*
 * Print a table of character strings, one per line.
 */
#include <stdio.h>

void print_strings(char **ptr, int n)
{
  char **endptr = ptr + n - 1;  /* pointer to last element */
  int j;                        /* index to individual item */

  for (; ptr <= endptr; ptr++)
  {
    for (j = 0; (*ptr)[j] != '\0'; j++)
      putchar((*ptr)[j]);
    putchar('\n');
  }
}
```

Figure 11.16 prstr5.c—Our final version of print_strings, which traverses the array using a pointer, and accesses the characters in the strings indirectly through that pointer.

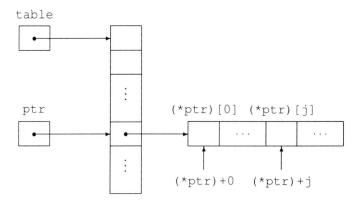

Figure 11.17 Accessing individual characters within an array of pointers to character strings when we're using a pointer to traverse them.

11-6 Rewrite `read_strings` to use a pointer to traverse the array. Do the same for `print_rev_strings`.

11-7 Modify the insertion sort program of Chapter 2 to work with strings instead of integers. Write both array subscripting and pointer indexing versions.

11-8 Write a string-searching function on top of the generic sequential search function in Chapter 7.

11-9 Modify the binary search function in Chapter 7 to work with strings.

11.3 **COMMAND-LINE ARGUMENTS**

There is one important application of arrays of pointers that we haven't yet examined—they are used to store command-line arguments. In DOS, when we run a program such as tc or tcc, we often provide not only the program's name but also the names of files the program will work with, as in

>   tcc queues.c inout.c handle.c wait.c

This is a *command line*, and its individual components are *command-line arguments*.

How can a program access these arguments? It turns out that when main is called, it is passed two parameters that together describe the command line that invoked the program. The first is the number of arguments on the command line. The second is an array of pointers to strings containing the various arguments. Traditionally, these are called `argc` and `argv`, respectively. We declare main's parameters in the same way as those of any other function.

```
int main(int argc, char *argv[])
```

By convention, `argv[0]` points to the first character of the program's name, so `argc` is always at least one (on pre-3.0 versions of DOS, the program's name is the null string). We use the other arguments to specify various program options, as well as external files the program should process. Exactly what constitutes a command line argument various from system to system, but individual arguments are usually delimited by white space. If you want white space within an argument, place the argument in quotes.

To illustrate command-line argument processing, we write a program, called echo, that simply prints each of its arguments minus the program name. If, in DOS, we supply the command line

>   echo turbo c is really wonderful

echo's output is

>   turbo c is really wonderful

For this command line, when main is called, argc is six and argv is an array of six pointers to strings, as shown in Figure 11.18.

Figure 11.19 contains a first implementation of echo, one that's straightforward, using array indexing to traverse argv and printing each of the entries except the

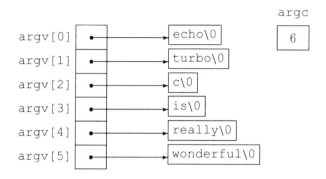

Figure 11.18 The initial values of `argc` and `argv` for our sample use of echo.

first (the program name). We write the arguments separated by spaces, with the last argument followed by a new line.

Figure 11.20 contains a second, trickier version. It uses a pointer to traverse `argv`. We can do this because `argv`, like any other array parameter, is really a pointer to the array's first element. We use our standard technique, setting a pointer, `argptr`, to point to the first array item we're interested in (in this case, the one pointed to by `argv + 1`, since we want to skip the program name), repeatedly incrementing it to traverse the arguments, and stopping when it points to the end of the array.

As with other arrays, using a pointer to traverse command-line arguments makes our programs run faster—but harder to read and understand. Either method of command-line-argument processing is acceptable, but master the pointer method, even if it isn't your favorite, as you will encounter it frequently in existing programs.

Command-Line Options

We'll illustrate the full power of command-line arguments with a program called ws, for word search. By default ws prints all of the lines in its input that contain any of the strings provided as its arguments. So, in DOS, typing the command line

> ws boolean true false < ws.c

prints any line in ws.c that contains the words "boolean", "true", or "false".

ws also allows some optional arguments. Traditionally, optional arguments begin with a dash ("-"). so ws's options are -n to print only those lines that don't match, -c to print only a count of those lines that do or don't match (depending on whether -n is used with it), and -l to precede its output with a line number.

```
/*
 * Echo arguments (using array subscripting).
 */
#include <stdio.h>

int main(int argc, char *argv[])
{
  int next;                     /* index to next argument */

  for (next = 1; next < argc; next++)
    printf("%s%c", argv[next], (next < argc - 1) ? ' ' : '\n');
  return 0;
}
```

Figure 11.19 echo1.c—Echo the program's arguments using array indexing.

```
/*
 * Echo arguments (using pointer indexing).
 */
#include <stdio.h>

int main(int argc, char *argv[])
{
  char **argptr = argv + 1;        /* ptr to first argument */
  char **endptr = argv + argc - 1; /* ptr to last argument */

  for (; argptr <= endptr; argptr++)
    printf("%s%c", *argptr, (argptr < endptr) ? ' ' : '\n');
  return 0;
}
```

Figure 11.20 echo2.c—Echo the program's arguments using pointer indexing.

>   ws -c boolean < ws.c   *count of lines that match*
>   ws -l -n boolean < ws.c *numbers, lines that don't match*

ws's design is typical of most programs that have options. The main program handles the options, and a separate function handles all the work, in this case doing the search. main first processes the optional arguments. We know we're done with the optional arguments when we encounter an argument that doesn't begin with a dash. When an argument does begin with a dash, we examine the next character and set a flag to record the option's value. An unrecognized option causes us to write an error message and quit. (Our program could be improved by allowing more than one

```c
/*
 * ws.c -- Search for strings provided in its arguments.
 */
#include <stdio.h>
#include "boolean.h"
#include "srchstr.h"
#include "inout.h"              /* prototypes for getline/putline */

#define MAXLEN 80

BOOLEAN number,                /* line number */
        nomatch,               /* print doesn't match lines */
        countonly;             /* just print match count */

main(int argc, char *argv[])
{
  char **argptr = &argv[1];        /* ptr to first real arg */
  char **endptr = &argv[argc - 1]; /* ptr to last arg */
  BOOLEAN badopt = FALSE;          /* bad option flag */
  void search_input(char **xptr, char **yptr);

  for (; argptr <= endptr && (*argptr)[0] == '-'; argptr++)
    if ((*argptr)[1] == '\0')
      badopt = TRUE;
    else
      switch ((*argptr)[1])
        {                       /* process next option */
          case 'C':
          case 'c':
                  countonly = TRUE;
                  break;
          case 'L':
          case 'l':
                  number  = TRUE;
                  break;
          case 'N':
          case 'n':
                  nomatch = TRUE;
                  break;
          default:
                  printf("ws: bad option %c\n", (*argptr)[1]);
                  badopt = TRUE;
        }
  if (badopt || argptr > endptr)                /* oops */
  {
    printf("usage: ws [-c][-l][-n] patterns...\n");
    return 1;
  }
  search_input(argptr, endptr);
  return 0;
}
```

```
/*
 * Do the actual search.
 */
void search_input(char **firstpatptr, char **lastpatptr)
{
  char line[MAXLEN + 1];        /* hold next line */
  long lines;                   /* count lines */
  long matched_lines = 0;       /* matched lines */

  for (lines = 1; getline(line, MAXLEN) != -1; lines++)
  {
    BOOLEAN found;

    found = search_strings(line, firstpatptr, lastpatptr) != NULL;
    if ((found && !nomatch) || (!found && nomatch))
    {
      matched_lines++;
      if (!countonly)
      {
        if (number)
          printf("%ld ", lines);
        putline(line);
      }
    }
  }
  if (countonly)
    printf("%ld\n", matched_lines);
}
```

Figure 11.21 ws.c—A program to search its input for the words provided as its arguments.

option to follow a single dash, but we leave that as an exercise.)

Once the options have been processed, we assume that any subsequent arguments are strings to process. We call a function search_input to do the searching, passing it pointers to the first and last arguments representing words to search for. It reads input lines with getline and uses search_strings to determine whether any of those words are in its input line. Like before, we use pointers to process the arguments. Figure 11.22 shows the relationships between the various pointers used to process the arguments.

Command-line options to control a program's functioning are a powerful and useful idea. Unfortunately, many programs use them to provide different and often unrelated features. These extra features are used infrequently, if at all, but they make the program significantly harder to read and debug. To avoid falling into this trap, first write a simple version of the program that performs its main task correctly. Options should be added only after the program has been used for a while, and adding certain

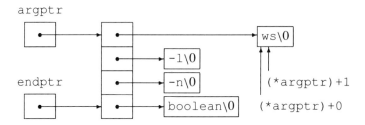

Figure 11.22 Processing the optional arguments. `argptr` points to the argument, `(*argptr)[i]` is the next character in the argument.

features will clearly make the program more useful.

EXERCISES

11-10 Add a -r option to `echo` that causes it to print its arguments in reverse order, First use array indexing, then use pointers.

11-11 Add two more options to `echo`: -n causes it to suppress the trailing newline, -s causes it to write each of its arguments on a separate line.

11-12 Write a program to count the number of words, lines, and characters in its input. Have options to request only a count of words, or only a count of lines, or only a count of characters.

11-13 Add a line-numbering option to our display program, `page` (Chapter 3). Also add an option that specifies the screen size.

11-14 Add three new options to the `uniq` program of Chapter 6. The first, `-c`, causes a count of the number of occurrences of any line of output to be printed before the line. The second, `-u`, causes only those lines that appear uniquely to be output. The last, `-d`, causes only those lines that are duplicated to appear in the output. What should `uniq` do when combinations of these options are specified?

11.4   ARRAYS OF POINTERS TO FUNCTIONS

Our arrays of pointers have contained only pointers to characters. But we can have arrays of pointers to any data type: pointers to `int`s, pointers to `float`s, or even pointers to functions.

We use arrays of pointers to functions in Figure 11.23, a program that prints a menu of choices

```
Your choices are:
        1) Add record
        2) Delete record
        3) Find record
        4) Print records
        5) Sort records
Or type a 0 to quit:
```

and then executes the function corresponding to the user's choice. The program keeps each menu entry in a table of strings

```
char *items[] =
{
  "Add record",  "Delete record",  "Find record",
  "Print records",  "Sort records"
};
```

and a pointer to each function in a table of functions.

```
extern void add_record(void), delete_record(void),
            find_record(void), print_records(void),
            sort_records(void);

void (*functable[])(void) =
{
  add_record, delete_record, find_record,
  print_records, sort_records
};
```

This declares `functable` as an array of pointers to functions that take no parameters and return no value. It also initializes it to hold pointers to five of these functions. We precede this initialization with prototypes for these functions so that the compiler knows they are function names and not variable names. In general, these functions would do things like add records to a data base, but for now we assume they simply print a message that the function has been called.

```
(*functable[choice - 1])();    /* execute the function */
```

Since `functable[choice - 1]` is a pointer to a function, dereferencing it and supplying an argument list executes the function to which it points.

EXERCISES

11-15 Modify our menu program so that it obtains the user's choice with `getdigit` rather than `getline`.

11-16 Write a program to manage a table of strings. The user should be able to add a string, delete a string, print a string, find all strings containing a particular string, sort the table of strings, and print the entire table. Let the user select choices from a menu.

```
/*
 * Simple menu program.
 */
#include "defs.h"
#include "inout.h"    /* once again, we use getline/putline */

#define MAXLEN 80

extern void add_record(void), delete_record(void),
            find_record(void), print_records(void),
            sort_records(void);

char *items[] =
{
  "Add record",  "Delete record",  "Find record",
  "Print records",  "Sort records"
};

void (*functable[])(void) =
{
  add_record, delete_record, find_record,
  print_records, sort_records
};

main()
{
  int choice;                        /* holds user's choice */
  int print_menu(char *table[], int n) ;
  int numitems = sizeof(items)/sizeof(char *);

  while ((choice = print_menu(items,numitems)) != 0)
    (*functable[choice - 1])();      /* execute the function */
  return 0;
}

int print_menu(char *table[], int n)
{
  int i;                             /* index */
  int num;
  char line[MAXLEN + 1];

  putline("Your choices are:");
  for (i = 1; i <= n; i++)
    printf("\t%d) %s\n", i, table[i - 1]);
  printf("Or type a 0 to quit: ");
  while (getline(line, MAXLEN) != -1)
    if (sscanf(line, "%d", &num) == 1 && INRANGE(0, n, num))
      return num;
    else
      printf("Enter a value between 0 and %d: ", n);
  return 0;
}
```

```
/*
 * The various functions (which simply print their names).
 */
void add_record()
{
  putline("In the add function");
}

void delete_record()
{
  putline("In the delete function");
}

void find_record()
{
  putline("In the find function");
} .

void print_records()
{
  putline("In the print function");
}

void sort_records()
{
  putline("In the sort function");
}
```

Figure 11.23   A program that prompts the user for a menu selection, and then uses the user's choice to select the appropriate function.

11.5   TYPE DECLARATIONS

We have presented a bewildering collection of types—arrays of pointers, pointers to arrays, pointers to functions, and so on—with each new type having a slightly more complicated syntax than the last. So far, you've simply had to memorize the form for the particular type you want to declare. Now it's time to explain the rationale underlying this seemingly senseless syntax, and to show you how to declare types of arbitrary complexity.

Declarators

A type declaration consists of a basic type followed by a *declarator*, and specifies the type of the identifier contained within the declarator. In the declaration

```
double (*funcptr)();
```

`double` is the basic type, `(*funcptr)()` is the declarator, and `funcptr` is the identifier contained in the declarator. As we saw earlier, this declares `funcptr` as a pointer to a function returning `double`.

The problem is to come up with the correct declarator. If we're declaring a variable with one of the basic types, it's simply a single identifier, as in

```
char x;               /* a character */
```

We can declare more complicated types by combining the identifier with a single `*`, `()`, and `[]`. Prefacing the identifier with `*` declares a pointer. Following it with `()`, possibly with an enclosed list of types, declares a function. And following the identifier with `[]` declares an array.

```
char *ptr;            /* pointer to a char */
char tab[MAX];        /* array of chars */
char func(int);       /* func takes an int, returns a char */
```

We declare more complex types, such as pointers to functions and arrays of pointers, by combining the pieces used to form the previous declarators.

```
char *tab[MAX];       /* an array of pointers to char */
char *func();         /* function returning ptr to char */
char (*funcptr)(int); /* ptr to func takes int, return char */
char (*rowptr)[10];   /* ptr to an array of 10 characters */
```

When we combine declarators, `*` has lower precedence than either `()` or `[]`, so to declare a pointer to an array or function, we have to use parentheses to override the normal precedence.

How do we declare even more complex types? It helps to think of the English description of an identifier's type as being composed of several pieces. Each piece of the description is either a basic type, "an array of," "a pointer to," or "a function returning." Suppose, for example, that we want to declare a table of pointers to functions, like the one we used in the previous section. We break its description into:

an array of   pointers to   functions taking `void` *and returning* `void`s

The last part of this description, `void`, is the base type of the identifier. To compose the declarator, we work through the description from left to right, examining each piece, deciding upon the C declarator for a variable with that type.

> `a[]`   `*p`   `f(void)`

Now we substitute the leftmost declarator for the identifier in the declarator to its immediate right.

> `*a[]`   `f(void)`

We repeat the process until only a single declarator remains, and then precede that declarator by the base type.

> `void (*a[])(void)`

Where did the parentheses come from? Because the precedence of `*` is less than that of either `()` or `[]`, we have to parenthesize pointer declarators when we substitute them in another declarator.

How do we understand complex type declarations? We take its declarator and find the innermost declarator within it, writing down its type. We then substitute an identifier for this innermost declarator, and repeat the process, until only a single identifier remains. At that point, we have determined the identifier's type. The hard part is locating the innermost declarator. The rule is that the innermost declarator is the identifier and an immediately following `[]` or `()`, or, if neither of these is present, an immediately preceding `*`. We ignore any parentheses surrounding the innermost declarator once we have determined its type.

To see how this works, suppose you were suddenly confronted with this confusing type declaration.

```
double *(*p[])(int, int)
```

Following the steps above results in:

Type Declaration	Center Piece	Resulting Type
`double *(*p[])(int, int)`	p[]	*an array of*
`double *(*s)(int, int)`	*s	*pointers to*
`double *f(int, int)`	f	*function returning*
`double *p`	p	*pointers to*
`double x`	x	`double`

The compiler can process these arbitrarily complex declarations—but most people can't. To keep declarations readable, it is a good idea to use `typedef` (Chapter 8) when declaring types more complex than arrays of pointers and pointers to arrays. A more readable way to declare a table of pointers to functions that take an `int` and a `double` and returning a `double` is:

```
typedef double (*PFD)(int,int);

PFD funcptr;
```

Type Specifications

When a declarator does not contain an identifier, we have a type specification instead of a variable declaration. These type specifications show up in three places: function prototypes, `sizeof`, and casts. The trick to writing a type specification is to first declare a variable of that type, and then omit the variable from the declaration. For example, we declare a pointer to a function returning a `double` with

```
double (*fp)();
```

So to find the number of bytes in a pointer to a function returning a `double`, we use

```
sizeof(double (*)())
```

Similarly, because we can declare a pointer to a row containing 10 elements as

```
int (*rowp)[10];
```

and a table of pointers to functions taking no arguments and returning `void` as

```
void (*functab[])(void)
```

we write the prototype for a function taking these values as arguments and returning an `int` as

```
int func(int (*)[10], void (*[])(void))
```

Type specifiers for casts, such as the one shown above, are difficult to read. Use `typedef` to simplify them.

```
typedef int (*ROWPTR)[10];   /* ptr to 10 element array */
typedef void (*VFP)(void);   /* ptr to void function */
    . . .
int func(ROWPTR, VFP);
```

EXERCISES

11-17 Write a function that walks through a table of pointers to functions, executing each function in turn, until one of them returns zero or all of the functions have been executed.

11-18 How do you declare a pointer to a pointer to a function returning a pointer to an `int`? An array of pointers to pointers to characters? A pointer to an array of 10 integers?

11-19 How would you cast an integer into a pointer to an array of pointers to functions returning `int`?

11.6   CASE STUDY—SORTING STRINGS

We conclude this long and depressingly detailed chapter with a short but surprisingly useful program that sorts its input using quicksort. We construct this program, shown in Figure 11.24, on top of the built-in `sort` function we first saw in Chapter 7. `qsort` does the sorting, all we have to provide are functions to build and print a table of strings, to compare two items in the table, and to handle any options.

To make the program more useful, we allow several options: -r reverses the sense of the sort, -b*N* begins sorting each string with the *N*th character in the string, and -l*N* limits the sort to a field of *N* characters.

The main program consists almost entirely of function calls. It uses a new function `handle_options` to process any optional arguments. `handle_options` is similar to the main function in the searching program we wrote earlier in the chapter. It's passed pointers to the first and last entries in `argv`, using the first pointer to traverse the argument array. When it encounters a -b or a -l, it uses `sscanf` to turn the subsequent characters into an integer. We could improve `handle_options` by making it do more error checking, as it currently ignores any unexpected characters.

```
/*
 * strsort.c -- String sorting program.
 */
#include <stdio.h>
#include <stdlib.h>
#include <string.h>
#include "boolean.h"
#include "strtab.h"

#define MAXLINES 1000
#define MAXLEN    80

typedef char *STRING;  /* ptr to 1st char in string */
typedef STRING *STRINGPTR;  /* ptr to ptr to 1st char */

BOOLEAN reverse;                    /* reverse sense of sort */
int     startcol = 0,               /* starting column */
        fieldlen = MAXLEN;          /* field length */

main(int argc, STRING argv[])
{
  STRING strings[MAXLINES];    /* input lines */
  int lines;                   /* count of input lines */
  int handle_options(STRINGPTR xptr, STRINGPTR yptr);
  void print_strings(STRING table[], int n);
  int sortcmp(const void *xptr, const void *yptr);

  if (argc > 1 || !handle_options(argv + 1, argv + argc - 1))
    return 1;  /* invalid arguments or options */
  if (!read_strings(strings, &lines, MAXLINES) && lines != 0)
  {
    printf("Ran out of memory after %d lines\n\n", lines);
    return 1;
  }
  if (lines == MAXLINES)
  {
    printf("More than %d lines of input\n\n", lines);
    return 1;
  }
  qsort((void *) strings, lines, sizeof(char *), sortcmp);
  reverse ? print_rev_strings(strings, lines)
          : print_strings(strings, lines);
  return 0;
}
```

```
/*
 * Handle various options.
 */
int handle_options(STRINGPTR argptr, STRINGPTR endptr)
{
  BOOLEAN goodopt = TRUE;      /* flag to indicate bad option */

  for (; argptr <= endptr && (*argptr)[0] == '-'; argptr++)
    if ((*argptr)[1] == '\0')
      printf("sort: missing option\n");
    else
      switch ((*argptr)[1])
        {                              /* process next option */
          case 'b':  if (sscanf(*argptr + 2, "%d", &startcol) != 1)
                       {
                         printf("sort: invalid starting column\n");
                         goodopt = FALSE;
                       }
                     break;
          case 'l':  if (sscanf(*argptr + 2, "%d", &fieldlen) != 1)
                       {
                         printf("sort: invalid field length\n");
                         goodopt = FALSE;
                       }
                     break;
          case 'r':  reverse = TRUE;  /* ignores anything */
                     break;           /*    after option */
          default:   printf("sort: bad option %c\n", *argptr[1]);
                     goodopt = FALSE;
        }
  if (argptr <= endptr)
  {
    printf("sort: extra arguments\n");
    goodopt = FALSE;
  }
  if (!goodopt)
    printf("Usage: sort [-r] [-bNUM] [-eNUM]\n");
  return goodopt;
}


int sortcmp(const void *xptr, const void *yptr)
{
  STRING x = * (STRINGPTR) xptr;
  STRING y = * (STRINGPTR) yptr;
  int i;

  for (i = 0; i < startcol && *x != '\0' && *y != '\0'; i++)
    x++, y++;
  return strncmp(x,y,fieldlen);
}
```

Figure 11.24 strsort.c—The heart of our sorting program.

The main program also uses several functions we wrote earlier in the chapter. `read_strings` reads the input into a table of strings, `print_strings` or `print_rev_strings` print the table. And it uses the library function `qsort` to sort it.

The main program has to pass a function to compare two values to `qsort`. Recall that `qsort` takes an array, the number of elements in it, the size of each element, and a pointer to a function that handles comparing array elements. While sorting, whenever it needs to compare two elements, it passes the comparison function pointers to two entries in this array. Since the entries in this array are pointers—specifically, pointers to the first character of a string—it is really passing our comparison function pointers to pointers to strings. The comparison function, `sortcmp`, dereferences these pointers to obtain pointers to the first characters in the strings to compare. It then increments these pointers until they point to the first character of the field upon which we sort, and compares these fields.

We've defined several types that keep our program readable,

```
typedef char *STRING;
typedef STRING *STRINGPTR;
```

`STRING` indicates a pointer to the first character to a string, `STRINGPTR` a pointer to a pointer to the first character in a string. To see how much these types help in making the program understandable, try to rewrite the program without using them.

EXERCISES

11-20 Modify the sorting program to have an option to sort in ascending or descending order. Add another option that allows it to sort numerically.

11-21 Write a generic quicksort, one that can not only sort integers and reals, but strings as well.

12 CONSTRUCTED TYPES

Arrays are the only data structure we have used so far. But arrays are limited—all their elements must have the same underlying type. In this chapter, we examine three new ways to represent collections of values: structures, unions, and enumerated types. We introduce structures, and show how they group together different values in a single variable. We introduce unions, and show how we can use them to have a single variable whose value varies in type. And finally, we introduce enumerated types, and show how they provide a convenient way to define many constants at one time. The chapter concludes with a small data base program for storing employee names and phone numbers that comes complete with a table-driven, menu-based front end.

12.1   STRUCTURES

Sometimes we want to combine data of different types into a single object. We might, for example, want to have a single variable hold an employee's name, employee number, phone number, and age. But we can't use an array because array elements all share the same underlying type. Instead, we must use a structure, which is similar to a Pascal record.

Defining Structures

Before we can use a structure, we must first define a structure type. We do so by following the keyword `struct` with the name of the structure type (called the *structure tag*) and declarations for each of the items it contains (called *fields*). We define a structure type to hold our employee information with

```
#define MAXNAME 40              /* longest name */

struct employee
{
  long number;                  /* employee number */
  char name[MAXNAME];           /* first and last name */
  char phone[13];               /* xxx-xxx-xxxx\0 */
  int age;                      /* age */
};
```

This declares a new type, `struct employee`, consisting of four fields: `number` (a `long`), `name` (an array of characters), `phone` (another array of characters), and `age` (a single `int`). Field names are in a special "name class" kept separate from variable names, so we can have field names that are the same as existing variable names, and we can use the same field name in different structure definitions without fear of conflict.

Once we've defined the structure type, we can declare variables with that type, as if it were one of C's built-in data types. For example,

```
struct employee emp;
```

declares a single variable, `emp`, with type `struct employee`. This forces the compiler to allocate at least enough storage for `emp` to hold the four fields within a `struct employee`. We can use structure variables like any others: we can assign to them, pass them to functions, and so on.

The fields within a structure can have any legal type, which means they themselves can be structures. The following

```
struct date                    /* to hold a single date */
{
  int month, day, year;
};

struct period                  /* to hold two dates */
{
  struct date start;           /* the starting date */
  struct date end;             /* the ending date */
}
```

defines a `date` structure type containing three integers, one each for the month, day, and year, and a `period` structure type that contains a starting and ending date. Following these definitions with

```
struct period x;
```

declares a variable `x` with two fields, `start` and `end`, each of which is a structure containing three integers.

Field Selection

Although it is convenient to treat a structure variable as a single unit, we also need a way to access its individual fields. To access a field, we follow the structure name with the field selection operator, '`.`', and the name of the desired field. Assuming that we've declared `emp` as a `struct employee`, we can assign values to `emp`'s fields with

```
emp.number = 1001;
emp.age = 22;
strcpy(emp.name, "merriweather, tammy");
strcpy(emp.phone, "818-555-1747");
```

The result is shown below.

	number	name	phone	age
emp	1001	merriweather, tammy\0	818-555-1747\0	22

The dot operator associates left to right. With x declared as a `struct period`, `x.start.month` refers to the month field within the start field of x. We can initialize x's fields with

```
x.start.month = 7;
x.start.day   = 20;
x.start.year  = 1981;
x.end.month   = 7
x.end.day     = 30;
x.end.year    = 1984
```

Compile-Time Initialization

Like other data types, we can initialize structures when we declare them. To initialize the fields of a structure, we follow the structure's declaration with a list containing values for each of its fields. We could initialize emp at compile time with

```
struct employee emp =
{
  1001,                          /* number */
  "merriweather, tammy",         /* name */
  "818-555-1747",                /* phone */
  22                             /* age */
};
```

This initializes the `number` field to `1001`, the `name` field to "`merriweather, tammy`," the `phone` field to "`818-555-1747`", and the `age` field to 22. Since the values for the `name` and `phone` fields are string constants, they are automatically terminated with a null character.

When we have fields that are themselves structures, we enclose the values of their fields in brackets.

```
static struct period x = { {7,20,1981}, {7,30,1984} };
```

We can omit the brackets surrounding a field when we provide all of its elements, but leaving them in clarifies which values are going to what fields.

Structures as Function Arguments

We can pass structures as arguments to functions. But unlike array names, which are always pointers to the start of the array, structure names are not pointers. When we pass a structure, the entire structure is copied. As a result, when we change a structure parameter inside a function, we don't affect its corresponding argument.

It turns out that we usually pass pointers to structures, rather than structures themselves. It is faster to pass a pointer, since the structure no longer has to be copied. This method is also more portable—although Turbo C allows structure parameters, many compilers don't.

Figure 12.1 illustrates both methods in a small program that declares, initializes, and prints the fields of several `struct employees`. We initialize the fields in the first employee, `emp`, by assigning them values at run time, and we print it by passing the entire structure to a function `write_emp`.

```
write_emp(emp);
```

We initialize the other employee, `other_emp`, at compile time rather than run time. Since we declare `other_emp` within `main`, we must declare it as `static`. We print `other_emp` by passing its address to a function `print_emp`.

```
print_emp(&other_emp);
```

The `printf` statements within `print_emp` must dereference the pointer to the structure, and then select the appropriate field. Assuming `ep` is a pointer to the structure, one way to do this is:

```
printf("Employee: %ld\n", (*ep).number);
```

We need parentheses when we dereference the pointer to the structure because the selection operator binds tighter (has higher precedence) than dereferencing. Without the parentheses, as in `*ep.number`, we're trying to dereference the value of a field in the structure (which doesn't make any sense in this case). It turns out, however, that dereferencing a pointer to a structure and selecting one of its fields is such a common operation that C provides a special shorthand operator for it, a right arrow, made up of a minus sign and a "greater than" symbol: `->`. We can use this operator to write the `printf` statements in `print_emp` more concisely, such as

```
printf("Employee: %ld\n", ep->number);
```

Structures and Operators

Only a few operators apply to structure variables. The first, `sizeof`, determines the number of bytes used by the structure. We could compute the size of a `struct employee` by taking the size of a variable with that type

```
sizeof(emp)
```

or by taking the size of the structure type itself

```
sizeof(struct employee)
```

You might think that we could also compute the size of a structure simply by adding together the size of each of its fields. In general, however, we can't. Although

```
printf("%d\n", sizeof(emp));
```

prints 70,

```c
/*
 * Program to write employee information.
 */
#include <stdio.h>
#include <string.h>

#define MAXNAME 40              /* longest name */

struct employee
{
  long number;                 /* employee number */
  char name[MAXNAME];          /* first and last name */
  char phone[13];              /* xxx-xxx-xxxx\0 */
  int age;                     /* age */
};

main()
{
  struct employee emp;
  static struct employee other_emp =
      {1023, "perl, doris", "213-555-6917", 22};
  void write_emp(struct employee);
  void print_emp(struct employee *);

  emp.number = 1001;
  emp.age = 22;
  strcpy(emp.name, "merriweather, tammy");
  strcpy(emp.phone, "818-555-1747");
  write_emp(emp);
  print_emp(&other_emp);
  return 0;
}

void write_emp(struct employee e)    /* take structure */
{
  printf("Employee: %ld\n", e.number);
  printf("Name:     %s\n",  e.name);
  printf("Age:      %d\n",  e.age);
  printf("Phone:    %s\n",  e.phone);
}

void print_emp(struct employee *ep)  /* take ptr to structure */
{
  printf("Employee: %ld\n", ep->number);
  printf("Name:     %s\n",  ep->name);
  printf("Age:      %d\n",  ep->age);
  printf("Phone:    %s\n",  ep->phone);
}
```

Figure 12.1   prstruct.c—Initialize and print a structure one field at a time.

```
          printf("%d\n", sizeof(emp.number) + sizeof(emp.name) +
                          sizeof(emp.phone) + sizeof(emp.age));
```

prints 69. Why? Because each data type has alignment restrictions, which may force the compiler to leave "holes" in a structure so that it can satisfy all the alignment constraints of the various fields within the structure. Although a char can start on a byte or word boundary, ints, longs, and other data types can usually begin only on a word boundary. In our structure, the 13-byte array containing the phone number ends on a byte boundary, so the single byte that follows it and precedes the age field (which must start on a word boundary) is left unused.

The next operator we can apply to structures, = (assignment), copies the contents of one structure into another.

```
          struct date old_date, date;
              .  .  .
          old_date = date;
```

One nice and perhaps not immediately obvious use of structure assignment is to conveniently copy arrays—we simply package the arrays in structures

```
          struct table              /* define the structure types */
          {
            int a[100];
          };

          struct table x, y;        /* declare the variables */
```

and then assign one structure to the other.

```
          x = y;
```

Some older compilers don't provide structure assignment, forcing us to do structure assignment one field at a time.

The final two operators that we can use with structures are the tests for equality and inequality, == and !=.

```
          struct date d1, d2;
              .  .  .
          printf("The dates are %s\n",
                  (d1 == d2) ? "the same" : "different");
```

These test whether all of the corresponding fields in two structures are the same. We can't use the other comparison operators, such as less than or greater than, because it isn't clear how to order arbitrary structures. Instead, we write our own functions to perform these types of comparisons, such as date_lt, shown in Figure 12.2. It compares two struct dates, and returns a nonzero value if the first is less than the second.

Arrays of Structures

We said earlier that we can have arrays of any type, even structures. One use for an array of structures would be to store a table of personnel records.

```
/*
 * Compare two dates (a function and a test program).
 */
#include <stdio.h>

struct date { int month, day, year; };

main()
{
  static struct date day1 = {11,18,63};
  static struct date day2 = {6,24,63};
  int date_lt(struct date *x, struct date *y);

  printf("%d/%d/%d %s less than %d/%d/%d.\n",
         day1.month, day1.day, day1.year,
         date_lt(&day1, &day2) ? "" : "not",
         day2.month, day2.day, day2.year);
  return 0;
}

int date_lt(struct date *x, struct date *y)
{
  if (x->year < y->year) return 1;

  return x->year == y->year &&
         (x->month < y->month ||
             (x->month == y->month && x->day < y->day));
}
```

Figure 12.2   datelt.c—Testing whether one date (stored in a structure) is less than another.

```
    struct employee emptab[SIZE];
```

This declares an array of SIZE elements, with each element in the array a struct employee containing number, name, phone, and age fields, as shown in Figure 12.3.

emptab is an array of structures, so we use the usual array-accessing methods to reach individual records and then the dot field selection operator to reach fields. We can, for example, assign a value to emptab[1] with

```
emptab[1].number = 1023;
emptab[1].age = 22;
strcpy(emptab[1].name, "perl, doris");
strcpy(emptab[1].phone, "213-555-6917");
```

We can also initialize a global or static array of structures when we declare it. The following declares and initializes emptab. We don't provide a size for the array, so the compiler determines it from the number of items we provide, seven in this case.

1001	merriweather, tammy\0	818-555-1747\0	22
1023	perl, doris\0	213-555-6917\0	22
1033	laforteza, nancy\0	714-555-2559\0	21
1036	masuda, debra\0	818-555-2999\0	24
1039	borromeo, irene\0	818-555-2718\0	22
1048	goebel, diane\0	213-555-4854\0	22
1047	ockert, veronica\0	213-555-4741\0	25

Figure 12.3 Array of `struct employees` showing the contents of an individual element.

```
static struct employee emptab[] =
{
  {1001, "merriweather, tammy", "818-555-5252", 22},
  {1023, "perl, doris", "213-555-6917", 22},
  {1033, "laforteza, nancy", "714-555-2559", 21},
  {1036, "masuda, debra", "818-555-2999", 24},
  {1039, "borromeo, irene", "213-555-2718", 22},
  {1047, "goebel, diane", "213-555-4854", 22},
  {1048, "ockert, veronica", "213-555-4741", 25}
};
```

We can index an array of structures in the same way we index any other array—either by array subscripting or by using pointers.

As an example, we'll write a program that initializes and prints an array of `struct employees`. The program has three parts. The first, premps.h, is a header file that defines a `struct employee`. The second, premps.c, is a main program that initializes the array and then calls the function `print_emps` to print each of the names. The final part is the file containing `print_emps`. Figure 12.4 contains premps.h, Figure 12.5 contains premps.c, and Figure 12.6 contains an array-subscripting version of `print_emps`.

`print_emps` takes two arguments—the address of the first element to print and the number of items we want to print. So to use `print_emps` we need to know how many items are in the array. But how can we figure this out automatically? We do so the same way we figure out how many items are in any other array—we divide the

```
/*
 * premps.h -- Definition of a struct employee.
 */

#define MAXNAME 40

struct employee   /* same definition as before */
{
  long number;                    /* employee number */
  char name[MAXNAME];             /* first and last name */
  char phone[13];                 /* xxx-xxx-xxxx\0 */
  int age;                        /* age */
};
```

Figure 12.4 premps.h—Header file defining the `struct employee` type.

```
/*
 * Print the name field of each element in a structure.
 */
#include <stdio.h>
#include "premps.h"

main()
{
  static struct employee emptab[] =
  {
    {1001, "merriweather, tammy", "818-555-1747", 22},
    {1023, "perl, doris", "213-555-6917", 22},
    {1033, "laforteza, nancy", "714-555-2559", 21},
    {1036, "masuda, debra", "818-555-2999", 24},
    {1039, "borromeo, irene", "213-555-2718", 22},
    {1047, "goebel, diane", "213-555-4854", 22},
    {1048, "ockert, veronica", "213-555-4741", 25}
  };
  void print_emps(struct employee table[], int);

  print_emps(emptab,sizeof(emptab)/sizeof(emptab[0]));
  return 0;
}
```

Figure 12.5 premps.c—A program to print an array of `struct employees`.

```
/*
 * Array printing function, using array subscripting.
 */
#include <stdio.h>
#include "premps.h"       /* for structure definition */

void print_emps(struct employee table[], int n)
{
  int i;                  /* use array indexing */

  for (i = 0; i < n; i++)
    printf("Name: %s\n", table[i].name);
}
```

Figure 12.6 premps1.c—A function `print_emps` to print an array of structures using array indexing.

```
/*
 * Improved version that uses pointer indexing.
 */
#include <stdio.h>
#include "premps.h"

void print_emps(struct employee *ptr, int n)
{
  struct employee *endptr = ptr + n;

  for (; ptr < endptr; ptr++)
    printf("Name: %s\n", ptr->name);
}
```

Figure 12.7 premps2.c—A new version of `print_emps`. This version uses pointer indexing.

total number of bytes in the array by the number of bytes in an individual item. So we can print the entire table with

```
    print_emps(emptab, sizeof(emptab)/sizeof(emptab[0]));
```

or

```
    print_emps(emptab, (sizeof(emptab)/sizeof(struct employee)));
```

In the example, we opted for the conciseness of the former over the readability of the latter.

Figure 12.7 shows an alternative version of `print_emps` that uses pointer indexing rather than array subscripting. We can use pointer indexing because pointer arithmetic is always done in units of the pointed-to type, so incrementing a pointer to a structure causes it to point to the next structure in the array.

Bitfields

So far, our integer fields have been at least one word in size. But when we are dealing with small integers—those integers that require less than 16 bits—this wastes space. Fortunately, C lets us to specify the number of bits required by an integer field, which lets us pack several different fields into a single word, saving space. Fields specified in terms of their size in bits are called *bitfields*.

We declare a bitfield the same way we declare any other structure field, with one exception and one restriction. The exception is that we must follow the field's name with a colon and the number of bits we need. The restriction is that bitfields must be signed or unsigned `ints`, from 1 to 16 (the number of bits in a Turbo C `int`) bits in length. Signed bitfields use the leftmost bit as the sign bit. Within a word, the fields are allocated right to left. For example,

```
struct date
{
    unsigned int year  : 7;    /* year is 7 bits */
    unsigned int day   : 5;    /* day is 5 bits */
    unsigned int month : 4;    /* month is 4 bits */
};
```

declares a structure with three bitfields: `year`, `day` and `month`, as shown below.

15 ⋯ 12	11 ⋯ 7	6 ⋯ 0
MONTH	DAY	YEAR

The entire structure fits in a single 16-bit word. `year` takes up 7 bits, `day` takes up 5 bits, and `month` takes up 4 bits.

The name of a bitfield is optional; an anonymous bitfield simply uses up space. And it turns out that a bitfield with size zero and no name causes the following field to be aligned on a word boundary.

We access bitfields in the same way we access any other structure field, using the `.` and `->` operators.

```
struct date bday;        /* holds a birthday */
     . . .
bday.month = 6;  bday.day = 24;  bday.year = 63;
```

There is one restriction, however. We can't take the address of a bitfield (which makes sense, since most machines aren't bit-addressable). This means, of course, that we can't use `scanf` to read values into a bitfield. Instead, we have to read into a temporary variable and then assign its value to the bitfield.

Figure 12.8 uses bitfields in a new version of the Chapter 4 program to pack employee information in a single word. We prefer the simplicity of using bitfields to the complexity of using our earlier bit-manipulating functions. But this doesn't mean that those functions are useless. They're still convenient when we don't know at compile time which combinations of bits we need to access.

EXERCISES

12-1 Write a function that prompts the user for the values of the individual fields within a `struct employee`.

12-2 Write functions to read a date, to print a date in a nice format, to determine if a date is valid, and to determine the number of days between two `struct dates`.

12-3 Define a structure type, `struct point`, for two-dimensional space coordinates (consisting of real values of *x* and *y*). Write a function, `distance`, that computes the distance between two `struct points`.

12-4 Write a program to read and sort an array of `struct employees`. Sort by employee name.

12-5 Repeat the previous exercise working with an array of `struct dates`. Then write a function to search an array of `struct dates` for a particular date. Write two versions of this function, one using linear search, the other using binary search.

12-6 Rewrite the previous exercise storing each date as a collection of bitfields.

12-7 Modify a `struct employee` so that the employee phone number is stored in a structure, with separate fields for the area code, the local prefix, and the final four digits. Write a function that prints the employee table, with entries sorted by area code.

12-8 Modify a `struct employee` to include an additional field containing the employee's birthdate. This field should be a structure containing bitfields. Write functions to initialize and print the modified table.

12-9 Implement the macros in ctype.h. One way to do so is to use a table of structures, containing one element per character. Each element contains a set of bitfields, one field for each possible property (uppercase, lowercase, digit, hexadecimal digit, and so on). If the property holds for a particular character, its corresponding bitfield contains a 1. If it doesn't, the field contains a zero.

12.2   UNIONS

Structures allow packaging together different types of values as a single unit. But we also often want to store values of different types in a single location. The mechanism that allows us to do this is called a *union*. A union may contain one of many different types of values (as long as only one is stored at a time).

We declare and use `unions` in the same way we declare and use `structs`. To declare a union type, we follow the keyword `union` with an optional union name

```
/*
 * New version of Chapter 4 program to pack employee information
 * into a single word, this time using bitfields.  This version,
 * like the earlier one, assumes information has been entered
 * correctly.
 */
#include <stdio.h>

#define SINGLE     0        /* marital status flags */
#define MARRIED    1
#define SEPARATED  2
#define DIVORCED   3
#define MALE       1        /* sex */
#define FEMALE     0

struct emp
{
  unsigned int mstat : 2;      /* marital status */
  unsigned int age : 7;        /* employee age */
  unsigned int sex : 1;        /* male or female */
  unsigned int years : 6;      /* years employeed */
};

main()
{
  unsigned int mstat, sex, age, years;
  struct emp info;         /* holds info on one person */

  printf("male=%d, female=%d? ", MALE, FEMALE);
  scanf("%d", &sex);
  info.sex = sex;
  printf("age? ");
  scanf("%d", &age);
  info.age = age;
  printf("single=%d, married=%d, separated=%d, divorced=%d? ",
         SINGLE, MARRIED, SEPARATED, DIVORCED);
  scanf("%d", &mstat);
  info.mstat = mstat;
  printf("years employed? ");
  scanf("%d", &years);
  info.years = years;
  printf("Here's the info:\n");
  printf("Sex: %d\n", info.sex);
  printf("Age: %d\n", info.age);
  printf("Marital status: %d\n", info.mstat);
  printf("Years employed: %d\n", info.years);
  return 0;
}
```

Figure 12.8 A new version of the Chapter 4 program to pack employee information in a single word.

and the alternative names and types it may hold. For example, we can declare a union type that can hold either an `int` or a `double` with

```
union number
{
  int    i;
  double d;
};
```

Once we've declared a union type, we can declare variables with that type.

```
union number x;
```

This declares a variable `x`, with type `union number`, which may contain either an `int` or a `double`. As with structures, we use the dot operator to access a union's individual fields. To assign to the `int` field of `x` we use `x.i`

```
x.i = 1234;
```

and to assign to the `double` field we use `x.d`

```
x.d = -123.345;
```

We can also access the fields of a union indirectly though a pointer, using the `->` operator.

```
union number *xptr;
   ...
xptr = &x;
x->d = -123.345
```

Internally, a union is allocated enough storage to hold its largest field. `x`, a `union number`, is allocated space sufficient for a `double` at all times, as shown below. That means, however, that a union may contain only one value (here, either an `int` or a `double`) at a time. *Warning: It's not portable to assign to one field of union and then use another.* A series of operations such as

```
x.d = -123.345;               /* assign a double */
printf("%d\n", x.i);          /* print "i" field */
```

is likely to produce results that differ from machine to machine.

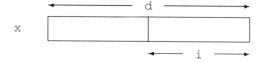

Figure 12.9 uses a union in a function, `getvalue`, that prints a prompt and obtains a value—either an `int`, `double`, or a string—from the user. The idea is

that we pass `getvalue` a prompt string, an indication of the type of value we want to read, and a pointer to a union that can contain either an `int`, a `double`, or a pointer. `getvalue` reads a line of input and fills the union with the desired type. If the type is numeric, `getvalue` uses `sscanf` to translate the characters it reads into the desired type. If the type is a string, `getvalue` uses `strdup` to allocate sufficient storage for it. The function returns -1 if there is any type of problem (as when the user doesn't enter a value of the appropriate type) and a 0 otherwise.

EXERCISES

12–10 Create a `union` with one field for each of C's basic data types. Store various values in the `union` and print each of the fields.

12–11 Extend `getvalue` to take two additional arguments that specify the minimum and maximum values the user should enter or the minimum and maximum length for a string.

12–12 Extend `getvalue` to read values of other types such as `short`, `long`, and `float`.

12.3   ENUMERATED TYPES

Sometimes we know a variable will have only one of a small set of values. In `getvalue`, for example, we know that the type should only hold the constants `INTEGER`, `REAL`, or `STRING`. In these situations, we can use an *enumerated type* to specify the possible values.

We define an enumerated type by giving the keyword `enum` followed by an optional *type designator* and a brace-enclosed list of identifiers. So

```
enum itype {INTEGER, REAL, STRING};    /* input types */
```

defines an enumerated type, `enum itype`, that has three possible values: `INTEGER`, `REAL`, and `STRING`. Internally, these are defined as constants with an integer value equal to their position in the list: `INTEGER` is zero, `REAL` is one, and `STRING` is two. Of course, we could have defined these as constants with `#defines` or `const`, but we find `enums` more convenient to use.

We are allowed to assign specific integer values to the items in an enumerated type. We do so by following the item with an equals sign and a value. The default value for any item is one more than the value of the item preceding it. So

```
enum itype {STRING = 2, INTEGER = 0, REAL};
```

assigns `STRING` a two, `INTEGER` a zero, and `REAL` a one, just like before.

All we've done so far is declare an enumerated type. We declare variables with that type in the same way we declared structures and unions.

```
enum itype type;
```

```
/*
 * unions.c -- A program that prompts and reads a value from
 *              the user using unions.
 */
#include <stdio.h>
#include <string.h>
#include <stddef.h>
#include "inout.h"

#define MAXLEN 80      /* longest input line */

#define INTEGER 0      /* used to indicate type */
#define REAL    1
#define STRING  2

union value            /* can hold an int, double, or char */
{
  int    i;
  double d;
  char   *s;
};

/*
 * Prompt and read value, placing value in provided union.
 */
int getvalue(char *prompt, int type, union value *up)
{
  char line[MAXLEN + 1];

  printf("%s", prompt);
  if (getline(line, MAXLEN) == -1)
    return -1;               /* error: no line */
  switch(type)
  {
    case INTEGER:            /* get int value */
      if (sscanf(line, "%d", &(up->i)) != 1)
        return -1;
      break;
    case REAL:               /* get double value */
      if (sscanf(line, "%lf", &(up->d)) != 1)
        return -1;
      break;
    case STRING:             /* get string value */
      if ((up->s = strdup(line)) == NULL)
        return -1;
      break;
    default:
      return -1;             /* error: bad code */
  }
  return 0;                  /* succeeded */
}
```

```
/*
 * main program using getvalue (quits on first error).
 */
main()
{
  int getvalue(char *, int, union value *);
  union value age, salary, name;

  if (getvalue("Enter name: ", STRING, &name) == -1)
    putline("Couldn't get name");
  else if (getvalue("Enter age: ", INTEGER, &age) == -1)
    putline("Couldn't get age");
  else if (getvalue("Enter salary: ", REAL, &salary) == -1)
    putline("Couldn't get salary");
  else
    printf("Name: %s, Age: %d, Salary: %7.2lf\n",
            name.s, age.i, salary.d);
  return 0;
}
```

Figure 12.9   unions.c—A package of functions for obtaining user input, including a main program that uses them.

This declares a variable, `type`, that can only hold a value of INTEGER, REAL, or STRING. While

```
    type = INTEGER;
```

is legal,

```
    type = 26;
```

is not.

The distinction between enumerated types and integers is a fuzzy one. Some compilers force us to cast them into an `int` before we use them as integers (such as if we were going to do arithmetic on them). Others, including Turbo C, let us use any enumerated type as if it were an integer. So why use enumerated types at all—why not simply use integers instead? Because enumerated types highlight variables that only hold one of a limited set of values, contributing to more readable programs. But even when we don't care about readability, we can still use them as a convenient way to define integer constants.

We illustrate the use of `enum`s in a new version of `getvalue`. To describe the expected input types, this version of `getvalue` is passed an `enum itype` instead of an integer. And `getvalue` now returns an `enum error` to describe what went wrong if it couldn't successfully read a value, rather than simply returning −1 or 0. These types are defined in getvalue.h, shown in Figure 12.10. `getvalue` itself is shown in Figure 12.11, along with several other useful functions. The first, `printerror`, takes an `enum error` and prints an error message appropriate for

```
/*
 * getvalue.h -- Define types for getvalue.
 */
#define MAXLEN 80    /* longest input line */

enum itype {INTEGER, REAL, STRING};
enum error {NOERROR, NOINPUT, NOSPACE, BADNUMBER, BADTYPE};

union value            /* can hold a long, double, or char */
{
  int    i;
  double d;
  char  *s;
};

int getinteger(char *prompt);
double getreal(char *prompt);
char *getstring(char *prompt);
```

Figure 12.10 getvalue.h—Header file defining types needed by getvalue.

it. The others—getinteger, getreal, and getstring—provide convenient interfaces for using getvalue to read an integer, real, or string. Figure 12.12 contains a sample main program that uses them.

EXERCISES

12-13 How can we define a boolean enumerated type? Is an enumerated boolean type preferable to using typedef or #define?

12-14 Modify getvalue to read the values without the user having to type a carriage return, as we did in the function getnumber, which we wrote in Chapter 3.

12-15 Define an enumerated type for the days of the week. Write functions to retrieve the next and previous days.

12-16 Write general predecessor and successor macros that work with any enumerated type (assuming that the values of the enumeration type represent integers consecutively from 0 to $n - 1$).

12-17 Write a function that is passed an array of enum_itypes describing the expected values on an input line and an array of unions that can hold these values. The functions reads the values and sticks them in the array. How should errors be indicated?

```c
/*
 * getvalue.c -- Read a value from the user.
 */
#include <stdio.h>
#include <string.h>
#include <stddef.h>
#include "getvalue.h"
#include "inout.h"

enum error
getvalue(char *prompt, enum itype type, union value *up)
{
  char line[MAXLEN + 1];

  printf("%s", prompt);
  if (getline(line, MAXLEN) == -1)
    return NOINPUT;
  switch(type)
  {
    case INTEGER: if (sscanf(line, "%d", &(up->i)) != 1)
                    return BADNUMBER;
                  break;
    case REAL:    if (sscanf(line, "%lf", &(up->d)) != 1)
                    return BADNUMBER;
                  break;
    case STRING:  if ((up->s = strdup(line)) == NULL)
                    return NOSPACE;
                  break;
    default:      return BADTYPE;
  }
  return NOERROR;                   /* succeeded */
}

void printerror(enum error code)
{
  switch(code)
  {
    case NOINPUT:   putline("Empty input line.");
                    break;
    case NOSPACE:   putline("Out of storage space.");
                    break;
    case BADNUMBER: putline("Invalid numeric value.");
                    break;
    case BADTYPE:   putline("Internal errorm, bad type");
                    break;
    default:        putline("Unknown error.");
                    break;
  }
}
```

```
/*
 * Additional functions built on top of getvalue:
 *      getinteger - read an integer.
 *      getreal    - read a real number.
 *      getstring  - read a character string.
 */
int getinteger(char *prompt)
{
  union.value x;
  enum error e;

  while ((e = getvalue(prompt, INTEGER, &x)) != NOERROR)
    printerror(e);
  return x.i;
}

double getreal(char *prompt)
{
  union value x;
  enum error e;

  while ((e = getvalue(prompt, REAL, &x)) != NOERROR)
    printerror(e);
  return x.d;
}

char *getstring(char *prompt)
{
  union value x;
  enum error e;

  while ((e = getvalue(prompt, STRING, &x)) != NOERROR)
    printerror(e);
  return x.s;
}
```

Figure 12.11 getvalue.c—A new version of `getvalue` that uses `enum`s to indicate the error.

12.4   CASE STUDY—A DATA BASE APPLICATION

We conclude this chapter by writing a small program to manage a data base of employee records. Its users can interactively add, delete, and print records, accessing the desired record by providing the corresponding employee number. When the program finishes, it prints the table. The program has a simple menu-driven interface, an extension to the one we developed in the previous chapter. Figure 12.13 shows a sample session with the program.

```
/*
 * A main program using getvalue.
 */
#include <stdio.h>
#include <alloc.h>
#include "getvalue.h"

main()
{
  int age = getinteger("Enter age: ");
  double salary = getreal("Enter salary: ");
  char *name = getstring("Enter name: ");

  printf("Name: %s, Age: %d, Salary: %lf\n", name, age, salary);
  free(name);    /* in general necessary, though not here */
  return 0;
}
```

Figure 12.12   tstgtval.c—A new version of the main program to test our `getvalue` function.

Storing the Data Base

The data base itself is kept as an array, `emptab`, of `struct employees`—but now we've made the structure's definition more general.

```
    struct employee          /* individual personnel record */
    {
      char *name, *phone;
      int number, age;
    };
```

The employee `name` and `phone` numbers are now pointers to `char` rather than arrays of `char`. This means that when we add a record we have to dynamically allocate the space for these fields. When we delete a record, we deallocate this space. We find the extra effort worthwhile, since it allows us to have arbitrarily long names and phone numbers without wasting storage.

To keep things simple, we don't bother to keep the array in sorted order. Instead, we add a new record by placing it after the last record, and we delete an existing record by replacing it with the last record, as illustrated in Figure 12.14. This organization allows us to quickly insert or delete a record, but slows searching—on the average we'll examine half of the items in the array.

The Data Base Program

Figure 12.15, the file database.c, contains the definitions of the employee structure, the main program, and the functions for adding, deleting, and printing data base records. Unfortunately, however, updating the employee table is only one part of the

```
Main Menu
  1) Add an employee
  2) Delete an employee
  3) Print an employee
Enter choice (0 to exit): 1

Add employee number? 10
Employee name: Alex Quilici
Employee phone: (213) 555-2115
Employee age: 26

Main Menu
  . . .
Enter choice (0 to exit): 1

Add employee number? 5
Employee name: Larry Miller
Employee phone: (213) 555-2738
Employee age: 39

Main Menu
  . . .
Enter choice (0 to exit): 1

Add employee number? 29
Employee name: Tony Quilici
Employee phone: (408) 555-7764
Employee age: 24

Main Menu
  . . .
Enter choice (0 to exit): 2

Delete employee number? 29

Main Menu
  . . .
Enter choice (0 to exit): 0

10, Alex Quilici, 26, (213) 555-2115
5, Larry Miller, 39, (213) 555-2738
```

Figure 12.13 Some sample input and output for our data base program.

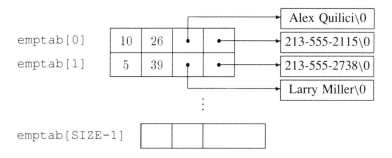

Figure 12.14 Diagram of the array after reading in and allocating several records.

data base program's job. It must also interact with the user, handling such chores as printing a menu, obtaining the user's choices, and executing the functions that carry them out.

These tasks are handled by the function `process_menu`, which we keep in a separate file. This function takes an array of `struct menuitems`, a string containing the menu's name, and the number of choices. A `struct menuitem` contains a string identifying the item and a pointer to a function to execute if the user chooses that entry.

```
struct menuitem
{
  char *item;       /* description of choice */
  void (*func)();   /* function to execute choice */
};
```

`process_menu` simply prints each of the table entries, requests a choice from the user, and then uses it as an index into the table to select the function to execute.

```
(*(menu[choice].func))();    /* execute function */
```

Figure 12.16 is the header file menu.h, which defines `struct menuitem`. Figure 12.17 is the source file menu.c, which defines `process_menu`.

Both database.c and menu.c use functions defined in getvalue.c, and `getvalue` makes use of `getline`, from inout.c, so both of these files must be compiled in as well. The project file for building the data base program is

```
database.c    (getvalue.h menu.h)
getvalue.c    (getvalue.h)
menu.c        (menu.h getvalue.h)
inout.obj
```

```c
/*
 * Data base program.
 */
#include <stdio.h>
#include <stddef.h>
#include <alloc.h>
#include "getvalue.h"
#include "menu.h"

#define SIZE 100                /* size of employee table */

struct employee                 /* individual person-
nel record */
{
  char *name, *phone;
  int number, age;
};

struct employee emptab[SIZE];   /* table */
int emps = 0;                   /* items in table */

void addentry(void);            /* functions to manipulate table */
void delentry(void);
void prentry(void);
struct employee *lookup(int num);

struct menuitem menu[] =         /* menu: choices + functions */
  {{"Add an employee",  addentry},
   {"Delete an employee", delentry},
   {"Print an employee", prentry}};

main()
{
  void printtable(struct employee *empptr, int n);

  process_menu(menu,"Main Menu", sizeof(menu)/sizeof(menu[0]));
  printtable(emptab, emps);
  return 0;
}

void printtable(struct employee *ptr, int n)
{
  struct employee *endptr = ptr + n - 1;

  for (; ptr <= endptr; ptr++)
    printf("%d, %s, %d, %s\n",
           ptr->number, ptr->name, ptr->age, ptr->phone);
  printf("%d employees\n", n);
}
```

```
/*
 * The data base operations and useful utilities:
 *    addentry - add a data base entry.
 *    delentry - delete a data base entry.
 *    prentry -  print a data base entry.
 *    lookup -   find and return a pointer to data base entry.
 */

void addentry(void)
{
  struct employee *emp;
  int newnum;

  if (emps == SIZE)
    printf("Employee table is full.\n");
  else
  {
    newnum = getinteger("Add employee number? ");
    if (lookup(newnum) != NULL)
      printf("Already an employee with that number.\n");
    else
    {
      emp = &emptab[emps++];
      emp->number = newnum;
      emp->name = getstring("Employee name: ");
      emp->phone = getstring("Employee phone: ");
      emp->age = getinteger("Employee age: ");
    }
  }
}

void delentry(void)
{
  struct employee *emp;
  int empnum = getinteger("Delete employee number? ");

  if ((emp = lookup(empnum)) == NULL)
    printf("No such employee!\n");
  else
  {
    free(emp->name);          /* get rid of name, phone */
    free(emp->phone);
    *emp = emptab[--emps];  /* copy last into old space */
  }
}
```

```
/*
 * database.c (continued).
 */

void prentry(void)
{
  struct employee *emp;
  int empnum = getinteger("Print employee number? ");

  if ((emp = lookup(empnum)) == NULL)
    printf("No such employee!\n");
  else
    printf("Employee #%d\n\tName: %s\n\tAge: %d\n\tPhone: %s\n",
           emp->number, emp->name, emp->age, emp->phone);
}

struct employee *lookup(int target)
{
  struct employee *ptr = emptab;
  struct employee *endptr = ptr + emps - 1;

  for (; ptr <= endptr; ptr++)
    if (ptr->number == target)
      return ptr;
  return NULL;
}
```

Figure 12.15 database.c—The main program for the data base manager.

```
/*
 * menu.h -- Header file for menu package.
 */
struct menuitem
{
  char *item;                  /* description of entry*/
  void (*func)();              /* function executing entry */
};

void process_menu(struct menuitem table[],  char *name, int n);
```

Figure 12.16 menu.h—Header file for the menu package.

```
/*
 * menu.c -- Display menu and obtain choice.
 */
#include <stdio.h>
#include "menu.h"
#include "getvalue.h"

void process_menu(struct menuitem menu[], char *name, int n)
{
  int choice;

  for(;;)
  {
    printf("\n%s\n\n", name);    /* write menu name and function */
    for (choice = 1; choice <= n; choice++)
      printf("  %d) %s\n", choice, menu[choice - 1].item);
    while ((choice = getinteger("Enter choice (0 to exit): ")) < 0
              && choice > n)     /* get user's choice */
      printf("Bad choice.  Choose between 0 and %d\n", n);
    putchar('\n');
    if (choice-- == 0)                 /* quitting time */
      break;
    (*(menu[choice].func))();     /* execute appropriate choice */
  }
}
```

Figure 12.17   menu.c—The function to deal with menus.

Obviously our data base program is far too simplistic to be suitable for any real-world application. The individual records aren't kept in any particular order, so finding a desired record can be time-consuming. And the data base is kept in memory, which means it has to be reentered each time the program is run. But we'll provide mechanisms for correcting these problems soon enough. The next chapter looks at alternative data structures for storing tables, and the one after that examines external files.

EXERCISES

12–18 Write a function to sort the items in database.c, and an appropriate menu entry.

12–19 Write a new version of the functions in database.c that maintain the data base in sorted order.

12–20 Write a program to handle a data base of events. An event includes the name of the event and its corresponding date. Provide operations to add, delete, and print events.

12-21 Write a program to manage a little black book. Each entry should include the person's name, address (broken into street number, street name, and apartment number), city, state, zip code, and phone number (broken into area code, prefix, suffix). Allow the retrieval of all phone numbers in a given city, state or zip code, as well as retrieval by specifying the person's name. Also provide a way to print the entire data base.

12-22 Write a program to manage a data base of information about an individual Compact Disc collection. Each entry includes the name of the group, the name of the CD, the year it was released, the price paid for it, and the total playing time. Allow the user to search for all the CDs released by a given group, or for all the information on a particular CD. The user should also be able to print the data base sorted by group name, by playing time, by year of release, or by price paid. Finally, allow the user to print aggregate information: the total cost of the collection, the number of CDs, the number of different groups, and so on.

12-23 Use the generic search routine of Chapter 7 to write a function to search for the information on a particular employee. Write a version that searches using the employee number as a key, and write another version that searches using the employee name.

13 LINKED LISTS

AND

TREES

There are several problems with using arrays to store tables of values. We can't conveniently and efficiently increase the table's size at run time. And, if we want to maintain the table in sorted order, we can't easily add or delete table entries. Instead, we're stuck with shifting array elements to make room for a new element or to close up the space used by an existing element. This chapter introduces two more dynamic data structures that don't have this problem—linked lists and binary trees—and uses them to write several new sorting programs. The chapter concludes by using them in a C program cross-referencer.

13.1   LINKED LISTS

Figure 13.1*a* shows a linked list of five integers. Each element of the list, called a *node*, has two fields, one containing data, the other a pointer to the next element in the list. The advantage of the linked list is that we can insert an element without shifting all of the elements that follow—we simply adjust the pointers appropriately, as shown in Figure 13.1*b*.

We illustrate linked lists by using them in an insertion sort routine, one that inserts each new input value into an already sorted list. But before we can do this, we need a way of representing a node. Since a node requires at least two fields, we can conveniently package an entire node as a structure.

```
struct node
{
  long value;          /* or whatever is needed */
  struct node *next;   /* pointer to another node */
};
```

The first value is the data item, the second a pointer to the next node in the list. A NULL pointer indicates the last item in a list. To clarify and simplify the use of this structure, we use a typedef that makes NODEPTR a synonym for the type "pointer to struct node."

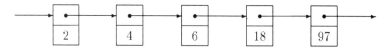

(*a*) A five-node linked list.

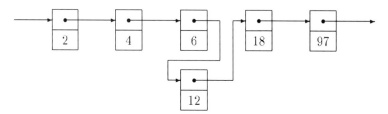

(*b*) The list with a new node containing 12 inserted into the middle.

Figure 13.1   What linked lists look like.

```
typedef struct node *NODEPTR;
```

Figure 13.2 is a simple program that sorts the numbers in its input, this time using a linked list rather than an array. The program repeatedly reads values, inserts them into their appropriate place in the list, and prints the list when it has finished building it. There are two big advantages to sorting numbers this way. The first is that we can sort an unlimited number of values—unlike the array version, for which we had to predeclare a maximum number of values to sort. The other and perhaps more important advantage is that we insert the new value into a linked list without shifting, thus speeding up our insertion sort algorithm.

Building a Sorted Linked List

The job of inserting a value into the correct place in a linked list is handled by the function `insert_list`. The function takes two arguments: the value to be inserted and a pointer to the linked list. To insert a new value in the list, `insert_list` determines where in the list the value should go, creates a new node for that value, and hooks this node into the list.

Figure 13.3*a* shows how we locate the correct place for a new value, and Figure 13.3*b* shows how we actually insert the node. We use two pointers, `curr` and `prev`, to search the list. We initialize `curr` to point the list's first node and `prev` to `NULL`, and move both down the list, one in trail of the other. Why do we need two pointers? Because we know we've found the correct place to insert only when we've gone one node past it. That is, as we move `curr` through the list, we compare the values it points to with the value to insert. When the value we're inserting is larger,

```c
/*
 * Sort integers using a linked list.
 */
#include <stdio.h>
#include <stddef.h>
#include <alloc.h>
#include "inout.h"

struct node
{
  long value;              /* value is single long integer */
  struct node *next;       /* pointer to another node */
};

typedef struct node *NODEPTR;

#define MAXLEN 80

main()
{
  NODEPTR listptr = NULL;   /* the sorted linked list */
  NODEPTR tempptr;          /* temporary list pointer */
  char line[MAXLEN + 1];    /* to hold input line */
  long x;                   /* input value */
  void print_list(NODEPTR ptr);
  void free_list(NODEPTR ptr);
  NODEPTR insert_list(NODEPTR ptr, long x);

  while(getline(line, MAXLEN) != -1)
    if (sscanf(line, "%ld", &x) != 1)
      putline("Bad input value.");
    else if ((tempptr = insert_list(listptr, x)) == NULL)
    {
      putline("Out of internal memory space.");
      return 1;                      /* quit early */
    }
    else
      listptr = tempptr;
  print_list(listptr);    /* print items */
  free_list(listptr);     /* free items, unnecessary here */
  return 0;
}

void print_list(NODEPTR ptr)
{
  for ( ; ptr != NULL; ptr = ptr->next)
    printf("%ld\n", ptr->value);
}
```

```
/*
 * Insert into list of long integers.
 */
NODEPTR insert_list(NODEPTR ptr, long x)
{
  NODEPTR curr = ptr,
          prev = NULL;
  NODEPTR temp;

  for (; curr != NULL && curr->value < x; curr = curr->next)
    prev = curr;                /* find element */
  if ((temp = (NODEPTR) malloc(sizeof(struct node))) == NULL)
    return NULL;                /* out of memory creating node */
  temp->value = x;              /* fill in value */

  temp->next = curr;            /* hook item into list */
  if (prev == NULL)
    ptr = temp;                 /* item is first in list */
  else
    prev->next = temp;          /* insert into middle */
  return ptr;                   /* pointer to first item */
}

/*
 * Return each element in "ptr" to the free storage pool.
 */
void free_list(NODEPTR ptr)
{
  NODEPTR temp;

  for (; ptr != NULL; ptr = temp)
  {
    temp = ptr->next;
    free ((char *) ptr);
  }
}
```

Figure 13.2   intlists.c—A linked-list insertion sort program for sorting `long` integers.

we know we should insert it in front of the current node. But since our list contains only pointers to the next node, we need to keep this *trailing link pointer*, `prev`, one node behind `curr`. The notion of a trailing pointer, one that points to the predecessor of a node, is a common technique with linked structures.

Once we find the place for the new value, we create a new node with `malloc`, requesting enough space for a `struct node`. Because `malloc` returns a pointer to `void`, we cast its return value to a `NODEPTR`. We then insert the node by manipulating pointers appropriately. First we set the new node's `next` pointer to `curr`. Then we make the previous node's `next` field point to the new node. And finally we return

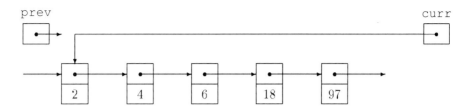

(*a*) Before searching the list.

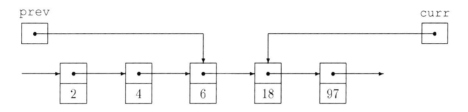

(*b*) When we find the desired node.

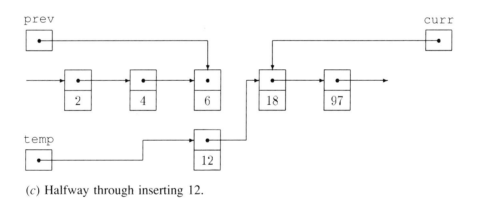

(*c*) Halfway through inserting 12.

Figure 13.3   How we insert a value into a linked list.

a pointer to the beginning of the list. But there is one exception to this simple scenario—when we insert an item into the beginning of the list, there is no previous item, so we simply return a pointer to the new node, which becomes the first item in the list.

Traversing a Linked List

Once we've built the sorted linked list, we use `print_list` to write its values. `print_list` does so by *traversing* the list, *visiting* each node, and printing its `value` field. We pass `print_list` a pointer, `ptr`, to the list's first element, which it uses to traverse the list. To go to the next node, we follow the `next` pointer.

```
ptr = ptr->next;
```

We stop once `ptr` is NULL, at which point we've reached the end of the list. To print a node, we simply use `printf` to print its value field.

```
printf("%ld\n", ptr->value);
```

Printing a list is not the only operation that requires its traversal. Another example is deallocating all of the nodes in a list. Because we dynamically allocate linked list nodes with `malloc`, we should deallocate them with `free` once we no longer need them. You might think we could deallocate a list simply by `free`ing the node's first element. But a single call to `free` returns only the single chunk of memory allocated by `malloc`. This means that we're forced to traverse an entire list to deallocate all of its nodes.

`free_list`, a slight variant on `print_list`, whereby "visit the node" becomes a call to `free`, accomplishes the job. Notice that we carefully save a copy of the node's `next` pointer before we `free` it. We do so because we must avoid accessing the contents of a block of storage that we have deallocated with `free`.

A Note on Insertion Sort's Efficiency

Although linked-list insertion sort avoids the time-consuming process of shifting data to make room for a new item, it isn't substantially faster than the array-based insertion sort. For each new value to be inserted, we still have to search the list for the correct place to insert, an operation that takes time proportional to m, if there are m values in the list or array. For all n input values, this takes a total amount of time proportional to n^2. If n doubles, sorting time goes up by a factor of 4; if n triples, it goes up nine times. Even so, the total sorting time for the same n inputs will be about twice as fast for linked lists as for array insertion.

EXERCISES

13-1 Write a function, `length_list`, that returns the number of elements in a list.

13–2 Write functions that implement the abstract data type *stack* using linked lists. A stack is a restricted access list: insertions and deletions may occur only at one end, the *top* of the stack. The operations are traditionally called *pushing* and *popping*.

13–3 Add the operations `count`, `top`, and `isempty` to the stack data type created in the previous exercise. `count` returns the number of elements on the stack, `top` returns the top element without popping the stack, and `isempty` returns nonzero only if there are elements on the stack.

13–4 Write functions that implement the abstract data type *queue*. A queue is another restricted list; additions are made to the end and deletions take place from the front. You should have functions to create the queue, to destroy the queue, to add to the queue's end, and to remove from the queue's front.

13–5 Write a function, `search_list`, that finds the first location of a given value in a list, and returns a pointer to it. The function header should be

```
NODEPTR search_list(NODEPTR, long)
```

If the value is not in the list, the function should return `NULL`.

13–6 Write a function, `delete_list`, that removes all nodes in a linked list with a given value. If the value is not in the list, the function does nothing. The function header is

```
NODEPTR delete_list(NODEPTR, long)
```

13–7 Write a function, `reverse_list`, that takes a pointer to a linked list, and reverses the order of the nodes. If the list contains nodes with 1, 2, 5, and 7, the list will point to the node with 7, which points to 5, and so on. No data movement should occur, only appropriate alteration of pointers.

13–8 A doubly linked list is one in which each node not only has a pointer to the following node but also one to the preceding node. Rewrite `insert_list` to work with a doubly linked list. Write the companion function `delete_list`.

13.2 SORTING STRINGS USING LINKED LISTS

Let's modify our current insertion sort program, which sorts integers, to sort character strings instead. Because integers always take up a fixed amount of storage, each node in a list is always the same size—room for the integer (the `value` field) plus room for the pointer to the next node (the `next` field). Unfortunately, strings can be different lengths, so to avoid wasting space, each node in a list of strings should contain a *pointer* to a string rather than the string itself, and we dynamically allocate the needed space for the string. The space for the node itself is a small, fixed amount: room for the string pointer, plus room for the pointer to the next node. Figure 13.4 shows what a simple list of strings looks like. The insertion sort algorithm is identical, the only difference is that we are now comparing strings. To do this, we use `strcmp` to compare the string to insert with the strings in the nodes of the list.

Figure 13.5 is the new version of insertion sort that sorts strings. This main program differs slightly from the previous one. Now when we read an input line, we

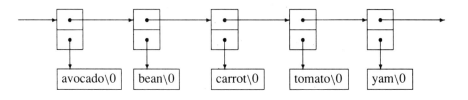

Figure 13.4 Linked list of nodes with pointers to a character string.

don't translate it into an integer. Instead we use `strdup` to make a newly allocated copy of the string. And we now pass `insert_list` a pointer to this space, rather than an integer as before. There are two other required changes. First, we change the type declaration for the `value` field in a node. Second, we must now rewrite `print_list` to print a string rather than an integer.

EXERCISES

13–9 Write a function, `size_list`, that determines the total number of bytes used to store a linked list. When is `size_list` useful?

13–10 Rewrite the `search_list`, `delete_list`, and `reverse_list` functions written in the exercises at the end of the previous section to work with lists of strings rather than lists of integers.

13–11 Rewrite Chapter 12's data base program to maintain the employee table as a sorted list of `struct employees`.

13–12 Write a program that maintains a list of events (event name and date) in sorted order.

13.3   GENERALIZED LINKED LISTS

Despite working with different data types, our two linked-list insertion sort programs are very similar—which makes sense, since we've used an identical algorithm. The only differences are in how `insert_list` compares the value to insert with values already in the list (using the less-than operation to compare numbers and `strcmp` to compare strings), and in how `print_list` prints the value in a node (using the `%ld` format of `printf` to print a `long` and the `%s` format to print a string). Rather than write almost identical versions of these functions for each new data type, we really want to somehow write generalized `insert_list` and `print_list` functions that work with lists of any data type.

In Chapter 7 we saw how to write generic array searching and printing functions. These functions handled the messy pointer manipulations required to efficiently tra-

```c
/*
 * Sort strings using a linked list.
 */
#include <stdio.h>
#include <string.h>
#include <alloc.h>
#include <stddef.h>
#include "inout.h"

struct node
{
  char *value;              /* string */
  struct node *next;        /* pointer to another node */
};

typedef struct node *NODEPTR;

#define MAXLEN  80
#define STRLT(x,y) (strcmp(x,y) < 0)

main()
{
  NODEPTR listptr = NULL;    /* the sorted linked list */
  NODEPTR tempptr = NULL;    /* temporary list pointer */
  char line[MAXLEN + 1];     /* to hold input line */
  char *x;                   /* newly allocated string */
  void print_list(NODEPTR ptr);
  NODEPTR insert_list(NODEPTR ptr, char *item);

  while (getline(line, MAXLEN) != -1)
    if ((x = strdup(line)) == NULL ||
        (tempptr = insert_list(listptr, x)) == NULL)
    {
      putline("Out of internal memory space.");
      return 1;              /* quit early */
    }
    else
      listptr = tempptr;
  print_list(listptr);
  return 0;
}

void print_list(NODEPTR ptr)
{
  for ( ; ptr != NULL; ptr = ptr->next)
    putline(ptr->value);
}
```

```
/*
 * Insert string into list.
 */
NODEPTR insert_list(NODEPTR ptr, char *x)
{
  NODEPTR curr = ptr,
          prev = NULL;
  NODEPTR temp;

  for (; curr != NULL && STRLT(curr->value,x); curr = curr->next)
    prev = curr;          /* find element */
  if ((temp = (NODEPTR) malloc(sizeof(struct node))) == NULL)
    return NULL;          /* out of memory (allocating node) */
  temp->value = x;
  temp->next = curr;      /* hook into list */
  if (prev == NULL)
    ptr = temp;           /* item is first in list */
  else
    prev->next = temp;    /* insert into middle */
  return ptr;             /* pointer to first item */
}
```

Figure 13.5 strlists.c—Revised version of `insert_list` that takes a string and inserts it into the proper place in a sorted linked list.

verse an array, but were passed pointers to functions to do any needed comparisons or printing. We can use the same technique for lists. But before we do, we'll have to change the definition of a node slightly. Now the item in the list is a pointer to void—a pointer to an object of unknown type—rather than a specific value or a pointer to string. This way the list nodes look the same regardless of the type of value they are supposed to contain, where it is an integer, string, or structure. Figure 13.6*a* shows what a generic list looks like in general; Figure 13.6*b* shows a generic list of integers.

The generic version of `insert_list` has arguments similar to those of the `insert_list` we wrote for inserting strings. The differences are that the pointer to the value to insert is now a pointer to void (to match the type within the list) and that it requires an additional argument, a pointer to a function that compares two items. Similarly, our generic version of `print_list` now takes a pointer to a function for writing an item. The new definition of a node is shown in Figure 13.7, the header file lists.h. The source file lists.c, which contains the new versions of the list-handling functions, is shown in Figure 13.8.

Figure 13.9 shows a new version of insertion sort that is written on top of these functions. Notice `insert_list`'s caller is responsible for allocating storage for the value to be inserted in the list, and for placing a copy of that value into this storage. That means that to insert an integer into the list, we must now `malloc` sufficient

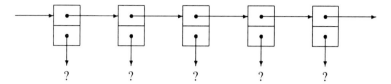

(*a*) A generic list.

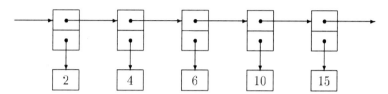

(*b*) A generic list of integers.

Figure 13.6   What generic lists look like.

```
/*
 * Generic linked lists.
 */
#include <alloc.h>
#include <stddef.h>

struct node
{
  void *value;            /* pointer to value */
  struct node *next;      /* pointer to next node */
};

typedef struct node NODE;
typedef NODE *NODEPTR;

typedef int (*CFPTR)(void *,void *);

extern NODEPTR
    insert_list(NODEPTR ptr, void *valptr, CFPTR cmpfunc);
extern void print_list(NODEPTR ptr, void (*prfunc)(void *));
```

Figure 13.7   lists.h—Header file for generic list functions.

```
/*
 * Generalized list handling functions.
 */
#include <stdio.h>
#include "lists.h"

NODEPTR insert_list(NODEPTR ptr, void *valptr, CFPTR cmpfunc)
{
  NODEPTR curr = ptr, prev = NULL,
          temp;

  for (; curr != NULL && cmpfunc(curr->value,valptr) < 0;
         curr = curr->next)
    prev = curr;       /* find element */
  if ((temp = (NODEPTR) malloc(sizeof(NODE))) == NULL)
    return NULL;       /* out of memory */
  temp->value = valptr;
  temp->next = curr;
  if (prev == NULL)
    ptr = temp;        /* item is first in list */
  else
    prev->next = temp; /* insert into middle */
  return ptr;          /* pointer to first item */
}

/*
 * Print a linked list
 */
void print_list(NODEPTR ptr, void (*prfunc)(void *))
{
  for ( ; ptr != NULL; ptr = ptr->next)
    (*prfunc)(ptr->value);
}
```

Figure 13.8   lists.c—Generic functions for inserting into a listing and printing a list.

storage for it, copy it into this storage, and then pass a pointer to it to insert_list. What insert_list does for us is determine where this integer belongs, creates a node whose value field points to the storage we allocated, and then hooks the node into the list. To determine where the node belongs, insert_list traverses the list, calling the comparison function once for each node, passing it the node's value field and a pointer to the value we are inserting. We use cmp_long as the comparison function. As before, the function dereferences the pointers it is passed to compare the values to which they point.

print_list is less complicated. We pass it a pointer to a function that writes a long integer. print_list calls this function once for each node, passing it the node's value field. We use prlong as our printing function. All it does is dereference the pointer it is passed, and passes it to printf, writing the value using an appropriate format.

Figure 13.10 shows a new version of string sort written on top of these functions. It is similar to Figure 13.9, except that it uses `cmpstr` as the comparison function, and `prstr` as the printing function.

The real payoff with generic functions is in using them to maintain linked lists of structures. Rather than having to write separate `insert_list` and `print_list` functions for each distinct structure, we simply write comparison and printing functions appropriate for the structure types we're using. The exercises provide some practice in doing so.

EXERCISES

13-13 Use the generic versions of `insert_list` and `print_list` to sort a list of dates. Use the definition for `struct date` found in the previous chapter.

13-14 Write generic versions of the list-manipulating functions (such as `delete_list`, `search_list`, and `reverse_list`) that you wrote as solutions to earlier exercises.

13-15 Rewrite Chapter 12's data base program to main the data base as a sorted list. Wherever possible, make use of the generic functions written in this chapter and the previous exercise.

13-16 Write a generic sorting function for linked lists.

13.4   BINARY TREES

We've seen that linked lists are lists where each node contains a pointer to the next node in the list. A binary tree is an extension to lists in which each node has two pointers, where each pointer is either NULL or a pointer to a binary tree. The top node in the tree is called the *root*.

Figure 13.11 is an example of a particularly useful type of binary tree, a *binary search tree*. In a binary search tree, the data value at each node partitions all of the data in its subtrees into two subsets. In the left subtree, every data item is less than the current node; in the right subtree, every data item is greater than the current node. In this section, we'll use these binary search trees to construct another, more efficient, sorting program, called *tree sort*. Unlike insertion sort, which takes time proportional to N^2, tree sort takes time proportional to $N log_2 N$. ($log_2 N$ is the x for which $2^x = N$.)

As with linked lists, we can define a binary tree as a structure, albeit with two pointers instead of one. Again, we use a `typedef` to keep things readable.

```
      struct tree
      {
        char *value;
        struct tree *left, *right;
/*
 * Insertion sort numbers.
 */
#include <stdio.h>
#include "lists.h"
#include "inout.h"

#define MAXLEN 80

main()
{
  NODEPTR listptr = NULL;    /* the sorted linked list */
  NODEPTR tempptr;           /* temporary list pointer */
  char line[MAXLEN + 1];     /* to hold input line */
  long x, *ptr;              /* input value, saved input value */
  int cmplong(void *xptr, void *yptr);
  void prlong(void *ptr);

  while(getline(line, MAXLEN) != -1)
    if (sscanf(line, "%ld", &x) != 1)
      putline("Bad input value.");
    else if ((ptr = (long *) malloc(sizeof(long))) == NULL ||
        (*ptr = x,
          (tempptr = insert_list(listptr, (void *) ptr, cmplong))
            == NULL))
    {
      putline("Out of internal memory space.");
      return 1;              /* quit early */
    }
    else
      listptr = tempptr;
  print_list(listptr, prlong);
  return 0;
}

int cmplong(void *xptr, void *yptr)
{
  long x = * (long *) xptr;
  long y = * (long *) yptr;

  return (x == y) ? 0 : ((x < y) ? -1 : 1);
}

void prlong(void *xptr)
{
  printf("%ld\n", *(long *) xptr);
}
```

Figure 13.9 intglist.c—Use insertion to build a sorted list of longs. The program is written on top of the generic insert list and print list functions.

```
/*
 * Insertion sort strings.
 */
#include <stdio.h>
#include <string.h>
#include "lists.h"
#include "inout.h"

#define MAXLEN 80

main()
{
  NODEPTR listptr = NULL;     /* the sorted linked list */
  NODEPTR tempptr = NULL;     /* temporary list pointer */
  char line[MAXLEN + 1];      /* to hold input line. */
  char *ptr;                  /* input value */
  void prstr(void *str);
  int cmpstr(void *xptr, void *yptr);

  while(getline(line, MAXLEN) != -1)
    if ((ptr = strdup(line)) == NULL ||
        (tempptr = insert_list(listptr, (void *) ptr, cmpstr))
            == NULL)
    {
      putline("Out of internal memory space.");
      return 1;                /* quit early */
    }
    else
      listptr = tempptr;
  print_list(listptr, prstr);
  return 0;
}

int cmpstr(void *xptr, void *yptr)
{
  return strcmp((char *) xptr, (char *) yptr);
}

void prstr(void *xptr)
{
  putline((char *) xptr);
}
```

Figure 13.10 strglist.c—A program using insertion sort to build a sorted list of strings. The program is written on top of the generic insert list and print list functions.

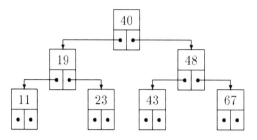

Figure 13.11 An example binary search tree. For every node, all of the items in its left subtree are less than the node, and all of the items in its right subtree are greater than the node.

```
    }

    typedef struct tree *TREEPTR;
```

Figure 13.12 is a program that sorts its input using tree sort. As it reads each value, it calls `insert_tree` to place the value in its correct place in the tree. When it has read and inserted all values, it calls `print_tree` to display the tree.

Inserting a value in an empty tree is easy—the value becomes the root of the tree. Inserting a value into a nonempty tree is more difficult, although we use a technique similar to that for inserting into a list. The idea is that we again have two pointers, `curr` and `prev`. Assuming the tree is not empty, we first set `curr` to its root, and `prev` to NULL. We then compare the value with the current node. If the value is less, we set `curr` to point to its left subtree. If the value is greater, we set `curr` to point to its right subtree. In either case, before changing `curr`, we save its value in `prev`. We keep repeating this process until `curr` becomes NULL, at which point we allocate a new node and make the appropriate pointer field of `prev` point to it.

Suppose we want to insert 27 into our tree. We first compare it with the value at the root; since 27 is less than 40, we move to the left. We then compare 27 with 19; it is greater, so now we move to the right. Finally, we compare 27 with 23 and again find that it is greater. We can't move right, since the right subtree of 23 is NULL, so we get a new node and attach 27 as the new right subtree of 23.

Once we've created a binary search tree, it isn't obvious how we can retrieve the values in a useful way. But we can do so by traversing the tree in a systematic way that corresponds to the way we constructed the tree. The idea is that, since all of the nodes in the left subtree of any node are less than its value, and all of the nodes in its right subtree are greater that its value, we can print the tree in sorted order by printing a node's left subtree, then printing the node, and then printing the node's right subtree. From this observation, we can easily code `print_tree`, which takes a pointer to a tree and prints it in order. `print_tree` calls itself recursively on the

```
/*
 * Insertion sort using trees instead of lists.
 */
#include <stdio.h>
#include <string.h>
#include <alloc.h>
#include <stddef.h>
#include "inout.h"

#define MAXLEN 80

struct tree
{
  char *value;
  struct tree *left, *right;
};

typedef struct tree *TREEPTR;

main()
{
  char line[MAXLEN + 1];
  char *dupline;
  TREEPTR root = NULL;
  TREEPTR temp;
  TREEPTR insert_tree(TREEPTR root, char *item);
  void print_tree(TREEPTR root);

  while (getline(line, MAXLEN) != -1)
    if ((dupline = strdup(line)) == NULL ||
        (temp = insert_tree(root, dupline)) == NULL)
    {
      putline("Out of memory");
      return 1;
    }
    else
      root`= temp;
  print_tree(root);
  return 0;
}

void print_tree(TREEPTR root)
{
  if (root != NULL)
  {
    print_tree(root->left);
    putline(root->value);
    print_tree(root->right);
  }
}
```

```
/*
 * Function to insert an item into a binary search tree.
 */
TREEPTR insert_tree(TREEPTR root, char *value)
{
  TREEPTR curr = root,
          prev = NULL;    /* parent */
  TREEPTR temp;

  while (curr != NULL)    /* find place to put node */
  {
    prev = curr;
    curr = (strcmp(value,curr->value) < 0)
               ? curr->left : curr->right;
  }
  if ((temp = (TREEPTR) malloc(sizeof(struct tree))) == NULL)
    return NULL;          /* problem creating new node */
  temp->value = value;
  temp->left = temp->right = NULL;
  if (prev == NULL)       /* insert node, updating correct */
    root = temp;          /* pointer in parent */
  else if (strcmp(value,prev->value) < 0)
    prev->left = temp;
  else
    prev->right = temp;
  return root;
}
```

Figure 13.12   treesort.c—Sort strings using binary tree insertion sort.

left subtree (printing those values), prints the node at the root of thee tree, and then calls itself recursively on its right subtree (printing those values).

A Note on the Efficiency of Tree Sort

In general, tree sort is substantially faster than insertion sort. Why? Because assuming that we're lucky and the binary tree is complete—that is, each node has exactly two nonempty subtrees, except for nodes at the bottom level—each comparison of an input value to a tree node reduces the search space by half. The result is that we only have do a few ($log_2 N$) comparisons to decide where to put the new node. We saw earlier that with insertion sort we will, on the average, examine half of the list ($N/2$). For a binary search tree, sorting time for N values averages $N log_2 N$; for insertion sort, it's N^2. As N gets large, so does the difference in speed between the two sorting methods. Of course, we're not always going to get lucky, and in the worst of all possible worlds (the input is already sorted), the tree degenerates into a list; each node will have, at most, one non-empty subtree. In this case, tree sort is no better than insertion sort. It turns out that there are ways to modify tree sort to prevent this degenerate case from happening—examine any data structures book for the details.

EXERCISES

13–17 Modify our tree sort to handle duplicate input lines. To do so, add a count field to each node. The count field is updated whenever an attempt is made to insert a value that is already in the tree. When printing the tree, use the count field to determine how many times to print a particular node.

13–18 Write a recursive function to insert a value into a binary search tree.

13–19 Write a function to delete a node from a binary search tree. There are three cases: the node has no children, the node has one child, and the node has two children.

13–20 Write recursive and iterative versions of a function search_tree that searches a binary search tree for a particular value, returning a pointer to the node that contains it or NULL if the value can't be found.

13–21 Write generic versions of the tree processing functions.

13.5   CASE STUDY—A CROSS-REFERENCE PROGRAM

Debugging programs is difficult, but can often be simplified by having a listing of the program's identifiers and the line numbers on which they appear. Such a listing is called a *cross-reference*, and a program to produce it is called a *cross-referencer*. To give you an idea of what such a program should produce, Figure 13.13 is the output of a cross-referencer run on our first C program from Chapter 1. We will build one that can be used for any file of words and, in particular, can be easily adapted for use with C or other programming languages.

Basically, all a cross-referencer does is maintain a table of words and the line numbers on which they appear. Whenever the program reads a word, it updates the table. After the program has read all of the words in its input, it prints the table in sorted order. The key question is: How do we organize the table of words?

Cross-Referencer Data Structure

To correctly choose an appropriate organization, it helps to list the characteristics that the table ought to have and see what they suggest.

The table must be able to contain an arbitrary number of words of varying size. This suggests that we dynamically allocate the table entries, and that each of these entries should contain a pointer rather than the word itself.

Table searches must be fast, because we do many searches. We have to search the table for each word to see if the word is already there, and we also need to be able to determine quickly whether a word has already occurred on the current input line. This suggests that there should be a list associated with each entry in the table: the

```
Balance             18
Generate            2
Interest            17
INTRATE             7, 17, 22
PRINCIPAL           6, 15
PERIOD              8, 19
Rate                17
Year                18
at                  13
accumulation        2
a                   2
balance             13 (2), 15, 21, 22 (3)
define              6, 7, 8
d                   21
end                 13
float               13
f                   17, 21
h                   4
interest            2, 7
int                 12
indicate            25
include             4
main                10
n                   17 (2), 18, 21
over                8
of                  7, 12, 13
program             25
printf              17, 18, 21
period              8, 12
return              25
rate                7
stdio               4
start               6
showing             2
that                25
table               2
worked              25
with                6
while               19
year                8, 12 (2), 13, 16, 19, 21, 23 (2)
```

Figure 13.13 The output of running the cross-referencer on our Chapter 1 interest rate program.

lines on which the word appears. So each table entry must not only have a pointer to the word, but also a pointer to a list of line numbers in which the word occurs.

It should be easy to print the table alphabetically by word, and in line number order for each word. To accomplish this objective, it seems reasonable to try to keep the table as a sorted list. But since the table might be large, adding a new word and searching for an existing word are likely to be time-consuming operations that, on the average, force us to examine half the words in the table. An alternative is to add new words at the end of the table, along with the current line number, and then sort the table just before printing. With this method, we can add an entry quickly, but sorting the table is costly.

No matter what, we want to avoid searching or sorting a lengthy list of words. A compromise provides a reasonable solution: We maintain separate, sorted lists of the words for each letter of the alphabet (both upper- and lowercase letters), packaged into a table of pointers. When we read a word, we use its first letter to select the appropriate table entry, and then we use insertion sort to place the word in this list. In the worst case (all words begin with the same letter), this method is no better than ordinary insertion sort. Fortunately, this worst case is unlikely, so we will rarely have to search a long list. And since the lists are kept sorted, we don't have to explicitly sort the table before we print it.

An example table with this organization is shown in Figure 13.14*a*. From examining the diagram, we can see that we need two different types of nodes: one for storing words, the other for storing line numbers. A *word node* includes a pointer to a word, a pointer to the first item in a list of line numbers, and a pointer to the following word node. And a *line node* includes a line number and a pointer to the next line node.

Actually, Figure 13.14*b* points out that there is still room for improvement. Because we always add line numbers to the end of the line number list, we want the word node to include an additional pointer, one that points to the last item in the line number list. This lets us add new line numbers without searching for the end of the list. And, rather than using multiple line nodes when a word occurs more than once in a single line, we include a *count* field that keeps track of the number of times a word appears on a given line. This should save some time-consuming allocation of nodes.

The Program

Now that we've decided on an organization for the cross-referencer's internal tables, we can worry about an organization for the cross-referencer itself. Essentially, we can divide the program, shown in Figure 13.16 into three tasks: reading the next word in the input, adding a word and line number to the table, and writing the table. We organize the program so that each of these tasks corresponds to a function— `word_get` returns the next word in the input, `table_add` adds a word to the table, `table_write` writes the table in sorted order. And furthermore, these functions correspond to the files xrefin.c, xreftab.c, and xrefout.c, respectively. To produce the runnable cross-referencer, we compile and link these files, along with the main program in file xref.c. We've placed the word table declarations in xreftab.h, which is

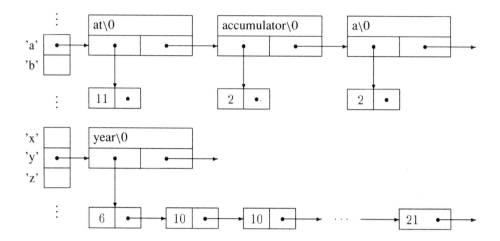

(a) Initial cross-referencer data structure.

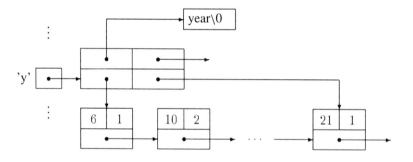

(b) Improved cross-referencer data structure.

Figure 13.14   Representing the cross-referencer word table.

included by the pieces of the program that need it. Figure 13.15 contains xreftab.h, Figure 13.16 contains xref.c, Figure 13.17 contains xrefin.c, Figure 13.18 contains xreftab.c, and Figure 13.19 contains xrefout.c.

Why did we choose this organization? Why, for example, didn't we put the entire program in one file? After all, it's a lot more work to have put the program in separate files. We had to create a header file and include it in the other source files. And we now have to use a fairly complicated project file to put the program together.

xrefout.c (xreftab.h)

```
/*
 * Header file defining word nodes and line nodes.
 */
#include <stdio.h>

#define MAXCHAR 256                     /* assume 8 bit chars */

#define SUCCESS 1
#define FAILURE 0

struct word    /* WORD NODE */
{
  char *text;                           /* value of the word */
  struct word *nextword;                /* next word */
  struct line *firstline;               /* first line node */
  struct line *lastline;                /* last line node */
};

struct line    /* LINE NODE */
{
  int lineno;                           /* value of line number */
  int count;                            /* times on line */
  struct line *nextline;                /* pointer to next line */
};

typedef struct word WORD;               /* word node */
typedef struct word *WORDPTR;           /* pointer to word node */
typedef struct line LINE;               /* line node */
typedef struct line *LINEPTR;           /* pointer to line node */
typedef WORDPTR WORDTABLE[MAXCHAR];     /* word table */

extern int word_get(char *word, int max, int *linenoptr);
extern void table_init(WORDTABLE table);
extern int table_add(WORDTABLE table, char *item, int lineno);
extern void table_write(WORDTABLE table, int wordlen);
```

Figure 13.15   xreftab.h—Handles the type definitions.

```
xreftab.c (xreftab.h)
xrefin.c
xref.c (xreftab.h)
```

The main reason is that we want to make it easy to change the internal organization of the table, or the definition of a word, or the format in which the table is written, without having to change and recompile the entire program. By placing the different pieces of the program in different files, when we change one function such as word_get, we don't have to recompile the rest of the program, which speeds program development.

There is another, more subtle, reason for breaking the program into small pieces.

```
/*
 * xref.c -- Main program of cross-referencer.
 */
#include <stdio.h>
#include "xreftab.h"

#define MAXWORD 20      /* longest word to read/write */

main()
{
  int line;
  char word[MAXWORD];
  WORDTABLE wordtable;

  table_init(wordtable);
  while (word_get(word, MAXWORD, &line) != 0)
    if (table_add(wordtable, word, line) != SUCCESS)
      printf("Out of memory at line %d\n", line);
  table_write(wordtable, MAXWORD);
}
```

Figure 13.16   xref.c—The cross-referencer program.

It is possible that at some point we'll want to change the internal organization of the table—perhaps because we find that some other data structure, such as a binary tree, is more suitable than the hybrid list structure we're currently using. When this happens, we want changes to the table's structure to affect as little of the program as possible. By having the code that directly accesses the table's elements in a different file than the main program or the input routines, we make it harder for other parts of the program to take advantage of the table's internal structure.

In fact, to ensure that the main program has no knowledge of how the table is implemented, we let it access the table only through a small set of interface functions—`table_add`, `table_write`, and `table_init` (a function to initialize the table). And we declare the variable holding the table with type `WORDTABLE` (a type we define with `typedef`), rather than as an array of pointers to word nodes. Doing so gives us the freedom of changing the table's implementation without having to rewrite the entire program.

To be honest, the main program is not completely isolated from the table's internal structure. The table may at some point fill up—either because we've implemented it as an array and we've used all the array elements, or because the table is dynamically allocated and there is no more available memory—and adding a new word to the table could fail. But we handle this possibility by having `table_add` return an error indication when it can't add a new entry. We don't let the main program examine the table itself.

The point is that we want our programs to be as modular as possible. Breaking the program up into separate pieces, each in its own file and communicating with the

```c
/*
 * xrefin.c -- Break the input into separate words.
 */
#include <stdio.h>
#include <ctype.h>

static int lineno = 1;              /* current line number */

/*
 * Read next input character updating global line count.
 */
static int nextchar(void)
{
  int c = getchar();
  extern int lineno;

  if (c == '\n')
    lineno++;
  return c;
}

/*
 * Fill in "word" and "*linenoptr".  Returns NULL when no
 * more words, otherwise word length.
 */
int word_get(char *word, int wordsize, int *linenoptr)
{
  int ch;                                /* next character */
  char *ptr = word,                      /* start of word */
       *endptr = word + wordsize - 1; /* end of word */
  int nextchar(void);

  while ((ch = nextchar()) != EOF && !isalpha(ch))
    ;                           /* skip non-letters */
  *linenoptr = lineno;        /* record line number */
  for (; ch != EOF && isalpha(ch); ch = nextchar())
    if (ptr < endptr)     /* save word up to max characters */
                          *ptr++ = ch;
  *ptr = '\0';
  return ptr - word;             /* return word length (or 0) */
}
```

Figure 13.17   xrefin.c—Handles reading input.

rest of the program only through a well-defined interface, makes it much easier for us to change or extend our program at some later time.

EXERCISES

13–22 Modify the cross-referencer so that it works for C programs. That is, so the program will *not* print C reserved words. What is the best form of the reserved word table?

13–23 After making the change suggested in the previous word, modify the program to have several tables of reserved words of various languages (C, Pascal, FORTRAN, and so on). Have command line options to select which reserved-word table the program uses.

13–24 Make the cross-reference so that it ignores words contained within comments and quoted strings.

13–25 Modify the cross-referencer to also include the position of a word on the line.

13–26 We can increase the modularity of the cross-referencing program even further. Write a function, `table_traverse`, that is passed a function which it applies to each word-line number pair stored in the table. The applied function is passed the word, a line number, a count, and an indication of whether the word is different from the previous word. Rewrite `table_write` to use `table_traverse`. Does this change suggest a different program organization?

13–27 Rewrite our cross-referencing program to use a different organization for the word table. Have it use an array of linked lists with one array element for each possible first letter of a word.

13–28 Rewrite our earlier data base program to use a binary tree to store its records. Use the employee number field as the key.

```
/*
 * xreftab.c -- Handles word table and line number references.
 */
#include <stdio.h>
#include "xreftab.h"

/*
 * Allocate word table, one entry per letter, and intialize
 * table entries to the NULL pointer.
 */
void table_init(WORDTABLE table)
{
  WORDPTR *ptr, *endptr;

  endptr = &table[MAXCHAR - 1];
  for (ptr = &table[0]; ptr <= endptr; *ptr++ = NULL)
    ;
}

/*
 * Allocate new line number for word and install in list.
 */
static int addlineno(WORDPTR currword, int lineno)
{
  LINEPTR currline = currword->lastline;   /* line node pointer */

  if (currline != NULL && currline->lineno == lineno)
  {
    currline->count++;                 /* already on this line */
    return SUCCESS;                    /* happy days */
  }

  if ((currline = (LINEPTR) malloc(sizeof(LINE))) == NULL)
    return FAILURE;                    /* couldn't allocate node */

  currline->lineno = lineno;           /* fill in node */
  currline->count = 1;

  currline->nextline = NULL;           /* hook into list */
  if (currword->firstline == NULL)
    currword->firstline = currline;  /* empty, goes in front */
  else                                 /* nonempty, goes in back */
    currword->lastline->nextline = currline;
  currword->lastline = currline;       /* update last pointer */
  return SUCCESS;
}
```

```
/*
 * Add a new word to the table.  We use the word's first letter
 * to index an appropriate list, and then insert the word there.
 */
int table_add(WORDTABLE table, char *text, int lineno)
{
  int cmpres;        /* result of comparing words */
  WORDPTR prevword = NULL,
          currword, temp;
  extern int addlineno(WORDPTR, int);

  for (currword = table[text[0]];
       currword != NULL &&
           (cmpres = strcmp(text, currword->text)) < 0;
       currword = currword->nextword)
    prevword = currword;
  if (cmpres == 0)
    return addlineno(currword, lineno);
  if ((temp = (WORDPTR) malloc(sizeof(WORD))) == NULL)
    return FAILURE;        /* out of memory */
  if ((temp->text = strdup(text)) == NULL)
  {                /* saving word failed */
    free(temp);                        /* out of memory */
    return FAILURE;                    /* die gracefully */
  }
  temp->firstline = NULL;     /* no lines yet */
  temp->lastline = NULL;
  temp->nextword = currword;  /* hook word into list */
  if (prevword == NULL)
    table[text[0]] = temp;
  else
    prevword->nextword = temp;
  return addlineno(temp, lineno);
}
```

Figure 13.18 xreftab.c—Handles building the word table.

```
/*
 * xrefout.c -- Print the table of word nodes in order.
 *              Uses new printf feature: %*s uses the
 *              next argument as the field width.
 */
#include <stdio.h>
#include <stddef.h>
#include "xreftab.h"

#define MAXLINENO 7    /* allow 7 line numbers per line */

void table_write(WORDTABLE table, int maxlen)
{
  WORDPTR *ptr = &table[0];
  WORDPTR *endptr = &table[MAXCHAR - 1];
  WORDPTR currword;      /* pointer to next node in word list */
  LINEPTR currline;      /* pointer to next line number node */
  int     count;         /* count of line nos for this word */

  for (; ptr <= endptr; ptr++)
    for (currword = *ptr;
         currword != NULL;
         currword = currword->nextword)
    {                    /* run through each word w/ that letter */
      count = 0;
      printf("\%-*s", maxlen, currword->text);
      for (currline = currword->firstline;
           currline != NULL;
           currline = currline->nextline)
      {                                  /* write the line numbers */
        if (count == MAXLINENO)
        {                                /* wrap to next line */
          printf("\n%-*s", maxlen, " ");
          count = 0;
        }
        printf(" %d" , currline->lineno);
        if (currline->count > 1)
          printf(" (%d)", currline->count);
        if (currline->nextline != NULL)   /* not last */
          putchar(',');
        count++;                 /* next */
      }
      putchar('\n');
    }
}
```

Figure 13.19   xrefout.c—Handles writing the word table.

14 EXTERNAL FILES

Our earlier programs have accessed files solely through their standard input and output. But that's a severe limitation—those programs can access only one input and one output file. Fortunately, C provides a well-stocked library of functions for manipulating external files. This chapter presents most of these functions, and uses them to write useful utilities to copy files, to compute a file's length, and to display a file's last few lines. We also write a small package that allows us to treat a file as though it were a large array. The chapter concludes with a electronic address book, one that stores the addresses and phone numbers in an indexed external file.

14.1 ACCESSING EXTERNAL FILES

Up to now, whenever we've wanted one of our programs to read or write an external file, we've redirected its standard input or output. But to be able to deal with more than one file at one time, we also need a way to access external files directly. In C, we do so using a set of library functions.

Before we can access a file, we have to *open* it. Opening a file does several things. It causes the system to set up any internal data structures, such as buffers, that are necessary for processing the file. And it gives us a handle that we can use to conveniently identify the file when calling I/O library functions. We open a file with the standard I/O function `fopen`. `fopen` takes two string parameters, a file name and a mode, and returns a pointer to a `FILE`. Unlike `int` and `float`, `FILE` is not one of C's basic data types. Instead, it is usually a structure (defined in stdio.h) that contains information useful to the library routines that process files. `fopen` returns `NULL` if there is an error and the file can't be opened.

The mode specifies how we plan to use the file. The basic modes are `"r"` (open for reading), `"w"` (open for writing), and `"a"` (open for appending). So

```
#include <stdio.h>
    ...
FILE *fp;
    ...
fp = fopen("phonenos", "r");    /* open phone number file */
if (fp == NULL)
  printf("Couldn't open phonenos.\n");
```

opens the file *phonenos* for reading.

We can open a file for reading only if it already exists. But there is no such restriction when we open a file for writing or appending. If the file doesn't exist, it is automatically created for us. If it does exist, opening it for writing wipes out its previous contents, and opening it for appending causes new writes to take place at the file's end.

In Turbo C, the mode also specifies the file's type—either *text* or *binary*. The difference between the two is that Turbo C does some additional processing on text files. Specifically, when reading from a text file, Turbo C ignores any carriage return (\r) that immediately precedes a line feed (\n). Similarly, when writing to a text file, Turbo C inserts a carriage return before every line feed. This extra mapping is necessary because many existing DOS programs, such as text editors and other utilities, create files that use the carriage-return/line-feed combination to indicate the end of a line.

Turbo C assumes by default that a file is a text file. We can make this assumption explicit by appending a t to the basic mode, as in "rt", "wt", or "at". We specify a binary file by appending a b, as in "rb", "wb", and "ab". In general, we use text mode when we think of the file as being divided into lines, such as in a program that prints every line containing a particular pattern. We use binary files when we don't care how the file is organized, as in a file copying program, or when we treat the file as being divided into records.

After we open a file, we can use any one of a large set of library functions to actually access its contents. When we're finished with a file, we use fclose to *close* it. This forces out any buffered output and frees up the file's FILE structure. fclose takes a single file-pointer argument, and returns EOF if there is an error in closing the file. Because most systems have a maximum number of files that can be open simultaneously (usually about twenty per program), we habitually close a file as soon as we no longer need it. All files, however, are automatically closed when our program terminates.

Character File I/O

There are several ways to access an open file. The simplest is a character at a time, using getc and putc, which are analogous to getchar and putchar. getc takes a file pointer and returns the integer representation of the next character in the file, or EOF if it encounters an end of file. putc takes the integer representation of a character and a file pointer and writes the character to the file. Both functions return EOF if an error occurs.

With getc and putc, we now have the pieces to write a useful utility program to copy files. This program, called filecopy and shown in Figure 14.1, takes two file-name arguments, copying the file named by its first argument into the file named by its second. For example,

filecopy paper paper.bak

copies the contents of the file paper into the file paper.bak.

filecopy begins by verifying that it was passed three arguments (the program name and the two file names), printing an error message if it wasn't. It then uses a function `filecpy` to actually perform the copy, passing it the two file names. `filecpy` opens the files, copies one into the other with `getc` and `putc`, and then closes the files. It returns the number of characters it copied, or −1 if it couldn't open both files successfully.

We don't care whether the files are divided into lines, so we open both of them in binary mode. Since opening a file for writing destroys the file's contents, we are careful to do the open for writing only after the open for reading has succeeded. In this way, we destroy the previous contents of the destination file only if there is something to copy. Finally, we also take care to perform the copy only if both opens are successful.

`filecpy` checks for only one error, a failed open, and ignores the possibility of other errors, such as a failed read or write. Although this is standard practice, it can cause problems in the unlikely event that an I/O error does occur, and we can make our programs more robust by checking for that possibility. (Usually such failures are caused by hardware errors, but write errors can also occur when a device becomes full and there is no room for the newly written characters.) The standard I/O output functions return `EOF` if they detect a write error, so `filecpy` should print an error message if `putc`'s return value is `EOF`. It should also check `fclose`'s return value, since output is usually buffered and it is possible that the final few characters aren't really written to the file until the file is closed.

Detecting read errors is more difficult, since `EOF` can indicate either an error or end of file. There are two library functions, `feof` and `ferror`, that help us distinguish between these two meanings. `feof` takes a file pointer and returns a nonzero value only when the end of the file has been reached. `ferror` is similar, taking a file pointer and returning nonzero only if an error has occurred in processing that file.

To keep our examples simple, we avoid the added complication of file I/O error handling—but at a cost. When an error does occur, our programs may behave abnormally, without indicating any error. Typically, an unchecked input error as `EOF` prematurely terminates input processing, and an unchecked output error results in lost output. In fact, filecopy now simply prints the number of characters in the source file, and relies on the user verifying that the destination file actually has this length (which can be done using the DOS dir command). Production quality programs check the values returned by the standard input and output library functions and provide appropriate error indications.

Formatted I/O to Files

As you might have guessed, both `printf` and `scanf` have counterparts that do formatted I/O on files. `fprintf` is like `printf`, with an additional file pointer argument that specifies the file to which we write.

> `fprintf` (*file-pointer*, *control-string*, ...)

And `fscanf` is like `scanf`, with an additional file-pointer argument that specifies the file from which we read.

```
/*
 * filecopy source dest (line-at-a-time file copying utility).
 */
#include <stdio.h>
#include <string.h>
#include <stddef.h>

#define MAXLEN  80              /* longest input line */

main(int argc, char *argv[])
{
  long copycnt;
  long filecpy(char *dest, char *source);

  if (argc != 3)
  {
    printf("Usage: %s source dest\n", argv[0]);
    return 1;    /* early exit; bad arguments */
  }
  if ((copycnt = filecpy(argv[2], argv[1])) == -1L)
  {
    printf("Copy failed\n");
    return 1;    /* early exit; file problems */
  }
  printf("Copied %ld characters\n", copycnt);
  return 0;
}

long filecpy(char *dest, char *source)
{
  FILE *sfp;                 /* source file pointer */
  FILE *dfp;                 /* destination file pointer */
  int c;
  long cnt = -1L;

  if ((sfp = fopen(source,"rb")) == NULL)
    printf("Can't open %s for reading\n", source);
  else
  {
    if ((dfp = fopen(dest,"wb")) == NULL)
      printf("Can't open %s for writing\n", dest);
    else
    {
      for (cnt = 0L; (c = getc(sfp)) != EOF; cnt++)
        putc(c,dfp);
      fclose(dfp);
    }
    fclose(sfp);
  }
  return cnt;
}
```

Figure 14.1 filecopy.c—A program to copy one file into another.

```
/*
 * Read up to "max" values into "a" from file "name".
 */
#include <stdio.h>
#include "getints.h"

#define TESTFILE   "table"
#define MAX        20

int main()
{
  int table[MAX], i;

  for (i = 0; i < MAX; i++)          /* some sample values */
    table[i] = i;
  if (fputints(TESTFILE, table, MAX) != MAX)
  {
    printf("Couldn't write array to file\n");
    return 1;      /* early exit; couldn't dump table */
  }
  if (fgetints(TESTFILE, table, MAX) != MAX)
  {
    printf("Couldn't read array from file\n");
    return 1;      /* early exit; couldn't load table */
  }
  printf("Wrote and read %d ints using %s\n", MAX, TESTFILE);
  return 0;
}
```

Figure 14.2   fints.c—A program to read and write arrays of integers onto a file.

> fscanf (*file-pointer*, *control-string*, ...)

Because of their similarity to `printf` and `scanf`, it is easy to forget to pass the file pointer to `fprintf` or `fscanf`. But if we've remembered to include stdio.h, which supplies prototypes for the various library functions, the compiler catches this error for us.

Figure 14.2 provides an example use of `fprintf` and `fscanf` in a small program to write an array to a file and then read the file back into the array. It uses two functions, `fgetints` and `fputints`. `fgetints` uses `fscanf` to read an array of integers from a file, `fputints` uses `fprintf` to write an array of integers to a file. Figure 14.3 contains their prototypes, and Figure 14.4 contains the functions.

We've hard-coded the file's name as a constant string. That's fine, but we have to be careful when we supply a path name. The call

> fgetints("c:\temp\table", table, MAX)   /* WRONG */

doesn't do what it is supposed to—the file open fails. Why? Because in DOS, a backslash indicates a directory name, but in C, a backslash indicates an escape

```
/*
 * getints.h - Prototypes for table-reading functions.
 */

int fputints(char *name, int *ptr, int max);
int fgetints(char *name, int *ptr, int max);
```

Figure 14.3   getints.h—The prototypes for table-reading functions.

```
/*
 * getints1.c -- Reading/Writing arrays.
 */
#include <stdio.h>

int fgetints(char *name, int a[], int max)
{
  int cnt = 0;
  FILE *fp = fopen(name, "r");

  if (fp != NULL)
  {
    for (; cnt < max; cnt++)          /* read values */
      if (fscanf(fp, "%d", &a[cnt]) != 1)
        break;
    fclose(fp);
  }
  return cnt;     /* number of values actually read */
}

int fputints(char *name, int a[], int num)
{
  int cnt = 0;
  FILE *fp = fopen(name, "w");

  if (fp != NULL)
  {
    for (; cnt < num; cnt++)
      fprintf(fp, "%d\n", a[cnt]);
    fclose(fp);
  }
  return cnt;          /* assumes write successful */
}
```

Figure 14.4   getints1.c—Two functions, `fgetints` and `fputints`, for reading and writing arrays.

sequence. This means that in the above name, the compiler substitutes a tab character for each \t in the file's name. Fortunately, the fix is straightforward: we simply provide two backslashes instead of one.

```
fgetints("c:\\temp\\table", table, MAX)    /* CORRECT */
```

Line-Oriented I/O

Many programs, such as uniq (Chapter 6), most naturally process their input a line at a time. The standard I/O library provides four functions that do line-at-a-time I/O. The most general of these functions are fgets and fputs.

fgets takes three parameters: a character array, its size, and a file pointer. It reads characters into the array, stopping when it encounters a newline or it finds that the array is full. Unlike our function getline, fgets includes the newline in the array. fgets terminates the array with a null, so it reads at most one less than the number of characters in the array. So the call

```
char buffer[MAXLEN + 1];
    . . .
fgets(buffer, MAXLEN + 1, fp)
```

reads up to MAXLEN characters, placing them into buffer. fgets returns NULL when the end of file is reached; otherwise, it returns its first argument, a pointer to a character.

If the line (including the trailing new line) is too long, we can keep calling fgets to read the rest of the line. Unfortunately, with fgets there is no way to determine if the entire input line was read without examining the returned string. This makes fgets much less useful than it would be if it returned the line length as getline does.

fputs takes a string and a file pointer and writes the string to the file. For example,

```
fputs("Hi Mom! Hi Dad! Send money!\n", fp);
```

writes a single line to the file specified by fp. It does not automatically terminate its output with a new line. fputs provides a convenient and more efficient way to print a string than fprintf, since it eliminates the overhead of parsing the control string. Its one drawback is that the file pointer is its last argument instead of its first argument, as with fprintf.

We use fgets and fputs in a new version of filecpy, shown in Figure 14.5. This line-copying version produces the same result as the character-copying version, albeit somewhat slower, since fgets and fputs are usually built on top of getc and putc, and because we have to determine the length of each line in the file.

The other two line-oriented functions, gets and puts, are closely related to fgets and fputs. Unfortunately, they are also just different enough to cause confusion. gets takes a character array, reads a line from the standard input, places it into the array, and terminates the array with a null. It returns a pointer to the array's first character, or NULL if it encounters an end of file. Unlike fgets, gets does

```c
/*
 * filecopy source dest (line-at-a-time file-copying utility).
 */
#include <stdio.h>
#include <string.h>
#include <stddef.h>

#define MAXLEN  80              /* longest input line */

int main(int argc, char *argv[])
{
  long copycnt;
  long filecpy(char *dest, char *source);

  if (argc != 3)
  {
    printf("Usage: %s source dest\n", argv[0]);
    return 1;      /* early exit, bad arguments */
  }
  if ((copycnt = filecpy(argv[2], argv[1])) == -1L)
  {
    printf("Copy failed\n");
    return 1;      /* early exit, file problems */
  }
  printf("Copied %ld characters\n", copycnt);
  return 0;
}

long filecpy(char *dest, char *source)
{
  FILE *sfp, *dfp;
  char line[MAXLEN + 1];
  long cnt = -1L;

  if ((sfp = fopen(source,"rb")) == NULL)
    printf("Can't open %s for reading\n", source);
  else
  {
    if ((dfp = fopen(dest,"wb")) == NULL)
      printf("Can't open %s for writing\n", dest);
    else
    {
      for (cnt = 0L; fgets(line, sizeof(line), sfp) != NULL;
           cnt += strlen(line))
        fputs(line,dfp);
      fclose(dfp);
    }
    fclose(sfp);
  }
  return cnt;
}
```

Figure 14.5 linecpy.c—A program to copy files line by line. Surprisingly, this is slower than character by character.

not place the terminating newline into the array. `puts` is simpler and more useful, taking a string and writing it and a trailing newline onto the standard output.

We use `puts` and `gets` most frequently to prompt the user for input and to read the response, as shown below.

```
char response[MAXLEN + 1];
    . . .
puts("What's your name?");
if (gets(response) != NULL)
  printf("Hi %s!  Do you like Turbo C?\n", response);
```

`gets` isn't all that useful. Because there is no way to limit the number of characters it reads, the program will "bomb" if the user enters more characters than the array can accommodate. We use `getline` instead.

EXERCISES

14-1 Make `filecpy` check for both read and write errors.

14-2 Write a function, `fileapp`, that appends one file to the end of another. Can `filecpy` and `fileapp` be combined into a single function? Is this a good idea?

14-3 Implement `fgets`, `fputs`, `puts`, and `gets`, using only `getc` and `putc`.

14-4 Write a function, `fgetline`, that is just like `getline` except that it reads its input from a file rather than the standard input.

14-5 Write a program to compare two files and print the line number of the first byte where they differ.

14-6 Write `wc`, a program that counts the number of words, lines, and characters in each of the files supplied as its arguments.

14-7 Make `uniq` work with external files.

14-8 Modify the cross-referencing program from the previous chapter so that it works with text files.

14.2   THE STANDARD FILES

When our programs start, four text files are automatically opened for us: the standard input, the standard output, and the standard error output. The corresponding file pointers are `stdin`, `stdout`, `stderr`, and `stdprn`, and are defined in stdio.h. These file pointers are constants, so we can't assign to them.

We've already been using `stdin` and `stdout`, even though we didn't know it. That is because `getchar` and `putchar` are defined as macros that expand into calls to `getc` and `putc`.

```
#define getchar()      getc(stdin)
#define putchar(c)     putc(c, stdout)
```

```
/*
 * Header file for fileopen/fileclose functions.
 */
#include <stdio.h>
#include <stddef.h>

extern FILE *fileopen(char *name, char *mode);
extern void fileclose(char *name, FILE *fp);
```

Figure 14.6   fileopen.h—Header file for file opening and closing functions.

Similarly, we can read from the standard input with either scanf(...) or with fscanf(stdin,...), and we can write to the standard output with either printf(...) or with fprintf(stdout,...).

We haven't used stderr yet. stderr is the place where we write error messages, since they will then show up on the console, even if the standard output has been redirected. That is, stderr is an output file like stdout, but it isn't redirected when we redirect stdout.

We use stderr in the functions fileopen and fileclose. Figure 14.6 supplies their prototypes and Figure 14.7 contains the functions themselves. fileopen is an extension to fopen, that not only opens the file for us, but it also writes an appropriate error message onto stderr if it fails. fileclose takes a file name and a file pointer, closing the file if it wasn't passed a NULL pointer, and writing an error message if necessary. These two functions simplify our file handling functions, since they no longer have to worry about error handling. We'll see just how convenient they are later in the chapter.

The final file pointer, stdprn, is a special addition to Turbo C that we can use to write to the printer. For example, we can modify Chapter 8's page-numbering program to actually print to a printer rather than just the standard output, simply by replacing its two printf statements

```
printf("\fPage Number: %d\n\n", ++pageno);
printf("%6lu %s\n", ++lineno, line);
```

with identical fprintf statements that write to stdprn.

```
fprintf(stdprn, "\fPage Number: %d\n\n", ++pageno);
fprintf(stdprn, "%6lu %s\n", ++lineno, line);
```

EXERCISES

14-9 Rewrite filecpy to use fileopen and fileclose.

14-10 Modify page (Chapter 3) to display the files given to it as arguments on the printer. It should use the standard input if no files are provided.

```
/*
 * Open and close files, writing an error message if it fails.
 */
#include "fileopen.h"

FILE *fileopen(char *name, char *mode)
{
  FILE *fp = fopen(name, mode);              /* open the file */

  if (fp == NULL)                            /* did open fail? */
  {
    fprintf(stderr, "Can't open %s for ", name);
    switch(mode[0])
    {
      case 'r': fprintf(stderr, "reading\n");
                break;
      case 'w': fprintf(stderr, "writing\n");
                break;
      case 'a': fprintf(stderr, "appending\n");
                break;
      default:  fprintf(stderr, "some strange mode\n");
                break;
    }
  }
  return fp;
}

void fileclose(char *name, FILE *fp)
{
  if (fp != NULL && fclose(fp) == EOF)
    fprintf(stderr, "Error closing %s\n", name);
}
```

Figure 14.7   fileopen.c—The functions `fileopen` and `fileclose` that open and close files, printing any necessary error message onto the standard error.

14-11 Write a program keep that prints only certain lines in the files provided as its arguments. The lines to print are specified as options. The command

keep -1-10 -50,52,54 *file*

prints the first 10 lines of *file* followed by lines 50, 52 and 54. keep should work with the standard input if no files are specified.

14-12 Write a program, cut, that prints only certain characters in the lines of the files provided as its arguments. As with `keep`, the relevant characters are provided as options. The command

cut -1-10 -50,52,54 *file*

prints each line without printing its first 10 characters or characters 50, 52, and 54.

14-13 Modify the file handling version of uniq (or any of the other file handling programs you wrote as solutions to earlier exercises) to use the standard input if it isn't provided with file-name arguments.

14.3   RANDOM FILE ACCESS

All our file processing has been sequential. That is, we started reading at the beginning of the file, and read characters one after the other until we hit its end. But we are sometimes interested in only part of a file, and we want to avoid reading all the preceding data. In effect, we want to treat a file like an array, indexing any byte in the file as we would an array element. Three standard I/O functions support this random file access: fseek, rewind, and ftell.

fseek moves the internal file pointer, which points to the next character in the file, to a specified location within the file. It takes three arguments—a file pointer, a long offset, and an int specifier—and computes the new location by adding the offset to the part of the file specified by the specifier. The specifier must have one of three values: 0 means the beginning of the file, 1 means the current position, and 2 means the end of the file. Here are some example fseek's:

```
long n;
    . . .
fseek(fp, 0L, 0);     /* goto the start of the file */
fseek(fp, 0L, 1);     /* don't move (not too useful!) */
fseek(fp, 0L, 2);     /* goto the end of the file */
fseek(fp, n, 0);      /* goto the nth byte in the file */
fseek(fp, n, 1);      /* skip ahead n bytes */
fseek(fp, -n, 1);     /* go backwards n bytes */
fseek(fp, -n, 2);     /* goto n bytes before the file's end */
```

Warning: Forgetting that fseek's *second parameter is a* long *produces strange and less-than-wonderful results.* fseek returns −1 if there is an error, such as attempting to seek past the file's boundaries, and zero otherwise. We have ignored fseek's return value in these examples; however, by checking it we can verify that the file position was changed.

rewind is a special case fseek which moves the internal file pointer to the beginning of the file, the equivalent of

```
fseek(fp, 0L, 0)
```

A rewind happens implicitly whenever we do an fopen for reading or writing (but not, of course, when we do an fopen for appending). Any input function immediately following a rewind begins its reading with the file's first character. rewind lets a program read through a file more than once without having to repeatedly open and close the file.

The final function, ftell, takes a file pointer and returns a long containing the current offset in the file, the position of the next byte to be read or written. So an ftell at the beginning of the file returns the position of the file's first byte, and an ftell at the end of the file returns the number of bytes in the file. Typically,

```
/*
 * filelen.c -- Find file's length in bytes.
 */
#include <stdio.h>
#include "fileopen.h"

int main(int argc, char *argv[])
{
  int i;                                 /* argument length */
  long len;                              /* next file's length */
  FILE *fp;                              /* file pointer */
  long filelen(FILE *fp);

  for (i = 1; i < argc; i++)
  {
    if ((fp = fileopen(argv[i], "rb")) != NULL)
      if ((len = filelen(fp)) == -1)
        fprintf(stderr,"Can't compute length of %s\n", argv[i]);
      else
        printf("%s: %d\n", argv[i], len);
    fileclose(argv[i], fp);
  }
  return 0;    /* don't worry about error codes */
}

long filelen(FILE *fp)             /* determine length of file */
{
  long oldpos, length;

  oldpos = ftell(fp);                        /* save old position */
  if (fseek(fp, 0L, 2) == -1) return -1; /* goto end of file */
  length = ftell(fp);                        /* compute length */
  return (fseek(fp, oldpos, 0) == -1) ? -1 : length;
}
```

Figure 14.8   filelen.c—A program to rapidly determine the size in bytes of a file.

programs use ftell to save their current position in a file so that they can easily return to it later, without having to read all the intervening data.

We use ftell and fseek in two programs. The first, length, shown in Figure 14.8, prints the number of bytes in the files provided as its arguments. It uses a function filelen to compute each file's length. filelen, in turn, uses ftell to save the current position in the file, fseek to go to the end of the file, ftell to record that position (which is the file's length), and another fseek to return to the previous position within the file. We are careful to test fseek's return value, because the file pointer's position doesn't change if we specify an invalid location to which to move.

Our second example is a program, tail, that prints the last 10 lines of each of the files specified as its arguments. It is especially useful for examining files, such as log files, in which new information is always appended to the end.

There is an especially easy way to write tail. We can use `fseek` to get to the file's end and then read the file backwards until the desired number of newlines have been seen. We can read backwards by first saving the current offset with `ftell`, reading a character with `getc`, and then using `fseek` to move to the character before the saved offset. Once we find the beginning of the appropriate line, we simply read and display the rest of the characters in the file. The problem with this simple-minded solution is that it is slow—several library calls are executed for each character we read.

We improve this scheme by reading a *block* of characters each time, and then counting the newlines within each block. A version of tail that works this way is shown in Figure 14.9. The program's surprising length arises from its substantial error checking.

EXERCISES

14-14 Modify tail to provide a command-line option that allows the user to select the number of lines to display.

14-15 Write a program, rev, that reverses the files provided as its arguments, one character at a time. This program is a useful April Fools' Day substitute for the dos type command.

14-16 Write a program that takes three arguments—a file name, a byte offset, and a byte count—and prints the specified bytes within the specified file.

14-17 Write a program, view, that allows a user to examine any specified line in a file. view should construct an index table, an array whose items hold the starting position of the corresponding line in the file. To get to the user-specified line, it uses this line as an index into the table, and then uses `fseek` to move to that position in the file.

14.4   BLOCK INPUT AND OUTPUT

The standard I/O library functions we have seen so far are designed to read and write characters. C also provides two functions to read and write blocks of bytes: `fread` reads an array of bytes from a file, and `fwrite` writes an array to a file. Both are passed four parameters: a pointer to the array's first element (`void *`), the size (in bytes) of an element, the number of elements in the array, and a file pointer. Both return the number of elements successfully read or written; zero indicates the end of file or an error.

We use `fread` and `fwrite` in Figure 14.10, which contains new versions of the functions `fgetints` and `fputints` (Figure 14.2). Now `fgetints` reads the array with a single `fread`, and `fputints` writes the array with a single `fwrite`.

```
/*
 * tail.c -- Print last 10 lines of a file.
 */
#include "fileopen.h"

#define LAST     10     /* last ten lines of the file */
#define MAXBUF  512     /* size of a block */

main(int argc, char *argv[])
{
  int i;                    /* count of newlines seen, index */
  long pos;                 /* position of newline within block */
  FILE *fp;
  long findpos(FILE *fp);
  void display(FILE *fp);


  for (i = 1; i < argc; i++)
    if ((fp = fileopen(argv[i],"rb")) != NULL)
    {
      if ((pos = findpos(fp)) == -1L || fseek(fp, pos, 0) == -1)
        fprintf(stderr,"Couldn't tail %s\n", argv[i]);
      else
        display(fp);
      fileclose(argv[1], fp);
    }
  return 0;         /* no special return value for error */
}

/*
 * Find position of first character in part of the file
 * we want to print by reading backwards through file.
 */
long findpos(FILE *fp)
{
  int  count = 0;      /* newlines seen */
  long pos;            /* position of desired newline within file */
  long blkend;         /* position of last char in block */
  int  blksize;        /* # of characters within block */
  int nextblock(FILE *fp, int max, int *cnt, int target);


  if (fseek(fp, 0L, 2) == -1)
    return -1;                    /* get to end of file */
  for (blkend = ftell(fp); blkend >= 0; blkend -= MAXBUF)
  {
    blksize = (MAXBUF > blkend) ? (int) blkend : MAXBUF;
    if (fseek(fp, blkend - blksize, 0) == -1)
      return -1;         /* couldn't go back one block */
    if ((pos = nextblock(fp, blksize, &count, LAST)) != -1)
      return blkend - blksize + pos;
  }
  return 0L;             /* start at beginning */
}
```

```
/*
 * The rest of tail.
 */
int nextblock(FILE *fp, int max, int *cnt, int target)
{
  char buffer[MAXBUF];      /* to hold block */
  char *ptr = buffer;       /* indexes buffer */
  char *endptr = buffer + max - 1;  /* end of buffer */
  int c;

  for (; ptr <= endptr && (c = getc(fp)) != EOF; *ptr++ = c)
     ;                         /* read next block of characters */
  *ptr = '\0';
  for (; ptr >= buffer; ptr--)
    if (*ptr == '\n' && (*cnt)++ == target)
       return ptr - buffer + 1; /* where to start reading */
  return -1;                    /* have to read another block */
}

/*
 * Display from current position to end of file.
 */
void display(FILE *fp)
{
  int c;

  while ((c = getc(fp)) != EOF)
    putc(c, stdout);
}
```

Figure 14.9 tail.c—A program to print the last 10 lines of each of the files specified as its arguments.

The new versions aren't exactly equivalent, however. To see why, note that our call to fwrite simply writes sizeof(int) × 10 bytes to the file, the first byte coming from &x[0]. And similarly, our call to fread reads the next sizeof(int) × max bytes from the file into the array a. No translation to and from ASCII characters takes place. This means the file is a binary file rather than a text file, and we are careful to specify the rb and wb modes when we open it.

fread and fwrite provide a convenient and efficient way to save internal tables between program runs. We often use fwrite to save an internal table when a program finishes and fread to read it the next time the program starts. This method is much more efficient than using fprintf and fscanf, but has the disadvantage that the saved table is not text and cannot be easily examined.

Warning: While the use of fread *and* fwrite *is portable, the files read and written by them are not.* To see why, consider a file containing 100 ints written using fwrite. If ints are 2 bytes, as on the PC, this file takes 200 bytes. Now

```
/*
 * getints2.c -- New versions of our earlier functions to read
 *               and write arrays.  Now they use fread/fwrite
 *               to write the arrrays all at once (rather than
 *               using getc/putc).
 */
#include <stdio.h>
#include "fileopen.h"

int fgetints(char *name, int a[], int max)
{
  FILE *fp = fileopen(name, "rb");
  int cnt = -1;

  if (fp != NULL)
    cnt = fread((void *) a, sizeof(int), max, fp);
  fileclose(name, fp);
  return cnt;  /* # of elements written or -1 */
}

int fputints(char *name, int a[], int num)
{
  FILE *fp = fileopen(name, "wb");
  int cnt = -1;

  if (fp != NULL)
    cnt = fwrite((void *) a, sizeof(int), num, fp);
  fileclose(name, fp);
  return cnt;  /* # of elements written or -1 */
}
```

Figure 14.10 getints2.c—New version of fgetints and fputints, functions to read and write arrays of integers.

suppose the file is moved to a machine with 4-byte ints, and we try to read it using fread, telling fread to read 100 ints. fread will try to read 400 bytes, which it won't be able to do. The moral: Don't use fwrite to create files to be transferred between machines.

EXERCISES

14-18 Rewrite filecpy to use fread and fwrite.

14-19 Have tail use fread to read the next block of bytes, and fwrite to display it.

14-20 Implement fread and fwrite using getc and putc.

14.5	**FILE UPDATING**

Turbo C provides three basic file modes we haven't yet mentioned: r+, w+, and a+. The trailing + means "open for update." When we open a file for update we are allowed to both read and write to it—with one important restriction. We can't immediately follow a read with a write or a write with a read; there must be an intervening fseek. Except for the ability to update, the modes have the same effects as their earlier counterparts. That is, when we open a file for "r+", the file must already exist. When we open a file for "w+", the file is either created or truncated. And when we open a file for "a+", the file is created if it doesn't exist, and the internal file pointer moved to the end of the file.

The update modes allows us to change a file's contents without completely rewriting it. We'll show how useful this is by writing a little package that allows us to create and access an array of any type, with its elements stored in a file rather than in memory. We call such an array an *external* array. External arrays are a convenient—but slow—way to store a large table when we have a limited amount of available memory. The package makes it easy for us to use files as arrays without forcing us to sprinkle lots and lots of fseeks, freads, and fwrites throughout our code.

Our package lets us access external arrays in the same way we access files. We first open them, which gives us a handle that we then pass to the functions that access or change an element's value. And when we are done, we close them.

We provide two ways to open an external array. The first, ea_create, creates a new external array. It takes two arguments: the name of the file in which the array is to be stored and the size in bytes of one of its elements. The function opens the file using mode w+b, which wipes out any previous contents and allows us to subsequently read or write the file. ea_create returns a pointer to an EXTARRAY. An EXTARRAY is a structure, like FILE, that contains information needed by the other functions in our package. Specifically, it contains a file pointer, the file's name, and the size of an element.

The other function, ea_open, lets us access an existing external array. It takes three arguments: the name of the file, the size in bytes of an element, and a pointer to variable to be filled in with the number of elements already in the array. Unlike ea_create, ea_open opens the file with mode r+b, which succeeds only if the file already exists. After opening the file, it computes the file's length (by seeking to its end and determining its offset) and determines how many elements are currently in it. Like ea_create, ea_open returns a pointer to an EXTARRAY.

Once we've opened an external array, we use ea_get and ea_put to access or change the values of its elements. Both take similar parameters: a pointer to an EXTARRAY, the index of the desired element, and a pointer to a buffer the size of an array element. ea_get determines the element's location within the file, uses fseek to move to that location, and then uses fread to read its value into the provided buffer. ea_put does the opposite: It writes the contents of the buffer to the appropriate position in the file. Both functions return zero if they can't successfully access the specified array element.

ea_put has a restriction that arises out of one of fseek's limitations. *Warning:*

```
 * extarray.h -- Define external arrays and provide prototypes
 *                for functions that manipulate them.
 */
#include <stdio.h>
#include <stddef.h>

struct extarray
{
  char *name;      /* name of file holding array */
  FILE *fp;        /* pointer to external file */
  int  size;       /* size of an element */
};

typedef struct extarray EXTARRAY;

/* PROTOTYPES */

EXTARRAY *ea_create(char *name, int size);
EXTARRAY *ea_open(char *name, int size, int *itemsptr);
void ea_close(EXTARRAY *ep);
int ea_get(EXTARRAY *ep, int index, void *table);
int ea_put(EXTARRAY *ep, int index, void *table);
int ea_init(EXTARRAY *ep, int items, void *table);
```

Figure 14.11   extarray.h—Header file for external arrays.

We can't use fseek *to move the internal file pointer past the end of the file.* That means we can use ea_put only to assign a new value to an existing array element or to append a single new element onto the end of the array. This isn't terrible, since we can create and initialize the elements of an external array by repeatedly using ea_put. But we also provide an alternative way to initialize an external array. This function, ea_init, takes an EXTARRAY pointer, an array, and a count, and initializes the EXTARRAY with the values in the provided array. It returns the number of array elements successfully initialized.

The package's final function, ea_close, closes an external array. It takes a pointer to an EXTARRAY, closes the file associated with it, and deallocates its EX-TARRAY structure.

Figure 14.11 contains a header file, extarray.h, that defines the EXTARRAY type and provides prototypes for the various external array operations. Figure 14.12, the file extarray.c, contains the operations themselves. We'll use these functions in writing the case study shown in the next chapter.

EXERCISES

```
/*
 * extarray.c -- Basic external array operations:
 *    ea_create - create an external array.
 *    ea_open   - open an existing external array.
 *    ea_init   - initialize an external array from internal array.
 *    ea_get    - read a single external array element.
 *    ea_put    - write a single external array element.
 */
#include <alloc.h>
#include <string.h>
#include "extarray.h"


EXTARRAY *ea_create(char *name, int size)
{
  FILE *fp = fopen(name, "w+b");
  EXTARRAY *make_extarray(FILE *fp, char *name, int size);

  return fp != NULL ? make_extarray(fp, name, size) : NULL;
}

EXTARRAY *ea_open(char *name, int size, int *numptr)
{
  FILE *fp = fopen(name, "r+b");   /* open file for read/update */
  long length;
  EXTARRAY *make_extarray(FILE *fp, char *name, int size);

  if (fp != NULL)                  /* couldn't open file */
    if (fseek(fp, 0L, 2) != -1 && (length = ftell(fp)) != -1)
    {
      *numptr = (int) (length / size);
      return make_extarray(fp, name, size);
    }
    else
      fclose(fp);
  return NULL;
}

void ea_close(EXTARRAY *x)
{
  fclose(x->fp);
  free((void *) x->name);
  free((void *) x);
}

int ea_init(EXTARRAY *x, int items, void *table)
{
  rewind(x->fp);
  return fwrite(table, x->size, items, x->fp);
}
```

```
int ea_get(EXTARRAY *x, int idx, void *element)
{
  return fseek(x->fp, (long) idx * x->size, 0) != -1 &&
         fread(element, x->size, 1, x->fp) == 1;
}

int ea_put(EXTARRAY *x, int idx, void *element)
{
  return fseek(x->fp, (long) idx * x->size, 0) != -1 &&
         fwrite(element, x->size, 1, x->fp) == 1;
}

static EXTARRAY *make_extarray(FILE *fp, char *name, int size)
{
  EXTARRAY *new = (EXTARRAY *) malloc(sizeof(EXTARRAY));

  if (new != NULL && (new->name = strdup(name)) != NULL)
  {
    new->fp = fp;
    new->size= size;
  }
  else
    fclose(fp);
  return new;
}
```

Figure 14.12   extarray.c—A library of functions for treating files as though they were arrays.

14-21   We can speed up our array-accessing functions by keeping a cache of the most recently accessed array elements. The cache is a small in-memory array. The idea is that whenever we access an array element, we first check the cache. If the value is there, we've saved a file access. If it isn't, we access the file element like before, except that we also add it to the cache, removing whatever item has been in the cache the longest (writing it to the file if its value has changed).

14-22   Write an insertion sort that works with external arrays. Use any of the earlier insertion sort programs as a starting point.

14-23   Rewrite Chapter 12's data base program to keep its data base in a file rather than in memory. Make use of external arrays.

14.6   CASE STUDY—AN INDEXED DATA BASE

We bring together many of the concepts covered in this text by implementing a small indexed data base containing names, addresses, and phone numbers—a computerized little black book. Our data base consists of two files, bb and bb.idx. bb is a text

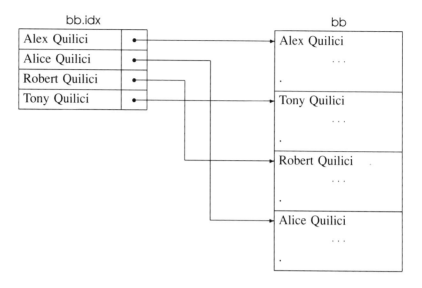

Figure 14.13 Our indexed data base: One file contains the data, the other a sorted index.

file that holds records that contain names, addresses, and phone numbers. The only requirements are that the first line of each record contain the person's name, and that the last line of each record contain a "." on a line by itself. bb.idx is a binary file that contains a person's name and the the starting position of their corresponding record in bb. We keep this index file sorted by name. Figure 14.13 shows a sample data base.

The idea is that we create and maintain bb using any ordinary text editor, but look up addresses and phone numbers using a special program. This program, lookup, doesn't simply do a slow sequential search of bb. Instead, it does a fast binary search through bb.idx to determine exactly where in bb the desired record is located, and then goes directly to this location to retrieve it. Unlike bb, however, we don't access bb.idx directly. We construct it by running another special program. This program, index, travels through bb, building a table of names and record locations. It then sorts the table and writes it to bb.idx. To ensure that the index file is up to date, we have to run index whenever we modify the file containing the names and addresses.

Both of these programs need the definition of an index structure, so we've placed it in a header file, index.h, shown in Figure 14.14. This header file also contains constants for the data base file names, the input line length, and the end-of-record delimiter. Both programs treat the index file as an external array, so index.h includes extarray.h.

Figure 14.15 contains index, which is surprisingly straightforward, despite its

```
/*
 * Definitions to use indexes.
 */
#include "extarray.h"                 /* for external array */

#define MAXLEN      80                /* maximum line length */
#define MAXKEY      40                /* maximum key size */
#define INDEXFILE   "idx"             /* the index file */
#define ENDREC(x)   ((*x) == '.')     /* end of a record */
#define MAXIDX      100               /* max number of records */

struct indexrec                       /* index record: */
{
  char key[MAXKEY];                   /*    name */
  long pos;                           /*    position */
};

typedef struct indexrec INDEX;
```

Figure 14.14   index.h—The data base header file.

long length. It opens the file provided as its argument, builds the name-location table with maketable, sorts it with qsort, and then writes it to an external file with savetable. savetable uses our external array functions to create and save this table as an external array.

lookup is also straightforward. It repeatedly prompts for names and prints the corresponding address and phone number. lookup, like index, treats the index file as an external array, but uses a new function, ea_search, to look up locations. ea_search is simply a modified version of our earlier binary search routine that uses ea_get to access the desired record in the file.

EXERCISES

14-24 Currently, when using lookup we have to specify an entire name in order to find its address. Modify lookup to allow partial matches and to print all records matching the given name.

14-25 Write a new main program for lookup that obtains the names it searches for from its command line arguments.

14-26 Write a program, labels, that prints the entire data base in a format suitable for mailing labels.

14-27 Use lookup and index to create and maintain Chapter 12's employee data base.

14-28 Write a little program that prints the indexing information for the data base. It should print each entry in the index file in a readable format. It should verify that the indexed

```c
/*
 * index.c -- Program to create the index table.
 */
#include <stdlib.h>
#include <string.h>
#include "index.h"                 /* definition of INDEX */
#include "fileopen.h"

int main(int argc, char *argv[])
{
  INDEX itable[MAXIDX];            /* holds index table */
  int items;                       /* items in table */
  char iname[MAXLEN + 1];          /* index file name */
  FILE *fp;                        /* text file name */
  int maketable(FILE *fp, INDEX table[]);
  int savetable(char *name, INDEX table[], int n);

  if (argc != 2)
  {
    fprintf(stderr,"Usage: %s file\n", argv[0]);
    return 1;    /* exit early, bad arguments */
  }
  if ((fp = fileopen(argv[1], "rb")) == NULL)
    return 1;    /* exit early, file problems */
  if ((items = maketable(fp, itable)) == -1)
  {
    fprintf(stderr,"Too many index entries\n");
    return 1;    /* exit early, index table problems */
  }
  qsort((void *) itable, items, sizeof(INDEX), strcmp);
  sprintf(iname,"%s.%s", argv[1], INDEXFILE);
  if (savetable(iname, itable, items) != items)
  {
    fprintf(stderr, "Couldn't build index file\n");
    return 1;    /* exit early, more index table problems */
  }
  fileclose(argv[1], fp);
  return 0;
}

int savetable(char *name, INDEX table[], int n)
{
  int cnt = -1;
  EXTARRAY *ep;

  if ((ep = ea_create(name, sizeof(INDEX))) != NULL)
  {
    cnt = ea_init(ep, n, (void *) table);
    ea_close(ep);
  }
  return cnt;
}
```

```
/*
 * Build the internal index table.
 */
int maketable(FILE *fp, INDEX table[])
{
  char line[MAXLEN + 1];    /* next line */
  long pos = 1L;            /* record's pos in file */
  int linecnt = 0;          /* # of lines in record */
  int cnt = 0;              /* count of records */

  while (fgets(line,sizeof(line), fp) != NULL)
  {
    if (linecnt++ == 0)              /* add a table entry */
    {
      if (cnt == MAXIDX)
        return -1;
      table[cnt].pos = pos - 1;
      line[strlen(line) - 2] = '\0';   /* strip \r\n */
      strncpy(table[cnt].key, line, MAXKEY);
      cnt++;                      /* update node count */
    }
    if (ENDREC(line))
    {
      linecnt = 0;
      pos = ftell(fp);
    }
  }
  return cnt;
}
```

Figure 14.15   index.c—The program that creates the indexed data base.

entry is indeed there, and print its length in bytes. And finally, it should print some summary information, including the total number of entries in the data base and the average size of an entry,

14-29 Modify index and lookup to allow fast access to records by phone number. You'll have to impose some additional structure on the file: The line containing the phone number must be easily identifiable.

14-30 Rewrite Chapter 12's data base program to store its information in a file. The program should keep an internal index table so that it can access records quickly. When the program terminates it writes this index table to a file. When the program starts it begins with the existing index table.

14-31 Write a program to manage a data base of student grades. The program should keep these grades in a single file, with one record per student. The record should include a name, an identification number, room for ten numeric grades, and room for a final letter grade. You should provide operations to add and delete students, to change

```c
/*
 * lookup.c -- Lookup addresses/phone numbers given name.
 */
#include <string.h>
#include "index.h"
#include "fileopen.h"
#include "inout.h"

int main(int argc, char *argv[])
{
  FILE *fp;                   /* black book */
  char iname[MAXLEN + 1];  /* index name */
  int findnames(FILE *fp, char *name);

  if (argc != 2)
  {
    fprintf(stderr, "usage: %s file\n", argv[0]);
    return 1;   /* exit early, bad argument */
  }
  if ((fp = fileopen(argv[1], "r")) == NULL)
    return 1;   /* exit early, file problems */
  sprintf(iname,"%s.%s", argv[1], INDEXFILE);
  if (findnames(fp, iname))
    return 1;   /* exit early, index file problems */
  fileclose(argv[1],fp);
  return 0;
}

/*
 * Prompt for name, find its location, and display that record
 */
int findnames(FILE *fp, char *name)
{
  int entries;              /* number of entries in file */
  EXTARRAY *ep;             /* external array */
  char line[MAXLEN + 1];  /* user input line */
  long pos;                 /* position of record */
  long ea_search(EXTARRAY *ep, int first, int last, char *target);
  long display_record(FILE *fp, long pos);

  if ((ep = ea_open(name, sizeof(INDEX), &entries)) == NULL)
  {
    fprintf(stderr,"Can't access index file %s\n", name);
    return 0;   /* oops... */
  }
  while (fputs("Name? ", stdout), getline(line, MAXLEN) != -1)
    if ((pos = ea_search(ep, 0, entries - 1, line)) == -1)
      fprintf(stderr, "Couldn't find: %s\n", line);
    else if (display_record(fp, pos) == -1)
      fprintf(stderr, "Couldn't display record at %ld\n", pos);
  ea_close(ep);
  return 1;      /* success */
}
```

```
/*
 * Print the contents of the desired record in the text file
 */
long display_record(FILE *fp, long pos)
{
  int rval;
  char line[MAXLEN + 1];    /* holds user input, record output */

  if ((rval = fseek(fp, pos, 0)) != -1)
    while (fgets(line, sizeof(line), fp) != NULL && !ENDREC(line))
      fputs(line,stdout);    /* print its record */
  return rval;
}

/*
 * Search file for desired record, returning position
 */
long ea_search(EXTARRAY *ep, int first, int last, char *target)
{
  int  mid = (first + last) / 2;    /* mid item */
  INDEX next;                       /* to hold record */
  int    cmp;                       /* holds comparison result */

  if (last < first || !ea_get(ep, mid, (void *) &next))
    return -1L;
  if ((cmp = strncmp(target, next.key, MAXKEY)) == 0)
    return next.pos;    /* found it */
  return (cmp < 0)  ? ea_search(ep, first, mid - 1, target)
                    : ea_search(ep, mid + 1, last, target);
}
```

Figure 14.16   lookup.c—Program to lookup records in the data base.

information about a student, and to add, delete, and change grades. Index the file by student identification number. You also need to provide operations to assign grades, to print the information on various students, and to print a grading summary for the entire data base.

15 MEMORY MODELS AND POINTER MODIFIERS

Our detailed discussion of Turbo C has assumed that we are writing small programs. Unfortunately, large real-world programs such as compilers, editors, spreadsheets, and data base managers require enormous amounts of memory. On a large computer that's not a problem. But on a small, personal computer accessing large amounts of memory directly detracts from the program's efficiency. This chapter worries about writing large programs. We first introduce Turbo C's memory models and show when each is most appropriate. We then present Turbo C's pointer modifiers and show how we can make the most efficient use of a particular memory model. The chapter concludes with an implementation of queues that runs efficiently under all of the memory models.

15.1 POINTERS REVISITED

Our previous discussion of pointers ignored the underlying architecture of the machine. We simply treated a pointer as a direct offset into memory and didn't worry about how pointers are actually represented or how address calculations are actually done. And doing so is not unreasonable—as long as our programs are small, requiring less than 64K of code and 64K of data. Unfortunately, however, this isn't true of most programs. To write these larger programs we need to understand how memory addressing takes place.

The 8086 Memory Architecture

The CPU of the IBM-PC and its clones is a member of the Intel 8086 family (which includes the 8088, 8086, 80186, 80286, and 80386 microprocessors). All of these CPUs use a *segmented* memory architecture. They treat memory as if it were broken into 64K segments. A segment must begin on a 16-byte boundary, but is allowed to overlap with other segments. To access a particular memory location, we supply a segment address and an offset into the segment. The 8086 computes the actual

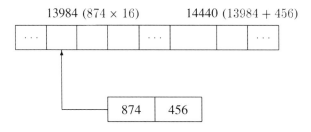

Figure 15.1   How the 8086 locates a desired memory location.

address by shifting the segment address left 4 bits (in effect, multiplying it by 16) and adding the offset.

Figure 15.1 illustrates the address calculation, assuming a segment address of 874 (0x036a) and an offset of 456 (0x01c8). We think of these addresses as *segment:offset* pairs (the segment and offset in hexadecimal notation), 036a:01c8 for the above example. That segment actually begins at memory location 874×16 or 13984 (0x36a0). The actual memory address we're accessing is memory location $13984+456$, or 14440 (0x3868).

The 8086 has both 32-bit and 16-bit pointers. Thirty-two-bit pointers explicitly specify both a segment and an offset. Sixteen-bit pointers merely provide an offset, relying on the value in one of the 8086's *segment registers* to specify the desired segment. Simply put, a segment register is a machine register that holds a segment address. The 8086 has four of them—CS, DS, SS, and ES—which point to a code segment (which contains machine instructions), a data segment (which contains global and static variables), a stack segment (which holds local variables and function return addresses), and an extra segment, respectively. A 16-bit pointer to a function is treated as offset in the code segment. Similarly, a 16-bit pointer to a local variable is treated as an offset into the stack segment.

Why are there two types of internal pointers? After all, with a 32-bit pointer we can address any location in memory, but with a 16-bit pointer can address data only within a single 64K segment. The problem is that 32-bit pointers require more space (two words each) and more time to manipulate (two fetches from memory to the CPU) than 16-bit pointers. So we have 16-bit pointers for speed and 32-bit pointers for addressing power.

Our previous programs have been small enough to use the Turbo C default of 16-bit pointers for both code and data. But we can't avoid using 32-bit pointers forever. To inform Turbo C of our pointer requirements, we must select an appropriate memory model.

Memory Models

A *memory model* specifies two things: the size of code and data pointers, and how our program is to be organized in memory. Turbo C provides six memory models:

TINY 16-bit pointers, with a single shared segment for code, data, and the stack. With this model, a complete program must fit in 64K, so we use it only when memory is very scarce.

SMALL 16-bit pointers, with one segment for code, and another shared segment for data and the stack. This model is appropriate for most programs, including all our earlier programs.

MEDIUM 32-bit pointers to code, 16-bit pointers to data. There are multiple segments for code, and a single shared segment for data and the stack. This model is suitable for large programs with little data.

COMPACT 16-bit pointers to code, 32-bit pointers to data. There is a single code segment, a single data segment, and a single stack segment. This model is used for small programs that require lots of data.

LARGE 32-bit pointers to code and data. There are multiple segments for code, a single data segment, and a single separate stack segment. This model is appropriate for large programs that need large amounts of memory.

HUGE Same as the LARGE model, except there can be more than one data segment. This model is used by large programs that use large amounts of static data.

Figure 15.2 illustrates each of the different organizations. From this diagram we can see that these models also differ in where they locate the heap, the place where malloc finds the space it allocates. In the TINY, SMALL, and MEDIUM memory models—the *small data* models—the heap is part of the data segment, and any remaining memory is used as an additional heap called the *far heap*. In the COMPACT, LARGE, and HUGE models—the *large data* models—the heap is the leftover memory.

These models have several restrictions. All the code that results from compiling a given source file must fit into a single 64K segment. And similarly, all its data must also fit within another 64K segment. These restrictions aren't particularly troublesome, since we can usually break our program into small enough pieces.

By default, we've been using the SMALL model, but it is straightforward to select a different memory model. With tcc, we use the -mX option, with X replaced by the first letter (lowercase) of the desired memory model. For example,

```
tcc -mt uniq.c
```

compiles a program named uniq.c using the TINY memory model. With tc, we select the appropriate entry in the OPTIONS/COMPILER/MODEL menu.

| CODE | DATA | HEAP-> | <-STACK | 64K |

(a) The TINY model.

CODE	<=64K
DATA	HEAP->	<-STACK	64K
FAR HEAP	Rest of memory

(b) The SMALL model.

| CODE | 64K |
| ... |
CODE	<=64K
DATA	HEAP->	<-STACK	64K
FAR HEAP	Rest of memory

(c) The MEDIUM model.

CODE	<=64K
DATA	64K
STACK	64K
HEAP	Rest of memory

(d) The COMPACT model.

| CODE | 64K |
| ... |
CODE	<=64K
DATA	64K
STACK	64K
HEAP	Rest of memory

(e) The LARGE model.

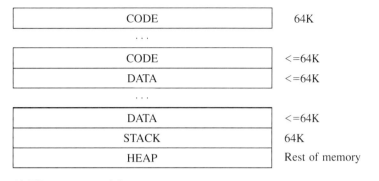

(f) The HUGE model.

Figure 15.2 What memory looks like under each of the various memory models.

Displaying Pointers

Sometimes it is useful to print addresses. When debugging we may discover that a pointer has gone out of bounds and want to print its value in various places to see where it's gone bad. In Turbo C, we write a data pointer using the %p format code. For example, assuming that x is a variable,

```
printf("%p\n", &x);
```

writes x's address in a format appropriate to the memory model we're using. If we're using a small data model, x is written as four hexadecimal digits. In a large data model, it is written in segment:offset notation.

In the small data models, we may want to know what x's absolute address is. To figure this out, we need to know the value in the data segment register. Turbo C allows us to directly access segment registers through the special variables _DS, _SS, _CS, and _ES. That means we can write x's absolute address with

```
printf("%p:%p\n", _DS, x);
```

We can use %p to write code pointers, so long as the memory model we choose has code and data pointers of the same size. If not, as in the MEDIUM and COMPACT models, we need to use two special printf format modifiers, N and F. %Np assumes that it's writing a 16-bit pointer regardless of the memory model we're using. %Fp is similar, but it assumes that it's writing a 32-bit pointer. In the COMPACT model (which has 16-bit code pointers and 32-bit data pointers) we can use

```
printf("%Np", main)
```

to write main's address. Similarly, in the MEDIUM model (which has 32-bit code pointers and 16-bit data pointers) we can use

```
printf("%Fp", main)
```

```
/*
 * Macros for writing pointers:
 *   PR_DPTR  - data ptr, size appropriate to model.
 *   PR_CPTR  - code ptr, size appropriate to model.
 *   PR_ADPTR - data ptr, always 32-bits.
 *   PR_ACPTR - code ptr, always 32-bits.
 */
#include <stdio.h>

#define PR_DPTR(ptr)   printf("%p", ptr)

#if defined(__TINY__) | defined(__SMALL__)  /* all 16-bit */

#define PR_CPTR(ptr)    printf("%p", ptr)
#define PR_ADPTR(ptr)   printf("%p:%p", _DS, ptr)
#define PR_ACPTR(ptr)   printf("%p:%p", _CS, ptr)
#endif

#if defined(__MEDIUM__)   /* 16-bit data, 32-bit code */
#define PR_CPTR(ptr)    printf("%Fp", ptr)
#define PR_ADPTR(ptr)   printf("%p:%p", _DS, ptr)
#define PR_ACPTR(ptr)   printf("%Fp", ptr);
#endif

#if defined(__COMPACT__)   /* 32-bit data, 16-bit code */
#define PR_CPTR(ptr)    printf("%Np", ptr)
#define PR_ADPTR(ptr)   printf("%Fp", ptr)
#define PR_ACPTR(ptr)   printf("%Np:%Np", _CS, ptr)
#endif

#if defined(__LARGE__) | defined(__HUGE__) /* all 32-bit */
#define PR_CPTR(ptr)    printf("%p", ptr)
#define PR_ADPTR(ptr)   printf("%p", ptr)
#define PR_ACPTR(ptr)   printf("%p", ptr)
#endif
```

Figure 15.3 prptr.h—A set of macros to print pointer addresses.

Ideally, however, we don't want to worry about which memory model we're using—we just want to write a pointer. Figure 15.3 defines four macros that help us do just that. PR_DPTR writes a data pointer as a 16-bit offset or 32-bit absolute address, whichever is appropriate for the particular memory model it's being used with. PR_CPTR is similar, but writes a code pointer. PR_ADPTR always writes a data pointer as a 32-bit absolute address. PR_ACPTR is similar, but writes a code pointer.

The trick is that we define different versions of these macros depending on which memory model we select when we compile our program. The preprocessor defines the name of the current memory model, so a simple test selects the appropriate macro.

```
/*
 * prptr.c -- Write the addresses of various pointers.
 */
#include "prptr.h"

#define MAX   100

int table[MAX];

main()
{
  /* addresses in 16-bit for small, 32-bit for large */

  PR_DPTR(table);  /* x's address */
  putchar('\n');
  PR_DPTR(table + MAX - 1);  /* last item's address */
  putchar('\n');
  PR_CPTR(main);  /* main's address */
  putchar('\n');

  /* addresses in 32-bit for all models */

  PR_ADPTR(table);   /* absolute address */
  putchar('\n');
  PR_ADPTR(table + MAX - 1);  /* last item's address */
  putchar('\n');
  PR_ACPTR(main); /* absolute address */
  putchar('\n');
  return 0;
}
```

Figure 15.4 prptr.c—A program that uses our pointer-printing macros.

Figure 15.4 shows how a program can use these macros to write various addresses.

EXERCISES

15–1 Compile and run the address printing program under each of the different memory models.

15–2 Compile one of the case studies from the last few chapters under each of the different memory models. Compare the size of the resulting object modules and executables, as well as their execution speed.

15–3 Write a program that requests segment/offset pairs from the user and then prints the underlying integer addresses. Then write a program to do the reverse: It takes integer addresses and writes them as a segment offset pairs.

15–4 Write a function to print all of the segment registers. Make the function work regardless of the memory model used.

15–5 In the LARGE and HUGE models, the stack segment is separate from the data segment. This means we can't use our macros to print data on the stack. Write PR_SPTR and PR_ASPTR that work like PR_DPTR and PR_ADPTR, except that they work with pointers to objects on the stack.

15.2   POINTER MODIFIERS

Sixteen-bit pointers are more efficient than 32-bit pointers, so we want to use them whenever possible. And this is easy to do as long as our programs stay small—we simply compile them with a memory model that uses 16-bit pointers. But a problem arises as our programs grow larger and we are gradually coerced into choosing a memory model that uses 32-bit data pointers by default. Then *all* of our data pointers are 32-bits, not just those that absolutely have to be. In the COMPACT model, for example, all data pointers are 32-bits, even though we need 32-bit pointers only to access dynamically allocated storage and can get by with 16-bit pointers to access static data and the stack.

We also run into trouble when we have a small program, one that runs under a memory model with 16-bit data pointers, and we want to access data outside its current data segment, such as an address in ROM, a task that requires a 32-bit pointer. We don't want to have to use a larger memory model when we really only a need a few 32-bit addresses.

What we do want is a mechanism that helps us avoid unnecessary overhead yet preserves addressing power—one that lets us specify the size of particular pointers, independent of the underlying memory model. In Turbo C, we can do so by providing one of the pointer modifiers near, far, or huge when we declare the pointer, as in the following examples.

```
int near *nptr;         /* nptr is a NEAR ptr to an int */
int func(int far *ip);  /* ip is a FAR ptr to an int */
char near *fp(int);     /* fp is a function taking an int */
                        /*   returning a NEAR ptr to a char */
double huge *hp;        /* hp is a HUGE pointer to an int */
```

Syntactically, these modifiers are like const: the modifier immediately precedes the pointer object it modifies. It helps to think of the modifier and the * indicating a pointer as a single unit. In fact, we can group them with parentheses.

```
int (near *) nptr;        /* nptr is NEAR ptr to an int */
int func(int (far *)ip);  /* ip is a FAR pointer to an int */
char (near *) fp(int);    /* fp is a function taking an int */
                          /*   returning a NEAR ptr to a char */
double (huge *) hp;       /* hp is a HUGE pointer to an int */
```

Use whichever form you find easiest to read.

By default, the TINY, SMALL, and MEDIUM models use near data pointers, and the COMPACT, LARGE, and HUGE models use far data pointers.

near **Data Pointers**

near pointers are 16-bit offsets into the data segment. We use them *only* when we want a 16-bit pointer in a program compiled using one of the memory models with 32-bit pointers as the default.

To illustrate, we'll write a new version of our Chapter 11 program to reverse its input. This version works in the same way as before: It fills a table with pointers to dynamically allocated character strings, one for each line of input, and then prints this table in reverse order. The difference is that our new version can store 1000 input lines, not just 100.

Because the original saved only 100 input lines, it required less than 10K of data and stack space (100 pointers, up to 100 strings of less than 80 characters, and some miscellaneous local variables) and fit easily into the SMALL model. Unfortunately, to save 1000 input lines, we need as much as 80K of dynamically allocated storage. So we can't simply change the number of table entries to 1000; we also have to recompile the program using the COMPACT model, which ensures a large enough heap.

The problem? Our program will run more slowly that it needs to, as it will be using 32-bit pointers throughout, not just to access items in the heap. The solution? Use explicit near pointers whenever we access something that's not in the heap—or in other words, whenever we access anything in the data segment. We need to examine our program, determine which pointers point to items in the data segment, and make these near pointers.

The main program is shown in Figure 15.5. It makes use of one array, strings, an array of pointers to strings on the heap. This table's entries must be 32-bit pointers, but the table itself is in the data segment, so we can use 16-bit pointers to traverse it, as illustrated in Figure 15.6.

Figure 15.7 contains prototypes for the two functions that traverse the table. The first is read_strings, the other print_rev_strings. Figure 15.8 contains the new versions of the functions themselves.

Within these functions, it's easy to declare the table entries—they're simply pointers to characters, and are 32-bits by default. But what about the pointers used to traverse the table? We want these to be 16-bit pointers, so we declare them as near pointers to pointers to characters.

```
char *(near *)ptr;   /* NEAR ptr to 32-bit ptr to char */
```

The parentheses aren't required, although they do make this complex declaration easier to read. Still, this declaration isn't aesthetically pleasing, so we've chosen instead to define a type CHARPTR for the table entries

```
typedef char *CHARPTR;
```

and to use it to define the pointers with which we traverse the table.

```
CHARPTR near *ptr;
```

When we're using different types of pointers within an expression or comparison, as we are in read_strings and print_rev_strings, we use casts to force the appropriate conversions. For example, the following declaration

```
/*
 * Reverse input, one line at a time (assumes COMPACT model).
 */
#include <stdio.h>
#include <stddef.h>
#include <string.h>
#include "inout.h"
#include "strtab.h"

#define MAXLINES  1000   /* lines to store */

main()
{
  static CHARPTR strings[MAXLINES];  /* 32-bit ptrs to strings */
  int lines = 0;                     /* input lines read */

  if (!read_strings(strings, &lines, MAXLINES))
  {
    printf("Ran out of memory after %d lines\n\n", lines);
    return 1;   /* early exit, no money */
  }
  if (lines == MAXLINES)
    printf("More than %d lines of input\n\n", lines);
  print_rev_strings(strings, lines);
  return 0;
}
```

Figure 15.5   revstr.c—A version of our input reversal program that runs efficiently under the COMPACT model.

```
    CHARPTR near *tabptr = (CHARPTR near *) table;
```

takes `table`'s 32-bit segment/offset address, converts it to a 16-bit offset into the data segment, and assigns this offset to `tabptr`. Figure 15.9 illustrates this conversion. *Warning: These conversions are potentially costly and should be avoided whenever possible.* In `read_strings` we could initialize `endptr`, a pointer to the last table entry, by assigning it `&table[n-1]`. But we avoid an unnecessary conversion by instead using

```
    CHARPTR near *endptr = tabptr + max - 1;
```

Similarly, in `print_rev_strings`, we need to determine when we've reached the table's first entry. One way to do this is to compare the traversing pointer with `table`. But this requires a conversion during each pass through the loop. So instead we assign `table` to a `near` pointer, `tabptr`, and use it in the comparison, which costs us only a single conversion.

It turns out that there is another array our input reversal program could manipulate more efficiently: the one into which `getline` reads characters. This array, `line`,

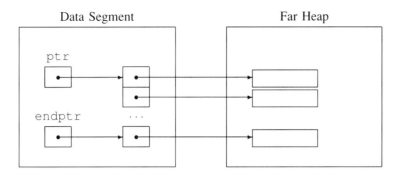

Figure 15.6   The layout of the table of strings and the pointers with which we traverse it.

```
/*
 * strtab.h -- Prototypes for our new versions of
 *             read_strings and print_rev_strings.
 */

typedef char *CHARPTR;

int read_strings(CHARPTR table[], int *cntptr, int max);
void print_rev_strings(CHARPTR table[], int n);
```

Figure 15.7   The prototypes for our new versions of our functions to read and print a table of strings.

is in the data segment, so we can modify getline to use near pointers to traverse it. We do just that in Figure 15.10, a new version of inout.h, and in Figure 15.11, a new version of inout.c.

Warning: Don't pass 32-bit pointers to functions expecting near *pointers.* get-line now expects its first parameter to be a near pointer, regardless of the memory model we're using. But when we use the COMPACT model, line (the name of the array used to hold the input characters) is a 32-bit pointer. How do we avert disaster? By providing a prototype for getline that explicitly states that its first parameter is a near pointer. This causes line to be automatically converted to a near pointer before being passed to getline. Had we failed to include our new prototype for getline, getline would be passed a 32-bit pointer when it was expecting a 16-bit

```
/*
 * strtab.c -- New version of read_strings and print_rev_strings.
 */
#include <stdio.h>
#include <string.h>
#include "strtab.h"
#include "inout.h"

#define MAXLEN 80

int read_strings(CHARPTR table[], int *cntptr, int max)
{
  CHARPTR sptr;                   /* ptr to new string */
  CHARPTR near *tabptr = (CHARPTR near *) table;
  CHARPTR near *ptr = tabptr; /* used to traverse table */
  CHARPTR near *endptr = tabptr + max - 1;
  static char line[MAXLEN + 1];

  *cntptr = 0;
  while (getline(line, MAXLEN) != -1 && ptr <= endptr)
    if ((sptr = strdup(line)) != NULL)
    {
      *ptr++ = sptr;
      (*cntptr)++;
    }
    else
      return 0;        /* failure; out of memory */
  return 1;            /* success */
}

void print_rev_strings(CHARPTR table[], int n)
{
  CHARPTR near *tabptr = (CHARPTR near *) table;
  CHARPTR near *ptr = tabptr + n - 1;

  for (; ptr >= tabptr; ptr--)
    printf("%s\n", *ptr);  /* can't use putline, why? */
}
```

Figure 15.8   strtab.c—A new version of our table reading and printing functions.

Segment   Offset   DS

| 1016 | 800 |

| 1000 |

(*a*) A 32-bit pointer before conversion. DS is the data segment register.

Offset

| 1056 |

(*b*) The 16-bit pointer that results from the conversion. The conversion is done by multiplying the difference between the DS and the segment by 16 and adding it to the offset.

Figure 15.9   How A 32-bit pointer into the data segment is converted into a 16 bit-offset.

```
/*
 * inout.h -- Prototypes for our new versions of getline
 *            and putline that run more efficiently under
 *            the compact model.
 */

int getline(char near *ptr, int max);
void putline(char near *ptr);
```

Figure 15.10   inout.h—Prototypes for versions of our string input and output functions that run efficiently in the COMPACT model.

pointer, and wouldn't work correctly.

Our new version of getline is a winner. We can use it with the small data models without change, since they use near pointers by default. And we've made it work more efficiently in the COMPACT model—*so long as it is passed a pointer to an object in the data segment*. But that's an important restriction. It means we can't pass getline a pointer to a dynamically allocated array, since we can't use near pointers to access objects on the far heap. It also means we can't pass getline a pointer to an automatic array. By default automatic arrays are placed on the stack. Since the COMPACT, LARGE, and HUGE memory models have separate data and stack segments, and near pointers are offsets into the data segment, we can't use them to access variables that reside on the stack.

The easiest solution is simple: avoid using automatic arrays. In Figure 15.5 and

```
/*
 * Read and save an input line (compact model)
 */
#include <stdio.h>
#include "inout.h"

int getline(char near *ptr, int max)
{
  int c;
  char near *startptr = ptr;        /* ptr to first char */
  char near *endptr = ptr + max;    /* ptr to last poss char */

  while ((c = getchar()) != '\n' && c != EOF)
    if (ptr < endptr)
      *ptr++ = c;
  *ptr = '\0';                      /* terminate with null */
  return (c == EOF) ? -1 : ptr - startptr;
}

void putline(char near *ptr)
{
  for (; *ptr != '\0'; ptr++)
    putchar(*ptr);
  putchar('\n');
}
```

Figure 15.11 inout.c—New versions of our string input and output functions that run efficiently under the COMPACT model.

Figure 15.8 we declared as static both arrays (table and line) we traverse using near pointers, which guarantees that they're in the data segment.

But we can't always avoid using near pointers to items on the stack. It's possible that we might not have sufficient space in the data segment for all the arrays we use. In these rare cases—when we want to use 16-bit pointers to access arrays on the stack, and we're stuck with using a larger memory model—we must use a special modifier to inform Turbo C that a particular pointer is an offset within the stack segment. It turns out that Turbo C provides four special modifiers—_ds, _ss, _cs, and _es—corresponding to the four segment registers. A pointer declared with the _ss modifier

```
    char _ss *local_ptr;
```

is treated as a 16-bit offset into the stack segment.

Suppose we change read_strings so that line is no longer static. That means line is now in the stack segment, so we can't pass it to getline, which expects an offset into the data segment. Instead, we have to write a new function, getline_ss, which expects the array it is passed to be in the stack segment.

```
    int get_line_ss(char _ss *, int);
```

```
/*
 * inoutss.h -- Prototypes for get_line_ss/put_line_ss.
 */

int getline_ss(char _ss *ptr, int max);
void putline_ss(char _ss *ptr);
```

Figure 15.12   inoutss.h—Header file for our stack segment oriented versions of our string input and output functions.

And within `getline_ss` we declare the pointers used to traverse this array as offsets into the stack segment. Figure 15.12 contains the new prototypes, Figure 15.13 the new functions.

Under the COMPACT model, the stack and data segments are the same and `getline_ss` behaves just like our earlier version of `getline`. But under the LARGE (and HUGE) models, we must ensure that we pass it an array in the stack segment. So long as we supply a prototype for `getline_ss` in any function that uses it, the compiler will flag as an error any attempt to pass it an array that isn't in the stack segment.

`near` pointers are never absolutely necessary. But the key to writing large, efficient programs is to use 16-bit pointers instead of 32-bit pointers wherever possible. So, sooner or later, we're going to need `near` pointers. We can stall, however, by initially writing large programs using only the default 32-bit pointers. Only if the resulting program runs too slowly do we need to modify it to use `near` pointers. And ideally, we'll be able to achieve a sufficient speedup merely by using them on a few frequently traversed arrays.

`far` **Pointers**

`far` pointers are 32-bit segment, offset addresses. They are stored as two words, with one word containing the segment and the other the offset. When we use the COMPACT, LARGE, and HUGE memory models, we obtain `far` data pointers by default. In the small data models, we use explicit `far` pointers to access data outside the current data segment. We might need to access a specific memory location, such as a particular location in ROM or an in-memory device control register. Or we may want to access storage obtained from the far heap.

Suppose, for example, that we want to examine the integer stored in memory location 0x3E8. To do so, regardless of the memory model we're using, we must convert this integer into a 32-bit pointer, which we then dereference. We do the conversion by casting 0x3E8 to a `far` pointer to an `int`.

```
printf("0x3E8 contains %d\n", * (int far *) 0x3E8);
```

Without the cast, we're trying to dereference an integer, an illegal operation. Figure 15.14 provides a more complete example, expanding this fragment into a little

```
/*
 * inoutss.c -- getline and putline for the larger (compact,
 *              large, and huge) memory models.  They assume
 *              the string they work with is on the stack.
 */
#include <stdio.h>
#include "inoutss.h"

int getline_ss(char _ss *ptr, int max)
{
  int c;
  char _ss *startptr = ptr;        /* ptr to first char */
  char _ss *endptr = ptr + max;    /* ptr to last poss char */

  while ((c = getchar()) != '\n' && c != EOF)
    if (ptr < endptr)
      *ptr++ = c;
  *ptr = '\0';                     /* terminate with null */
  return (c == EOF) ? -1 : ptr - startptr;
}

void putline_ss(char _ss *ptr)
{
  for (; *ptr != '\0'; ptr++)
    putchar(*ptr);
  putchar('\n');
}
```

Figure 15.13 inoutss.c—New versions of our string input and output functions that run efficiently under the COMPACT model.

program that obtains memory locations from the user and prints their contents. Be careful when running it, as some values are likely to cause addressing exceptions.

When writing programs for the PC, we don't usually work with integer addresses. Instead, we usually have a segment and an offset. Turbo C provides several macros for examining or modifying a memory location, given a segment and an offset.

```
int peek(unsigned int segment, unsigned int offset)
void poke(unsigned int segment, unsigned int offset, int value)
```

These are defined in the header file dos.h. peek takes a segment and an offset and returns the integer found there. Similarly, poke takes a segment, an offset, and a value, and assigns the value to that location. So peek(0,0x3E8) returns the integer at location 1000, and poke(0,0x3E8,1) puts a 1 into location 1000.

How are peek and poke written? One possible implementation is shown in Figure 15.15 and Figure 15.16. It takes advantage of another macro found in dos.h, MK_FP.

```
void far *MK_FP(unsigned int segment, unsigned int offset)
```

```
/*
 * Read integer addresses and print their contents.
 */
#include <stdio.h>
#include "inout.h"

#define MAXLEN 80

main()
{
  static char line[MAXLEN + 1];
  long addr;
  int far *ptr;

  while (printf("Address: "), getline(line, MAXLEN) != -1)
    if (sscanf(line, "%lx", &addr) != 1)
      putline("Not a valid long integer");
    else
    {
      ptr = (int far *) addr;
      printf("%Fp contains %d\n", ptr, *ptr);
    }
  return 0;
}
```

Figure 15.14   explore.c—A program to print the contents of specified memory locations.

MK_FP takes a integer segment address and an integer offset address and combines them into a single far pointer (by returning an unsigned long with the segment address in the high word, and the offset in the low word). Both peek and poke then dereference this to access the desired value. We use MK_FP to hide the details of how far pointers are actually represented.

In the small data models, we also use far pointers to access storage allocated on the far heap. These memory models use a single shared segment for data, the stack, and the heap, which leaves little leftover space for malloc to allocate. When we need large amounts of dynamically allocated storage, one solution is to compile our program using a larger memory model, as we did with our input reversal program. The problem with this approach is that the library functions in the larger memory models use 32-bit pointers, which limits the amount of optimization we can do.

As an alternative, we can use two special Turbo C functions, farmalloc and farfree. These work analogously to malloc and free, except that they allocate storage from the far heap and work with far pointers (farmalloc also differs from malloc in that it takes an unsigned long instead of an int, which means we can use it to allocate arrays larger than 64K, a feature we'll take advantage of shortly). The idea is that we use far pointers to access this storage, while all our

```
/*
 * peekpoke.h -- Prototypes for our peek and poke.
 */

int
ourpeek(unsigned int segment, unsigned int offset);

void
ourpoke(unsigned int segment, unsigned int offset, int value);
```

Figure 15.15 peekpoke.h—Prototypes for the functions found in peekpoke.c.

```
/*
 * peekpoke.c -- Examine or modify a memory location.
 */
#include <dos.h>

int ourpeek(unsigned int segment, unsigned int offset)
{
  return * (int far *) MK_FP(segment, offset);
}

void ourpoke(unsigned int segment, unsigned int offset, int value)
{
  int far *addr = (int far *) MK_FP(segment, offset);


  *addr = value;
}
```

Figure 15.16 peekpoke.c—One possible implementation of peek and poke.

other pointers, including those used by the library functions, are 16-bit pointers by default.

Figure 15.17, Figure 15.18, and Figure 15.19 use these functions in another version of our input reversal program. It, too, can handle 1000 lines of input, but it runs under the SMALL memory model.

As before, the table entries are 32-bit pointers to dynamically allocated character strings. Since we're running under a small data model, we must declare them as far pointers. For convenience, we again declare a type CHARPTR and use it to declare these table entries.

```
typedef char far *CHARPTR;  /* far ptr to character */
```

Now, however, 16-bit pointers are the default, so we no longer have to declare the pointers we use to traverse the table as near pointers.

```
/*
 * Reverse input, one line at a time (small/medium model).
 */
#include <stdio.h>
#include "strtab2.h"

#define  MAXLINES   1000      /* lines to store */

main()
{
  static CHARPTR strings[MAXLINES];  /* 32-bit ptrs to strings */
  int lines = 0;                     /* input lines read */

  if (!read_strings(strings, &lines, MAXLINES))
  {
    printf("Ran out of memory after reading %d lines\n\n", lines);
    return 1;      /* early exit; out of memory */
  }
  if (lines == MAXLINES)
    printf("More than %d lines of input\n\n", lines);
  print_rev_strings(strings, lines);
  return 0;
}
```

Figure 15.17   revtab2.c—An input reversal program that can handle 1000 lines of input and run under the SMALL memory model.

Despite its advantages in terms of efficiency, this approach has a devastating draw-back. The SMALL model library functions, such as strcpy and strcmp, all expect to work with near pointers—which means we can't use them on our dynamically allocated strings. One way to work around this problem is to copy whatever we've allocated into the data segment before we manipulate it. Another is to write our own versions of the library functions that work with far pointers. Neither is pleasant. In this example, we've chosen the latter and effectively written our own versions of strdup and strcpy.

Actually, a few library functions let us tell them which type of pointer we're passing. We saw earlier that printf allows us to specify whether a pointer is near or far by preceding the format type with an F or an N. We use %Fs to print the table entries, since they are all pointers to dynamically allocated strings.

```
        printf("%Fs\n", *ptr);
```

When we need large amounts of dynamically allocated storage, how do we decide whether to use a small or large data model? Usually, we decide based on the program's use of existing library functions. Do we use them most often on dynamically-allocated storage? Then using a large data model makes sense. Do we use these library functions

```
/*
 * strtab2.h -- Prototypes for string table functions.
 *    read_strings - read and allocate a table of strings.
 *    print_rev_strings - print a table of strings in
 *                        reverse order.
 */
typedef char far *CHARPTR;  /* ptr to char far heap */

int read_strings(CHARPTR table[], int *cntptr, int max);
void print_rev_strings(CHARPTR table[], int n);
```

Figure 15.18 strtab2.h—The prototypes for our table-manipulating functions.

most often on objects in the data and stack segments? Then using a small data model is most appropriate.

huge **Pointers**

far pointers have one major limitation. We can't use them to traverse large arrays, those containing more than 64K bytes. This restriction arises because the 8086 does pointer arithmetic only on the offset and not the segment. Adding one to the far pointer 0000:FFFF gives 0000:0000, an undesirable outcome.

huge pointers are far pointers stored in a special form that overcomes this restriction. A huge pointer always has an offset between 0 and 15. When we do arithmetic on a huge pointer, the result is converted to a pointer in this *normalized* form. This means that when we add one to 0FFF:000F, the huge equivalent of 0000:FFFF, we get 0FFF:0010, which is then converted to the huge pointer 1000:0000. The point is that modifying the offset has changed the segment, which allows us to use a single pointer to access data in more than one segment.

Figure 15.20 shows an example use of huge pointers in a simple function to allocate an array of 25000 longs and set all of its elements to zero. Our first choice is to declare and initialize the array at compile time, but we can't—no memory model allows the static data in one file to exceed 64K. Our next choice is to use malloc to allocate the array. But we can't do that either, since an array of 25000 longs requires 100K, so we're stuck with using farmalloc to allocate the array.

Once we've allocated it, we initialize all of its elements to zero by using a pointer to traverse the array. But the array is too large to use a far pointer, so instead we use a huge pointer. The drawback is the extra overhead, which is the price we have to pay for the ability to manipulate very large arrays.

EXERCISES

```
/*
 * strtab2.c -- New version of read_strings and print_rev_strings.
 */
#include <stdio.h>
#include <string.h>
#include <alloc.h>
#include "inout.h"
#include "strtab2.h"


#define MAXLEN 80

int read_strings(CHARPTR table[], int *cntptr, int max)
{
  /* pointers used to traverse table */
  CHARPTR near *tabptr = (CHARPTR near *) table;
  CHARPTR near *ptr = tabptr; /* used to traverse table */
  CHARPTR near *endptr = tabptr + max - 1;

  /* pointers used to deal with newly allocated string */
  CHARPTR sptr;        /* pointer to string */
  CHARPTR cptr;        /* pointer into string */

  /* stuff to deal with running through input line */
  char line[MAXLEN + 1];  /* input line */
  char *lptr;             /* pointer into line */
  int len;                /* characters read */

  *cntptr = 0;
  while ((len = getline(line, MAXLEN)) != -1 && ptr <= endptr)
    if ((sptr = farmalloc((unsigned long) len + 1)) != NULL)
    {
      lptr = line; cptr = sptr;
      while ((*cptr++ = *lptr++) != '\0')
        ;
      *ptr++ = sptr;  /* store line in array */
      (*cntptr)++;
    }
    else
      return 0;        /* failure; out of memory */
  return 1;            /* success */
}

void print_rev_strings(CHARPTR table[], int n)
{
  CHARPTR *ptr = table + n - 1;

  for (; ptr >= table; ptr--)
    printf("%Fs\n", *ptr);  /* can't use put_line, why? */
}
```

Figure 15.19   strtab2.c—Our string table traversing functions rewritten to work with the SMALL model.

```
/*
 * Allocate an initialize a HUGE table of longs.
 */
#include <stdio.h>
#include <stddef.h>
#include <alloc.h>

main()
{
  long huge *table;
  long huge *make_table(int);

  printf("Initializing table...\n");
  if ((table = make_table(25000)) == NULL)
  {
    printf("Couldn't allocate table\n");
    return 1;
  }
  farfree((void far *) table);
  return 0;
}

long huge *make_table(int items)
{
  long huge *temp;
  long huge *ptr;
  long huge *endptr;

  temp = (long huge *)
           farmalloc((unsigned long) items * sizeof(long));
  if (temp != NULL)
    for (ptr = temp, endptr = ptr + items; ptr < endptr; ptr++)
      *ptr = 0L;   /* initialize items */
  return temp;
}
```

Figure 15.20 huge.c—An example program manipulating huge arrays.

15–6 Rewrite Chapter 11's string sorting program to work efficiently under the compact model.

15–7 Rewrite Chapter 12's data base program to allocate storage from the far heap.

15–8 Repeat the previous exercise for Chapter 13's linked list insertion sort program.

15–9 Rewrite Chapter 13's cross-referencer to work efficiently using the LARGE memory model.

15–10 Turn the octal dump program from Chapter 5 into a function that dumps memory rather than its standard input. Assume that it is running in one of the SMALL models. It takes two arguments, the starting and ending addresses to dump. How can this

```
/*
 * newfact.c -- Compute n! for n >= 0.
 */
#include <stdio.h>

main()
{
  long near fact(int n);      /* compute factorial */

  printf("%ld\n", fact(10));  /* test it */
  return 0;
}

long near fact(int n)         /* fact is a NEAR function */
{
  return (n > 1) ? n * fact(n-1) : 1L;
}
```

Figure 15.21 newfact.c—A new version of our factorial program that works efficiently even when compiled in the larger code models.

function be used to dump just the code segment? The data segment? All of memory?

15.3   FUNCTION MODIFIERS

By now we're painfully aware that 16-bit pointers are preferable to 32-bit pointers for accessing data. They are just as desirable for accessing functions. When we call a function, the caller does a goto to the function's address, after saving a return address on the stack. When a function returns, it does a goto to the saved address. All of this address manipulation is more efficient with 16-bit rather than 32-bit function addresses; that is, when we're using offsets into the code segment.

It turns out that Turbo C lets us apply the near, far, and huge modifiers to pointers to functions

```
int (near *nfp)(int);   /* nfp is a NEAR pointer to a function
                            returning an int */
int *(huge *ffp)(int);  /* ffp is a FAR ptr to function
                            returning a pointer to an int */
```

and to functions themselves (the name of a function is a pointer to it), as we've done in a new version of fact shown in Figure 15.21.

By default, the TINY, SMALL, and COMPACT models use near functions, and the MEDIUM, LARGE, and HUGE models use far functions.

near **Functions**

By default, the TINY, SMALL, and COMPACT models have a single code segment, and all code pointers are 16-bit offsets. In contrast, the MEDIUM, LARGE, and HUGE memory models have one code segment for each source file, which means all code pointers are 32-bit absolute addresses. In these models, we improve the efficiency of our programs by using 16-bit code pointers. We do this by using near functions.

In near functions, the calling address and return address are stored as 16-bit offsets, rather than full 32-bit pointers, with a corresponding increase in speed and decrease in size. Figure 15.21 uses near calls to guarantee that fact will use 16-bit calls and returns, even if the program is compiled under one of the larger memory models. This saves storage, both in the code segment and on the stack, and makes our program run faster.

Since these 16-bit code pointers are offsets into the code segment, a near function must reside in the same code segment as its caller. In practice, that means that we can only declare a function or pointer to a function to be near if it is defined in the same file as its caller. Figure 15.22 provides an example in a more sophisticated version of search, our earlier function to search an array of ints. search selects the search technique it uses based on the number of values in the array. It uses binary search if there are 25 or more values, and sequential search otherwise. It actually does the search by calling an appropriate function, bsearch for binary search; ssearch for sequential search. Figure 15.23 is an example program using search.

Suppose that we're using search as part of a larger program, one that requires a memory model that uses 32-bit code pointers. Since bsearch and ssearch are only called from within search, and they are defined in the same module, we make search more efficient by using 16-bit pointers to call these functions. To do so, we define both as near functions, and provide prototypes for them within search.

far **Functions**

far functions use 32-bit calls and returns. There are two reasonable uses for them. One is to let us mix memory models. That is, to let us compile one module with the SMALL model, compile another with the LARGE model, and then link the two together into a single executable.

Why would we want to mix models? We often write generally useful modules, such as sets or queues, that we want to compile separately and link in with more than one program. The problem is that the programs to which we link may be compiled under any one of the different memory models. We could simply compile a module under each of the different memory models—but this takes extra time to do the compiles and extra space to store the different object modules. We would prefer to somehow do just one compile, under a single memory model, and to then link the resulting object module with any programs that need it, regardless of the memory model they happen to use.

To illustrate mixed model programming, let's suppose we've used the LARGE model to compile a module containing the two functions min and max. Let's also suppose we've used the SMALL model to compile a main program that uses them.

```
/*
 * Searching functions (efficient calls in any memory model).
 */
#include <stdio.h>
#include <stddef.h>

#define FASTSEQ  25     /* < 25 sequential search is faster */

typedef int *INTPTR;

INTPTR search(int *minptr, int *maxptr, int target)
{
  INTPTR near bsearch(int *minptr, int *maxptr, int target);
  INTPTR near ssearch(int *minptr, int *maxptr, int target);

  return (maxptr - minptr > FASTSEQ)
            ? bsearch(minptr, maxptr, target)
            : ssearch(minptr, maxptr, target);
}

static INTPTR near
bsearch(int *minptr, int *maxptr, int target)
{
  int *midptr = minptr + (maxptr - minptr) / 2;

  if (maxptr < minptr)                /* value in table? */
    return NULL;
  if (target == *midptr)              /* middle is target? */
    return midptr;
  return (target < *midptr)           /* search correct half */
            ? bsearch(minptr, midptr - 1, target)
            : bsearch(midptr + 1, maxptr, target);
}

static INTPTR near
ssearch(int *minptr, int *maxptr, int target)
{
  for (; minptr <= maxptr; minptr++)
    if (*minptr == target)
      return minptr;         /* found, return pointer to it */
  return NULL;               /* failure, return null */
}
```

Figure 15.22   nrsearch.c—A generalized search function that uses sequential search for less than 25 elements and binary search otherwise.

```
/*
 * Test search routine (compile with any memory model).
 */
#include <stdio.h>
#include "search.h"

#define MAXSIZE 1000
#define MAXLEN  80

main()
{
  int table[MAXSIZE];
  int i, target;
  INTPTR t;

  for (i = 0; i < MAXSIZE; i++)   /* some initial value */
    table[i] = i;
  while (printf("Search for: "), scanf("%d", &target) == 1)
    if ((t = search(table, table + MAXSIZE - 1, target)) == NULL)
      printf("Couldn't find the %d.\n", target);
    else
      printf("%d is in position %d.\n", target, t - table);
  return 0;
}
```

Figure 15.23 tstsrch.c—A program that uses our new search function.

Now, unless we do something special, when we try to link these two modules together, we have a problem: main will be doing 16-bit calls to min and max, even though they are located in a different code segment—a recipe for disaster. And we would have a similar problem if instead we compiled min and max using the SMALL model and the main program with the LARGE model. In this case, min and max would be doing 16-bit returns to a main program in a different code segment—another way to cause bizarre behavior.

Figure 15.24, Figure 15.25, and Figure 15.26 show how we solve this problem. We must somehow ensure that we're using 32-bit calls to min and max, which we can do by defining them as far functions and providing appropriate prototypes in the caller. The prototypes guarantee that min and max will be called using a 32-bit address, and their definitions assure that they will do 32-bit returns.

Although far functions allow us to mix memory models, we generally avoid doing so. We find that it usually takes only a little extra time to create object modules for each of the memory models. And, as we'll see in the case study that concludes this chapter, we can use the preprocessor to help us tune a source file to the memory model under which it's compiled.

The other use of far functions occurs when we're using a memory model with

```
/*
 * Header file for min and max.
 */

int far min(int x, int y);
int far max(int x, int y);
```

Figure 15.24   minmax.h—Header file for module containing `min` and `max`.

```
/*
 * Source file for min and max.  Compile this with the large
 * model.
 */

int far min(int x, int y)
{
  return x > y ? y : x;
}

int far max(int x, int y)
{
  return x > y ? x : y;
}
```

Figure 15.25   minmax.c—Source file for the functions. The `far` calls allow the calling function to have been compiled under any of the different memory models.

16-bit code pointers and we want to call a function outside the current code segment, perhaps to execute some machine code in ROM or some code we've placed in the data segment. We don't do either of these very often.

huge **Functions**

huge functions are similar to `far` functions except that they are allowed to change the data segment register. We use them only when we want to use `near` data pointers in the HUGE memory model. Why? Because the HUGE model has one code segment and one data segment per module, we need a way of specifying the data segment to which a particular `near` pointer refers. huge functions provide the mechanism for doing so. When we call a `huge` function, it places the address of its module's data segment into the data segment register. And when a `huge` function exits, it restores this value.

We illustrate `huge` functions in a version of our queues package that runs efficiently when compiled with the HUGE model. Figure 15.27 contains the header file

```
/*
 * Main program using min and max.  Compile it with the small
 * model and link in the small model libraries.
 */
#include <stdio.h>
#include "minmax.h"

main()
{
  int i,j;

  i = min(6,3);      /* a "far" call and return */
  j = max(6,3);      /* another "far" call and return */
  printf("min = %d, max = %d\n", i, j);
  return 0;
}
```

Figure 15.26 tstmnmx.c—A main program testing `min` and `max`.

```
/*
 * queues.h -- Prototypes for queue functions.
 */
#define MAXQUEUE 100           /* maximum number of items. */

typedef int ITEM;             /* queue items */
typedef ITEM near *ITEMPTR;   /* pointer to queue item */

void huge enqueue(ITEM);      /* add item to queue */
ITEM huge dequeue(void);      /* take item away from queue */
int huge emptyqueue(void);    /* is queue empty? */
```

Figure 15.27 queues.h—Header file for queues compiled with HUGE model.

and Figure 15.28 contains the queue-handling functions. Because we placed these functions within a single module, and because we use `near` pointers to traverse the `queues` array, we must declare them as `huge` functions. Otherwise, the `near` pointers they use would be offests into the wrong data segment—the data segment of their callers.

`huge` functions, like `huge` pointers, require additional overhead. One way to avoid them is to avoid using 16-bit pointers when we use the HUGE model. This is easy to do, but may make our program run much more slowly. A better way to avoid them is to place as many of our arrays on the stack as possible and use `_ss` pointers to access them. This is reasonable, but we're limited in how much stack data we can have. Unfortunately, it seems, for some programs we have no choice but to use the

```
/*
 * queues.c -- Queue manager that runs efficiently under the
 *             huge model.
 */
#include "queues.h"        /* include prototypes */

ITEM queue[MAXQUEUE];      /* holds the queue */
ITEMPTR qptr = queue;      /* pointer to queue */
ITEMPTR fptr = queue;      /* pointers to front and */
ITEMPTR rptr = queue;      /*    rear of queue */

static ITEMPTR near next(ITEMPTR ptr)
{                          /* update ptr to nxt item */
  return (ptr == qptr + MAXQUEUE - 1) ? qptr : ptr + 1;
}

void huge enqueue(ITEM item) /* add item to queue */
{
  *rptr = item;
  rptr = next(rptr);
}

ITEM huge dequeue(void)    /* take top item off queue */
{
  ITEM temp = *fptr;

  fptr = next(fptr);
  return temp;
}

int huge emptyqueue(void) /* does queue have items left? */
{
  return fptr == rptr;
}
```

Figure 15.28 queues.c—Queues that work under any memory model.

HUGE model.

EXERCISES

15-11 Rewrite the set package in Chapter 8 to use near functions where appropriate.

15-12 Write a sorting function that uses insertion sort for fewer than 25 values and quicksort otherwise.

15-13 Modify the cross referencing program to run efficiently under the HUGE memory model.

```
/*
 * queues2.h -- Prototypes for queue functions.
 */

#define MAXQUEUE 100              /* maximum number of items */

typedef int ITEM;                /* queue items */
typedef ITEM near *ITEMPTR;      /* pointer to queue item */

#if defined(__HUGE__)
  void huge enqueue(ITEM);       /* add item to queue */
  ITEM huge dequeue(void);       /* take item away from queue */
  int huge emptyqueue(void);     /* is queue empty? */
#else
  void enqueue(ITEM);            /* add item to queue */
  ITEM dequeue(void);            /* take item from queue */
  int emptyqueue(void);          /* is queue empty */
#endif
```

Figure 15.29 queues2.h—New version that can run efficiently under any memory model.

15–14 Modify the sets package to work efficiently under the LARGE model.

15–15 Modify the sets package to work efficiently under the HUGE model.

15.4   CASE STUDY—REIMPLEMENTING QUEUES

We saw earlier that when we write a generally useful package of functions, such as sets or queues, we may want to link it with programs compiled under any of the different memory models. One solution is to use far functions and to compile the package under a particular memory model. But it isn't the most efficient, because in the smaller memory models we'll be using 32-bit function calls even though we don't need to.

A more efficient alternative is to write different versions of the package, each optimized for the particular memory model we use to compile it. That's what we've done in Figure 15.30, a new version of our earlier queues package.

Although we want to compile the queues package into one object module for each of the different memory models, we don't want to have multiple versions of queues.c. Instead, we want one version that's efficient, regardless of the memory model we're using.

To accomplish this, we need to use 16-bit pointers wherever possible. Since near pointers speed up programs compiled with the larger models, and don't slow down programs compiled with the smaller models, it never hurts to declare a pointer using near. But there are several constraints. When we compile into the LARGE model,

```
/*
 * queues2.c -- Queue manager that runs efficiently under the
 *              each of the different memory models.
 */
#include "queues2.h"         /* include prototypes */

ITEM queue[MAXQUEUE];        /* holds the queue */
ITEMPTR qptr = queue;        /* pointer to queue */
ITEMPTR fptr = queue;        /* pointers to front and */
ITEMPTR rptr = queue;        /*    rear of queue */

static ITEMPTR near next(ITEMPTR ptr)
{                            /* update ptr to nxt item */
  return (ptr == qptr + MAXQUEUE - 1) ? qptr : ptr + 1;
}

#if defined(__HUGE__)
  void huge enqueue(ITEM item) /* add item to queue */
#else
  void enqueue(ITEM item)
#endif
{
  *rptr = item;
  rptr = next(rptr);
}

#if defined(__HUGE__)
  ITEM huge dequeue(void)    /* take top item off queue */
#else
  ITEM dequeue(void)
#endif
{
  ITEM temp = *fptr;

  fptr = next(fptr);
  return temp;
}

#if defined(__HUGE__)
  int huge emptyqueue(void) /* does queue have items left? */
#else
  int emptyqueue(void)
#endif
{
  return fptr == rptr;
}
```

Figure 15.30 nqueues.c—Queue functions that work under any memory model.

our `near` pointers must point only to objects in the data segment. And when we use the `HUGE` model, we must ensure that the data segment register has been set up appropriately when call functions in different modules, and we must restrict our use of `near` pointers to point to data defined in the current module.

In this case, we use pointers only to access the queue items. Since the array representing the queue is global, and is therefore in the data segment, we can use `near` pointers to traverse it regardless of the memory model. But because we'd like to understand how queues work without being distracted by the type of pointers we're actually using, we declare the variable using a new type, `ITEMPTR`, that we define with `typedef`. For efficiency, we also want to declare any function used only within queues.c as a `near` function. Here, only `next` meets this criterion.

The one potential problem comes when we use the `HUGE` model. Since `enqueue`, `dequeue`, and `emptyqueue` are called from other modules, we must make sure they reset the data segment register appropriately. We do this by making them `huge` functions. But we want them to be `huge` functions only when we compile under the `HUGE` memory model. This means we have to test which memory model we're using and declare each function appropriately.

```
#if defined(__HUGE__)
  void huge enqueue(ITEM item)       /* add item to queue */
#else
  void enqueue(ITEM item)            /* add item to queue */
#endif
```

We make a similar test in the header file supplying the prototypes.

To be honest, this example does have one major simplification: Our functions aren't passed arrays. In the `LARGE` and `HUGE` models it's difficult to write an efficient function that works whether or not the array is it is passed is in the data segment or on the stack. Generally, most functions use the default-sized pointers for traversing these arrays, or work only with arrays in the data segment, or arrays in the stack, but not both.

EXERCISES

15–16 Rewrite the sets package to work efficiently under any memory model.

15–17 Write the function, `instack`, that takes a pointer to an array and the array's length, and returns whether or not the array falls completely within the stack segment.

15–18 Make `getline` work efficiently under any memory model. In the `LARGE` and `HUGE` models, `getline` should use `instack` to detect whether it is passed an array in the stack. Otherwise, it can assume it is passed an array in the data segment. But be careful: Since `getline` is being passed an array it can't use `near` pointers to traverse it when it's compiled under the `HUGE` model.

16   PORTABILITY

By now you've been introduced to almost all of Turbo C's features and should feel fairly comfortable using it to write large, useful programs. But what about when we want to take one of the programs we wrote using Turbo C and compile it with a different compiler, or run it on a different machine, or use it with some other operating system? This short chapter discusses the problems we're likely to run into and how we can best avoid them. We present a series of problems that arise when porting programs, along with a set of reasonable solutions. The chapter concludes with a case study that develops device-independent input and output routines.

16.1   PRINCIPLES OF PORTABILITY

What do we mean by portability? Ideally, a portable program doesn't need to be changed to run under a different compiler or operating system, to run on a different computer, or to run with different input or output devices. Unfortunately, however, the ideal is almost always impossible to attain. Compilers differ in the length of variable names they allow, how much of the language they implement, and the library functions and additional features they provide. Operating systems provide different system calls. Computers differ in word sizes, character sets, and amount of available memory. Input can be typed on the keyboard, entered with a mouse or joystick, or selected with cursor input keys. And displays can be black and white or color. There are so many differences that we must carefully design and code our programs to achieve any degree of portability between different systems.

Since writing portable programs requires extra effort, why do we care about portability at all? If we *always* develop and run our programs using Turbo C on an IBM-PC, we don't. But few of us will write programs that spend their entire lifetime on a single machine. We've found that many programs we've written on the PC are just as useful running on an Apollo or a Sun. And because we work so hard to write large programs, especially highly interactive or graphics-based programs, we'd like to be able to move them effortlessly from one environment to another.

So, assuming that we care about portability, how can we attain it? By doing two things. We have to avoid constructs that are known to be nonportable. And, when that's impossible, we have to package any nonportable constructs within a portable interface. These principles are relatively easy to follow—given a list of portable and nonportable constructs. So now we'll look at some common portability pitfalls and how we get around them.

```
/*
 * inout.h -- Prototypes for getline and putline.
 */
#include <stdio.h>

#if defined(__TURBOC__)
  typedef char near *LINEPTR; /* Use near pointers */
#else
  typedef char *LINEPTR:       /* No near pointers */
#endif

int getline(LINEPTR ptr, int max);
void putline(LINEPTR ptr);
```

Figure 16.1   inout.h—Header file for a more portable version of getline and putline.

16.2   PORTABILITY ACROSS COMPILERS

Different compilers provide different features. Although there is a soon-to-be-released C standard, not every compiler conforms to it. Some provide additional features; others lack supposedly standard features. Turbo C, for example, allows the near, far, and huge pointer modifiers. Turbo C provides this nonstandard feature because it is very useful for programs running on personal computers. On the other hand, most early PC compilers didn't provide standard features such as enumerated types, structure assignment, or variable names longer than eight characters. And, even though function prototypes are in the new C standard, very few compilers provide them yet.

Using Special Features

To write portable programs we should ignore special features like Turbo C's—but we need them to write efficient programs. We have to somehow set things up to take advantage of this feature when we compile using Turbo C and to ignore the feature when we use other compilers. To do so, we make use of the preprocessor, as in the new versions of inout.h and inout.c shown in Figure 16.1 and Figure 16.2.

The basic idea is simple. We use #if to determine whether we're compiling under Turbo C. If we are, we use versions of getline and putline that take advantage of near pointers. Otherwise, we use a version with normal C pointers. But rather than writing two versions of these functions and using an #if to choose between them, we've chosen to have them declare their pointers using a type LINEPTR that we define as char near * for Turbo C and char * otherwise. The advantage of this approach is that if we make later changes to this pointer type, we only have to do them in one place.

```
/*
 * inout.c -- getline and putline, once again.
 */
#include <stdio.h>
#include "inout.h"

int getline(LINEPTR ptr, int max)
{
  int c;
  LINEPTR startptr;                     /* ptr to 1st char */
  LINEPTR endptr = ptr + max;        /* ptr to next char */

  while ((c = getchar()) != '\n' && c != EOF)
    if (ptr < endptr)
      *ptr++ = c;
  *ptr = '\0';                          /* terminate with null */
  return (c == EOF) ? -1 : ptr - startptr;
}

void putline(LINEPTR ptr)
{
  for (;*ptr != '\0'; ptr++)
    putchar(*ptr);
  putchar('\n');
}
```

Figure 16.2 inout.c—More portable version of getline and putline.

Using Function Prototypes

A similar problem occurs when we want to write a program that's portable to compilers missing standard features. Suppose we want a Turbo C program that uses function prototypes and new-style function definitions, like those for getline and putline, to compile correctly under an old style C compiler. The problem is that these compilers don't allow us to specify the type of variables in function prototypes. But this feature is a wonderful part of the new C standard. Again, we have a problem. And again, the preprocessor rides to the rescue.

The solution requires two steps. First, we modify the header file so that it defines complete prototypes when we're running a standard C compiler, such as Turbo C, and partial prototypes under other compilers.

```
#ifdef __TURBOC__
  int getline(LINEPTR ptr, int max);  /* full prototype */
#else
  int getline();                        /* no full prototype */
#endif
```

And second, when we define the functions, we use the preprocessor to select between the old and new styles of parameter declarations. Figure 16.3 and Figure 16.4 contain

```
/*
 * inout2.h -- Prototypes for getline and putline.
 */
#include <stdio.h>

#ifdef __TURBOC__
  typedef char near *LINEPTR;  /* Use near pointers */
#else
  typedef char *LINEPTR:       /* No near pointers */
#endif

#ifdef __TURBOC__
  int getline(LINEPTR ptr, int max);
  void putline(LINEPTR ptr);
#else
  int getline();
  void putline();
#endif
```

Figure 16.3 inout2.h—An even more portable version of header file input.h.

even more portable versions of `getline` and `putline`.

Since we're now assuming that our program might not run on a standard compiler, we can no longer use `#if` to do the test and we have to use `#ifdef` instead. That's because many current compilers don't yet support `defined`.

Identifier Names

Another area in which many current C compilers fail to achieve the current standard is in how many characters are significant within a variable name. The standard states that the first 31 characters in an internal name and the first 8 characters in an external name are significant (the distinction arises because many linkers weren't written with C in mind and can't be easily changed). But many older compilers treat only the first 8 characters in any name as significant, and many linkers ignore case and consider only the first 5 or 6 characters of a name.

To ensure portability, we must write our program so that all names differ within the first five characters. When two names are identical in the first five characters, we can rename them slightly so they vary. For example, we can rename several variables used to access a data base

```
    int *tableptr_first, *tableptr_last, *tableptr_next;
```

so that they differ in their first few characters rather than their last

```
    int *first_tableptr, *last_tableptr, *next_tableptr;
```

We can also use `#define` to provide readable names. Suppose we have an existing program with a large number of variables such as

```
/*
 * inout2.c -- getline and putline, once again.
 */
#include <stdio.h>
#include "inout2.h"

#ifdef __TURBOC__
  int getline(LINEPTR ptr, int max)
#else
  int getline(ptr, max)
  LINEPTR ptr;
  int max;
#endif
{
  int c;
  LINEPTR startptr = ptr;          /* ptr to 1st char */
  LINEPTR endptr = ptr + max;      /* ptr to next char */

  while ((c = getchar()) != '\n' && c != EOF)
    if (ptr < endptr)
      *ptr++ = c;
  *ptr = '\0';                     /* terminate with null */
  return (c == EOF) ? -1 : ptr - startptr;
}

#ifdef __TURBOC__
  void putline(LINEPTR ptr)
#else
  void putline(ptr)
  LINEPTR ptr;
#endif
{
  for (;*ptr != '\0'; ptr++)
    putchar(*ptr);
  putchar('\n');
}
```

Figure 16.4 inout2.c—An even more portable version of getline and putline.

```
        int *tableptr_first, *tableptr_last, *tableptr_next;
```

We simply redefine these long names to shorter names, and place the definitions in a header file included by the program containing the long names.

```
        #define tableptr_first    tpf
        #define tableptr_last     tpl
        #define tableptr_next     tpn
```

There are several potential problems with this practice. The first is that only the preprocessor ever sees the longer names, so that error messages will refer to the shorter names. And the other is that we might accidentally `#define` two long names to the same short name, a mistake that may be hard to detect.

Libraries

One very subtle portability problem can arise from assuming that library calls never fail. It arises most frequently when dealing with dynamic allocation and when opening files.

When we assume that `malloc` (or one of its derivatives) always succeeds, we're making an assumption that there will always be some available memory. This may be reasonable in a small program using a large memory model and running on a machine with 1 megabyte of memory. But it is much less reasonable if the program is running in the small model on a machine with 128K. Why is not checking `malloc`'s return value a portability problem? Because our program will usually bomb if it runs out of memory, which will happen on some machines but not on others.

Similarly, we shouldn't assume that a file open or write can never fail. It is possible for a file open to fail if the file doesn't exist, and for a file write to fail if there isn't sufficient room on the disk. And while one machine may have a 100-megabyte hard disk that never fills up, another may be running with a 320K floppy that is almost always full.

Not checking these return values could make our program work fine on one machine but fail miserably on another. We would hate to use a text editor that promptly died if it couldn't open our file or allocate enough space to hold it in memory, or failed to at least warn us if a disk was full and it couldn't write the file. To write portable programs, we must always check the return values of system calls and library functions.

EXERCISES

16–1 Are the queue routines in the case study in the last chapter portable? Make whatever changes are necessary to guarantee that they work with both Turbo C and other C compilers.

16–2 Write a set of routines for managing a stack of `int`s. Name them `int_stack_push`, `int_stack_pop`, `int_stack_empty`, and `int_stack_count`. Now pretend you have to port this program to a system that supports only 5 significant characters in an identifier name.

16–3 Rewrite our linked-list insertion sort so it is portable to C compilers that don't provide function prototypes. Do the same thing for Chapter 13's cross-referencer.

16.3   PORTABILITY ACROSS OPERATING SYSTEMS

Most of the programs we've written are useful not only on machines running DOS but also on machines running UNIX or AEGIS or any number of additional operating

```
/*
 * filesize.h -- Prototype for filesize.
 */
#include <stdio.h>

#define  UNKNOWNSIZE     -1L

#ifdef  __TURBOC__
  long filesize(char *file);
#else
  long filesize();
#endif
```

Figure 16.5 filesize.h—Header file for the function file_size.

systems (O/S). This is problematic because we often have to make use of operating-system-specific function calls to accomplish different tasks.

It is obviously a bad idea to simply thread O/S-specific calls throughout our code, as it makes porting programs much more difficult. We would have to thoroughly examine our code, flushing out these calls and replacing them with the appropriate calls for whatever O/S we want to port to. We can make our programs more portable by placing all system calls in generically named routines. By *generic* we mean that routines should be named to indicate the function they perform. The idea is that this generic function takes account of any operating system dependencies, limiting any nonportable code to a small part of our program.

Figure 16.5, Figure 16.6, and Figure 16.7 contain a portable function to print the size of a file, its prototypes, and a main program that uses it. We wrote one version of this function earlier. It computed the length of a file by opening it, seeking to the end, and returning that position. That's a completely portable way of doing it, since we are using only standard C library functions. But DOS and UNIX provide different system calls that find a file's length in a more efficient way. So to keep our program portable, when we need the length of a file, we don't include direct references to these system calls. Instead we call the function filesize. filesize itself use #ifdefs to compile into the appropriate version for DOS or UNIX.

Placing all of the operating-system-specific code within filesize makes the code within the function harder to read. But the main program itself is actually more readable, since the purpose of the strangely named system calls is now clearer.

EXERCISES

16–4 filesize gives up if there is no system call that returns the length of a file. Modify it to use a default way of computing the length of a file.

```
/*
 * filesize.c -- Determine the size of the given file.
 *                Returns UNKNOWNSIZE if it can't do so.
 */
#include "filesize.h"

#ifdef __TURBOC__
  long filesize(char *file)
#else
  long filesize(file) char *file;
#endif
{
#ifdef __MSDOS__
#include <io.h>
  FILE *fp = fopen(file, "r");

  if (fp != NULL)
  {
    long len = filelength(fileno(fp));

    fclose(fp);
    return len == -1L ? UNKNOWNSIZE : len;
  }
#endif

#ifdef unix
#include <sys/types.h>   /* UNIX specific include file */
#include <stat.h>        /* UNIX specific include file */
  struct stat s;

  if (stat(file, &s) != -1)
    return s.st_size;
#endif

  return UNKNOWNSIZE;
}
```

Figure 16.6   filesize.c—A function to determine the number of bytes in a file.

16–5 Write exists, a function that takes a single file name argument and returns 1 if a file with that name exists, and a 0 otherwise. Write it so that it works with DOS and UNIX. The UNIX version should use stat, which returns -1 if the file doesn't exist. The DOS version can simply try to open the file for reading.

```
/*
 * A main program to test filesize.
 */
#include "filesize.h"

main(int argc, char *argv[])
{
  long fs;

  if (argc != 2)
  {
    printf("Usage: %s filename\n", argv[0]);
    return 1;
  }
  if ((fs = filesize(argv[1])) == UNKNOWNSIZE)
  {
    puts("Can't get size of junk\n");
    return 1;  /* exit early on failure */
  }
  printf("Size of junk: %ld\n", fs);
  return 0;     /* everything worked */
}
```

Figure 16.7 tstfs.c—A main program using `filesize` to determine the length of a file.

16.4   MACHINE DEPENDENCIES

C differs from most high-level languages in that it was designed to help us implement programs efficiently and to let us directly access the underlying machine. Although these are two of its most attractive features, they are also a source of machine dependencies that lead to portability problems.

Data Type Sizes

Most machines work most efficiently on integers when they are stored in a single word. But the size of a word can differ from machine to machine. This means that `int`s vary in size from 16 bits (as on the PC), to 32 bits (as on VAXs, Suns, and 386-based UNIX systems), to 60 bits (on the Cray). The result is that we must never assume that an `int` can hold a value outside the range of -32768 to 32767. Since Turbo C uses `int`s at least as small as those on other machines, we don't have to worry. But suppose we have to take a program written for a bigger machine, such as a VAX, and make it run on the PC. We're in trouble if they've assumed that `int`s have 32 bits.

`char`s also vary in size from machine to machine. They range from 6 bits on CDC machines, to 7 bits on the PDP-7, to 8 bits on most minicomputers, to 10 bits on the Cray. How can this cause portability problems? Suppose we use a `char` to

```
/*
 * Header file for defining "Short CouNTer" type.
 */
#if defined(__TURBOC__)
  typedef unsigned char SCNT;     ./* 8-bit chars */
#endif

#if defined(__PDP7__)
  typedef unsigned short SCNT;    /* 7-bit chars */
#endif
```

Figure 16.8 ourtypes.h—Header file defining names for our types.

hold small integers in the range of 0 to 128. That's safe if our characters are 8 bits, but what if we go to a machine with 6-bit characters? Once again, we're in trouble.

One way to minimize portability problems is to use `long`s for all our integers. But the drawbacks to this approach should be obvious: Our programs will run slower and take up more space. A better way is to carefully define types that reflect their uses, and to define these types differently on different machines.

Suppose, for example, that we want a type for dealing with small counters, that is, counters that range in size from 0 to 255. And further suppose that we have an array of 1000 of these. That means that we can save 1000 bytes by declaring these types as `unsigned char`s instead of `short`s or `int`s. But then we would have a problem if we tried to port our program to a machine such as the PDP-7 that has 7-bit characters. So we instead define a new type, SCNT, and use it to declare all our counters. On some machines, such as the PC, this type is defined as an `unsigned char`. But on others it might be a `short`. This extra work lets us use space efficiently without hurting portability. Figure 16.8 shows how to define the type, Figure 16.9 gives an example use of it.

Pointer Problems

Pointers are another area where portability problems frequently arise. The problems stem from a common false assumption—that all pointers are the same size and have the same internal representation.

In Turbo C, with its `near` and `far` pointers, that's obviously not true. And other machines exist where it is possible for pointers to different data types to be different sizes and to have different internal representations. That means that assigning a pointer of one type to a pointer of another type without a cast could conceivably cause a program to work on one machine yet fail on another. The solution is obvious: Cast from one pointer type to the other. We've consistently done so with the pointer (of type `void`) returned by `malloc`.

```
        int *temp = (int *) malloc(sizeof(int));
```

```
/*
 * Program using the types.
 */
#include <stdio.h>
#include "ourtypes.h"                    /* type definitions */

#define MAXCNT 20

main()
{
  SCNT table[MAXCNT];                    /* array of that type */
  SCNT i;

  for (i = 0; i < MAXCNT; i++)           /* some initial values */
    table[i] = i;
  for (i = 0; i < MAXCNT; i++)           /* print them */
    printf("%u\n", table[i]);
}
```

Figure 16.9   ourtypes.c—Using the defined types to isolate the underlying types.

This is portable, since if void pointers somehow differ from int pointers, the cast will cause the correct conversion to take place.

Character Set Differences

Different machines can have different underlying representations for characters. The two most common are ASCII and EBCDIC. This causes problems when we make direct use of the underlying representation. It is clearly unportable to use

```
if (c == 48)
  printf("Character is a '0'\n");
```

to check whether we've read the character '0'. Although 48 is the ASCII representation for the character '0', it represents a different character in EBCDIC. The solution is to always use the character rather than its integer representation. If we need a nonprinting character, we can use its octal code, but to aid portability we should define a symbolic name for it.

```
#define ACK '\004'          /* acknowledge packet received */
```

The mistake shown earlier results from assuming that the integer representation of a character is the same across different character sets. But a similar mistake occurs from the less odious assumption that a group of characters is always contiguous.

```
if (c >= 'a' && c <= 'z')
  printf("lower case letter\n");
```

In ASCII, this assumption holds for lowercase letters, for uppercase letters, and for digits. In EBCDIC, the assumption only holds for digits. The functions in the character-testing library discussed in Chapter 3 provide a more portable way of making these comparisons.

```
#include <ctype.h>
    . . .
if (islower(c))
  printf("lower case letter\n");
```

In fact, using the library functions is also more readable. The only possible sacrifice we might be making is in efficiency. But since these functions are actually macros, and they usually expand into an index into a table of information about various characters, they may be even more efficient than the nonportable comparison.

Sign Problems

We pointed out in Chapter 3 that C doesn't specify the results of conversions between signed and unsigned types, particularly when there is a change in the length of the data type. For example, suppose we assign the `unsigned short` 65535 (all 16 bits on) to a `long`.

```
unsigned short y = 65535;
long x = y;
```

Some compilers will zero extend, which results in x being assigned 65535, as we would expect. But other compilers sign extend, which causes x to be assigned -1. The solution to this portability problem is to use a cast.

```
unsigned short y = 65535;
long x = (unsigned long) y;
```

The cast guarantees that y is zero extended before being assigned to x.

Another potential sign problem occurs when we do right shifts on signed numbers. Again, some compilers fill with zeros, others propagate the sign bit. The solution is to do right shifts only on unsigned quantities. Luckily we don't have a problem with left shifts, since they always shift in zeros.

Byte Ordering

Unfortunately, the order of bytes in a word also differs between machines. On some the high byte is most significant; on others the low byte is most significant, as illustrated in Figure 16.10. This is a problem if we access the individual bytes within a word, as we've done in Figure 16.11.

This program declares a variable that's a `union` of a `short` and a 2-byte character array. It assigns the `short` the value 0x08F0, and then prints the values of the two entries in the byte array. On some machines the output will be 0x08 followed by 0xF0; on others the values will be reversed. The solution is to avoid directly accessing bytes within integers.

1	0
08	_F_0
MSB	LSB

(_a_) On some machines the most significant byte (MSB) is the high byte.

1	0
_F_0	08
LSB	MSB

(_b_) On other machines, it's the low byte.

Figure 16.10   Differences in most significant versus least significant bytes.

```
/*
 * Nonportable program with byte-order assumptions builtin.
 */
#include <stdio.h>

union word
{
  short x;          /* use as word */
  char bytes[2];    /* use as bytes */
};

main()
{
  union word w;

  w.x = 0x08F0;     /* 08 F0 */
  printf("LSB=%x, MSB=%x.\n", w.bytes[0], w.bytes[1]);
  return 0;
}
```

Figure 16.11   bytetest.c—A program with a nonportable assumption about byte ordering.

EXERCISES

16–6 Find out what the machine-dependent operations (such as right shifts of negative integers) actually do on the PC. Do any of your programs take advantage of them? If any do, can you rewrite your programs to avoid these operations?

16–7 Write a program that prints the contents of a long, one byte at a time, using a union as we did in Figure 16.11.

16–8 Write a function that can print the contents of any type, including structures, one byte at a time. What might such a function be useful for?

16.5   **CASE STUDY—PORTABLE I/O DEVICE HANDLING**

We don't want a program wedded to a particular input or output device. But if we directly call the low-level calls needed to manipulate the keyboard or display, we're going to be in trouble once we change to a different device or to a system with different calls. To avoid this problem, we have to treat keyboards and displays as *virtual* devices. That means that, rather than directly calling whatever low-level calls are required to actually access the display, we make use of a package of high-level functions that do things such as reading a key or moving the cursor. This gives us the flexibility to reimplement these functions for many different devices on different systems.

We'll illustrate our point by writing two functions for displaying output on the standard pc monitor: delete_text and move_cursor. (Turbo C 1.5 provides similar library functions to do these tasks, but earlier versions of Turbo C don't.)

It turns out that Turbo C provides a library call, int86, for accessing resources like the display. int86 has a strange name and even stranger arguments.

```
int86(unsigned int, union REGS *, union REGS *)
```

The name is shorthand for "execute an 8086 interrupt function." An interrupt function is a low-level system routine, one that is built into the operating system. When we call int86, it *interrupts* our program's normal execution and passes control to the operating system, which then executes the specified routine. Once the routine has completed, our program resumes where it left off. Table 16.1 lists the interrupt functions we use most often.

int86's first argument is an integer identifying the interrupt function we want to execute. 0x10 selects the one that handles screen I/O, 0x17 selects printer I/O, and so on. Its second argument specifies the action we want the interrupt function to perform and any arguments to that action. This is the argument we use to tell the screen handler that we want to move the cursor and to provide its new location. Table 16.2 lists some of the more common actions.

The argument itself is a pointer to an object with a new type, union REGS, that is defined in dos.h.

ENTRY   FUNCTION

0x5	Print screen
0x10	Screen I/O
0x13	Disk I/O
0x14	Serial Port I/O
0x16	Keyboard I/O
0x17	Printer I/O
0x19	Bootstrap loader
0x1A	Time and date
0x21	DOS entry point

Table 16.1   The more common interrupt functions.

AH	WHAT IT DOES	REGISTERS
0	Set video mode	AL=mode (value between 0-6)
1	Set cursor lines	CH=start of line, CL=end of line
2	Set cursor pos	BH=page, DH=row, DL=column
3	Get cursor pos	BH=page, DH=row, DL=column, CX=mode (lines)
5	Set video page	AL=page
6	Scroll up	AL=lines (clear if AL=0), CH=srow, CL=scol
		BH=color, DH=torow, DL=tocol
7	Scroll down	same arguments as scroll up
8	Read character	BH=page (sets AL=char, AH=attribute)
9	Write character	BH=page, CX=number, AL=char, BL=attribute

Table 16.2   Table of various screen actions.

```
struct WORDREGS
       {unsigned int ax, bx, cx, dx, si, di, cflag};
struct BYTEREGS
       {unsigned char al, ah, bl, bh, cl, ch, dl, dh};

union REGS
{
  struct WORDREGS x;  /* for dealing with word registers */
  struct BYTEREGS h;  /* for dealing with byte registers */
};
```

These funny two-letter names correspond to the names of machine registers. Interrupt functions examine these registers to determine exactly what it is they are supposed to do. The screen handler, for example, examines the ah register to determine what

```
/*
 * Screen output operations (from 0,0 to 23,79).
 */
void move_cursor(int row, int col);
void delete_text(int srow, int scol, int erow, int ecol);

#define clear_screen()        delete_text(0, 0, 23, 79)
#define delete_line(row)      delete_text(row, 0, row, 79)
#define clear_toeol(row,col)  delete_text(row, col, row, 79)
```

Figure 16.12   screen.h—Header file for screen operations.

action to perform, according to the chart shown in Table 16.2. If this value is 2, which means "move the cursor," it then takes `dh` as the row number and `dl` as the column number. The idea is that we fill one of these `union REGS` with initial values for the registers and then pass a pointer to it. `int86` then loads these register with the values we provide and executes the interrupt function. The reason for the union is that sometimes we provide the values for word-size registers, and at other times for byte-size registers.

`int86`'s last argument is also a pointer to a `union REGS`. It is filled in with the values of the registers after the interrupt function has been called.

Now we've got the pieces to write our screen I/O functions, shown in Figure 16.12 and Figure 16.13. All these functions work the same way. First, they declare variables to hold the initial and final values of the registers.

```
union REGS inregs, outregs;  /* hold in/out registers */
```

Second, they fill in `inregs` with the initial values of the registers. The screen handler expects the `ah` register to select the action, but which other registers it examines depends on the particular action. Because we have a union, we have to first select one of the structures within it (h or x, depending on whether we want to access word registers or byte registers), and then the field within that structure.

```
inregs.h.ah = 2;   /* OP: set cursor position */
```

Third, they call `int86`, passing it pointers to the two unions declared earlier.

```
int86(0x10, &inregs, &outregs);
```

Most actions don't change the registers, so we can usually get by with a single union as both of `int86`'s second and third arguments. But the actions that return information, such as finding the current cursor position, place the values in registers. For these we generally use a second union and examine it after the call.

These screen functions are nice, but how is this discussion related to portability? The point is that `int86` is difficult to use and inherently nonportable. But we need to use it to write nice, highly interactive programs. What we've tried to do here is localize the nonportable code in a few specialized routines. That way, only these routines

```
/*
 * The screen handling functions themselves.
 */
#include <dos.h>
#include "screen.h"

void move_cursor(int row, int col)
{
  union REGS regs;

  regs.h.ah = 2;            /* OP: set cursor position */
  regs.h.bh = 0;            /* page to move to (always 0) */
  regs.h.dl = col;          /* row to move to */
  regs.h.dh = row;          /* column to move to */
  int86(0x10, &regs, &regs);
}

void delete_text(int startrow, int startcol,
                 int endrow, int endcol)
{
  union REGS inregs, outregs;

  inregs.h.ah = 6;              /* OP: scroll up code */
  inregs.h.al = 0;              /* clear */
  inregs.h.ch = startrow;
  inregs.h.cl = startcol;
  inregs.h.dh = endrow;
  inregs.h.dl = endcol;
  inregs.h.bh = 7;              /* attribute: black background */
  int86(0x10, &inregs, &outregs);
}
```

Figure 16.13   screen.c — A set of functions for doing operations directly to the screen.

have to be changed and recompiled to use a different display, not the remainder of our program. To illustrate, we've used the functions in Figure 16.14, a new version of the Life program's output routine. Not only do they make this routine more portable, but they make it more readable as well.

Here we've dealt only with output displays, but we can apply the same technique to input device drivers. In fact, we already have. In Chapter 3 we wrote getkey, a function to read a key, which we wrote on top of the low-level bioskey system call.

EXERCISES

16–9 How portable are the programs in the book? Pick two or three of the case studies and

```c
/*
 * Print generation using direct cursor addressing.
 */
#include <stdio.h>
#include "screen.h"
#include "life.h"

#define HEADER_ROW      0   /* row containing header */
#define BORDER_ROW      1   /* row containing top border */
#define BORDER_COL      0   /* col containing left border */
#define TOP_CELL_ROW    2   /* first row with cells */
#define LEFT_CELL_COL   1   /* first column with cells */

void putworld(WORLD world)
{
  int c, r;
  static int printed = FALSE;      /* first printing? */
  extern int rows, cols, gen, endgen;

  if (!printed)
  {
    clear_screen();
    move_cursor(BORDER_ROW, BORDER_COL);
    for (c = 0; c <= cols + 1; c++)        /* top border */
      putchar(BORDER);
    for (r = TOP_CELL_ROW; r <  TOP_CELL_ROW + rows; r++)
    {                                    /* other borders */
      move_cursor(r, BORDER_COL); putchar(BORDER);
      move_cursor(r, LEFT_CELL_COL + cols); putchar(BORDER);
    }
    move_cursor(BORDER_ROW + rows + 1, BORDER_COL);
    for (c = 0; c <= cols + 1; c++)      /* bottom border */
      putchar(BORDER);
    printed = TRUE;
  }
  move_cursor(HEADER_ROW, BORDER_COL);
  printf("Generation %d out of %d", gen, endgen);
  for (r = TOP_CELL_ROW; r < TOP_CELL_ROW + rows; r++)
  {
    move_cursor(r, LEFT_CELL_COL);
    for (c = 1; c <= cols; c++)
      putchar(world[r][c] ? MARKER : ' ');
  }
  move_cursor(BORDER_ROW + rows + 2, BORDER_COL);
}
```

Figure 16.14   outworld.c—A new version of the Life output routines using these portable I/O functions.

run them on another machine.

16-10 If you have access to more than one machine, take a sizeable program that you have written and used on one machine and port it to another. Where were your portability problems? Does the program have identical run-time behavior on both machines?

16-11 Suppose you have to write a program that requires a 100,000 element array of integers and that, in addition, it must be able to run on a machine with 16 megabytes of virtual memory and on a machine with only 128K of memory where arrays are limited to 64,000 bytes. Assume that the only operations on the table are to access an element and to store a value in an array element. Write functions for these operations that use an in-memory array if there is enough room or store the array in an external file if there is not. Should the callers of these functions be aware of how the array is actually accessed?

17 EFFICIENCY

We've learned how to write large, portable Turbo C programs. Now it's time to learn how to make these programs run more quickly and use less space. This chapter studies program efficiency. But we don't provide devious machine-dependent tricks that make our code much less portable and only slightly faster. Instead, we simply suggest some likely sources of inefficiencies and show how we can best eliminate them. The chapter concludes with several case studies in efficiency—a simple memory allocator that allocates fixed-size blocks, and a short function for reading integers into an array.

17.1 SOME BASICS

We've tried to show that we get efficient, easily modified programs by designing our programs well, by selecting algorithms carefully, and by using appropriate data structures. And usually the simplest, most direct method of solving a problem is the most efficient way, particularly when we consider programmer time.

There are times, however, when we have to make a program run faster or require less space. Fortunately, there are many areas that we can attack to make our programs more efficient. But before we do so we need an idea of what we mean by program efficiency and how we might go about measuring it. One common measure is the time a program takes to run s a function of the size of its inputs. We used this measure back in Chapter 2 when we studied insertion sorting. That routine takes time proportional to the *square* of the number of input values. Double the number of values to be sorted and computing time goes up by a factor of 4; triple the input size, time goes up by a factor of 9, and so forth.

This measure is an excellent way to examine an algorithm's performance with average data. But there may be special conditions that make it particularly good or bad for a special set of values. What happens if the values are already sorted? Or if they are sorted in reverse order? When selecting an algorithm or designing a data structure, we have to take this *asymptotic performance* into account.

This measure also says little about how a particular implementation of the algorithm will run on a particular machine, with its particular operating system and compiler. And how we actually implement the algorithm can have a considerable effect on how fast it runs. Our job is not over once we've selected an appropriate algorithm and chosen our data structures—we still have to worry about how to make the program run as efficiently as possible within its environment. And that's the topic of the remainder of this chapter. But before you read on, do the following exercises.

EXERCISES

17–1 Take a program you've written, perhaps a solution to one of the more complicated exercises you encountered earlier in the text, and find three places where you can improve its efficiency.

17–2 Make the improvements you suggested in the previous exercise. Do they result in a noticeable speedup?

17.2   COMMON SOURCES OF INEFFICIENCY

Many sources of inefficiency result from sloppy programming. And making a program efficient is often a matter of going through it looking for unintentional uses of expensive language features. Two of the most common efficiency traps are unnecessary conversions and unneeded arithmetic.

Unnecessary Conversions

Conversions are convenient, but they are also costly, and we want to avoid them wherever possible. Unfortunately, they often creep in without our realizing it, unnecessarily slowing down our program.

Unneeded conversions frequently happen in seemingly innocuous assignment statements. What could possibly be wrong with the following?

```
f = 1;
```

Nothing, so long as f is an int. But suppose f is a long. Then a conversion must take place, placing zeros in f's high word. This conversion isn't difficult to avoid; all we have to do is assign f a value of the correct type, 1L instead of 1.

This situation is even worse if f is a double, because then the conversion also involves a representation change, which may require several additional instructions. But once again we can easily avoid any conversion, this time by assigning 1.0.

Comparisons are another likely source of conversions. A test as simple as f == 0 becomes costly when f isn't an int. The same conversions that take place within an assignment take place here. And we saw earlier how costly these can be when we do things like compare near and far pointers.

Parameter passing is also similar to assignment, and is yet another likely source of unwanted conversions. When we supply function prototypes, Turbo C automatically converts the actual parameter to whatever type the function expects. That's good because we can write a single function that takes doubles but also works for ints and longs. But it's bad because we'll be doing expensive conversions whenever we pass ints.

To avoid these conversions we need to write separate versions of the function, one to handle longs and another to handle ints. The math library, for example, provides several different functions to compute absolute values: abs returns the absolute value of an int, labs returns the absolute value of a long, and fabs returns the absolute value of a `double`. It provides these functions even though C's automatic conversions would let us use `fabs` with any of the other types.

An assignment can only cause a single conversion, but an arithmetic expression can cause multiple conversions, many of which may be unnecessary. With a declared as a `char` (perhaps because it always contains a small integer), b declared as an `int`, and c as a `long`, the assignment

```
x = (a + b) * c;
```

causes several conversions. First, a's value is converted to an `int` before being added to b. Then that result is converted to a `long` before being multipled with c. And, if x happens to be an `int`, still another conversion takes place: that result is converted back to an `int` before it's assigned to x. How do we cut down on the conversions? The simplest solution, assuming that c must be a `long`, is to make a, b, and x `long`s as well.

Things are worse with floating point, since by default all floating point arithmetic takes place using `double`s. With x and y declared as `float`s,

```
x = y / 2.0;
```

causes y to be converted to a `double` before the division takes place, with the result converted back to a `float` before being assigned to x. The problem disappears if we declare x and y as `double`s instead of `float`s.

In general, automatic conversions take place whenever we have two different data types within the same expression—which means that we should try to limit expressions to a single data type. In the above examples, we did so by making sure that we declared all our variables using the same type, and by making sure that any constants we used were also of the appropriate type. But sometimes we're stuck with arithmetic involving different types. In these cases, the best we can hope for is to minimize the number of conversions that take place, either by rearranging the expression or making use of explicit temporary variables.

Suppose, for example, that we have the assignment,

```
d = a * c + b * c;
```

along with the constraints that a and b must be `int`s, and that c and d must be `float`s. The way the expression is currently written, a, b, and c are all converted to `double`s, and the result of the computation is converted to a `float`. But we can eliminate at least one conversion by rewriting the expression.

```
d = (a + b) * c;
```

Now a and b are left as `int`s, and only their result is converted to a `double`.

Unnecessary Arithmetic

Programs frequently spend much of their execution time doing arithmetic. To make them more efficient we want to avoid arithmetic whenever we can, and when that's impossible, we want to use integer arithmetic ·rather than floating point arithmetic. C's floating point arithmetic is especially slow, since C does it using `double`s.

Unnecessary floating point arithmetic often occurs in expressions involving constants. Consider the following expression, assuming `a` is a `double` and `i` is an `int`.

```
a = i * 2.0;
```

Here `i` is converted to a `double`, multiplied by 2.0 using `double` arithmetic, and the result stored in `a`. But we can do better with

```
a = i * 2;
```

Even though there's still an automatic conversion, this is faster because it uses only integer arithmetic.

A single `float` in an expression can cause the entire expression to be evaluated using floating point. Take an assignment as simple as

```
x = d * i * j * k;
```

and suppose that `d` is a `double` and all the other variables are `int`s. Depending on the order the compiler chooses for evaluating the multiplications, it is possible that all will be done in floating point, which is highly undesirable. If we really want to guarantee that integer arithmetic is used, we have to use a temporary variable.

```
temp = i * j * k;    /* integer arithmetic */
x = d * temp;        /* floating point arithmetic */
```

There are some cases where even integer arithmetic is unnecessary, as in these naive macros for determining whether a particular integer is odd or even.

```
#define ODD(x)  ((x) % 2 == 1)   /* odd integer? */
#define EVEN(x) ((x) % 2 == 0)   /* even integer? */
```

These work by examining a remainder, which requires a division. A better way avoids arithmetic entirely by directly checking whether the leftmost bit has been set.

```
#define ODD(x)  ((x) & 01)       /* odd integer? */
#define EVEN(x) !ODD(X)          /* even integer? */
```

We can also use the bitwise operators to speed up some special case multiplications and divisions. For example, if we need to compute x^n, and we know that `x` will be a small power of two, we can use `x << n` to do the computation efficiently.

Unneeded arithmetic often occurs because we're doing the same computation more than once, as in this loop to sum the first n elements of an array.

```
sum = 0;
for (ptr = a; ptr < a + n; ptr++)
  sum += *ptr;
```

What's wrong with it? It's computing the address $a + n - 1$ every single time it goes through the loop. But it really needs to do so only once. By assigning the result to a temporary variable before the loop and using it in the comparison, we eliminate one extra computation each time through the loop, which can result in substantial savings.

```
sum = 0;
endptr = a + n;
for (ptr = a; ptr < endptr; ptr++)
  sum += *ptr;
```

We can find ourselves repeatedly doing the same computation without even being in a loop. Often we have expressions in which the same subexpression appears multiple times. Although we can compute a^4 with

```
result = (a * a) * (a * a);
```

we do better by computing a^2 once, storing it into a temporary variable, and then multiplying the temporary variable by itself.

```
temp = a * a;              /* save pow(a,2) */
result = temp * temp;
```

In the above example, the redundant computation is obvious, but what about this obviously harmless program fragment?

```
a[i][j] = a[i][j] + value;
```

We realize its not so harmless once we remember that `a[i][j]` is really a shorthand notation for `*(*(a + i) + j)`, a complex computation involving at least two additions. And it's a computation that the we're doing twice. In this case, all we have to do to fix things is use an assignment operator.

```
a[i][j] += value;
```

EXERCISES

17–3 What's the drawback to defining `BOOLEAN` as an `unsigned char`? How can we get around this?

17–4 Pick one of the larger programs in this book and see if you can improve it by eliminating unnecessary conversions or arithmetic.

17.3   C EFFICIENCY AIDS

We've shown how to recognize and remove several sources of unnecessary sluggishness. Now we turn to special features of C that help us write more efficient programs. These features, which aren't available in many other high-level languages, are compile-time initialization, pointers, and macros.

Compile-Time Initialization

Compile-time initialization lets us initialize arrays without having to use a potentially lengthy run-time loop. Rather than setting all of an array's elements to zero with

```
int a[N];
int i;
    . . .
for (i = 0; i < N; i++)
  a[i] = 0;
```

we simply make the array `static`, provide any needed initial values at compile-time, and let the compiler and linker do the initializing for us.

```
static int a[N];    /* zero by default */
int i;
```

In the above example, it's obvious that we can make use of compile-time initialization. But there are many other cases where we can do so as well. Suppose, for example, that our program needs to compute x^y for integers x and y, $1 \le x \le 5$ and $0 \le y \le 10$. We could use the math library function `pow(x,y)` to compute them.

```
#include <math.h>
     . . .
result = pow(x,y);
```

But `pow` works with `doubles`, which means that some conversions are necessary. And in any case, it still has to do some computing. We could write our own version of `pow` that works with integers, but this merely avoids the conversions and not the calculations.

What we can do instead is precompute the necessary powers; using either a calculator or another program, and stick them into a table. Then we can write a function on top of `pow` that first examines a table with these precomputed values and computes the necessary powers only if doesn't already know about them. That function is shown in Figure 17.1.

Using Pointers

Throughout this text we've emphasized that we gain efficiency by using pointers instead of array subscripting when we traverse arrays. We'll now provide one final example, three new versions of `search`, our Chapter 7 sequential search function.

Our new versions of `search` use a special trick to eliminate a comparison. The old `search` had two tests to determine whether it could exit the loop used to travel through the array. One checked whether we had found the value we were looking for, the other whether we had reached the end of the array. Now `search` cheats. It expects the array to have an additional empty element at the end, and it assigns this element the value for which it's searching. That guarantees that it will always find the value and eliminates the check for the end of the array.

The first version, Figure 17.2, uses array accessing. And as we're by now well aware, the problem is that each time we access `a[i]`, the compiler has to take i, multiply it by the size of an element of a, and then add it to a.

The second version, Figure 17.3, corrects this problem by using a pointer to traverse the array. But it isn't just using a pointer that improves efficiency. Had we simply used `*(a + i)` to access the array element, we would get no improvement, even though it looks like we're using a pointer. Why? Because the compiler still has to do the address calculation, just like before. What makes it more efficient is our incrementing the pointer each time we go through the loop—we've eliminated much of the address calculation required to locate a particular array element.

The final version, Figure 17.4, is a more compact pointer version. Now we combine dereferencing the pointer with incrementing it, which can often be done in

```c
/*
 * Compute powers using table of commonly accessed powers.
 */
#include <stdio.h>
#include <math.h>

#define MAXEXP 10
#define MAXRDX  5

long power(int x, int y)
{
  static long twos[] =
    {1, 2, 4, 8, 16, 32, 64, 128, 256, 512, 1024};
  static long threes[] =
    {1, 3, 9, 27, 81, 243,729, 2187, 6561, 19683, 59049L};
  static long fours[] =
    {1, 4, 16, 64, 256, 1024, 4096, 16384, 65536L,
     262144L, 1048576L};
  static long fives[] =
    {1, 5, 25, 125, 625, 3125, 15625, 78125L,
     390625L, 1953125L, 9765625L};

  if (x >= 1 && x <= MAXRDX && y >= 0 && y <= MAXEXP)
    switch((int) x)
    {
      case 1: return 1L;
      case 2: return twos[y];
      case 3: return threes[y];
      case 4: return fours[y];
      case 5: return fives[y];
    }
  return pow(x,y);
}

main()  /* a test program for pow */
{
  printf("2^5: %ld\n", power(2,5));
  printf("5^8: %ld\n", power(5,8));
  printf("4^1: %ld\n", power(4,1));
  printf("7^3: %ld\n", power(7,3));
  printf("3^6: %ld\n", power(3,6));
  printf("2^14: %ld\n", power(2,14));
  return 0;
}
```

Figure 17.1   fastpow.c—Efficiently computing powers by precomputing common ones in a table.

```
/*
 * New linear search function (assumes extra array element).
 * Array subscripting version.
 */
#include <stddef.h>

int *search(int a[], int num, int value)
{
  int i;

  for (a[num] = value, i = 0; a[i] != value; i++)
    ;
  return (i < num) ? &a[i] : NULL;
}
```

Figure 17.2 Original array-subscripting version of a linear search function.

```
/*
 * New linear search function (assumes extra array element).
 * Pointer indexing version.
 */
int *search(int *ptr, int num, int value)
{
  int *endptr = ptr + num;

  for (*endptr = value; *ptr != value; ptr++)
    ;
  return (ptr < endptr) ? ptr : NULL;
}
```

Figure 17.3 A pointer-indexing version.

a single instruction. This version is slightly harder to read, so we use it only when we're trying to squeeze the last ounce of performance from our program.

Using Macros

Macros are the last performance aid that we'll examine. They allow us to keep the readability of a function call without its overhead.

Figure 17.5 provides a good example of where using a macro can aid efficiency. It contains a new version of reverse_tab, a Chapter 7 function to reverse an array in place. It runs two pointers through an array, one from the front and the other from the back, and exchanges the pointed to elements. reverse_tab does the exchange with a function swap—which makes it clear and concise, but also somewhat slow,

```
/*
 * New linear search function (assumes extra array element).
 * More compact, pointer indexing version.
 */
int *search(int *ptr, int num, int value)
{
  int *endptr = ptr + num;

  *endptr = value;
  while (*ptr++ != value)
    ;
  return (--ptr < endptr) ? ptr : NULL;
}
```

Figure 17.4   An even faster pointer version.

```
/*
 * Reverse an array (using earlier swap function).
 */
void reverse_tab(int *ptr, int first, int last)
{
  int *endptr = ptr + last - 1;

  for (ptr += first; ptr <= endptr; ptr++, endptr--)
    swap(ptr, endptr);
  }
}
```

Figure 17.5   Rewriting `reverse_tab` to use a function to exchange two values.

since it calls a function each time it goes through the loop.

We can improve it by replacing this function call with a macro, as we've done in Figure 17.6. Using a macro eliminates the extra instructions used to call and return from the function and to handle parameter passing.

Since macros are more efficient than functions, why don't we turn every function into a macro? Because there's a tradeoff between speed and size. A macro executes faster but takes more space, since the entire code into which the macro expands appears each time we call it. We really only want to turn small functions into macros, those functions for which the cost of the function call and return constitutes most of the cost of using the function. Generally, that means functions such as `swap` that can be turned into a single expression.

```
/*
 * Reverse an array (using swap macro).
 */
#define SWAP(var, px, py) (var = *px, *px = *py, *py = var)

void reverse_tab(int *ptr, int first, int last)
{
  int *endptr = ptr + last - 1;
  int temp;

  for (ptr += first; ptr <= endptr; ptr++, endptr--)
    SWAP(temp, ptr, endptr);
}
```

Figure 17.6 Rewriting `reverse_tab` to use a macro.

EXERCISES

17–5 Modify our search function to save the position and value of the last few items it looked up. Whenever the function is called, it should check this list before searching the larger table. Of course, this technique only pays off when there are certain items that we frequently search for.

17–6 Rewrite the string-handling functions we wrote earlier as concisely as possible, making sure that pointers are incremented only when they are used within an expression. Are the resulting functions faster? Are they harder to read?

17–7 Rewrite the Game of Life program so that it increments pointers only when it uses them in expressions.

17–8 What functions throughout this book could have been better written as macros? Start by examining the larger programs, such as the cross-referencer.

17.4   SHRINKING SPACE REQUIREMENTS

Our discussion of efficiency has so far been devoted to making our programs run faster. But when we're writing programs for small personal computers, it also becomes important to use less storage. Often, shrinking a program's storage requirements results in a program that works in a smaller memory model and therefore runs faster.

We have two basic techniques for saving storage. The first is to eliminate any unused storage space hidden within a data structure, the other is to eliminate any information we store that we really don't need. Both of these techniques are likely to increase the running time of our program, but can lead to substantial space savings.

Eliminating Unused Storage

Many of our programs don't store data as compactly as they could. As a simple example, consider our earlier method for storing a date—we declared a structure with three integers, one for the month, day, and year.

```
struct date
{
    int month, day, year;
};
```

`month`, `day`, and `year` are all integers, but do they have to be? Since there are only twelve possible values of month, we really only need 4 bits to store it. Similarly, the day can range only from 1 to 31, so 5 bits are sufficient for it. The year is more difficult, but if we assume it's an offset into this century (a value that's added to 1900 before processing it), we can fit it within 7 or 8 bits.

C doesn't have 4 or 5 bit integers, but we can use an `unsigned char` as an 8 bit integer. Keeping this in mind, we can use a more compact structure.

```
typedef unsigned char DATE_PART;   /* part of a date */

struct date
{
    DATE_PART month, day, year;
};
```

Now we use half the storage we used before. If our program stores only a single date, the three bytes we save here isn't a big deal. But the savings add up rapidly if our program has a thousand element array of dates.

There is a tradeoff here, though. Our program is going to run slower. Since C always converts characters to integers before comparing them, every time we use the components of a date to perform arithmetic or as part of a comparison, there is going to be an automatic conversion.

We can actually use even less storage for a date: The 4 bits we need for the day, the 5 bits for the month, and the 7 for the year can be packed into a single 16-bit word, using bitfields.

```
struct date
{
    unsigned int day : 4;
    unsigned int month : 5;
    unsigned int year : 16;
};
```

Of course, now we have to use the field selection operators to access the relevant pieces of a date. And, unfortunately, these operators aren't always efficient, since they usually compile into instructions that do some type of bit shifting.

Eliminating unused gaps by compressing the data is a generally useful technique for saving space. But beware that it may also slow your program down considerably.

Eliminating Extra Information

We saw earlier that a big advantage of linked lists over an array is that we can insert and delete items without shifting. But we pay a price, the extra pointer we store with each element and the overhead of each call to `malloc`. That may not seem like its worth worrying about, but suppose we're keeping a list of integers. Then exactly half our storage is extra information used solely for maintaining the list. To save storage, we can eliminate this overhead by using an array—although this brings us back our original problems with inserting and deleting values. If storage is crucial, use an array and suffer the cost of slow insertions and deletions. If speed is crucial, use a linked list and try to save space elsewhere.

This sort of choice between finite acess and storing less information is hard to avoid. In fact, the language's built-in strings are an example of where this choice was made. Many other languages store strings as a structure containing a length and a pointer to the characters it contains. And doing so makes operations that require the length of a string (such as reversing a string, or accessing its nth-to-last character) much faster. Unfortunately, it also makes strings one word longer. By eliminating this extra information we save some additional storage.

EXERCISES

17-9 Implement the basic string library functions on strings as structures consisting of a length and a pointer to the first character, with no null character terminating the string. What functions can be improved if we the string's length is handy?

17-10 Suppose we have a program with a number of boolean variables that we use as flags. What's the most space-efficient way to store them?

17-11 Modify Chapter 13's linked list routines to keep a count of the number of times a value appears, rather than having separate nodes.

17.5   CASE STUDY—REPLACING LIBRARY ROUTINES

As a general rule, a function to do a specific task is more efficient than one to do a more general task. And since many library routines are written to handle a wide range of situations, we can improve efficiency by replacing them with versions that handle only the single, specific situations that are relevant to us.

We illustrate this principle with two examples. The first is a set of routines for managing a free storage pool. The other is a function that reads an array of integers.

Managing Our Own Free Storage Pool

Earlier we wrote a linked-list version of insertion sort. Most of its work was done in a routine called `insert_list`. That function took a value and a pointer to an already-sorted list and installed the value in its correct place. It used `malloc` to

```
/*
 * Prototypes for routines that manage free storage pool.
 */
long fsp_init(long n);
NODEPTR fsp_alloc(void);
void fsp_free(NODEPTR ptr);
```

Figure 17.7   fsp.h—Prototypes for routines that manage our own free storage pool.

allocate the node. Since we built the list just once, that was a perfectly reasonable way to implement it.

But suppose that we have a program, such as a linked-list version of our earlier data base manager, that has to repeatedly add and delete items. Then we can do better by managing our own free storage pool. The idea is that we'll build our own free storage pool by calling `malloc` a fixed number of times at the start of our program. And then when we need a node, we'll call our own storage-allocation function, which grabs storage off this free storage pool.

Figure 17.7 provides the prototypes for our allocation functions and Figure 17.8 contains the functions themselves. There are three functions: `fsp_init` allocates the initial storage, `fsp_alloc` provides a single node, and `fsp_free` releases a single node. To use this package, we first call `fsp_init` to allocate space for all the nodes we're likely to need. Then we call `fsp_alloc` anywhere we would have called `malloc` to allocate a node, and we call `fsp_free` anywhere we would have called `free` to throw away a node.

Figure 17.9 shows how these routines work. Our free storage pool is a linked list of nodes, pointed to by a global pointer `fsp`. `fsp_init` builds this linked list by allocating nodes with `malloc` and inserting them in the front. `fsp_alloc` simply removes the first node from this list and adjusts `fsp` appropriately. `fsp_free` puts a node back by inserting it on the front of the list.

Why go to all of the trouble of writing these routines? Why not simply use `malloc` and `free` as before? The answer is that our routines are faster than the system-supplied `malloc` and `free`. Our routines deal only with fixed-size blocks, but `malloc` and `free` are general purpose storage allocation routines that must be able to deal with blocks of arbitrary size. This means that they have additional over-head, including searching for a block of the appropriate size and combining adjacent free blocks.

But our handler does have one disadvantage. It allocates all the blocks at one time, at the beginning of the program, much like we would allocate a fixed-size array. In fact, our version is really a compromise between fixed size arrays and the arbitrary allocation and size of dynamic structures. For insertion sorting, linked lists give us the advantage that we can sort with no data shifting, so linked-list insertion sorting is likely to be faster than array-based insertion sort.

We've included these functions as replacements for `malloc` and `free` for linked-

```
/*
 * Routines to manage our own free storage pool.
 */
#include  <stdio.h>
#include  "lists.h"      /* definition of a node */
#include  "ourfsp.h"

static NODEPTR fsp;       /* ptr to start of free storage pool */

long fsp_init(long n)     /* create our free storage pool */
{
 .NODEPTR ptr;            /* ptr to space returned by malloc */
  long    i=0L;           /* loop index */

  for (fsp = NULL;
         i < n &&
         (ptr = (NODEPTR) malloc(sizeof(struct node))) != NULL;
       i++)
  {
    ptr->next = fsp;
    fsp = ptr;
  }
  return i;      /* number of nodes allocated */
}

NODEPTR fsp_alloc(void)       /* allocate a node */
{
  NODEPTR ptr = fsp;

  if (fsp != NULL)
    fsp = fsp->next;
  return ptr;
}

void fsp_free(NODEPTR ptr)  /* free a node */
{
  if (ptr != NULL)
  {
    ptr->next = fsp;
    fsp = ptr;
  }
}
```

Figure 17.8   ourfsp.c—Routines to manage our own free storage pool.

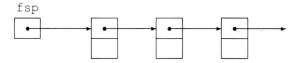

(*a*) Nodes in free storage pool.

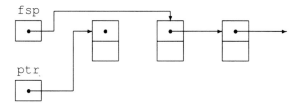

(*b*) Allocating a node from the front of the list.

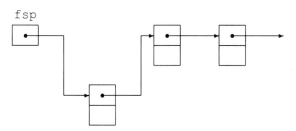

(*c*) Returning a node to the front of the list.

Figure 17.9   How we manage our own free storage pool.

list versions of several of the programs in this book, including our data base program. On the average, we achieved a savings of 10-15 percent.

Writing Our Own Input Handler

scanf is powerful, flexible, and convenient, a function that can read an arbitrary number of values of arbitrary types. But all this power and flexibility produces a problem—scanf must process a control string to determine what its input is, an extra step that requires some additional time-consuming overhead. And when we use scanf to read an array of values, it must do this additional work once for each array element. The result is that we should be able to improve our program's performance by writing our own function to read an array of ints. And that's exactly what we did. Figure 17.10 contains a new version of data that reads the values into the array without using scanf.

```
/*
 * A function to read an array of positive integers,
 * avoiding scanf, and assuming one integer per line.
 */
#include <stdio.h>
#include <ctype.h>

int get_data(int table[], int max)
{
  int *ptr = table;          /* ptr to next array element */
  int *endptr = ptr + max;   /* ptr to last array element */
  int c;                     /* next character */

  for (*ptr = 0; ptr < endptr; ptr++)
  {
    while (!isdigit(c = getchar()) && c != '\n' && c != EOF)
      ;                          /* find a digit */
    if (isdigit(c))
      do                       /* translate number */
        *ptr = *ptr * 10 + (c - '0');
      while (isdigit(c = getchar()));
    else
      *ptr = -1;                   /* -1 indicates bad number */
    while (c != '\n' && c != EOF)  /* skip rest of line */
      c = getchar();
    if (c == EOF)                  /* reached EOF */
      break;
  }
  return ptr - table;          /* # of values read */
}
```

Figure 17.10   getdata.c—A fast function to read an array of `int`s.

We used the program in Figure 17.11 to compare the efficiency of this version with a modified version of our earlier `get_data` (which we changed to use pointers to traverse the array). We ran both on a 5000-value file, with one `int` on each line. The version which didn't use `scanf` took approximately one-third the time, a substantial savings.

EXERCISES

17-12 Rewrite `far_alloc` and `far_free` as macros.

17-13 Toward the end of Chapter 6 we wrote a little program that reversed all the numbers on each of its input lines. Modify that program to use our storage pool manager.

17-14 Modify the data base program to use a linked list to store its items, and to use our storage pool routines to manage its storage. Is there a noticeable performance

```
/*
 * Use get_data to fill in an array with values.
 */
#include <stdio.h>

#define MAX 100

main()
{
  int tab[MAX], values, i;
  int get_data(int table[], int max);

  values = get_data(tab, MAX);
  printf("%d lines read\n", values);
  for (i = 0; i < values; i++)
    if (tab[i] == -1)
      printf("Bad value for line %d.\n", i);
  return 0;
}
```

Figure 17.11   tstdata.c—A program using `get_data` to fill an array.

improvement when dealing with many additions and deletions?

17-15 Our free storage pool manager is slow to start up. After all, it has to allocate a bunch of nodes right at the start. It can be improved by initializing parceling out storage from a preallocated array of nodes. That saves the initial call to `malloc`.

17-16 `printf` is a complex, general purpose output formatting routine. Write an output converter that prints a single floating point number. That is, it takes a `float` as input and writes its value a character at a time to the output. Compare its running time with that of `printf` in writing 5000 `floats`.

17-17 Write a function that writes an array of `floats` without calling `printf`. Is this function faster than the one you wrote in the previous exercise?

17-18 In this book we've usually focused on readability rather than efficiency. That means that most of the programs in the book can be made to run somewhat faster. Pick some program we've written and make it run faster. Some especially good candidates are Chapter 2's insertion sort, Chapter 10's Game of Life, Chapter 11's string sorting program, Chapter 12's data base program, and Chapter 13's cross-referencing program.

18   TURBO C'S
GRAPHICS
LIBRARY

Turbo C 1.5 provides a rich collection of routines for graphics programming and for manipulating characters in different sizes and styles. These routines work on a broad selection of graphics boards and displays, everything from 40x25 monochrome character displays to 640x480 full-color displays. This lengthy chapter examines Turbo C's graphics library and its capabilities, discusses methods of isolating your routines from the individual differences between processors and displays, and concludes with an implementation of a function plotter that ties everything together. Despite its length, however, it covers only the basics—a detailed examination of your reference manual will turn up many additional functions.

18.1   INTRODUCTION

Graphics is all about drawing pictures—lines, arcs, circles, and polygons. To draw these pictures, we treat the display as a large two-dimensional array of *pixels*, and turn different pixels on and off. The Turbo C graphics library is a set of high-level function calls that draw objects by accessing the appropriate pixels.

Actually, it's not that simple—we don't access the display directly. Instead, we go through a piece of hardware, called a *graphics board*, that actually controls turning pixels on and off. There are many different graphics boards, which differ in the number of pixels and the number of colors they can support. Table 18.1 lists the ones supported by Turbo C. You can only use the Turbo C graphics library if you have a board that's listed here, or a board that can emulate one of the listed boards.

The *resolution* of a device is the number of pixels in a row × the number of rows, as illustrated in Figure 18.1. On typical PC displays, this ranges from 320×200 to 640×480, the higher the better. To support multiple colors, each pixel must be able to be in one of many different states, each representing a different color. Some displays have only two colors (white and black); others have up to sixteen.

Because there are so many different graphics boards, our programs don't access them directly—they go through a *graphics driver* instead. A graphics driver is an implementation of all of the functions in the Turbo C graphics library for one particular

GRAPHICS BOARD	GRAPHICS MODE	RESOLUTION: COLUMNS × ROWS	COLOR PALETTE
CGA	CGAC0	320×200	Color 0
	CGAC1	320×200	Color 1
	CGAC2	320×200	Color 2
	CGAC3	320×200	Color 3
	CGAHI	640×200	2 color
MCGA	MCGAC0	320×200	Color 0
	MCGAC1	320×200	Color 1
	MCGAC2	320×200	Color 2
	MCGAC3	320×200	Color 3
	MCGAMED	640×200	2 color
	MCGAHI	640×480	2 color
EGA	EGALO	640×200	16 color
	EGAHI	640×350	16 color
EGA64	EGA64LO	640×200	16 color
	EGA64HI	640×350	4 color
EGAMONO	EGAMONOHI	640×350	2 color
HERC	HERCMONOHI	720×348	2 color
ATT400	ATT400C0	320×200	Color 0
	ATT400C1	320×200	Color 1
	ATT400C2	320×200	Color 2
	ATT400C3	320×200	Color 3
	ATT400MED	640×200	2 color
	ATT400HI	640×400	2 color
VGA	VGALO	640×200	16 color
	VGAMED	640×350	16 color
	VGAHI	640×480	16 color
PC3270	PC3270HI	720×350	2 color

Table 18.1 Graphics boards and modes supported in Turbo C.

device. That means there's a graphics driver for a CGA board, another for the EGA board, and so on. In this way, using the Turbo C graphics calls lets us write programs that are independent of any particular display device. And anyone who has tried to write even a simple routine to change the color of a particular pixel can appreciate the advantage of having these routines already written and compiled for us.

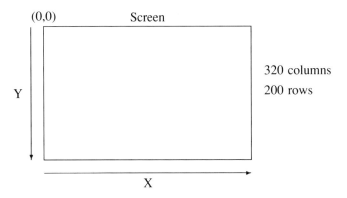

Figure 18.1 Screen resolution is measured in terms of lines, and pixels (picture elements) per line.

Using the Graphics Library

Normally our displays are in *text mode*. In text mode, the screen is treated as a large array of characters rather than an array of pixels. To use the graphics routines, we have to place the screen in *graphics mode*. We do that using `initgraph`.

```
void initgraph(int *driver, int *mode, char *path)
```

`driver` is an integer specifying which graphics driver we're using. `mode` is the graphics mode it's opened in. And `path` is the place (directory) where the driver program is actually found. In Turbo C, the graphics drivers are in files whose names end in .bgi (for "Borland Graphics Interface"). We usually use the null path, which requires that the .bgi files be in the current directory.

We don't have to specify a particular driver. We can use the special driver DE-TECT, which tells Turbo C to automatically detect the installed graphics system, and then set the graphics mode to the highest available resolution for the particular device (a highly desirable feature, since detecting which graphics hardware is actually being used and setting the mode require examining several different specific memory locations and registers). There's also a special call `detectgraph`

```
void detectgraph(int *grboard, int *grmode)
```

which fills in its arguments with the type of board and mode being used, but doesn't automatically place us in graphics mode.

When we're all done with whatever graphics calls we need, we use `closegraph` to leave graphics mode and to return to text mode.

```
void closegraph(void)
```

Figure 18.2 provides a simple example, with a program that draws a little box on the screen, waits for a key press, then quits. The program includes graphics.h

```
/*
 * Draw a filled box on the screen.
 */
#include <stdio.h>
#include <conio.h>
#include <stdlib.h>
#include <graphics.h>

/* box goes from 100,20 (upper left) to 200,50 */

const int left = 100, top = 20, bottom = 50, right = 200;

main()
{
  int grboard = DETECT;       /* auto detect graphics board */
  int grmode;                 /* filled in with mode */
  int grresult;               /* result of calls */

  initgraph(&grboard, &grmode, "");
  if ((grresult = graphresult()) < 0)
  {
    fprintf(stderr, "%s\n", grapherrormsg(grresult));
    return 1;   /* exit early, couldn't setup graphics */
  }
  bar3d(left, top, right, bottom, 10, 1);    /* box */
  getch();                    /* wait for key press */
  closegraph();
  return 0;
}
```

Figure 18.2 box.c—A simple program that draws a box on the screen.

to provide the prototypes and constants for the various functions and constants in the graphics library.

It turns out that Turbo C treats the graphics library differently than the other system-supplied libraries: It doesn't automatically link it with your program. With tcc this isn't that big a problem, since we can just add graphics.lib to the command line when our programs need it. But with tc we have to create a project file containing graphics.lib for every program that uses graphics—unless we take advantage of the OPTIONS/LINKER/GRAPHICS menu entry. Setting this entry to ON causes the graphics library to be automatically linked in with our program.

Error Handling

Graphics calls can fail. Perhaps the most common causes of failure are that we make a call to initgraph and there isn't any graphics board attached, or that we request a specific graphics board or mode, and that particular one isn't available, or that we don't have sufficient memory to load the graphics driver or font files. Two functions helps us detect and display error information in the graphics library: `graphresult` and `grapherrormsg`.

```
int graphresult(void);
char *grapherrormsg(int errorcode);
```

When a routine fails, it sets a global error code rather than return an error indication. We can check for these errors by calling `graphresult`, which returns zero if the last call succeeded, or a value less than zero indicating the type of error if the call failed. There are many different error codes; `graphresult` lets us handle them cleanly without worrying about exactly what the error was.

In our example, we call `graphresult` to determine whether `initgraph` succeeded. If it failed, we call `grapherrormsg`, which returns a string containing an error message corresponding to its integer argument, and print this returned string.

Obtaining Screen Information

All of the various library functions deal with integer arguments representing screen coordinates (measured in pixels). The origin (0,0) is the upper left-hand corner of the display; the coordinate of the lower right-hand corner is equivalent to the resolution of the device. We can determine this value by calling two special library functions: `getmaxx` and `getmaxy`.

```
int getmaxx(void);
int getmaxy(void);
```

These functions return the largest possible X and Y values for the specific graphics device and mode we're using. We use them most frequently to ensure that a program places objects in the same relative place, regardless of the resolution of its output device. The center of the screen, for example, is always at (`getmaxx()/2`, `getmaxy()/2`).

Entering graphics mode, checking for errors, and obtaining information about the device we're using is done so frequently that we've written a special function, `gropen`, to handle it. The prototype for `gropen` and a macro, `grclose`, that exits graphics mode are shown in Figure 18.3. The function itself is shown in Figure 18.4.

`gropen` is passed three arguments, pointers to objects to be filled in with the largest X coordinate, the largest Y coordinate, and something called the *aspect ratio*. On most displays pixels are taller than they are wide (we usually have many more X pixels than Y pixels). That means if we drew a box ten pixels high and ten pixels wide, it probably won't come out square. Instead, it's going to be much taller than it is wide. If we really want a square, we can multiply the number of X pixels we're writing by the aspect ratio to compute the corresponding number of Y pixels we need. `gropen` uses the library function `getaspectratio` to compute this value.

```
void getaspectratio(int *xasp, int *yasp);
```

```
/*
 * Prototypes for gropen and definition of grclose.
 */
#include <graphics.h>

int gropen(double *aratio, int *maxx, int *maxy);

#define grclose()  closegraph()    /* close macro */
```

Figure 18.3 gropen.h—Prototypes for a convenient way to get in and out of graphics mode.

```
/*
 * Initialize and graphics routines, computing aspect ratio,
 * maxx, and maxy.
 */
#include <stdio.h>
#include "gropen.h"

int gropen(double *ratio, int *maxx, int *maxy)
{
  int grboard = DETECT;    /* auto detect graphics board */
  int grmode;              /* filled in with mode */
  int grresult;            /* result of calls */
  int xr, yr;              /* used for aspect ratio */

  initgraph(&grboard, &grmode, "");
  if ((grresult = graphresult()) < 0)
  {
    fprintf(stderr, "%s\n", grapherrormsg(grresult));
    return -1;            /* early exit */
  }
  if (ratio != NULL)
  {                        /* ratio computed only if space for it */
    getaspectratio(&xr, &yr);
    *ratio = (double) xr / yr;
  }
  *maxx = getmaxx();     /* maximum x and y */
  *maxy = getmaxy();
  return grmode;
}
```

Figure 18.4 gropen.c—Our function to deal with initializing graphics mode.

yasp is always normalized to 10000, xasp is some value that's less than or equal to 10000. Dividing xasp by yasp gives us the desired value.

EXERCISES

18–1 Write a little program that prints a message describing your graphics board and mode. Make sure that you handle any errors appropriately.

18–2 Extend the program in the previous exercise to print the resolution of the screen and its aspect ratio (determining them dynamically).

18–3 Modify box.c to print a square box in the center of the screen.

18.2   DRAWING OBJECTS

Turbo C provides a large collection of function for drawing objects of various types. These range from primitive functions to produce lines and arcs, to more complicated functions to produce circles, rectangles, and even polygons.

Lines and Polygons

The most primitive drawing routines produce simple lines, and line is the simplest of these routines.

```
void line(int x1, int y1, int x2,int y2)
```

All it does is draw a line from (x1, y1) to (x2, y2), with the coordinate origin at the upper left of the screen.

Often we need to connect a series of line segments together. We could do this by repeatedly calling line, making sure the starting point of the any call the same as the ending point of the previous call. But there's an easier way. We first move to the place where the initial segment starts, and then we use lineto.

```
void lineto(int x1, int y1)
```

lineto draws a line segment from the *current position* on the display (CP) to the point (x1, y1), and then resets the CP to (x1, y1). The current position starts at the origin. Another line drawing routine, linerel, is similar, drawing a line from the CP to (cpx+dx, cpy+dy), with CP reset.

```
void linerel(int dx, int dy)
```

How do we set the initial current position? The obvious but wrong way would be to use line to do write the first line segment. Unfortunately, line doesn't modify the current position. Luckily, the moveto call does.

```
void moveto(int x1,int y1)
```

```
/*
 * Draw a square centered around (x1,y1) with x-radius xrad.
 */
#include <stdio.h>
#include <graphics.h>

int draw_square(int x1, int y1, int xrad, double aratio)
{
  int yrad = (int) (xrad * aratio);

  line(x1 - xrad, y1 - yrad, x1 + xrad, y1 -yrad);   /* top     */
  line(x1 - xrad, y1 + yrad, x1 + xrad, y1 + yrad);  /* bottom */
  line(x1 - xrad, y1 - yrad, x1 - xrad, y1 + yrad);  /* left    */
  line(x1 + xrad, y1 - yrad, x1 + xrad, y1 + yrad);  /* right   */
  return yrad;
}
```

Figure 18.5 square1.c—A first version of a function to draw a square.

This sets the current drawing position (CP) to (x1,y1). There's also a similar function, moverel,

```
        void moverel(int dx, int dy)
```

that resets CP to (cpx+dx, cpy+dy).

Figure 18.5 contains a function, draw_square, that uses repeated calls to line to draw a square. Figure 18.6 contains a version of draw_square that uses moveto, lineto, and linerel. And Figure 18.7 contains a main program that uses it to draw a large square in the center of the screen.

While we could use line and its siblings to draw more complicated objects like squares, rectangles, and arbitrary polygons, Turbo C provides several additional drawing primitives that take care of these tasks for us. The first is rectangle, a function which draws a rectangle using straight-line segments—it's an outline, not a solid object (we'll see how to draw those later).

```
        void rectangle(int left, int top, int right, int bottom);
```

The rectangle starts with its upper left at (left, top) and its lower right at (right, bottom). Given rectangle, it's straightforward to write draw_square as a macro.

```
        #define draw_square(xc, yc, xrad, aratio) \
                rectangle(xc - xrad, yc - (int) (xrad * aratio), \
                        xc + xrad, yc + (int) (xrad * aratio))
```

To draw a more complex figure, a *polygon*, we use drawpoly:

```
/*
 * Draw a square centered around (x1,y1) with x-radius xrad.
 */
#include <stdio.h>
#include <graphics.h>

int draw_square(int x1, int y1, int xrad, double aratio)
{
  int yrad = (int) (xrad * aratio);

  moveto(x1 - xrad, y1 - yrad);
  linerel(0, yrad + yrad);             /* left */
  linerel(xrad + xrad, 0);             /* bottom */
  linerel(0, -yrad - yrad);            /* right */
  lineto(x1 - xrad, y1 - yrad);        /* top */
  return yrad;
}
```

Figure 18.6   square2.c—A second version of our square drawing function.

```
/*
 * Draw a large square in the center of the screen.
 */
#include <conio.h>
#include "gropen.h"

main()
{
  int draw_square(int x1, int y1, int xside, double aratio);
  int xmax, ymax;
  double aratio;

  if (gropen(&aratio, &xmax, &ymax) == -1)
    return 1;        /* exit early; no graphics mode */
  draw_square(xmax / 2, ymax / 2, 100, aratio);
  getch();           /* wait for character */
  grclose();         /* get out of graphics mode */
  return 0;
}
```

Figure 18.7   squares.c—A program using our square drawing function to draw a large square in the center of the screen.

```
/*
 * Draw a square centered around (x1,y1) with radius xrad.
 */
#include <stdio.h>
#include <graphics.h>

int draw_square(int x1, int y1, int xrad, double aratio)
{
  int yrad = (int) (xrad * aratio);
  int pts[10];

  pts[0] = x1 - xrad; pts[1] = y1 - yrad; /* initial */
  pts[2] = x1 + xrad; pts[3] = y1 - yrad; /* top right */
  pts[4] = x1 + xrad; pts[5] = y1 + yrad; /* bottom right */
  pts[6] = x1 - xrad; pts[7] = y1 + yrad; /* bottom left */
  pts[8] = x1 - xrad; pts[9] = y1 - yrad; /* top left */
  drawpoly(5, pts);
  return yrad;
}
```

Figure 18.8 square3.c—A final version of our square drawing function.

```
void drawpoly(int n, int *points)
```

A polygon is drawn using n points. points is a pointer to the first element in an array of 2 × n integers. Each pair of integers represents the X and Y values of a point on the polygon. Though the routine implies it draws a polygon (and might suggest that the last point is automatically connected to the first), we're actually responsible for closing the figure—the last point in the array should be the same as the first for the polygon to be properly closed. That means that we can write yet another version of draw_square, this time using drawpoly, which we've done in Figure 18.8.

Arcs and Circles

Turbo C provides another set of functions for drawing smoothly curved features. arc is the simplest, drawing a circular arc.

```
void arc(int x, int y, int start_angle, int end_angle,
         int radius);
```

The other two are built on top of arc. circle draws a circle, and ellipse draws an elliptical arc (different major and minor axes—it is the most general of these three routines).

```
void circle(int x, int y, int radius);
void ellipse(int x, int y,
             int start_angle, int end_angle,
             int xradius, int yradius);
```

All three of these functions center the object at (x, y). For `arc` and `ellipse`, `start_angle` is the starting, and `end_angle` is the ending angle for the arcs, measured counterclockwise from three o'clock. In `arc` and `circle`, `radius` is the circle's radius (or arc from the circle). In `ellipse`, `xradius`, and `yradius` are half the axes for the ellipse. When we draw an elliptical arc, its axes are aligned with the X and Y coordinate axes.

Here are some examples. We can use any of the following to draw a circle with a radius of 30 pixels, and a center at (100,50).

```
arc(100, 50, 0, 360, 30);
circle(100, 50, 30);
ellipse(100, 50, 0, 360, 30, 30);
```

We can draw a right-facing semicircle at the same location with:

```
arc(50,50,270,90,40);
```

And we can draw half an ellipse, 50 pixels high and 20 pixels wide and facing upwards, with:

```
ellipse(50,50,0,180,25,10);
```

Figure 18.9 is a short program that uses these functions to draw a cute little robot. Run it!

Filled Objects

In addition to the line drawing and circle/arc routines, Turbo C provides routines for creating solid objects—objects that are outlined and then filled with a solid color or pattern.

Two routines draw filled rectangles: `bar` and `bar3d` (their names derive from their common use to draw bar charts). `bar` draws and optionally fills a two-dimensional rectangle.

```
void bar(int leftx, int topy, int rightx, int lowy);
```

`bar3d` is similar, except that it gives the bar a depth, as if we are looking at a perspective view of a solid object, as seen in Figure 18.10.

```
void bar3d(int leftx, int topy, int rightx, int bottomy,
           int depth, int hastop);
```

`bar3d` has two additional arguments that `bar` doesn't—a depth (in pixels) for the three-dimensional part of the bar, and a flag indicating if a three-dimensional top is to be placed on the bar. It turns out a depth of about one quarter the width of the bar works well for bar charts. If we don't provide a top, the bar appears to be an empty box; with it, the top is closed off. To get an outlined box, use a depth of 0 and request a top:

```
bar3d(lt, top, rt, bottom, 0, 1);
```

```
/*
 * robot.c -- Draws a very simple (hopefully, cute) robot.
 */
#include <stdio.h>
#include <conio.h>
#include "gropen.h"

main()
{
  int xc, yc;               /* center of body */
  int xmax, ymax;           /* largest x, largest y */
  int yrad;                 /* height of body */
  const int xrad = 50;      /* 100-pixel wide body */
  double aratio;
  int headyc;               /* y center of head */
  int basey, topy, rightx, leftx;
  int draw_square(int x1, int y1, int xrad, double aratio);

  if (gropen(&aratio, &xmax, &ymax) == -1)
    return 1;
  xc = xmax/2;                        /* center robot body */
  yc = ymax/2;
  yrad = draw_square(xc, yc, 50, aratio);

  headyc = yc - yrad - yrad;          /* center of head */
  basey = yc + yrad;                  /* base of body */
  topy = yc - yrad;                   /* top of body */
  rightx = xc - xrad;                 /* left of body */
  leftx = xc + xrad;                  /* right of body */

  circle(xc, headyc, xrad);           /* head */
  line(xc - xrad / 2, basey,          /* left leg */
  rightx - xrad, basey + yrad);
  line(xc + xrad / 2, basey,          /* right leg */
  leftx + xrad, basey + yrad);
  arc(rightx, topy, 180, 270, xrad);  /* left arm */
  arc(leftx, topy, 270, 360, xrad);   /* right arm */
  circle(xc - xrad / 4, headyc - .3 * yrad,
         xrad / 8);                   /* left eye */
  circle(xc + xrad / 4, headyc - .3 * yrad,
         xrad / 8);                   /* right eye */
  ellipse(xc, headyc + .3 * yrad,
         180, 360, xrad / 2, .3 * yrad);   /* mouth */
  getch();
  closegraph();
  return 0;
}
```

Figure 18.9 robot.c—A simple program that draws a little robot.

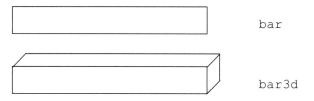

Figure 18.10   A two-dimensional bar and a three-dimensional bar.

Figure 18.11 uses `bar` to produce a simple horizontal bar chart, whose bars correspond to the value of an array's entries. In this program, we keep it simple and initialize this array at compile time.

We can draw arbitrarily complex solid figures using `fillpoly`, a routine similar to `drawpoly`, except that it also fills the polygon. *Warning: If the polygon isn't closed, your whole screen may be filled.*

```
void fillpoly(int n, int *points)
```

The final filled-object drawing routine we'll examine is `pieslice`. It draws an arc and fills the swept out area—voila, a pie slice.

```
void pieslice(int x, int y, int start_angle, int end_angle,
              int radius);
```

Figure 18.12 is a simple example that uses it to draw a pie with a single piece filled. We use `pieslice` to draw the single pie slice. and then we use `arc` to draw the rest of the pie.

EXERCISES

18–4   Write a program to produce a histogram of its input. Use `bar3d`. Have a command-line option select whether the orientation of the histogram is horizontal or vertical.

18–5   Write a program to produce a bar chart that illustrates the frequency of different characters in its input. Start with one of the character-counting programs in Chapter 5.

18.3   COLORS

Turbo C supports all current color modes for most of the available PC color boards and displays. Unfortunately, each class of color PC boards has a somewhat different

```
/*
 * Print horizontal bar chart of table (assume positive values).
 */
#include <conio.h>
#include "gropen.h"

const int sep_y = 2;   /* separation between bars */

main()
{
  int table[] = { 8, 23, 18, 35, 47, 67, 19, 25, 30, 56};
  int n = sizeof(table)/sizeof(int);   /* # of values */
  double aratio;
  int xmax, ymax;
  int i, scalex, scaley, max = -1;
  int start_x, start_y;        /* border on left, top */
  int end_x, end_y;            /* border on right, bottom */

  if (gropen(&aratio, &xmax, &ymax) == -1)
    return 1;
  start_x = xmax / 10;         /* 10% border surrounding chart */
  end_x = xmax - start_x;
  start_y = ymax / 10;
  end_y = ymax - start_y;

  for (i = 0; i < n; i++)      /* find largest value */
    if (max < table[i])
      max = table[i];
  scalex = (end_x - start_x) / max;
  scaley = (end_y - start_y) / n;
  for (i = 0; i < n; i++)      /* draw bars */
    bar(start_x,                               /* left */
        start_y + i * scaley,                  /* top */
        start_x + scalex * table[i],           /* right */
        start_y + (i + 1) * scaley - sep_y); /* bottom */
  getch();                           /* wait for key */
  grclose();
  return 0;
}
```

Figure 18.11 barchart.c—A program to print a bar chart.

```
/*
 * pieslice.c -- Draw pie with extended pieslice.
 */
#include <stdio.h>
#include <stddef.h>
#include <conio.h>
#include "gropen.h"

#define SLICEPCNT  0.25     /* slice of 25% of pie */

main()
{
  double aratio;
  int angle = 360 * SLICEPCNT;   /* angle for slice */
  int xc, yc;                     /* center */
  int xmax, ymax;
  int pierad;                     /* radius of pie */
  int xextend;                    /* make slice stick out */
  int yextend;

  if (gropen(&aratio, &xmax, &ymax) == -1)
    return 1;                     /* early exit; no graphics */
  xc = xmax/2;  yc = ymax/2;
  pierad = xc / 2;                /* radius 1/4 width of screen */
  xextend = pierad / 8;           /* extend 1/8 of that */
  yextend = aratio * xextend;
  arc(xc, yc, angle, 360, pierad);      /* pie except for slice */
  pieslice(xc + xextend, yc - yextend, /* draw filled slice */
           0, angle, pierad);
  line(xc, yc, xc + pierad, yc);        /* lines around slice */
  line(xc, yc, xc, yc - pierad * aratio);
  getch();                              /* wait for key */
  grclose();
  return 0;
}
```

Figure 18.12 pieslice.c—A program to print a pie chart.

way of dealing with colors—which makes it difficult for us to write programs that behave reasonably across display types.

Color boards for the PC fall into two major classes. The first is the original IBM color board, the CGA (for Color Graphics Adaptor), the other is the EGA (Extended Graphics Adaptor) and VGA (Video Graphics Array). These boards differ in how many colors they have and in how we select which colors we're using. The CGA boards support the colors listed in Table 18.2.

The EGA boards support 64 colors, including the 16 colors that CGA supports. The differences are that these colors have EGA_ prepended to their names and that

COLOR	VALUE	COLOR	VALUE
BLACK	0	DARKGRAY	8
BLUE	1	LIGHTBLUE	9
GREEN	2	LIGHTGREEN	10
CYAN	3	LIGHTCYAN	11
RED	4	LIGHTRED	12
MAGENTA	5	LIGHTMAGENTA	13
BROWN	6	YELLOW	14
LIGHTGRAY	7	WHITE	15

Table 18.2 CGA colors and the values.

many of them have different values. Thus WHITE is named EGA_WHITE, BLACK is EGA_BLACK, and so on. Their values and the other EGA colors can be found by examining graphics.h.

Regardless of which board we use, however, we can only have a few colors on the screen at any one time. This group of colors is called a *palette* or *color lookup table*. On a color board, a pixel is represented by an index into this table. A value of 0 means the pixel will display as the zeroth color in the palette, a value of 1 means it will display as the first color, and so on. This means that the number of bits in a pixel determines how many colors we can have on the screen at any one time.

Although both boards use the same basic scheme for displaying colors, the details vary.

CGA **Color Control—Low Resolution**

The CGA board allows two different resolution/color combinations: 320×200 low resolution, with four colors on the screen at one time, and 640×200 high resolution, with two colors.

On the CGA low-resolution mode we can display four colors at one time, selected from four predefined palettes, shown in Table 18.3. Actually, the palettes are not quite predefined; we can set the first entry, the one that's used for the background color, to whatever we want. We use setgraphmode to select the palette (by setting the mode of the driver). For a CGA driver we use

```
setgraphmode(CGACn)
```

where n is 0 through 3. So setgraphmode(CGAC0) selects palette 0 (the one with lightgreen, lightred, and yellow), and so on. *Warning:* setgraphmode *clears the screen to the background color.* We can also use initgraph to initialize the graphics system with a particular driver and mode, but we'd better be sure that the named driver is actually available.

PALETTE	COLOR ASSIGNED TO INDEX		
NUMBER	1	2	3
0	LIGHTGREEN	LIGHTRED	YELLOW
1	LIGHTCYAN	LIGHTMAGENTA	WHITE
2	GREEN	RED	BROWN
3	CYAN	MAGENTA	LIGHTGRAY

Table 18.3 Turbo C graphics palettes for CGA.

The program in Figure 18.13 detects the graphics board, and, if it is a CGA board, sets it to low-resolution mode, using palette 3. (For non-CGA boards it simply exits). The MCGA and ATT400 boards are similar, so we'll allow these as well. After the program selects the palette, it draws a magenta circle in the center of a screen with a green background color.

Since there are several colors in the palette, we need to choose which one we're going to use to actually draw objects, called the *foreground* color. We do so with setcolor. And we can use setbkcolor to set the background color to any one of the 16 colors CGA supports.

```
void setcolor(int color);
void setbkcolor(int color);
```

To determine the current foreground and background colors, use getcolor and getbkcolor.

```
int getbkcolor(void);
int getcolor(void);
```

CGA Color Control—High Resolution

For the CGA high resolution mode, only two colors are available: the background color, which is *always* black, and a programmer-setable foreground color (unlike low resolution where it's the background color that can be changed). Strangely enough, however, we use setbkcolor to change the foreground color. That's because the palette in this mode has two entries: a background color, and black. Since the background color is user-setable, it's the one that's used to draw objects. This means that setcolor has no effect in CGA high resolution mode.

Figure 18.14 does the same thing the previous program did—drawing a magenta circle on a green background—but it uses high-resolution CGA graphics.

EGA/VGA Color Control

EGA/VGA boards let us manipulate palettes in a slightly different way. They start off with a default palette using the 16 CGA colors we saw earlier (which are usually

```
/*
 * Selecting CGA colors (low resolution mode only).
 */
#include <stdio.h>
#include <conio.h>
#include <stdlib.h>
#include <graphics.h>

main()
{
  int  grboard, grmode;

  detectgraph(&grboard, &grmode);
  switch (grboard)
  {                       /* select palette three */
    case CGA:      grmode = CGAC3;      break;
    case MCGA:     grmode = MCGAC3;     break;
    case ATT400:   grmode = ATT400C3;   break;
    default:
         fprintf(stderr, "Needs CGA compatible board\n");
         return 1;
  }
  initgraph(&grboard, &grmode, "");  /* assume it worked */
  setcolor(MAGENTA);                      /* set drawing color */
  setbkcolor(GREEN);                      /* background color */
  circle(getmaxx() / 2, getmaxy() / 2, getmaxy() / 4);
  getch();                                /* wait for key press */
  closegraph();
  return 0;
}
```

Figure 18.13 cgalow.c—A program that draw a magenta circle on a green background using low-resolution CGA graphics.

more than sufficient). We can use setcolor as before, to select any one of these colors as the current drawing color. We can use

```
    setcolor(EGA_RED);
```

to set the current drawing color to red.

But setbkcolor works somewhat differently. We no longer specify a particular background color. Instead, we specify a particular position in the palette, and setbkcolor *copies* a color from a particular position in the palette to position zero, the background color. So

```
    setbkcolor(2);
```

changes the background color to the color in the second position within the palette, whatever color that is. We set the color in a particular position in a palette with setpalette.

```
/*
 * Selecting CGA colors (high resolution).
 */
#include <stdio.h>
#include <conio.h>
#include <stdlib.h>
#include <graphics.h>

main()
{
  int grboard, grmode;

  detectgraph(&grboard, &grmode);    /* default is highest res */
  switch(grboard)
  {
    case CGA:
    case MCGA:
    case ATT400:
        initgraph(&grboard, &grmode, "");
        break;                         /* in high-res mode */
    default:
        fprintf(stderr, "Needs CGA board or CGA compatible\n");
        return 1;

  }
  setbkcolor(MAGENTA);                 /* drawing color */
  circle(getmaxx() / 2, getmaxy() / 2, getmaxy() / 4);
  getch();
  closegraph();
  return 0;
}
```

Figure 18.14 cgahigh.c—A program that writes a magenta circle on a black background using CGA high resolution.

```
    void setpalette(int pos, int color);
```

To ensure that the second color in the palette is green, we simply do

```
    setpalette(2, EGA_GREEN);
```

Figure 18.15 uses these functions in yet another version of our program that draws the magenta circle on a green background. This one works with an EGA graphics board.

EXERCISES

18-6 Modify the box-drawing program to change the color of the box each time the user hits a key (for as many different colors are possible on your graphics board).

```
/*
 * Selecting EGA colors.
 */
#include <stdio.h>
#include <conio.h>
#include <stdlib.h>
#include <graphics.h>

main()
{
  int  grboard, grmode;

  detectgraph(&grboard, &grmode);
  switch (grboard)
  {
    case EGA:      grmode = EGAHI;      break;
    case EGA64:    grmode = EGA64LO;    break;
    case VGA:      grmode = VGAHI;      break;
    default:       fprintf(stderr, "Needs EGA compatible board\n");
                   return 1;
  }
  initgraph(&grboard, &grmode, "");  /* assume it worked */
  setcolor(EGA_MAGENTA);                /* drawing color */
  setpalette(2, EGA_GREEN);      /* place green in palette */
  setbkcolor(2);                        /* background color */
  circle(getmaxx() / 2, getmaxy() / 2, getmaxy() / 4);
  getch();                             /* wait for key press */
  closegraph();
  return 0;
}
```

Figure 18.15   ega.c—A program using EGA graphics mode to draw a magenta circle on a green background.

18-7 Modify the robot-drawing program to use different colors for the robot's head, body, and appendages. (This assumes CGA low-resolution or EGA.)

18-8 Write a program to produce a checkerboard pattern on the screen. Have it first produce it in black and white, then in whatever other color combinations are possible on your machine.

18.4   STYLES

So far we've used Turbo C's default styles for drawing lines and filling boxes. But we can have dashed, dotted, and straight lines, and there are many different ways to

STYLE	DESCRIPTION
SOLID_LINE	Solid line
DOTTED_LINE	Dotted line
CENTER_LINE	Centered line
DASHED_LINE	Dashed line
USERBIT_LINE	Use a user-defined style

Table 18.4   Different line styles.

fill boxes, bars, and pie slices. In fact, we can even create our own styles.

Setting Line Drawing Styles

We use `setlinestyle` to select one of four standard styles or a style of our own, and to set the thickness of the line.

```
void setlinestyle(int style, unsigned upattern, int thickness);
```

`style` can be any one of the names listed in Table 18.4. `thickness` is either NORM_WIDTH or THICK_WIDTH. Normal lines are drawn one pixel wide; thick lines are three pixels wide. `upattern` is normally zero, unless we've selected USER-BIT_LINE as our `linestyle`. In that case, `pattern` is a 16-bit pattern describing the line: a 1 bit in the pattern turns on a pixel when the line is drawn, a 0 bit turns it off. After the call,

```
setlinestyle(DASHED_LINE, 0, THICK_WIDTH);
```

we'll obtain thick dashed lines. And

```
setlinestyle(USERBIT_LINE, 0xf5f5, NORM_WIDTH);
```

gives us a dash-dot-dot line (1111010111110101). If `setlinestyle`'s arguments are in any way invalid, no change is made to the current line drawing properties.

Once we've selected a line style with `setlinestyle`, it stays selected, which means that all future lines will be drawn with that style. To draw a single object in a particular style, we have to save the original settings before we draw the object and then restore them when we're done. We use `getlinesettings` to access the original settings.

```
void getlinesettings(struct * linesettingstype lineinfo);
```

This function takes a pointer to a `struct linesettingstype` and fills it in with the current line style, user pattern, and thickness.

```
struct linesettingstype
{
  int       linestyle;
  unsigned  upattern;
  int       thickness;
};
```

```
/*
 * Draw several squares, illustrating different line
 * styles and thicknesses.
 */
#include <conio.h>
#include "gropen.h"

int xmax, ymax;
double aratio;

main()
{
  void centered_square(int style, int thickness);

  if (gropen(&aratio, &xmax, &ymax) == -1)
    return 1;         /* exit early; no graphics mode */
  centered_square(DASHED_LINE, NORM_WIDTH);
  getch();
  centered_square(DASHED_LINE, THICK_WIDTH);
  getch();
  centered_square(DOTTED_LINE, THICK_WIDTH);
  getch();
  grclose();          /* get out of graphics mode */
  return 0;
}

void centered_square(int style, int thickness)
{
  struct linesettingstype old;
  void draw_square(int left, int top, int xside, double aratio);

  getlinesettings(&old);
  setlinestyle(style, 0, thickness);
  draw_square(xmax / 2, ymax / 2, 100, aratio);
  setlinestyle(old.linestyle, old.upattern, old.thickness);
}
```

Figure 18.16 newsq.c—A program that draws several different squares to illustrates different line styles.

Figure 18.16 uses these functions in a new program that draws squares using different line styles and thicknesses.

Getting and Setting Fill Patterns

Just as we can change the style of the lines that comprise objects, we can also change the style with which objects are filled. We can use setfillstyle to select the pattern and color used to fill an object.

NAME	FILL WITH
EMPTY_FILL	background color (the default)
SOLID_FILL	named color
LINE_FILL	horizontal lines
LTSLASH_FILL	slashes
SLASH_FILL	thick slashes
BKSLASH_FILL	thick backslashes
LTBKSLASH_FILL	backslashes
HATCH_FILL	light cross-hatching
XHATCH_FILL	heavy cross-hatching
INTERLEAVE_FILL	interleaving lines
WIDE_DOT_FILL	widely spaced dots
CLOSE_DOT_FILL	closely spaced dots
USER_FILL	user-defined pattern

Table 18.5 Turbo C fill patterns.

```
void setfillstyle(int pattern, int color);
```

pattern can be any of the predefined fill patterns in Table 18.5. color can be any of the colors the particular graphics board supports (selecting EMPTY_FILL as the pattern uses the background color).

In fact, it's possible to draw a filled object in one color, with a second color as the border, and a third color as the background. The following:

```
setbkcolor(WHITE);
setcolor(RED);
setfillstyle(SOLID_FILL, BLUE);
bard3d(lt, top, rt, bottom, 0, 1);
```

draws a solid blue bar with a red border on a white background on a low-resolution CGA board.

We can also define our own fill patterns. When we call setfillstyle, we use USER_FILL as the pattern. We then call setpattern, passing it a pointer to a string supplying the fill pattern.

```
void setfillpattern(char *upattern, int color);
```

upattern points to an 8-byte sequence used as an 8×8 fill pattern. Each 1 bit in the pattern will be drawn in the fill color; each 0 bit in the background color. The pattern is simply repeated endlessly until the figure is filled. We can specify a checkboard pattern, something like:

```
setfillpattern("\xF0\x0F\xF0\x0F\xF0\x0F\xF0\x0F", RED);
```

Besides these two routines to set the fill pattern and color, there are two routines that get the current values. The routines are getfillsettings and getfill-pattern.

```
void getfillsettings(struct fillsettingstype * fillinfo);
void getfillpattern(char * upattern);
```

getfillsettings takes a pointer to a struct fillsettingstype, which despite its long name is a rather simple structure.

```
struct fillsettingstype
{
  int  pattern;
  int  color;
};
```

The pattern field is set to one of the twelve predefined pattern types, or to USER_FILL (which assumes there has been a previous call to setfillpattern). color is set to the current fill drawing color.

getfillpattern takes a pointer to an 8-byte area, and copies the user-defined pattern, which should have been set via a previous call to setfillpattern. Obviously before calling getfillpattern, we need to call getfillsettings to determine that USER_FILL was the pattern used. Figure 18.17 contains a new version of our square-drawing program that illustrates some of the more commonly used fill patterns.

EXERCISES

18-9 Write a program to produce a checkerboard pattern on the screen using different fill settings rather than different colors.

18-10 Modify pieslice.c to produce the pie slice in one color, the pie in another, and the background in a third.

18-11 Write a program that reads in a small table of values, and then displays their percentage of the total in a pie slice representation.

18-12 Modify the program in the previous exercise to use different colors to represent the pieslice, depending on its size. It might, for example, use green for a pieslice of under 20% of the pie, yellow for between 20-50%, and red for anything larger.

18.5 ## SCREEN AND VIEWPORT MANIPULATION

Sometimes we want to map out a particular area on the screen, perhaps to write a menu, or to overlay a figure. To do so, we need to use viewports. A viewport is a rectangular area on the screen where graphics output is drawn. The default viewport is the entire screen, but we can create a new viewport in a specified location with

```
/*
 * Draw several squares, illustrating different fill patterns.
 */
#include <stddef.h>
#include <conio.h>
#include "gropen.h"

int xmax, ymax;
double aratio;

main()
{
  void centered_square(int fillstyle);

  if (gropen(&aratio, &xmax, &ymax) == -1)
    return 1;        /* exit early; no graphics mode */
  centered_square(SLASH_FILL);
  getch();
  centered_square(INTERLEAVE_FILL);
  getch();
  centered_square(CLOSE_DOT_FILL);
  getch();
  grclose();         /* get out of graphics mode */
  return 0;
}

void centered_square(int fill_style)
{
  struct fillsettingstype old;

  getfillsettings(&old);
  setfillstyle(fill_style, old.color);
  bar(xmax / 2 - 50, ymax / 2 - 50 * aratio,
      xmax / 2 + 50, ymax /2 + 50 * aratio);
  setfillstyle(old.pattern, old.color);
}
```

Figure 18.17 newsq2.c—Draw squares using different fill patterns.

```
    void setviewport(int left, int top, int right, int bottom,
                      int clip_flag);
```

We can have more than one viewport on the screen at any one time, but only one is *active*. All drawing commands are relative to the currently active viewport. That is, a line from $P1$ to $P2$ will actually be drawn relative to the viewport's origin; (left, top) is treated as (0,0), with x running 0 to (right-left), and y running from 0 to (bottom-top), as illustrated in Figure 18.18.

It's possible that a line is too long for a viewport, or lies entirely outside the viewport. In this case, the line can be *clipped* against the viewport boundaries, if the

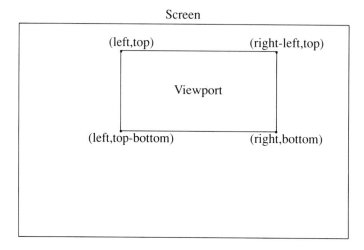

Figure 18.18   Viewports and relation to coordinate origin in terms of screen coordinates. Within the viewport (left,top) is 0,0, and (right,bottom) is (right−left, top−bottom).

last parameter to `setviewport` is nonzero. Assuming we've created a viewport from 100,100 to 150,150, a line from 0,0 to 200,200 would be clipped against the upper right and lower left corners of the viewport. *Warning: Not setting the clip flag means that lines aren't clipped at viewport boundaries.*

When we create a viewport, nothing changes on the screen. This means that in general the first thing we do is erase its contents. `clearviewport` clears the viewport to the current background color (which defaults is black) and sets the current graphics position to the viewport origin. `cleardevice` is similar, except that it clears the entire screen, not just the current viewport.

```
void clearviewport(void);
void cleardevice(void);
```

Figure 18.19 shows an example use of overlapping viewport. It places a circle in the center of the screen, and waits for a keystroke. Then it draws a box in an outlined viewport that covers this circle, and waits for another keystroke. Finally, it erases the covering viewport and restores the original circle.

Outlining the viewport is actually a little more difficult than it might at first appear to be. The problem is we want to write a general function, `outline_vp`, that can place a border around any size viewport. But ideally we don't want to have to pass it the size of the viewport. The solution, shown in Figure 18.20, involves a new

```
/*
 * Draw a circle, replace with box, and then restore circle.
 */
#include <conio.h>
#include <stdio.h>
#include <stdlib.h>
#include <stddef.h>
#include "gropen.h"

main()
{
  int xmax, ymax;              /* largest x and y coordinates */
  int vp1top, vp1bot, vp1left, vp1right;    /* viewport coords */
  void *orgimage;              /* holds saved viewport */
  void *draw_box(int vptop, int vplift, int vpright, int vpbot);

  if (!gropen((double *) NULL, &xmax, &ymax))
    return 1;       /* exit early; no graphics */
  circle(xmax/2, ymax/2, ymax/4);   /* draw centered circle */
  getch();
  vp1top = ymax / 4;           /* viewport has one-quarter */
  vp1bot = vp1top * 3;         /* screen border around it */
  vp1left = xmax / 4;
  vp1right = vp1left * 3;
  orgimage = draw_box(vp1top, vp1left, vp1right, vp1bot);
  getch();
  setviewport(0, 0, xmax, ymax, 1);   /* restore circle */
  putimage(vp1left, vp1top, orgimage, COPY_PUT);
  getch();                     /* wait for key press */
  grclose();
  return 0;
}

void *draw_box(int vptop, int vpleft, int vpright, int vpbot)
{                         /* place box in center of a viewport */
  int xc, yc;
  void *saveimage;        /* for saving whatever's underneath */
  void outline_vp(void);  /* outline current viewport */


     /* save what's in the current viewport */
  saveimage = malloc(imagesize(vpleft, vptop, vpright, vpbot));
  getimage(vpleft, vptop, vpright, vpbot, saveimage);
     /* border around the current viewport */
  setviewport(vpleft, vptop, vpright, vpbot, 1);
  clearviewport();        /* get rid of any junk in viewport */
  outline_vp();           /* draw outline around viewport */
  xc = (vpright - vpleft) / 2;   /* compute center x,y */
  yc = (vpbot - vptop) / 2;      /* of viewport */
  bar3d(xc - 20, yc - 20, xc + 20, yc + 20, 10, 1);
  return saveimage;
}
```

Figure 18.19 viewpt.c—A program illustrating the use of viewports.

```
/*
 * Draw a border around the current viewport.
 */
#include <graphics.h>

void outline_vp(void)
{
  struct viewporttype vp;      /* save viewport settings */

  getviewsettings(&vp);
  rectangle(0, 0, vp.right - vp.left, vp.bottom - vp.top);
}
```

Figure 18.20 outlinev.c—A function to draw a border around a viewport.

function, `getviewsettings`.

```
    getviewsettings(struct viewporttype *vp);
```

It fills in a structure with information on the current coordinates of the viewport.

```
    struct viewporttype { int right, left, top, bottom;};
```

`outline_vp` simply passes these coordinates to `rectangle`.

Since we have a viewport that's covering part of the screen, we have a problem: How do we restore the parts of the original screen that we wiped out? We need to use three new functions: `imagesize`, `getimage` and `putimage`.

```
    int imagesize(int left, int top, int right, int bot);
    void getimage(int left, int top, int right, int bot,
                  void *buffer);
    putimage(int startx, int starty, void *buffer, int type);
```

The idea is that before we place an image on the screen, we use `getimage` to save the part of the screen it will overwrite into a temporary location. We use `imagesize` to determine how much space we need for the image. When we want to restore the image, we redraw it with `putimage`. This function's last argument describes how the saved image will be combined with the image already at that location: COPY_PUT copies the saved image, overwriting what's on the screen; XOR_PUT performs an exclusive OR with the existing image; OR_PUT bitwise ORs the saved image; AND_PUT bit-wise ANDs the saved image; and NOT_PUT inverts the bits in the saved image.

This program may not seem particularly useful as written. But imagine that each of the viewports contained different representations of a program's input—one a bar chart, another a pie slice, still another a graph. Then our program is much more useful, since by hitting one key the user can see these different representations. The exercises have you make these modifications.

EXERCISES

18–13 Write a function to draw a viewport of a specified size and location, returning the saved image behind it. This function should optionally draw an outline around the viewport.

18–14 Write a function to produce a bar chart within a viewport. The function takes a table of values, the number of values, and the viewport location. Write similar functions to produce a pie diagram within a viewport, and to produce a simple graph.

18–15 Write a program that uses the functions from the previous exercise to produce a bar chart, pie slice, and graph representation of its input. Each time the user hits the key, a different bar chart should be brought to the foreground (that is, should have nothing obscuring it).

18.6   TEXT OUTPUT IN GRAPHICS MODE

So far all we've done in graphics mode is draw pictures. We can also display text, although we can do so only through a special set of functions.

We write strings using one of two functions, `outtext` and `outtextxy`.

```
void outtext(char *string);
void outtextxy(int x, int y, char *string);
```

`outtext` writes the string at the current position, `outtextxy` writes the string at the specified (x,y) location.

There are also two other functions that are very useful: `textheight` and `textwidth`. `textheight` returns the height in pixels of a given string, `textwidth` returns its length in pixels.

```
int textheight(char *string);
int textwidth(char *string);
```

Figure 18.21 combines all these in a function, `waitkey`, that writes the message "Hit any key to continue" within a rectangle that just surrounds it.

By default strings are written in a fixed-width font. But we can select any of the fonts in Table 18.6 using `settextstyle`.

```
void settextstyle(int font, int direction, int charsize);
```

`direction` is either `HORIZ_DIR` or `VERT_DIR`, depending on whether we want to write strings horizontally or vertically. `charsize` is a scaling factor that behaves differently when used with the default bit-mapped font or with the vector fonts. When we provide a bit-mapped font, we provide a value between zero and 10, which is used to magnify the characters (so with a magnification of 10, the 8×8 characters are blown up to an 80×80 area). When we provide a vector font, we provide a zero, which by default magnifies the characters by a factor of 4.

It turns out that blowing up the bit-mapped font produces unaesthetic blocky results. That means for large characters, we need to use the vector fonts and a special function `setusercharsize`.

```
/*
 * waitkey.c -- Write a message and wait for a keystroke.
 */
#include <graphics.h>
#include <conio.h>

void waitkey(int x, int y)
{
  char *msg = "Hit any key to continue.";

  outtextxy(x, y, msg);
  rectangle(x - 1, y - 1 - textheight(msg),
            x + 1 + textwidth(msg), y + 1);
  getch();   /* get keystroke */
}
```

Figure 18.21   waitkey.c—Write a message and wait for a keystroke.

FONT NAME	DESCRIPTION
DEFAULT_FONT	Standard 8×8 bit-mapped font
TRIPLEX_FONT	Triplex (triple line stroked) font
SMALL_FONT	A small stroked font
SANSSERIF_FONT	A sans-serif font
GOTHIC_FONT	A gothic (Olde English) font

Table 18.6   Fonts and descriptions for graphics text.

```
void setusercharsize(int multx, int divx, int multy, int divy);
```

This function scales the vector fonts separately in width (x) and height (y). The scale factor is determined by

```
ScaleX = multx / divx;
ScaleY = multy / divy;
```

Normally text is output (in horizontal mode) starting at the current graphics position CP, and moving to the right; CP is reset to the end of the string. For vertical text, justification is at the top of the string. You can change the direction that text is output from CP (move left, or center around CP) by a call to settextjustify.

```
void settextjustify(int horiz, int ver);
```

Its arguments can be any of the constants described in Table 18.7.

Figure 18.22 contains a function that to write a string in the gothic vector font, scaled up by a factor of 1.5 in width and 2 in height. The main program uses this

NAME	DESCRIPTION
LEFT_TEXT	Left horizontal justification (default)
CENTER_TEXT	Center text horizontally or vertically
RIGHT_TEXT	Right horizontal justification
BOTTOM_TEXT	Bottom vertical justification
TOP_TEXT	Top vertical justification (default)

Table 18.7   Justification constants for settextjustify.

function to write the string "Alex Was Here" in the center of the screen. It turns out that whenever Turbo C programs use these special fonts, settextstyle makes use of files that describe each of the characters in the font. These files, whose names end in .chr must be in whatever directory we passed as initgraphs third argument. Since we're using gropen, these files must be in the current directory.

EXERCISES

18–16   Write a program that puts up a pop-up menu with these options: help, draw, and quit. help displays a description of the menu, draw causes our earlier robot to be drawn, quit causes the program to exit. The menu's title should be directly above it, in a sans serif font.

18–17   Modify our earlier data base program to use a pop-up menu like the one you wrote in the previous exercise. Have its input come from one viewport and its output go to another.

18–18   Extend the programs written in the previous exercises to display the pop-up menu in a different color than the rest of the screen.

18.7   TEXT OUTPUT IN TEXT MODE

So far this chapter has concentrated on what we can do in graphics mode. But graphics mode is often overkill—all we really want is a way to add and delete characters from particular places on the display. Turbo C 1.5 provides a small set of functions that do just that.

In text mode there is a notion similar to the viewports of graphics mode—*text windows*. A text window is a rectangular area of the screen, with its origin in the upper left, just like a viewport. But, unlike a viewport, its basic unit is characters, not pixels, and its coordinates run from (1, 1) to the maximum number of text *lines* and text *columns* the display can handle. For most display drivers this is 25 lines by 80

```
/*
 * Write string in large gothic font near center of screen.
 */
#include <stdio.h>
#include <stdlib.h>
#include "gropen.h"

main()
{
  int maxx, maxy;
  void waitkey(int x, int y);
  void big_gothic(int xc, int yc, char *string);

  if (gropen((double *) NULL, &maxx, &maxy) == -1)
    return -1;   /* exit early; no graphics */
  big_gothic(maxx / 2, maxy / 2, "Alex Was Here");
  waitkey(5, maxy - 5);    /* near bottom left of screen */
  grclose();
  return 0;
}

void big_gothic(int x, int y, char *string)
{
  setusercharsize(3, 2, 2, 1); /* scale 1.5 in x, 2 in y */
  settextstyle(GOTHIC_FONT, HORIZ_DIR, 0);
  settextjustify(CENTER_TEXT, CENTER_TEXT);
  outtextxy(x, y, string);        /* centered around x & y */
  settextstyle(DEFAULT_FONT, HORIZ_DIR, 1);   /* restore */
  settextjustify(LEFT_TEXT, LEFT_TEXT);       /* defaults */
}
```

Figure 18.22 title.c—A program that shows how to use fonts of different sizes.

columns, although some new display drivers (the VGA for example) can display 43 to 50 lines of text, and some older drivers only display 40 columns. As with graphics viewports, there can be several simultaneous text windows, but only one of them can be active at any one time. And just as with graphics viewports, there are a set of functions for manipulating text windows. To use them we must include conio.h.

Manipulating Text

The default text window is the entire screen. We can, however, use window to set up a subset of the screen as the currently active text window.

```
void window(int left, int top, int right, int bottom)
```

Its arguments are similar to those for creating a viewport. Once we have an active window, we can do various operations to it: move the cursor to a location within it, add text, and erase text.

We use `gotoxy` to move the cursor to a particular row and column within the current text window.

```
gotoxy(int x, int y)
```

In case we forget, `wherex` and `wherey` tell us where we are.

```
int wherex(void);
int wherey(void);
```

When we're dealing with text windows, we need to use special versions of our standard I/O functions that write to the current text window instead of just to the standard output. These are `cprintf`, which is like `printf`, except that it returns the number of bytes written; `cputs`, which is like `puts`; and `putch`, which is like `putchar`. In addition, there is a special function, `insline`, that inserts a blank line at the current cursor position. The lines below it scroll down one position.

There are also several special operations for erasing text.

```
void clrscr(void);
void clreol(void);
void delline(void);
```

`clrscr` erases the contents of the current text window, `clreol` erases text from the cursor to the end of the current line, and `delline` erases the previous lines, with all of the text underneath it shifting up one row.

Character Attributes

In *text* mode, characters have several attributes we can modify: the foreground and background colors, whether or not they're highlighted, and whether or not they blink.

We can set the background or foreground to any of the CGA colors we saw earlier. To do so, we use two functions, `textcolor` and `textbackground`.

```
void textbackground(int color);
void textcolor(int color);
```

For the foreground, there is also an additional color, BLINK, which causes the character to behave like its name would suggest. As before, once we set a color it stays set until we change it. As an example, to write a string in yellow or a red background, set the colors and then write the string.

```
textbackground(RED);
textcolor(YELLOW);
cprintf(string);
```

To set things up so characters blink, add BLINK to the color.

```
textcolor(YELLOW + BLINK);
```

Of course, as before, you're limited to the colors your board supports.

We can reset the default intensity to high intensity or low intensity with:

```
void highvideo(void);
void lowvideo(void);
```

There is only one text font available in text mode—the standard fixed-width font. If you want something else, you have to work in graphics mode.

Figure 18.23 illustrates some of these functions in a new version of the output function for Chapter 10's Game of Life. This version is a little fancier than the previous version: It writes the border in high-intensity and centers the displayed world.

EXERCISES

18–19 Modify the interface to Chapter 12's data base program so that it uses text windows.

18–20 Modify the output function for Game of Life to use graphics mode instead of text mode.

18–21 Write a simple screen oriented editor. At the very least, allow the user to insert and delete lines, to insert and delete characters within a line, and go to a particular place in the file.

18.8   CASE STUDY—A FUNCTION PLOTTER

This chapter is a long one that's covered a lot of material. To try and put all of it in perspective, we'll use many of the library functions we've discussed in a simple—but very useful—function plotting program. The plotter reads a file containing (x,y) points to plot, ordered in x. We generate this file from another program that evaluates some interesting function at 500 or so values between x_{min} and x_{max}.

Overview of the Function Plotter

The task of plotting a function from an already-generated table of values divides nicely into two parts. The first is to read the table from a file into x and y arrays, determining the smallest and largest values of x and y. The other is to plot each of these points to a viewport, connecting them by a straight line. Why do we need to know the maximum and minimum values? Because we have to scale the data to whatever viewport we're using to plot the function.

Reading in the values is straightforward. We expect the user to provide the file's name on the command line, but if we don't find one, we use the standard input instead. The program simply reads the values, one per line, placing them into the array. To keep things simple, it assumes that the values in the input file are ordered in x so points can be connected by straight lines (we can relax this assumption by sorting points, but it's not an unreasonable assumption to make).

Plotting the function isn't much more difficult. As always, we start by initializing the graphics environment. We then set up the viewport and call a routine to actually plot the points. To further illustrate the use of viewports, we set up a second viewport and plot the routine again. After doing all this, the program waits for a keystroke, and then terminates.

```c
/*
 * Print generation using direct cursor addressing.
 */
#include <stdio.h>
#include <conio.h>
#include "life.h"

#define HEADER_ROW      1    /* row containing header */
#define BORDER_ROW      2    /* row containing top border */
#define BORDER_COL      1    /* col containing left border */
#define TOP_CELL_ROW    3    /* first row with cells */
#define LEFT_CELL_COL   2    /* first column with cells */

const int MAX_ROWS = 24, MAX_COLS = 80;   /* assume 24x80 */

void putworld(WORLD world)
{
  int c, r;
  static int printed = FALSE;     /* first printing? */
  extern int rows, cols, gen, endgen;

  if (!printed)
  {
    clrscr();
    window((MAX_COLS - cols) / 2, (MAX_ROWS - rows) / 2,
           MAX_COLS, MAX_ROWS);
    gotoxy(BORDER_COL, BORDER_ROW);
    highvideo();
    for (c = 0; c <= cols + 1; c++)        /* top border */
      putch(BORDER);
    for (r = TOP_CELL_ROW; r <  TOP_CELL_ROW + rows; r++)
    {                                      /* other borders */
      gotoxy(BORDER_COL, r); putch(BORDER);
      gotoxy(LEFT_CELL_COL + cols, r); putch(BORDER);
    }
    gotoxy(BORDER_COL, BORDER_ROW + rows + 1);
    for (c = 0; c <= cols + 1; c++)     /* bottom border */
      putch(BORDER);
    printed = TRUE;
    lowvideo();
  }
  gotoxy(BORDER_COL, HEADER_ROW);
  cprintf("Generation %d out of %d", gen, endgen);
  for (r = TOP_CELL_ROW; r < TOP_CELL_ROW + rows; r++)
  {
    gotoxy(LEFT_CELL_COL, r);
    for (c = 1; c < cols; c++)
      putchar(world[r][c] ? MARKER : ' ');
  }
  gotoxy(BORDER_COL, BORDER_ROW + rows + 2);
}
```

Figure 18.23 outworld.c—A new version of the function to display a Game of Life world.

The Plotter Itself

Figure 18.24 contains the function plotter. The program itself is divided into two basic parts: A main program that reads in the values and determines the largest and smallest points, and a function `plot_graph` to actually plot the points in a given viewport.

`plot_graph` clears the viewport, draws an outline around it (that doesn't happen by default), and then plots the points in it. To plot the points, we want to simply `moveto` the first one, and then do `lineto`s to each of the others. But there are two problems with this simple approach.

The first problem is that the points don't correspond to pixels. Suppose we're plotting $\sin(x)/x$, and we run x from about 0 to about 10; y always falls somewhere between -0.2 and 1.0. But the PC uses integer coordinates from 0 to 350 or more in x and 0 to 200 or more in y. That means we have to *scale* the data to the screen, or our plot will end up in a tiny, tiny corner of the viewport. But scaling points is simple. We shift each value to the origin, and then multiply it by a scaling factor that maps any value within the data `xmin` to `xmax` into the range in the viewport, `vp.right` to `vp.left`.

The second problem is more subtle. Turbo C uses a coordinate origin in the *upper* left of the screen, while normal geometric coordinates are in the *lower* left. So we have to adjust the scaled points to account for the differing origins. But that's not so simple: It requires "moving" all y values down by the size of the viewport; to do this we need to know the size of the viewport. Luckily, we can obtain this information with a call to `getviewsettings`.

Run the function plotter. You'll be impressed with its output!

EXERCISES

18–22 Use the plotter program to explore capabilities of your own graphics board. Add options to the plotter program that describe the line drawing methods, colors, and viewport positions.

18–23 Extend the function plotter so that it labels the x and y axes. Then modify it to add tick marks on the axes and label them with appropriate values.

18–24 It is often useful to plot two different functions into the same viewport (rather than one function into two viewports). Modify and extend the function plotter so that it reads plotting data for multiple data files, whose names are specified in the command line.

18–25 Modify the function plotter to do color plots.

```
/*
 *   Plot a graph into two viewports.
 */
#include <stdio.h>
#include <stdlib.h>
#include <conio.h>
#include <graphics.h>
#include "boolean.h"

#define  MAXPTS    500   /* max nbr of points to plot */
#define  vpleft    5                /* viewport coordinates */
#define  vpright   (getmaxx() - 5)
#define  vptop     5
#define  vpbottom  (getmaxy() - 25)

struct point { float x, y; };       /* to make life easier? */

main(int argc, char *argv[])
{
  register int i = 0;
  int    gr_device = DETECT, gr_mode;
  float  x[MAXPTS], y[MAXPTS],     /* data points */
         xmin, xmax, ymin, ymax;
  struct point yb, yt,      /* bottom & top of Y axis */
               xl, xr;      /* left & right of X axis */
  FILE  *fptr;                   /* input data file ptr */
  void waitkey(int col, int row);
  void plot_graph(float x[], float y[], int npts,
                  float minx, float maxx, float miny, float maxy,
                  struct point Yb, struct point Yt,
                  struct point Xl, struct point Xr);

  if ((fptr = (argc < 2) ? stdin : fopen(argv[1], "rt")) == NULL)
  {
    fprintf(stderr, "Couldn't obtain points.\n");
    return 1;
  }
  for (; i < MAXPTS &&     /* read X-Y data */
       fscanf(fptr, "%f%f", &x[i], &y[i]) == 2; i++)
  {
    if (i == 0)    /* first time through */
    {
      xmin = max = x[0]; ymin = ymax = y[0];
      continue;
    }
    if (x[i] < xmin)
      xmin = x[i];
    else if (x[i] > xmax)
      xmax = x[i];
    if (y[i] < ymin)
      ymin = y[i];
    else if (y[i] > ymax)
      ymax = y[i];
  }
```

```
/*
 * Set points for x and y axis and then plot the graph.
 */
 xl.x = xmin;   xl.y = 0.0;   xr.x = xmax;   xr.y =  0.0;
 yt.x = 0.0;    yt.y =  ymin; yb.x = 0.0;    yb.y =  ymax;

 initgraph(&gr_device, &gr_mode, "");
 if (gr_device < 0)
 {
   fprintf(stderr, "Can't initialize graphics.  Exiting\n");
   return 1;
 }
                  /* create first viewport */
 setviewport(vpleft, vptop, vpright, vpbottom, 1);
 plot_graph(x, y, i, xmin, xmax, ymin, ymax,
           yb, yt, xl, xr);
                  /* plot same graph in a smaller viewport */
 setviewport(vpleft+150, vptop+50, vpright-75, vpbottom-50, 1);
 plot_graph(x, y, i, xmin, xmax, ymin, ymax,
           yb, yt, xl, xr);
 getch();        /* key press to exit */
 closegraph();
 return 0;
}

void plot_graph (          /* plot points, w/axis */
  float          x[],      /* table of values */
  float          y[],
  int            npts,     /* nbr of points */
  float          minx,     /* min & max vals...*/
  float          maxx,     /* ...of x and y */
  float          miny,
  float          maxy,
  struct point   Yb,       /* bottom of Y axis */
  struct point   Yt,       /* top of Y axis */
  struct point   Xl,       /* left of X axis */
  struct point   Xr)       /* vpright of X axis */
{
  float  axis_x[2],        /* X coords of an axis */
         axis_y[2],        /* Y coords of an axis */
         x1[MAXPTS],       /* holds scaled points */
         y1[MAXPTS];
  void outline_vp(void),
       scale(float x[], float y[], float x1[], float y1[],
             int npts,
             float minx, float maxx, float miny, float maxy),
       plot(float x[], float y[], int npts);
```

```
/*
 * plot.c (continued)
 */
  clearviewport();
  outline_vp();

/* draw X axis: scale & plot */
  axis_x[0] = Xl.x;   axis_x[1] = Xr.x;
  axis_y[0] = Xl.y;   axis_y[1] = Xr.y;
  scale(axis_x, axis_y, x1, y1, 2, minx, maxx, miny, maxy);
  plot(x1, y1, 2);

/* draw Y axis: scale & plot */
  axis_x[0] = Yt.x;   axis_x[1] = Yb.x;
  axis_y[0] = Yt.y;   axis_y[1] = Yb.y;
  scale(axis_x, axis_y, x1, y1, 2, minx, maxx, miny, maxy);
  plot(x1, y1, 2);

/* plot the function: scale & plot */
  scale(x, y, x1, y1, npts, minx, maxx, miny, maxy);
  plot(x1, y1, npts);
}

/*
 * Scale a set of x-y values to the current viewport.
 */
static void
scale(float x[], float y[],
      float x1[], float y1[], int npts,
      float minx, float maxx, float miny, float maxy)
{
  struct viewporttype  vp;
  register int         i;
  register float       xscale, yscale;

  getviewsettings(&vp);
  xscale = (vp.right-vp.left)/(maxx-minx);
  yscale = (vp.top-vp.bottom)/(maxy-miny);

  for (i = 0; i < npts; i++)
  {
    x1[i] = xscale * (x[i] - minx);
    y1[i] = yscale * (y[i] - miny);
  }
}
```

```
/*
 * Plot points to the current viewport,
 */
static void plot(float x1[], float y1[], int npts)
{
  register int         i;
  register float       vp_ht;
  struct viewporttype  vp;

  getviewsettings(&vp);
  vp_ht = vp.top - vp.bottom;
  moveto(x1[0], y1[0] - vp_ht);
  for (i = 1; i < npts; i++)
    lineto(x1[i], y1[i] - vp_ht);
}
```

Figure 18.24   plot.c—Our function plotter program.

19   DEBUGGING TURBO C PROGRAMS

The interactive version of Turbo C 2.0 provides a powerful symbolic debugger, a program that can help us quickly locate many of our programming mistakes. In this chapter, we introduce that debugger and use it to debug several short Turbo C programs. We focus on its two most important features: its ability to display the values of variables and expressions, and its ability to let us execute various pieces of the program one statement or a group of statements at a time. The chapter concludes with a list of common Turbo C programming errors and suggestions for avoiding them.

19.1   INTRODUCTION

It would be a wonderful world if all our programs worked perfectly the first time we tried to run them. Unfortunately, however, no matter how carefully we design and code, some bugs crawl in when we're not looking and cause our programs to misbehave—especially the first few programs we write in an unfamiliar programming language. In fact, far too much programmer time is spent trying to flush out and exterminate these bugs.

One common technique for finding bugs is to flood programs with `printf` statements that display the values of important variables. The hope is that this debugging output will provide a clue as to where things first went awry. But although this approach quite often proves successful, it's also too often slow and inconvenient. Tracking a single variable's value may require many, many `printf` statements, spread out over several source files. It takes time to insert all these `printf`s, to recompile the program, and to remove them once we're done debugging. And it takes even more time to plow through page after page of output, trying to put our finger on the place where we made our mistake.

Luckily, there's a convenient alternative to this tedious and time-consuming process. The Turbo C interactive environment comes with a *debugger*, a tool that gives us control over the program we're running. We can use the debugger to temporarily stop our program's execution or to execute the program one statement at a time through

```
/*
 * Buggy program to find the smallest and largest values in
 * its input, as well as the average value.
 */
#include <stdio.h>

main()
{
  long min, max;         /* smallest and largest values */
  long value;            /* next value */
  long sum = 0L;         /* total */
  int n;                 /* number of values */

  for (n = 0; scanf("%ld", &value) == 1; n++)
  {
    if (n == 0)
      min = max = value;
    else if (value > min)
      min = value;
    else if (value < max)
      max = value;
    sum += n;
  }
  printf("Values: %d\nAverage: %f\n", n, (double) sum / n);
  printf("Min: %ld\nMax: %ld\n", min, max);
  return 0;
}
```

Figure 19.1 minmax.c—A buggy program that's supposed to find its smallest and largest input values.

sections we suspect are problematic. We can use it to poke around its memory to our heart's content, examining and even changing the values of variables. And we can use it to automatically display a variable's value every time it stops.

19.2   DEBUGGER BASICS

We'll start off by using the debugger to debug the short program shown in Figure 19.1. This program is supposed to read in a set of values and then print the number of values it read, the average value, and the smallest and largest values. Unfortunately, when run with the input values

```
10
20
15
5
25
```

its sadly incorrect output is:

```
Values: 5
Average: 2.000000
Min: 25
Max: 0
```

The only part of this output that's correct is the number of values, which really is 5. But the average isn't 2.000000, it's 15; the smallest value isn't 25, it's 5; and the largest value isn't 0, it's 25. So this program obviously contains some bugs. Since this program is so short, we probably need only study it for a short while to discover what those bugs are. But even with such a short program, the debugger helps locate bugs more quickly.

Starting the Debugger

So far we've been running our programs by hitting *CTRL-F9* or selecting the RUN/RUN menu entry. This caused the program to run from start to finish, without making use of the debugger. To use the debugger we have to do two things differently.

The first is that we have to make sure that the DEBUG/SOURCE DEBUGGING entry is set to EXE/OBJs before we try to compile the program. This guarantees that the compiler will include extra information needed by the debugger in the object module. What kind of information? Basically a table that connects the machine level instructions the compiler generates with the source-level statements from which they were compiled.

The other is that we have to run our program by hitting *F7* or using the equivalent RUN/TRACE INTO menu entry. This causes the debugger to place a *highlight bar* on the line defining `main` in the edit window. This highlight bar indicates the next line of the program to be executed. As we execute different statements, the highlight bar shifts throughout the source file.

Executing Statements

Quite obviously, the point of using the debugger is to find bugs. In our program, there were several. One is that the smallest and largest values were incorrectly computed. This seems to indicate that there's some sort of problem with the `if` statement contained in the `for` loop that reads the program's input. So to find this bug it makes sense to execute the program one statement at a time through the body of this loop.

Pressing *F8* (or selecting the RUN/STEP OVER menu entry) executes the next line of the program. In this case, hitting *F8* simply moves the highlight bar to the declaration of `sum`. Why here? Because the debugger skips over any lines in the source file that don't produce any machine-language instructions. These lines include blank lines, comments, the braces that indicate the beginning and end of statement groups, and declarations that don't include an explicit initialization. Hitting *F8* again executes this declaration, initializing `sum` to zero, and moving the highlight bar to the `for` statement.

Actually, there's a faster way to get to the `for` statement. When the highlight bar was on `main`, we could have moved the cursor down to the `for` and hit *F4* (or selected the RUN/GO TO CURSOR menu entry). *F4* causes the debugger to execute statements until it gets to the one the cursor is on. There is one caveat, however. *Warning: Don't put the cursor on a line in the source file that precedes the one the highlight bar is on.* If you do and then hit *F4* the program simply runs to completion.

Let's use *F8* to single step through one iteration of the for loop. Hitting *F8* executes the for, which executes scanf to read an input value. This causes the debugger to temporarily display the I/O screen instead of the normal tc display. Now we can enter the first input value, 10. At this point the debugger returns to the normal tc display, with the first line of the if highlighted. (Remember that hitting *ALT-F5* returns you to the I/O screen.) Hitting *F8* again evalutes the if, which causes the highlight bar to go to the next line, the statement that assigns value (the value read) to min and max. That's what we expect the first time through the loop. Hitting *F8* once again gets us out of the if and places the highlight bar on the assignment to sum. And hitting *F8* once more executes this assignment, placing the highlight bar back on the line containing the for.

So far so good—we made it through the for loop once without anything going wrong. But we still haven't found our bug. Perhaps one more iteration through the loop will provide a clue. Hitting *F8* executes the for, which once again displays the I/O screen—giving us the chance to enter the next value (20)—and then highlights the if. Hitting *F8* once more moves the highlight bar to the first else-if, the one that tests whether the next value is the smallest. Since this isn't the first time through the loop, that's what we expect. But now hitting *F8* again moves the highlight bar down one line to the statement assigning the current value to min. That's unexpected, since the current value of 20 is *not* the smallest so far. That means the test succeeded when it shouldn't have. A bug! From examining the if, we can see that the problem is that we accidentally reversed the test, using value > min instead of value < min. We really want to assign to min only when the value is smaller than the current minimum. Strangely enough, we made a similar mistake on the next test, the one to determine whether the next value is the largest so far.

After we fix these two tests and run the program, we get the correct output for the smallest and largest values—but the average is still wrong.

Displaying Variables

When running our buggy program, we assumed that it was reading values correctly. That wasn't such a bad assumption, since the bug we found had to do with our if and not with our for. But what if we had wanted to know what value was actually read, or had needed to know the values of other variables, such as sum or min or max? It turns out that whenever the debugger is stopped and a statement is highlighted, we can examine and modify variables.

Let's suppose we're back in the debugger again, with the debugger stopped at the beginning of the if statement. To find out what value we just read, we need to hit *CTRL-F4*. This causes a pop-up window containing three fields—EVALUATE, RESULT, and NEW VALUE—to appear on the screen. We then type the name of the variable we want to examine into the EVALUATE field and hit *ENTER*. In this case, that's value. The debugger displays its value in the RESULT field. What's the NEW

VALUE field useful for? We can use it to change the value of a variable. All we have to do is enter the desired value.

We can use this ability to display variables to track down our remaining bug, the incorrect average. The average is computed using sum, so we need to ensure that sum was computed correctly. To do so, we start up the debugger and get to the line that assigns to sum. Hitting *CTRL-F4* gives us the evaluate window, into which we enter sum. And its value when displayed is 0, as it should be at this point. Hitting *F8* executes the assignment—but did sum get updated correctly? We can find out by hitting *CTRL-F4* and entering sum once again. And when we do its value is still 0. What's going on here? The problem is in how we're updating sum: We're adding n to it. But that's not what we want to do—n is the loop index, not the value we read. And the first time through the loop, n is zero, which explains why sum is zero.

Now we're reasonably sure that we've found the problem. But to be sure, we'll execute the rest of the program, changing sum to its correct value before we execute the final few printf statements. That way we can make sure that we're correctly computing the average. Moving the cursor to the first printf and hitting *F4* finishes the loop. Then, hitting *CTRL-F4*, entering sum, and then entering 75 (the value it's supposed to have at this point) changes sum's value. Now hitting *F8* several times finishes executing the program, printing the correct average, 15.000000. The corrected program is shown in Figure 19.2.

A Word of Warning

Debuggers are great for finding bugs—but the best way to get rid of bugs is to avoid putting them in your program in the first place. That's not always possible, but careful coding eliminates many bugs early, helping you avoid spending time using the debugger to track them down. When careful coding isn't enough and your program still misbehaves, don't rely on using the debugger to find all your mistakes. A quick glance at your code is often enough to locate the problem.

Save the debugger for those times when, despite your best efforts at coding your program correctly, it has a troublesome flaw that you can't find by examining the code. Even then, don't just blindly single-step through your entire program or display the value of every variable in sight. Instead, try to narrow down the possibilities where it might be going wrong. With our example program, we narrowed it down to a problem within the loop before we started up the debugger. In general, it helps a great deal to make an educated guess of where the bug is likely to be before you go searching for it.

Keep in mind that the debugger only helps find problems once you're aware of them. It's up to you to bring those bugs to the surface by carefully testing your program and analyzing its behavior. For example, we claimed that our version of minmax.c works. But what happens if we don't provide it with any input? We get strange values for min and max, and an average that's computed by dividing by zero. That's because we forgot to check for that particular case. How did we find that bug? By thinking about the different cases our program must handle—not by using the debugger.

```
/*
 * Find the smallest, largest, and average values (corrected).
 */
#include <stdio.h>

main()
{
  long min, max;         /* smallest and largest values */
  long value;            /* next value */
  long sum = 0L;         /* total */
  int n;                 /* number of values */

  for (n = 0; scanf("%ld", &value) == 1; n++)
  {
    if (n == 0)
      min = max = value;
    else if (value < min)        /* BUG FIX! */
      min = value;
    else if (value > max)        /* BUG FIX! */
      max = value;
    sum += value;                /* BUG FIX! */
  }
  printf("Values: %d\nAverage: %f\n", n, (double) sum / n);
  printf("Min: %ld\nMax: %ld\n", min, max);
  return 0;
}
```

Figure 19.2 minmax2.c—The corrected version of our earlier buggy program.

EXERCISES

19–1 Write a program that finds the three largest and three smallest values in its input. Use the debugger to track down any bugs. Make sure your program works even when there are less than three values in its input.

19–2 Write a program to strip comments from C programs, leaving blank lines in their place. Again, use the debugger to track down any bugs.

19.3   A SECOND DEBUGGER EXAMPLE

Displaying variables and single-stepping through statements are powerful features of the debugger worth examining in more detail. We'll further illustrate them by debugging a second program, one that's supposed to reverse each of its input lines. The program itself is shown in Figure 19.3. The problem with this program is that, regardless of the input lines we provide it, its output is one carriage return per input line and nothing else—not at all what we wanted.

```
/*
 * A program to reverse each of its input lines.
 */
#include <stdio.h>
#include <string.h>
#include "inout.h"          /* From Chapter 8 */

#define MAXLEN 256
#define SWAP(var, x, y)     (var = *x, *x = *y, *y = var)

main()
{
  char line[MAXLEN + 1];
  void reverse(char *string);

  while (getline(line, MAXLEN) != -1)
  {
    reverse(line);
    putline(line);
  }
  return 0;
}

void reverse(char *string)
{
  char *fptr = string;
  char *rptr = string + strlen(string);
  char temp;

  for (; fptr < rptr; fptr++)
    SWAP(temp, fptr, rptr);
}
```

Figure 19.3 A buggy program to reverse each line in its input.

The program works by using `getline` to read an input line into a variable `line`, using a function `reverse` to reverse `line`, and then using `putline` to print `line` (The code for `getline` and `putline` first appears in Chapter 8). We'll try to find our mistake by single-stepping through the main program, repeatedly displaying `line`'s value, hoping to see where it becomes null. Doing so is surprisingly simple. We enter the debugger and repeatedly hit *F8*. And every time the debugger stops we hit *CTRL-F4* and enter `line`. Because `line` is an array of characters, the debugger by default displays the entire string. In this case, after `getline` executes, `line` contains whatever input line we typed. And after `reverse` executes, `line` displays as a null string. Aha! We've narrowed down the problem to somewhere within `reverse`.

Tracing Into Functions

Now we need to examine `reverse` in more detail, since that's where our bug seems to be. But pressing *F8*, when we were in the main program with `reverse` highlighted, executed `reverse` and went to the next line. How do we get into `reverse` so we can single-step through it? It turns out that we use *F7*, the same key we used to start stepping through `main`. *F7* is exactly like *F8*, except that it doesn't *step over* function calls; it *traces into* them.

Let's run the program from the beginning and trace through it again, this time diving into the details of `reverse`. We can restart the program by hitting *CTRL-F2* (or selecting the RUN/PROGRAM RESET menu entry). Hitting *F8* a few times gets to the line containing the call to `reverse`, and then hitting *F7* gets us into `reverse`. When we use *F7* to step into a function, it places the highlight bar at the first line of the function's definition (just like it did with `main` at the start of our program). Now we can single-step through `reverse`, displaying the relevant variables.

Displaying Expressions

When debugging `reverse`, we want to find out to which characters `fptr` and `rptr` point. But the default action when we display either of these pointers is to print the entire string, not just the first character. While that's not incredibly irritating—it's easy enough to locate the first character in a string—we would prefer to display only the first character.

That's easy to do. The debugger actually lets us enter entire expressions in the EVALUATE window; we're not limited to variables. So to display the single character to which `fptr` points, we enter the expression `*fptr`. The debugger evaluates the expression and displays its value. We can enter almost any legitimate expression, with several obvious restrictions. First, we can't use function calls. Second, we can't use `#defined` macros. And third, we can't refer to local variables that aren't defined in the current function.

When the debugger displays an expression, it uses a default format appropriate for the expression's type. Already, we've seen that integers are displayed as decimal integers, and arrays of characters are displayed as character strings. Table 19.1 lists the defaults for various types.

Usually, the defaults are appropriate. But what about when we want to actually display the address of a character pointer? Or want to display an integer in hex? Or want to display a pointer in decimal? Fortunately, the debugger provides a mechanism for supplying an alternative format. All we have to do is follow the variable we're displaying with a comma and one of the formatting codes shown in Table 19.2. Entering

```
fptr,p
```

in the EVALUATE window will display the address contained in `fptr` in pointer format, rather than doing the default action of displaying the string to which it points.

Let's put all this together to debug `reverse`. Once we're in `reverse`, hitting a couple of *F8*'s brings us to the `for` loop. But before we execute the `for`, let's

TYPE	FORMAT
char	as we'd enter it in C (ie, \n or \003)
int, long	decimal integer
float	floating point (7 significant digits)
double	floating point (15 significant digits)
long double	floating point (18 significant digits)
char *	character string
pointer	segment:offset notation, in hex
enumerated	decimal followed by member name
array of char	character string
other arrays	elements enclosed in braces
structure	values of each field

Table 19.1   Default format used to display variables.

make sure the pointers have the appropriate values. string should be the entire
input line, fptr should point to the beginning of the string, rptr to the character
before the trailing null. Hitting *CTRL-F4* pops up the EVALUATE windows. Entering
string displays the entire input line. Entering *fptr displays the first character of
the input line, as it should. Entering *rptr, however, displays a '\0'. But didn't
we expect rptr to point to the last character in the string, not the trailing null? The
problem is that we initially assigned it

```
string + strlen(string)
```

which gives us a pointer to the trailing null. We need to subtract one from that to
point to the character before the null.

Without even having to trace all the way through reverse, we've managed to
find a bug. Unfortunately, it's not the only bug.

EXERCISES

19-3   Take the insertion sort program from Chapter 1 and use the debugger to display the
addresses of all the variables it uses. Also use the debugger to display each element
as it's read.

19-4   Write a simple program that uses a variable with an enumerated type day to index
and print a table of days of the week. Use the debugger to single-step through this
program, printing the values of this variable and the strings in the table.

CHARACTER	DISPLAY FUNCTION
d	decimal integer
h	hexadecimal integer
x	hexadecimal integer
fN	floating point (N is optional # of significant digits to display)
s	special character (as coded in C)
c	raw character (as it normally displays)
p	segment/offset pointer in hex
ph	segment/offset pointer in hex
pd	segment/offset pointer in decimal
r	structure (display field names and values)
Nm	N bytes of memory

Table 19.2 Format characters recognized in debugger expressions.

19.4   BREAKPOINTS

After we fix the bug we found in our reversal program, it still doesn't produce the correct output. When we give it the input line

```
What's up doc?
```

the output is

```
?What's up doc
```

It appears as though we haven't found all of the bugs in reverse. All reverse appears to be doing is shifting characters over one position in the array and moving the last character to the front. This behavior makes it likely that there's a problem with the for loop—possibly with the pointers used to traverse the array.

To track down this bug, what we want to do is run the program until the for loop, and then repeatedly run through the loop examining the values of the pointers after each pass through the loop. While we could use *F4* or *F7* to get to the for, and then use *F8* to repeatedly single-step through the loop, there's an easier way.

What we want to do is set a *breakpoint* at the SWAP statement. A breakpoint causes the debugger to temporarily stop execution every time it's encountered. So we no longer have to single-step through the loop; we can just hit *CTRL-F9* to run until the next breakpoint, which causes it to stop each time it's about to exchange characters.

Setting and Using Breakpoints

How do we set a breakpoint? It's easy: We simply move the cursor to the line where we want the breakpoint and hit *CTRL-F8* (or select the BREAK/TOGGLE menu entry). In this case, we move the cursor to the line in `reverse` that contains the `SWAP` statement, and hit *CTRL-F8*. Once a breakpoint has been set, the line is highlighted, although in a slightly different way than the highlight bar we're used to. Now if we rerun our program, execution stops when it hits this line, and we can use *CTRL-F4* to display the values of the various pointers.

The first time we hit the breakpoint, we display `*fptr`, which is 'W', and `*rptr`, which is '?', just as they should be. We also display `fptr` and `rptr` in pointer format, and their values are DS:FEC2 and DS:FECF, respectively. Hitting *CTRL-F9* causes the program to continue running until it hits the same breakpoint again. Now when we display `*fptr`, we see an 'h', as we should. When we display `*rptr`, however, we see a 'W', which is strange, since we expected to see a 'c', the letter preceding the question mark. So something has gone wrong. But what? Examining the pointers provides a clue: `fptr` is now DS:FEC3, so it was incremented successfully, but `rptr` is still DS:FECF—it hasn't changed. Ah, that's it. We just forgot to decrement it each time through the loop. A simple fix, shown in Figure 19.4, and the program now works correctly.

Finding and Removing Breakpoints

Once we set a breakpoint, it stays set throughout the remainder of our session with tc— even when we edit different source files—until we explicitly remove it. The usual way to get rid of a breakpoint is to go to the line containing the breakpoint and hit *CTRL-F8*. But we can remove all breakpoints in a program by selecting the BREAK/CLEAR ALL BREAKPOINTS entry. And we can selectively remove breakpoints by repeatedly selecting the BREAK/VIEW NEXT BREAKPOINT entry, and hitting *CTRL-F8* at the breakpoints we no longer need. This menu entry causes the cursor to move to the next breakpoint in the file.

tc tries to keep track of breakpoints even when we're inserting and deleting lines in the source files we're debugging. (Of course, if we delete a line that contains a breakpoint, that breakpoint goes away.) *Warning:* tc *can, however, occasionally get confused about which lines in the source file correspond to breakpoints.* This can occur when we edit a source file and then continue on within the debugger without recompiling and relinking. And it can occur if we set breakpoints in a file, make changes to it, and then fail to save them. In these situations, it's possible that tc will highlight the wrong lines in the source file as breakpoints. But with a little care they are easily avoided.

EXERCISES

19-5 Take an earlier program you wrote that uses pointers to traverse an array, and use breakpoints and displaying variables to verify that all of its pointers have the appropriate values before and after the array is traversed.

19-6 Rewrite our reversal program so it not only reverses each line of input but also prints

```
/*
 * Reverse a string in place (corrected version)
 */
#include <stdio.h>
#include <string.h>
#include "inout.h"

#define MAXLEN 256
#define SWAP(var, x, y)     (var = *x, *x = *y, *y = var)

main()
{
  char line[MAXLEN + 1];
  void reverse(char *string);

  while (getline(line, MAXLEN) != -1)
  {
    reverse(line);
    putline(line);
  }
  return 0;
}

void reverse(char *string)
{
  char *fptr = string;
  char *rptr = string + strlen(string) - 1;     /* BUG FIX! */
  char temp;

  for (; fptr < rptr; fptr++, rptr--)            /* BUG FIX! */
    SWAP(temp, fptr, rptr);
}
```

Figure 19.4   reverse2.c—The fixed version of our program to reverse its input lines.

these lines in reverse order. Use the debugger to help get rid of any bugs your program
may have.

19.5   **WATCH EXPRESSIONS**

When we're debugging a program we often find ourselves examining the same values
each time we go through a loop. That happened to us when we were trying to find the
pointer bug in the input reversal program. We found ourselves repeatedly displaying
an entire of set of values: the pointers, and the characters and strings to which they
pointed.

In that particular example, it wasn't so bad since we only had to go through the
loop twice to find the bug. But suppose we hadn't figured out the bug so quickly and

that we needed to go through the entire string before the cause of the problem dawned on us. Then it would have been a lot of work to keep hitting *CTRL-F4* and entering each of the expressions. Once again, there's a better way. The debugger provides something called a *watch expression*, an expression whose value is automatically updated and displayed in the watch window whenever the debugger stops.

Hitting *CTRL-F7* (or selecting the BREAK/ADD WATCH menu entry) lets us add a new watch expression. This displays a small pop-up window into which we enter the expression whose value we want to watch. This expression and its value is then displayed in the watch window, with the last watch expression added at the top of the window. We can have as many watch expressions as we like, with the watch window growing to provide enough room for them. Actually, the watch window is limited to half the screen; if we want to have more expressions we're forced to scroll through the window to see them all.

How can we use watch expressions to debug our earlier reverse program? Assuming that we've set a breakpoint at the SWAP statement, we first run the program until it hits that breakpoint. At this point we enter the various expressions we want to watch (`rptr`, `fptr`, `*rptr`, `*fptr`, and `string`), one at a time. Now every time we hit *CTRL-F9* to continue the program, it will stop at this breakpoint and display in the watch window whatever expressions we entered.

Once we find a bug, we're likely to want to get rid of some of our watch expressions. To do so, we use *F6* to move the cursor into the watch window, and then use the usual cursor movement keys to move the cursor onto the expression we wish to delete. Once we've selected the expression, we can delete it simply by selecting the BREAK/DELETE WATCH entry.

We can edit expressions in a similar way. We select the expression we want to edit and then select the BREAK/EDIT WATCH. This causes another small window to appear on the screen containing the selected expression. We can then modify this expression—for example, adding or changing a format modifier—hitting *ENTER* when we're done with any changes.

EXERCISES

19–7 How could we have combined watch expressions with breakpoints to more quickly debug our first example? Do so.

19–8 Write a program that identifies which of its input strings are palindromes (strings that are identical forwards or backwards). Use the debugger to debug it.

19.6   A FINAL DEBUGGER EXAMPLE

There are still a few debugger features we haven't yet covered. We'll use them to debug the sorting program shown in Figure 19.5. This program is behaving strangely. When we present it with the input

```
75 15 23 98 17 11 50 3
```

it produces

```
3
11
15
```

as output. It's correct as far as it goes—the values it prints are sorted—but it only prints a few of the values.

The sorting program consists of two basic functions: `insert`, which places a value in its correct place in the array, and `print_table`, which prints the sorted array. It appears that `insert` is working correctly and that `print_table` is the problem. To verify that hypothesis, we would like to use the debugger to somehow display the sorted array. All we have to do is hit *CTRL-F4* and enter the name of the array. By default, the debugger displays the contents of the entire array. To display just part of the array, we need to make use of a new debugger feature: the *repeat count*. If we follow a single array element with a comma and an integer *n*, the debugger will display the next *n* elements of the array. So entering

```
table[0],8
```

displays the first 8 array elements. It turns out that we can also follow a pointer with a repeat count, as in `table,8`. The debugger will print 8 elements starting at the location pointed to by the pointer.

To debug our sorting program, we'll first do two things. We'll start by setting a breakpoint at the call to `print_table` and running the program until it gets to that breakpoint. At this point, we can display the `table` array. And, lo and behold, the array is sorted correctly. So there must be a problem with `print_table`. To find out what it is, we'll use *F7* to trace into that function.

Before we spend a lot of time single stepping through `print_table`, it would be nice to make sure that the function was passed the correct parameters. To do so, we hit *CTRL-F3* (or select the DEBUG/CALL STACK entry). This creates a small pop-up window that lists the current *call stack*—the list of currently active functions and their parameters. In this case, there are only two: `print_table` and `main`. According to the call stack, `print_table` was passed an address and an integer 3.

What are the values of these parameters supposed to be? The first is the address of the array we're printing. In the main program, that's `table`. We'd like to verify that this is the address we passed `print_table`. But simply entering `table` won't work while we're in `print_table`. That's because `table` is defined in `main`, not in `print_table`. To examine `table`'s value, we need to tell the debugger which function it's in, which is called *qualifying* a name. When we want to examine a local variable defined in another function, we precede its name with a period, the name of the module containing the function, a period, the function name, and another period. So entering `.isort.main.table` into the evaluate window will display `table`'s address. Actually, we can leave off the module name if the current module contains the function. So entering `.main.table` would work just as well. Of course, we're limited to displaying local variables of functions that are on the current call stack. (There's one other time we need to qualify names—when we're accessing `static` variables in other modules. In that case, we don't need to provide a function name.)

```c
/*
 * Read a table of values and sort them using "insertion sort."
 */
#include <stdio.h>

#define   MAX    100        /* maximum number of values to sort */

main()
{
  int n,                    /* number of values in table */
      res,                  /* value returned by scanf */
      table[MAX],           /* table of values */
      next;                 /* current value */
  void insert(int a[], int val, int num);
  void print_table(int a[], int num);

  for (n = 0; n < MAX && (res = scanf("%d", &next)) == 1; n++)
    insert(table, next, n);
  if (res != EOF)           /* check for input errors */
    printf("Error while reading input.\n");
  print_table(table, next);
  return 0;
}

/*
 * Place value in correct place in array.
 */
void insert(int a[], int val, int num)
{
  int *ptr;

  for (ptr = a + num; ptr > a && val < *(ptr - 1); ptr--)
    *ptr = *(ptr - 1);
  *ptr = val;
}

/*
 * Print array in sorted order.
 */
void print_table(int a[], int num)
{
  int *ptr;

  for (ptr = a; ptr < a + num; ptr++)
    printf("%d\n", *ptr);
}
```

Figure 19.5   isort.c—A buggy version of our insertion sort program.

In this case, we find that the two addresses are the same. But what about `print_table`'s other parameters. That's supposed to be the number of entries in the table, 8 in this case. Why is it 3 instead? Because we made a mistake—we're passing `next`, the last value we read, to `print_table` rather than n, the number of items in the array. Fixing this mistake gives us the correctly working insertion sort program we first presented in Chapter 2.

EXERCISES

19–9 Combine watch expressions and breakpoints to use the debugger to display the entire array, right before it returns from `insert`. It should also display the value of the element it inserted, and the position where it inserted the element.

19–10 Modify the insertion sort program so that it sorts strings. Use the debugger to track down any mistakes.

19.7   COMMON MISTAKES

There are an almost infinite number of ways to go wrong when writing C programs. But some of these mistakes seem to happen far more frequently than others. Here are the five most common mistakes, along with their symptoms and some hints on how to avoid them.

- *Failing to initialize a local variable before using it.*

Too often C programmers assume that local variables start off as zero—but they don't. Unless they're explicitly initialized, local variables start off with whatever happens to be in the memory locations assigned to them. Should we happen to use an uninitialized local variable in an arithmetic expression, we're likely to get the wrong answer—but at least our program usually won't behave abnormally or terminate early. We're in big trouble, however, if we use an uninitialized pointer or use an uninitialized integer variable in a pointer expression. Why? Because we're going to end up accessing a random address. If we're lucky, our program will die at that point or soon thereafter. But if we're unlucky, the program may modify some bizarre memory location and keep right on running. Or if we're really unlucky, sometimes the right value will happen to be in the memory location and our program will work one time and fail the next.

Uninitialized local variables often lead to bugs that are hard to track down. Fortunately, there's a simple way around this problem: Initialize every local variable at the time you declare it. This is especially crucial with counters and pointers. Initialize counters and accumulators to zero. And make sure that any pointer initially points to a reasonable location.

- *Using an inappropriate formatting code with* scanf *or* printf.

For some strange reason, we frequently find ourselves trying to read or print a long with %d. When reading a value, what happens depends on what value we're reading and what's already in the memory location into which we're reading. If we're reading a value that fits in an int and we're reading it into a location that's been initialized to zero, our program may work as expected. Otherwise, however, we're going to get strange values—a combination of the low 16 bits of the input values and the high 16 bits of the memory location into which we're reading. When printing, we'll simply see the low 16 bits of whatever value we're printing. And, in any case, if we don't get the formatting code right for any one value, all the other values we read or write are going to turn out wrong.

The obvious way to avoid this type of mistake is to get the printfs and scanfs right in the first place. But that's hard to do when we use a single printf to write the value. An alternative approach defines and uses several macros to print the values.

```
#define PRINT_LONG(l)    printf("%ld", l)
#define PRINT_INT(i)     printf("%d", i)

#define READ_LONG(lptr)  scanf("%ld", lptr)
#define READ_INT(iptr)   scanf("%d", iptr)
```

The problem with this method is that it's slow: printing three values now requires three function calls, rather than one. But it takes only a small decrease in run-time efficiency to forestall a possibly large decrease in programmer efficiency.

- *Accessing a nonexistent array element.*

In languages such as Pascal, when we try to access an element using an invalid subscript, the language's run-time system catches it, produces a nice error message, and then stops. But as we've pointed out, these errors go undetected in C—there's no run-time bounds checking. That means that simple bugs such as accessing one element past either end of an array (caused by a slightly incorrect loop-termination test) can cause havoc. We simply wipe out whatever value used to be in that location—which may have been another local variable, a header field of a dynamically allocated record, or some other similarly important value. Unfortunately, these errors happen frequently, especially with programmers used to languages in which array indexing starts at 1 rather than 0.

Most bugs that somehow involve accessing an incorrect address are going to be hard to hone in on, so it makes sense to do everything in our power to prevent them. One technique that helps takes advantage of indexing macros.

```
#define INDEX_UP(a, elements, ptr) \
        for (ptr = &a[0]; ptr < &a[elements]; ptr++)
#define INDEX_DOWN(a, elements, ptr) \
        for (ptr = &a[elements - 1]; ptr >= &a[0]; ptr--)
```

Rather than explicitly using a for to travel through the array, we let the INDEX_UP and INDEX_DOWN macros do it for us.

```
int table[100];                 /* table of elements */
int *tabptr;                    /* pointer into table */

INDEX_UP(table, 100, tabptr)    /* initialize table to zero */
  *tabptr = 0;
```

The problem with this technique is that when we start using lots of macros, our programs stop looking like C, and it becomes harder for other people to read them. But using these macros does guarantee that we won't go off the end of arrays.

- *Using incorrect operators or assuming incorrect operator precedence.*

C has more operators than most programming languages, and this leads to two major problems for novice C programmers. The first is using one operator when another is meant. At one point or another, almost every C programmer has used bitwise AND (&) instead of logical AND (&&) or used the assignment operator (=) instead of the equality-testing operator (==). These mistakes usually lead to some conditional expression is unexpectedly either always true or always false. The second is forgetting that some operators have lower precedence than might be expected. The bit-shifting operators have lower precedence than the arithmetic operators, which means that

```
i << 2 + 1
```

shifts i 3 bits to the left, not 2 as is usually expected. With these mistakes, we simply get strange results.

How do we get around problems with operators? Our technique of using macros to hide the troublesome part of C is once again a reasonable solution. Many C programmers define macros for the equality-testing and logical AND and OR operators.

```
#define EQUALS ==
#define AND    &&
#define OR     ||
```

The easiest way to avoid problems with operator precedence is to fully parenthesize all expressions. But that takes time and actually makes some expressions less readable. Since most of the problems with precedence occur with the bitwise operators, however, it's usually sufficient to parenthesize any expression containing these operators.

- *Passing the incorrect number of parameters or parameters with the wrong type.*

Since functions are frequently defined in a different place from where they are called, it's extremely easy to forget exactly what the parameters are that a particular function expects. And this can cause nasty bugs when we provide too few parameters or parameters of the wrong type, since some parameters will be uninitialized and others will have nonsensical values.

Fortunately, Turbo C provides a simple mechanism for preventing these bugs: *function prototypes.* If we supply a function prototype whenever we call a function, the compiler will catch this error for us—before we ever run our program. And that's the best place for bugs to be discovered—long before we've spent several frustrating hours in the debugger!

EXERCISES

19-11 Take insertion sort and implement the preceding suggestions. Is the program noticeably less readable?

19-12 Take one of the larger case studies in this text and implement the preceding suggestions. Is the program more readable or less readable?

A CONFIGURING TURBO C

This appendix describes how to install and use the command-line and interactive versions of Turbo C. We show how to use the installation program that comes with Turbo C, and show how to install Turbo C without using it. We also explain how to set up and modify configuration files. But before reading through this appendix and setting up your system, be sure to make backup copies of the original Turbo C disks—just in case something goes wrong.

A.1   INSTALLING TURBO C

Turbo C consists of a large collection of programs and files. The programs, listed in Table A.1, include the command-line and interactive versions of Turbo C and a set of useful utilties. (See the *Turbo C Reference Manual* for a detailed description of what these programs do.) The remaining files are the header, library, and object files needed to compile and link your programs, and a few miscellaneous files that provide help and documentation. The header files are described in Appendix D; the library files are listed in Table A.2. There are several versions of most of the library files, one for each memory model. The *x* in their names is actually a letter that identifies the particular memory model—either t (TINY), s (SMALL), c (COMPACT), m (MEDIUM), l (LARGE), and h (HUGE).

Before we can use Turbo C, we have to install it on our system. The easiest way to do this is to run install, a program you'll find on the disk labelled *Installation Disk*. To run it, place this disk in drive A, type A: and hit *ENTER*, and then type install and hit *ENTER*. install takes you step-by-step through the installation process—just do what it tells you to do!

Exactly what install does depends on whether or not you have a hard disk. On hard disk systems install creates a directory called \turboc and two subdirectories, \lib and \include. It places the header files in \include, the library and object files into \lib, and the various programs and help files in \turboc.

The installation process is more complex when you don't have a hard disk. To run install you'll need to have three freshly formatted floppies handy. The first becomes your *Turbo C diskette*, the second is your *system* or *library diskette*, and the third is your *source diskette*. install places tc on the Turbo C diskette; it places the library files, the include files, the compiler, and the linker on the system diskette; and it places

PROGRAM	FUNCTION
tcc.exe	Command-line Turbo C compiler
tlink.exe	Turbo C linker
tcinst.exe	Turbo C customization program
cpp.exe	Turbo C preprocessor
make.exe	Turbo C MAKE program
touch.exe	Turbo C file redating utility
grep.exe	Fast searching program
tlib.exe	Turbo C librarian
bgiobj.exe	Converts graphics drivers and fonts
objxref.exe	Object module cross referencer
readme	Special information (not in the manuals)
readme.com	Displays the special information
tchelp.tch	Turbo C Help file

Table A.1   Turbo C programs and important files.

NAME	FUNCTION
c0x.obj	Start-up object code
cx.lib	C library functions
math$x$.lib	Math library functions
fp87.lib	Floating point coprocessor library
emu.lib	Floating point emulation library
graphics.lib	Graphics library

Table A.2   Turbo C library files and object modules.

the Turbo C help file on the source diskette. Actually, it only places the library files for a single memory model on the system diskette. That's because there isn't enough room for more than one memory model on the usual 360K diskette. Fortunately, most programs in this book can be run with the SMALL memory model. In the long run, however, you'll probably use them all, so you'll likely end up running install several times.

A.2   **USING TURBO C**

When a hard disk is available, it's easy to access the Turbo C: We simply enter tc or tcc at the DOS command line. But using Turbo C is less convenient without a hard disk.

To use tc when we have two floppy drives and no hard disk, we first place the Turbo C diskette into drive A and execute tc. Once tc has been loaded, we place the source diskette (which contains the program we're working on and the system help files) into drive A and the system diskette (which contains the system libraries and header files) into drive B.

Those of you with only one floppy drive should run right out and purchase a second. If you're really stuck with only one drive, you can still run tc—but it's a pain. What you end up having to do is creating a single source/library diskette that contains your program and the system library and include files. The problem is that this doesn't leave any room for the help files, and you're stuck exchanging diskettes whenever you need help.

To use tcc when we don't have a hard disk, we need two diskettes, one for each drive. One contains the compiler, linker and libraries. The other diskette contains our program's source. We can't use tcc on a system with only one floppy drive.

A.3   **CONFIGURATION FILES**

tc and tcc make an important assumption—that your library and include files are in the same directory as your source file. But the way install sets things up, that's obviously not true. Fortunately, there are several ways to tell these commands where the files are located.

With tcc, we can use the command-line options -L and -I, with -L specifying the location of the library files and -I specifying the location of the include files. (We can give a list of files by using semicolons to separate the file names.) The command line

```
tcc -La:\lib -Ia:\include b:filename.c
```

compiles the file filename.c under the two-floppy configuration suggested above. Those of you with a hard disk use a command line with the same options but different locations:

```
tcc -Lc:\turboc\lib -Ic:\turboc\include filename.c
```

There is an alternative to all of this onerous typing. We place the command-line options on a single line in a file turboc.cfg (in the same directory as your source file). Under the two-floppy disk configuration, the file contains the single line

```
-La:\lib -Ia:\include
```

For the hard disk scheme, the file contains

```
-Lc:\turboc\lib -Ic:\turboc\include
```

The file can also include any other desired compiler options (Appendix C contains a complete list of these options).

With tc, the process is much easier. We simply select the appropriate entries on the OPTIONS/ENVIRONMENT menu, and specify the new locations. We can then write our options into the configuration file tcconfig.tc by selecting the OPTIONS/SAVE entry. If we want to, however, we can create that file ourselves and place the appropriate command-line options in it directly (as we did with tcc).

A.4   ## SETTING THE SEARCH PATH

We've been assuming that tcc and tc are available on the same disk as the program or in a location that is part of our DOS search path. If it is not, simply typing tcc or tc won't execute it. Instead, we'll have to provide a full path name, as in

        c:\turboc\bin\tcc b:filename.c

or

        c:\turboc\bin\tc b:filename.c

But we can avoid typing this full path name every time we run tcc or tc by adding their location to our DOS search path. We do this with the DOS path command. Assuming our original path was the single entry \system, the single DOS command

        path=c:\system;c:\turboc\bin

is sufficient to update our path appropriately. Consult a DOS manual for more information.

B THE TURBO C EDITOR

This appendix is a *brief* summary of the Turbo C interactive editor. The editor is very similar to WordStar and SideKick, so if you know these editors you'll have few problems using this one, and can use this appendix as a reference. But if you haven't used either of them, don't worry—this appendix should quickly bring you up to speed. And don't forget—hitting *F1* while in the editor window provides help in using the editor.

B.1 ENTERING TEXT

Choosing EDIT when in Turbo C's main menu, places you in the edit window of the Turbo C editor. By default, anything you type is entered into the window, as is. When you are done with a line, hitting *ENTER* takes you to the next line. There are, however, several text-entering modes that modify this default behavior. The edit window status line, located just above the edit window, tells you which of these modes you're in.

The first is *insert* mode. In insert mode, typing any character automatically inserts it in front of the character under the cursor. When not in insert mode, typing any character replaces the current character. Hitting the *INS* key toggles insert mode.

The second is *autoindent* mode. In autoindent mode, hitting *ENTER* moves the cursor to the next line, at the position of the first nonblank on the current line. When not in autoindent mode, the cursor is moved to the beginning of the next line. Hitting *ctrl-O I* turns autoindent mode on and off.

The third is *tab* mode. In tab mode, typing a *ctrl-I* places a tab character into the text (assuming a tab stop of 8). When it's off, spaces are inserted instead. Hitting *ctrl-O T* turns tab mode on and off.

The fourth is *fill* mode. When in *tab* mode and *fill* mode simultaneously, the editor will optimally fill the beginning of each line with tab characters and spacing. Hitting *ctrl-O F* turns fill mode on an off.

The last one is *unindent* mode. In this mode, backspace goes back one level of indentation whenever the cursor is on the first nonblank character of a line or on a

MOVEMENT	KEY
Left one character	*ctrl-S* or ←
Right one character	*ctrl-D* or →
Left one word	*ctrl-A* or ←
Right one word	*ctrl-F* or →
Left to beginning of line	*ctrl-Q S* or Home
Right to end of line	*ctrl-Q D* or End
Up one line	*ctrl-E* or ↑
Down one line	*ctrl-X* or ↓
Up a group of lines	*ctrl-W*
Down a group of lines	*ctrl-Z*
Up one page	*ctrl-R* or PgUp
Down one page	*ctrl-C* or PgDown
Up to top of window	*ctrl-Q E*
Down to bottom of window	*ctrl-Q X*
Up to top of file	*ctrl-Q R*
Down to bottom of file	*ctrl-Q C*
Up to beginning of block	*ctrl-Q B*
Down to end of block	*ctrl-Q K*
To last cursor position	*ctrl-Q P*

Table B.1   Cursor movement commands.

blank line.

B.2   BASIC EDITING COMMANDS

Editing commands fall into two categories: cursor movement and text manipulation.

Table B.1 lists the cursor movement commands. There are two types of cursor movement commands. The local movement commands are single keystroke commands that move the cursor one unit, such as left one character and right one word. The nonlocal commands are two keystroke commands that begin with a *ctrl-Q*. These commands move the cursor "all the way," such as to the beginning of the file or to the end of a line.

Table B.2 lists the text-manipulating commands. Unlike WordStar or SideKick, you can undo your last change. Hitting *ctrl-Q L* restores the current line to the state it was in before the last insert or delete action (provided you haven't yet left it).

Block commands allow you to do actions to an arbitrary piece of text. The basic idea is straightforward: We mark the start and end of a block, and then specify the action we want to affect on it.

ACTION	KEY
Insert line	*ctrl-N*
Delete line	*ctrl-Y*
Delete to end of line	*ctrl-Q Y*
Delete character at cursor	*ctrl-G* or Del
Delete character left of cursor	*ctrl-H* or Backspace
Delete word right of cursor	*ctrl-T*
Mark block start	*ctrl-K B*
Mark block end	*ctrl-K K*
Mark one word	*ctrl-K T*
Copy block	*ctrl-K C*
Delete block	*ctrl-K Y*
Hide/display block	*ctrl-K H*
Move block	*ctrl-K V*
Read block	*ctrl-K R filename*
Write block	*ctrl-K W filename*
Find	*ctrl-Q F*
Find and replace	*ctrl-Q A*
Repeat last find	*ctrl-L*
Find place marker	*ctrl-Q number*
Set place marker	*ctrl-K N number*
Abort operation	*ctrl-U*
Find matching delimiter forward	*ctrl-Q ctrl-[*
Find matching delimiter backward	*ctrl-Q ctrl-]*

Table B.2   Basic text-manipulating commands.

Find and replace commands let you quickly find and modify a string. When you do a find or a find and replace, you'll be prompted for a search string. This string is the piece of text you're trying to locate. It can be up to 30 characters in length. Several characters are special. A *ctrl-A* is a wildcard that matches any other character. A *ctrl-M J* matches a line break. To enter a control character in the string, you must preface it with *ctrl-P* (you can use this to enter control characters in your text as well, although in general we don't recommend doing so).

Once you've entered the search string, Turbo C prompts you for search options. Normally, the editor searches forward from the current cursor position to the next occurrence. The *B* option causes it to search backwards instead. The *G* option causes it to search the entire text, starting from the beginning. The *N* option simply tells it to find the next occurrence in the current direction. The *number* option means find the *number*th occurrence. Finally, the *W* option says to search for complete matches, skipping matches embedded within words. These search options can be combined in the obvious way.

If you're doing a find and replace, after you've entered the replace string, you have two additional options. An *N* means replace without asking (normally you're asked for confirmation at each substitute), and a number *n* means replace the next *n* occurrences.

C MENU ITEMS AND COMMAND OPTIONS

This appendix describes the contents of each of menus in the interactive version of Turbo C, and lists the options available for the command line version. When we select a menu entry, it can either cause another menu to pop up, or it can execute a specific command. We've indicated commands by following them with an asterisk.

C.1 THE MAIN MENU

This menu describes the highest level tasks you can do in tc.

FILE	Handles files, directories, accessing DOS
EDIT*	Switch to Turbo C Editor Window
RUN	Compile, link and run program
COMPILE	Compile, or compile and link program
PROJECT	Helps manage project file
OPTIONS	Select compiler options
DEBUG	Control the debugger
BREAK/WATCH	Set breakpoints and watch expressions

C.2 THE FILE MENU

This menu helps you manage files and access DOS.

LOAD*	Load a new file
PICK*	Load a previously loaded file
NEW*	Specifies that file is new
SAVE*	Save Editor Window to current file
WRITE*	Write Editor Window to different file
DIRECTORY*	Display files in specified directory
CHANGE DIR*	Change to specified directory
OS SHELL*	Invoke temporary DOS shell
QUIT*	Exit Turbo C

C.3   THE RUN MENU

This menu helps you control your program's execution.

RUN*	Compile, link, and execute the program
RESET*	Cancel current debugging session
GOTO CURSOR*	Run until line cursor is on
TRACE INTO*	Execute statement (going into function)
STEP OVER*	Execute statement (skip over function)
USER SCREEN*	Display execution screen

C.4   THE COMPILE MENU

This menu actually deals with compiling and linking, not just compiling.

COMPILE*	Compile file into .obj file
MAKE*	Do a Project Make to create an .exe file
LINK*	Link from .objs to .exe (No Project Make)
BUILD ALL*	Do an unconditional Project Make
PRIMARY*	Specify default C file to compile
GET INFO*	Provide information on current program

C.5   THE PROJECT MENU

This menu specifies defaults for the program builder.

PROJECT NAME*	Specify project file name
BREAK MAKE	When Project Make should quit
AUTO DEPEND	Recompile all needed C files on disk
CLEAR PROJECT*	Clear project name
REMOVE MESSAGES*	Erase messages from message window

Its BREAK MAKE entry causes another pop-up menu to appear that allows you to specify whether a Project Make should stop on Warnings, Errors, Fatal Errors, or before Linking.

C.6   THE OPTIONS MENU

This menu is tc method for setting command-line options.

COMPILER	Specify compiler options
LINKER	Specify linker options
ENVIRONMENT	Specify where various files are
ARGUMENTS*	Specify command-line arguments to program
SAVE OPTIONS*	Save options to config file
RETRIEVE*	Retrieve options from config file

The three submenus in this menu are worth discussing in some detail.

The COMPILER submenu lets us specify compiler options. We use it to select an appropriate memory model, to select various code generation and optimization options, to specify special characteristics of the source file, and to specify how the compiler should deal with errors.

There are many code-generation options. We can specify the calling convention (C or Pascal), the target CPU (8086 or 80186), the type of floating point processor (direct 8087, emulation 8087 if not present, no floating point), the default type of character (signed or unsigned), whether duplicate strings should be merged, whether data should be word- or byte-aligned, whether a standard stack frame should be generated (extra code for debugging), whether there should be a check for stack overflow, whether an underscore is prepended to externals, and whether line numbers should be included in the object model.

There are also several optimization options. We can choose whether to optimize for size or for speed, whether or not register declarations should be ignored, whether to suppress redundant loads (doesn't work with indirect register modification), and whether to eliminate redundant jumps and reorganize loops.

Among the source characteristics we can specify are the number of significant characters in an identifier, whether comments can be nested, and whether the compiler should recognize ANSI keywords only.

Finally, there are a few error handling options. We can tell the compiler when to stop compiling (how many errors and how many warnings), and whether the compiler should display warnings (and which types: Portability warnings, ANSI violations, Common Errors, and Less Common Errors).

The LINKER submenu provides only a few linker options. The most important options are whether the linker should automatically link in the graphics library, whether the linker should produce a memory map, whether it should warn us about duplicate symbols, and whether linking should be case sensitive. But we can also use this menu to specify whether the linker should initialize uninitialized segments, whether it should limit itself to Turbo C's default libraries, and whether it should warn us if there is no stack.

The ENVIRONMENT submenu lets us specify several directories. We can specify the include directories (where standard include files are), the output directory (where .obj, .exe, and .map files go), the library directory (where Turbo C libraries are), the Turbo C directory (where help and configuration files are). It also lets us specify some options. Should the Edit Window be saved automatically? Should the source file be backed up automatically? Should new messages be appended to or replace the current message window? And should Edit or Message Windows be expanded automatically?

Finally, the DEBUG submenu deals with error message output (although it also happens to display how much memory is currently available). It lets you specify how messages should be tracked, clear the messages from the Error Window, and specify whether previous error messages should be kept during the compile.

C.7	## THE DEBUG MENU

The debug menu is used to access debugger features.

EVALUATE*	Evaluate a C expression
CALL STACK*	Currently active functions
FIND FUNCTION*	Displays function definition
REFRESH DISPLAY*	Restore editor screen
DISPLAY SWAPPING*	When to display execution screen
SOURCE DEBUGGING*	Compile with debugging info

C.8	## THE BREAK/WATCH MENU

The break/watch menu is used to manipulate breakpoints and watch expressions.

ADD WATCH	Add a new watch expression
DELETE WATCH	Delete current watch expression
EDIT WATCH	Edit current watch expression
REMOVE WATCHES*	Delete all watch expressions
TOGGLE BREAKPT*	Add/Delete breakpoint
CLEAR BREAKPTS*	Delete all breakpoint
VIEW NEXT BREAKPT*	Go to next breakpoint

C.9	## COMMAND-LINE OPTIONS

Most of tc's menu items correspond to tcc options. These options are listed, grouped by function, in Table C.1. Appending a dash to toggle options turns the option off. -f links floating point libraries, -f- doesn't. This feature is useful for overriding options set in the configuration file.

OPTION	FUNCTION
-c	Compile but don't link
-o*file*	Name object *file*.obj
-e*file*	Name executable *file*.exe
-n*directory*	Place any new .obj and .EXE files in *directory*
-I*directory*	Search *directory* for include files
-L*directory*	Get library from *directory*
-M	Have linker produce a full memory map
-S	Create .asm file
-A	ANSI keywords only
-C	Allow comment nesting
-D*name*	Define *name* as a space
-D*name=string*	Define *name* as *string*
-U*name*	Undefine *name*
-i*num*	*num* significant characters in identifier
-K	`char` defaults to `unsigned char`
-g*num*	Stop compile after *num* warnings or errors
-j*num*	Stop compile after *num* errors
-w*???*	Turn warnings on and off
-1	Generate extended 186/286 instructions
-mc	Use COMPACT memory model
-mh	Use HUGE memory model
-ml	Use LARGE memory model
-mm	Use MEDIUM memory model
-ms	Use SMALL memory model (default)
-mt	Use TINY memory model
-a	Align integer-size items on word boundaries
-f	Use 8087 if present, otherwise emulate (default)
-f87	Use 8087 floating point chip
-f-	Don't link floating point libraries
-d	Merge duplicate strings
-G	Choose speed over size
-N	Add code to detect stack overflow
-y	Include line numbers in object file (for debugger)
-Y	Generate standard stack frame (aids debugger)
-v	Extra debugging info in object module
-O	Optimize loops/switch/jumps
-p	Generate calls using Pascal parameter-passing sequence

Table C.1 Compiler options.

D TURBO C HEADER FILES

This appendix lists the header files available in Turbo C. These header files define constants and types needed by various library functions, as well as providing prototypes for these functions. We've divided them into two sections. First, we list the standard header files. Second, we list those header files that are unique to Turbo C or that are used to make use of operating system functions.

D.1 ANSI C HEADER FILES

assert.h	`assert` debugging macro
ctype.h	Character testing macros
errno.h	Constants for error codes
float.h	Parameters for floating point
limits.h	Ranges of integers and compile-time limits
math.h	Prototypes for the math library
setjmp.h	Data types and prototypes for nonlocal gotos
signal.h	Constants and prototypes for signal-handlers
stdargs.h	Macros for handling variable argument lists
stddef.h	Common data types and macros
stdio.h	Types and macros for standard I/O library
stdlib.h	Prototypes for commonly used routines
string.h	Prototypes for string- and memory manipulation
time.h	Data types and prototypes for time-conversion

D.2	**TURBO C-SPECIFIC HEADER FILES**	
	alloc.h	Prototypes for memory management
	bios.h	Prototypes for DOS BIOS functions
	conio.h	Prototypes for direct console I/O functions
	dir.h	Prototypes for directory access functions
	dos.h	Prototypes for DOS-specific functions
	fcntl.h	Constants used by low-level file-handlers
	io.h	Prototypes for low-level file-handlers
	graphics.h	Prototypes for graphics library
	mem.h	Prototypes for memory manipulation functions
	process.h	Prototypes for process-management functions
	share.h	Parameters used by file-sharing functions
	sys\stat.h	File system information
	sys\timeb.h	Prototypes for time-manipulating functions
	sys\types.h	Special data types
	values.h	Declares machine-specific constants

E THE STANDARD LIBRARIES

This appendix describes many of the library functions we didn't get to earlier, and provides additional details about some of those we did. For each of these functions, we provide a header and a *brief* description Because of space limitations, we limit ourselves to the most frequently used standard C library functions standard C and ignore those available in DOS environments.

E.1 THE STANDARD I/O LIBRARY

The functions in the standard I/O library are part of standard C and are portable to other C compilers (we explicitly note any exceptions). To use these functions, we need to include stdio.h.

`clearerr` clears the error indicator set by `feof` and `ferror`.

```
void clearerr(FILE *file)
```

`getw` returns the next integer (written as a 16-bit binary value) from the file, returning EOF on end of file or error. Since EOF is the symbolic constant -1, a valid integer value, we must call `feof` or `ferror` to determine that one of these conditions has actually occurred. `putw` is the inverse of `getw`, writing a single integer to a file.

```
int getw(FILE *file)
int putw(int c, FILE *file)
```

Neither of these routines are standard C; use `fread` and `fwrite` instead.

`fcloseall` calls `fclose` on all open files except `stdin`, `stdout`, and `stderr`, and returns the numbers of files successfully closed.

```
int fcloseall(void)
```

`fcloseall` isn't standard C, and usually isn't necessary, since all open files are automatically closed when a program exits.

`fgetc`, `fgetchar`, `fputc`, and `fputchar` are functions that behave the same as the macros `getc`, `getchar`, `putc`, and `putchar`, respectively.

```
int fgetc(FILE *file)
int fgetchar(void)
int fputc(int c, FILE *file)
int fputchar(int c)
```

fflush clears an input file buffer, or dumps an output file buffer onto the file. flushall does an fflush to every open file.

```
int fflush(FILE *file)
int flushall(void)
```

Both return 0 if they were successful and EOF otherwise. flushall isn't standard C, and is usually unnecessary, since when the program terminates all open files are flushed.

freopen creates a new file pointer for an already-opened file.

```
FILE *freopen(char * name, char *mode, FILE *stream)
```

It returns a file pointer, or NULL, as with fopen, but closes the old file even if it can't open the new file. We can use freopen to redirect stdin, stdout or stderr, as in

```
freopen("datafile", "r", stdin)
```

perror writes a string to stderr that describes the most recent system error.

```
void perror(char *string)
```

It writes the string, a colon, the system error message (corresponding to the global variable errno), and a new line.

setbuf provides a buffer for a file. If the buffer is NULL, the file is unbuffered. Otherwise, the buffer should be BUFSIZE bytes long. setvbuf is similar, but if the buffer is NULL, malloc is used to allocate a buffer of size bytes.

```
void setbuf(FILE *file, char *buf)
int setvbuf(FILE *file, char *buf, int type, unsigned size)
```

type is one of _IOFBF, _IOLBF, or _IONBF. _IOFBF is fully buffered (next input tries to fill entire buffer, next output happens when buffer has been completely filled), _IOLBF is line buffered (the next input tries to fill entire buffer, but next output occurs whenever a newline character is written), and _IONBF is unbuffered. setvbuf returns 0 on success, and a nonzero value otherwise. When used, both these functions should be called immediately after opening the file.

ungetc sets things up so that its single-character argument is the next character read by getc. ungetch is identical to ungetc to the standard input. It is not standard C.

```
int ungetc(char c, FILE *file)
int ungetch(int c)
```

Both return the saved character. Subsequent calls to ungetc erase the previous saved character, as does doing an fseek to that file.

TYPE	INPUT EXPECTED
d	signed decimal integer
u	unsigned decimal integer
o	unsigned octal integer
x	unsigned hex integer
c	next character(s)
s	string (nonwhitespace characters)
f, e, g	signed float

Table E.1 `scanf`'s format types.

E.2   FORMATTED INPUT/OUTPUT

We've seen that the standard library provides a large set of functions to handle formatted input and output. In this section, we expand on the different formatting instructions.

`scanf`'s format string contains a list of format specifiers. A format specifier looks like

%[*width*]*type*

Any character that isn't part of a format specifier is expected to match the next character in the input exactly. `scanf` skips over intervening white space, except when reading a character.

Table E.1 lists the possible *types*. We indicate a `short` by preceding an integral type with an h, and a `long` with an l. Preceding a floating type with l indicates a `double`.

width specifies the maximum number of characters to read when reading the field. `%5d` means read at most 5 digits. `%10c` means we want to read exactly 10 characters. `%10s` means we want to read a 10-character string, starting with the first nonwhitespace character. A width field of * means skip the current field. For example,

    scanf("%*d%*d%d", &x)

reads three integers, placing the third to `x`.

The functions in the `printf` family work in a similar way. Normally, characters in the format string are written as is, except for format specifiers.

% [*flags*] [*width*] [*.precision*] *type*

type indicates the type of the expression or value. It must be one of the values from Table E.2. Preceding one of these types with a l indicates a `long` or a `double`, depending on whether the type is an integer or a real. Turbo C also supports the characters N and F for `near` and `far` pointers, respectively.

width is an optional value that sets a minimum width for the output field. If the field's value doesn't fit, it isn't truncated—it simply overflows the output field. The width is an integer number of characters, such as `%10d` or `%010d`. A leading zero indicates that the field should be padded on the left with zeros. The width can also be an asterisk, which means that the next value in the expression list provides the width. This statement

TYPE CHAR   OUTPUT FORMAT

d	Signed decimal integer
o	Unsigned octal integer
x	Unsigned hex integer (uses `a - f` for the values 10 through 15)
X	Unsigned hex integer (uses `A - F` for the values 10 through 15)
f	Signed float value in form `[-]dddd.ddd`
e	Signed float value in form `[-]d.dddd e [+|-]ddd` (scientific notation)
E	Same as `e` but prints `E` instead
g	Signed value using either `e` or `f` form, based on value and precision (trailing 0s and decimal point printed only if necessary)
G	Same as `g` but prints `E` instead
c	Single character
s	Prints characters until a null character, or until precision number of characters is printed
%	Print a single percent character
n	Stores in the location pointed to by the next argument (which must be the address of an `int`), a count of the characters written so far
p	Prints the value as a pointer (Turbo C specific: `far` pointers printed as `XXXX:YYYY`; near as `YYYY` (offset only)

Table E.2 `printf` format types and their meaning.

```
printf("Val: %*d", width, val);
```

prints the value of `val` (an integer) using the width given as the value of `width` (also an integer).

A *precision* specifier indicates the amount of space for the decimal part of a floating point value, or the amount of space for zero padding for integers. If no precision is given, or a precision of `.0` is given, the default is used (1 for `d, i, o, u, x, X`; 6 for `e, E, f`; all significant digits for `g` and `G`; all characters up to the null for `s`). If the precision is `.n` (where n is a constant), *n* characters or decimal places are printed as specified in Table E.3. As with the width, the precision can be an `*`, with the same meaning.

Finally, *flags* is an optional list of characters indicating whether the number is signed, whether and how it is justified, whether it has leading or trailing zeros. A *flag* is either −, +, a blank, or #. The − flag left justifies the value or string, padded to the right with blanks; without it, the value is left justified and is padded on the left with

TYPE CHARACTER	EFFECT OF PRECISION SPECIFIER
d, i, o, u, x, X	At least n digits are printed, with the output padded on the left if it has less than n digits, and no truncation occurring if the input has more than n digits
e, E, f	n digits are printed after the decimal point, with the least significant digit *rounded*
g, G	At most n digits are printed
c	No effect
s	No more than n characters are printed

Table E.3   Effect of *precision specifier* on printf formats.

FORMAT	EXPRESSION	OUTPUT
"[%15d]"	val	[-15]
"[%-15d]"	val	[-15]
"[%15d]"	val2	[87]
"[%+15d]"	val2	[+87]
"[%-15d]"	val2	[87]
"[%f]"	fval	[43.717999]
"[%15.0f]"	fval	[44]
"[%-15.0f]"	fval	[44]
"[%+15.0f]"	fval	[+44]
"[%10.5f]"	fval	[43.71800]
"[%.5f]"	fval	[43.71800]
"[%30s]"	s	[I love rock and roll]
"[%-30s]"	s	[I love rock and roll]
"[%15x]"	val	[fff1]
"[%#15x]"	val	[0xfff1]

Table E.4   Examples of different printf formats.

blanks (or zeros if the width has a leading zero). The + flag says that both positive and negative values should be printed with a sign. A blank flag says that a blank should be printed in front of positive numbers, and a minus sign in front of negative numbers. And the # flag uses an alternate output format. Octal and hex values are preceded with 0, 0x, or 0X, as appropriate. And floating pointer values will always contain a decimal point, with trailing zeros not removed.

Table E.4 shows some examples, using the following values.

```
int    val = -15;
int    val2 = 87;
float  fval =  43.718;
char   *s = "I love rock and roll";
```

There are also several functions dealing with console I/O that we ignored in the text.

`cgets` reads characters from the console keyboard, until a *linefeed, cr* combination, which is replaced by a null, or until it has read the maximum number of characters. This number is specified in advance in `string[0]`. On return, `string[1]` contains the actual number of characters read, and the characters themselves begin in `string[2]`.

```
char *cgets(char *string)
```

`cscanf` is similar to `scanf`, taking a format specifier and an optional list of addresses.

```
int cscanf(char *format [, address-list])
```

E.3   THE STANDARD STRING FUNCTIONS

C provides a set of functions for manipulating strings. We must include string.h to use them.

`strcpy` copies the contents of `s2` into `s1`, returning a pointer to `s1`. `strncpy` is similar, but only copies the first n characters of `s2`. If `s2` is shorter than n, `s1` is padded with null characters up to length n. If `s2` is at least n characters long, `s1` is not null-terminated.

```
char *strcpy(char *s1, char *s2)
char *strncpy(char *s1, char *s2, int n)
```

`strcat` copies `s2` onto the end of `s1`, returning a pointer to `s1`. `strncat` is similar, but only copies the first n characters of `s2`.

```
char *strcat(char *s1, char *s2)
char *strncat(char *s1, char *s2, int n)
```

In general, the string arguments passed to any of these string copying functions should be distinct.

`strcmp` compares two strings and returns an integer less than zero if the first is less than the second, zero if they are equal, and an integer greater than zero if the first is greater than the second. `strncmp` is similar, but only compares up to the first n characters or a `null` character, whichever comes first. `strcmpi` and `strncmpi` are identical to `strcmp` and `strncmp` respectively, except that perform the comparison without case sensitivity.

```
int strcmp(char *s1, char *s2)
int strncmp(char *s1, char *s2, int n)
int strcmpi(char *s1, char *s2)
int strncmpi(char *s1, char *s2, int n)
```

`strchr` returns a pointer to the first occurrence of c in s, or NULL if c doesn't occur in s. `strrchr` is also similar to `strchr` except that it returns a pointer to the last occurrence of c in s. `strstr` returns a pointer to the first substring in a given string.

```
char *strchr(char *s, char c)
char *strrchr(char *s, char c)
char *strstr(char *s, char *substr)
```

strrbrk returns a pointer to the first character in s that is also in set, or NULL if s and set don't intersect. strrpbrk is similar, except it returns a pointer to the last character in the set.

```
char *strpbrk(char *s, char *set)
char *strrpbrk(char *s, char *set)
```

strset sets all characters in a string to a given character. strnset sets the first n characters in string to the given character. It stops early if it hits a null character.

```
char *strset(char *s, int ch)
char *strnset(char *s, int ch, int n)
```

strlwr converts uppercase letters in a string to lowercase, returning a pointer to the converted string. strupr is similar except that it converts lowercase letters to uppercase. strrev reverses a string in place, returning a pointer to the string's first character.

```
char *strlwr(char *s)
char *strupr(char *s)
char *strrev(char *s)
```

strlen returns the number of characters in s that precede the trailing null. strcspn returns the number of characters in s that precede a character in set. Returns strlen(s) if no characters in set are also in s. strspn is similar, but it returns the number of characters before encountering a character that is not in s.

```
int strlen(char *s)
int strspn(char *s, char *set)
int strcspn(char *s, char *set)
```

strdup makes a dynamically allocated copy of s and returns a pointer to it.

```
char *strdup(char *s)
```

strdup returns NULL if it can't allocate enough memory.

E.4   MEMORY-MANIPULATION FUNCTIONS

Turbo C also provides a set of functions for manipulating blocks of bytes. These functions are very similar to the string-manipulating functions except that they don't stop when they encounter a null character. To use them include either string.h or mem.h.

memcpy copies a block of n bytes. memccpy is similar except that it stops early if it encounters the character c. memmove is also similar to memcpy except it works successfully even if the the two blocks overlap. memset sets n bytes of a block of memory to a particular value.

```
void *memcpy(void *dest, void *src, int n)
void *memccpy(void *dest, void *src, int c, int n)
void *memmove(void *dest, void *src, int n)
void *memset(void *dest, int c, int n)
```

All these functions return a pointer to the first byte in the destination block.

memcmp compares two blocks for a length of exactly n bytes. Its return value is the same as strcmp. memcmpi is similar, but it ignores case. memchr searches n bytes for a particular character, returning a pointer to the first matching byte or NULL if no byte matches.

```
int memcmp(void *s1, void *s2, int n)
int memcmpi(void *s1, void *s2, int n)
char *memchr(void *s, int c, int n)
```

E.5   STORAGE-ALLOCATION FUNCTIONS

These functions allocate and free storage. The storage-allocation functions return a pointer to a contiguous block of storage of at least the requested size, guaranteed to be properly aligned to the requirements of the underlying hardware. The storage-freeing routines require a pointer to one of the contiguous blocks of storage, and return the pointed-to block to the free storage pool. To use them, include alloc.h.

malloc allocates a single block of storage containing at least size bytes and returns a pointer to the first byte in the block. calloc allocates n blocks of storage, each of size bytes, and sets all bits in the allocated space to zero.

```
void *malloc(unsigned int size)
void *calloc(unsigned int n, unsigned int size)
```

realloc takes a pointer to a block of storage and "grows" it to the requested size, returning a pointer to the new block.

```
void *realloc(void *ptr, unsigned int size)
```

free returns space previously allocated by malloc or calloc to the free storage pool.

```
void free(void *ptr)
```

farmalloc returns a pointer to storage allocated on the far heap (which is the same as the heap in the large data models). farfree returns that storage.

```
void far *farmalloc(unsigned long size)
void farfree(void far *ptr)
```

E.6   ADDITIONAL LIBRARY FUNCTIONS

The standard library also provides a set of functions for performing various tasks such as converting strings to numbers and searching and sorting tables. To use these functions, we must include stdlib.h.

The *atox* functions convert a string representing a double, int, or long into an appropriate numeric value.

```
double atof(char *nptr)
int atoi(char *nptr)
long atol(char *nptr)
```

The string must contain a string of digits, optionally preceded by leading white space (blanks or tabs) and a single plus or minus sign. With atof, the string of digits may be in scientific notation (that is, followed by a decimal point, and optionally, an e or E and a possibly signed integer. The string is converted until the first character that can't be part of a number. If the value causes overflow, the result is undefined. The functions return the converted value, or 0 if no conversion occurs occur.

strtod converts a string to a double, and strtol converts a string to a long in the specified base.

```
double strtod(char *s, char **endptr)
long strtol(char *s, char **endptr, int base)
```

If endptr isn't NULL, both functions set *endptr to point to the first character that couldn't be successfully converted. With strtol, if base is zero, the string's first few characters determines the base. If they are 0x or 0X, the base is hex. If they are 01 through 07, the base is octal. Otherwise, the base is decimal. strtol returns 0 if given an illegal base, with *endptr set to the first character in s.

The *xtoa* functions convert an integer to a string, using the given radix, storing the result in string, which must be large enough to store the converted value.

```
char *itoa(int val, char *string, int radix)
char *ltoa(long val, char *string, int radix)
char *ultoa(unsigned long val, char *string, int radix)
```

itoa converts an integer, which requires up to 17 bytes. ltoa and ultoa require up to 33 bytes. radix is the base used for converting—it must be a value between 2 and 36. Both functions return a pointer to string.

The *xcvt* functions convert a floating point value to a null-terminated string, which is assumed to be large enough to hold digits characters.

```
char *ecvt(double val, int digits, int *decpt, int *sign)
char *fcvt(double val, int digits, int *decpt, int *sign)
char *gcvt(double val, int digits, char *buff)
```

ecvt places the position of the decimal point in the location pointed to by decpt, and places a nonzero in the location pointer to by sign if the number is negative, and a zero otherwise. fcvt is the same as ecvt, except that it uses FORTRAN-style rounding. gcvt uses e-style output if there isn't enough space.

qsort uses quicksort to sort an array beginning at base and containing nelems, each containing width bytes. The items are compared with the function fcmp, which is passed pointers to the items.

```
void qsort(void *base, int nelem, int width,
           int (*fcmp)(const void *, const void*));
```

The comparison function should return an integer less than 0 if its first argument is less than the second, 0 if they are equal, and an integer greater than 0 if the first argument is greater than the second.

bsearch searches a sorted array for target using binary search. The comparison function works the same way qsorts does.

```
void bsearch(void *target, void *base, int nelem, int width,
             int (*fcmp)(const void *, const void *));
```

lfind does a linear search through an array. lsearch is like lfind, but it appends the item to the table if it isn't already in it. The comparison function should return 0 if the items are identical, and nonzero otherwise.

```
void lfind(void *target, void *base, int nelem, int width,
           int (*fcmp)(void *, void *));
void lsearch(void *target, void *base, int nelem, int width,
             int (*fcmp)(void *, void *));
```

rand returns a pseudo-random number between 0 and $2^{15} - 1$. srand provides the initial seed.

```
int rand(void)
void srand(unsigned seed)
```

system takes a single string containing a DOS command, executes it, and returns to the program. It returns the exit status of the command, or -1 if it couldn't execute it

```
int system(char *string)
```

exit terminates the program and returns its argument as the command's exit status. To use it, we also need to include process.h.

```
void exit(int status)
```

E.7   THE MATH LIBRARY

C has a sizeable library of math functions. To use them, include math.h. Many of these functions expect a double, but as long you include the prototypes, you can pass floats to them without any problems. All of the trigonometric functions expect their arguments in radians.

sin, cos, and tan return the sine, cosine, and tangent of x, respectively.

```
double sin(double x)
double cos(double x)
double tan(double x)
```

asin returns the arc sine, acos the arc cosine, and atan the arc tangent of x, respectively. These functions return zero if $-1 \leq x \leq 1$. atan2 returns the arc tangent of x/y, for $y \neq 0$.

```
double asin(double x)
double acos(double x)
double atan(double x)
double atan2(double y, double  x)
```

sinh returns the hyperbolic sine, cosh the hyperbolic cosine, and tanh the hyperbolic tangent of x. These functions return the largest possible double on overflow, and unpredictable results on underflow.

```
double sinh(double x)
double cosh(double x)
double tanh(double x)
```

exp returns ϵ^x, or the largest possible double on overflow. log returns the $\log_\epsilon x$, while log10 returns $\log_{10} x$. Both assume $x \geq 0$.

```
double exp(double x)
double log(double x)
double log10(double x)
```

ldexp returns $x \times 2^y$. frexp finds f and n such that $0.5 \leq f \leq 1.0$ and $f \cdot 2^n = x$. It returns f and puts n into *nptr.

```
double ldexp(double x, int y)
double frexp(double x, int *nptr)
```

pow returns x^y. It is an error if $x < 0$ and y is not an integer, or if $x = 0$ and $y \leq 0$. sqrt returns $\sqrt{x}$ for $x \geq 0$, and 0 otherwise.

```
double pow(double x,  double y)
double sqrt(double x)
```

abs, fabs, and labs return the absolute value of x.

```
int abs(int x)
double fabs(double x)
long labs(long x)
```

ceil returns x rounded up to the nearest integer, and floor returns x rounded down to the nearest integer.

```
double ceil(double x)
double floor(double x)
```

fmod returns the remainder of x/y. modf splits x into a fraction and an integer, returning the fraction and putting the integer in the place pointed to by nptr.

```
double fmod(double x,  double y)
double modf(double x,  double *nptr)
```

F NUMBERING SYSTEMS

A value can be represented in any number of different base systems. This appendix discusses some of the more common ones: binary (base 2), octal (base 8), decimal (base 10), and hexadecimal (base 16). We focus on how to understand values in different bases, and how to convert from one base to another.

F.1   INTRODUCTION

In a base system, a value is represented by a string of symbols. In binary the allowable symbols are 0 and 1. In octal the symbols used are 0, 1, 2, 3, 4, 5, 6, and 7. In hexadecimal the symbols are 0, 1, ..., 9, and A, B, C, D, E, and F. The letters represent the values 10, 11, 12, 13, 14, and 15, respectively. Each of these base systems is centered on an integer, other than zero or one, called the *base* or *radix*. For binary it's base 2, for octal it's base 8, and for hexadecimal it's base 16.

Each place occupied by a symbol corresponds to a power of the base. The rightmost place corresponds to the base raised to the zero power (which is one for any choice of base). Each move to the left multiplies the current place by the value of the base. In octal, the rightmost place corresponds to 1s; the next place to the left corresponds to 64s, and so on. In hexadecimal, the rightmost place also corresponds to 1s, but the next place on the left corresponds to 16s, and the one after that to 16*16s, or 256s, and so on.

The correspondence between position and value in binary, octal, and hexadecimal is shown below.

Base		Position				
	n	4	3	2	1	0
binary	2^n	16	8	4	2	1
octal	8^n	4096	512	64	8	1
hexadecimal	16^n	65536	4096	256	16	1

Positions are numbered starting from zero, going from right to left (this way the position's value is equal to the power of the base).

We compute the base 10 value of a number $a_n a_{n-1} \cdots a_1 a_0$ in base B by computing $\sum_{i=0}^{n} a_i * B^i$. For example, to convert 742_8, we need to compute $(7 * 8^2) +$

$(4 * 8^1) + (2 * 8^0)$, which gives us 482_{10}. To convert $A2C_{16}$ to base 10, we evaluate $(10 * 16^2) + (2 * 16^1) + (12 * 16^0)$, which evaluates to 2604_{10}.

F.2   BASE CONVERSIONS

There is a simple and direct relationship between binary, octal, and hexadecimal numbers. To convert from binary to octal, group the number from the right in three-bit units and convert each group to an octal number. To convert to hexadecimal, group the number from the right in four-bit units and convert each group to a hexadecimal number (for hexadecimal, remember that 10 converts to A, 11 to B, 12 to C, 13 to D, 14 to E, and 15 to F). Here's an example:

```
Binary   0 100 001 110 111 010
Octal    0   4   1   6   7   2

Binary     0100 0011 1011 1010
Hex          4    3    B    A
```

To convert a number X from base 10 to base B, divide X by B. The remainder becomes the leftmost digit of the converted number. The quotient becomes the next X, and is divided by B, with the process completing when the new quotient is finally zero.

G CHARACTER SETS

Every implementation uses some underlying representation for characters. This appendix presents the ASCII character set, the character set Turbo C uses. To find a character's integer representation, add its row number to the number at the top of its column. For example, the internal representation for the character 'A' is $64 + 1$, or 65.

G.1

THE ASCII CHARACTER SET

	0	16	32	48	64	80	96	112
0	^@	^P	space	0	@	P	'	p
1	^A	^Q	!	1	A	Q	a	q
2	^B	^R	"	2	B	R	b	r
3	^C	^S	#	3	C	S	c	s
4	^D	^T	$	4	D	T	d	t
5	^E	^U	%	5	E	U	e	u
6	^F	^V	&	6	F	V	f	v
7	^G	^W	'	7	G	W	g	w
8	^H	^X	(	8	H	X	h	x
9	^I	^Y	)	9	I	Y	i	y
10	^J	^Z	*	:	J	Z	j	z
11	^K	esc	+	;	K	[	k	{
12	^L		,	<	L	\	l	|
13	^M		−	=	M	]	m	}
14	^N		.	>	N	^	n	~
15	^O		/	?	O	_	o	del

543

INDEX